Contents

JOANNA

The NOTORIOUS QUEEN *of* NAPLES,
JERUSALEM *and* SICILY

NANCY GOLDSTONE

PHOENIX

For my parents

A PHOENIX PAPERBACK

First published in Great Britain in 2010
by Weidenfeld & Nicolson
This paperback edition published in 2011
by Phoenix,
an imprint of Orion Books Ltd,
Orion House, 5 Upper St Martin's Lane,
London WC2H 9EA

An Hachette UK company

This edition published by arrangement with
Walker Publishing Company, Inc,. New York

1 3 5 7 9 10 8 6 4 2

Copyright © Nancy Goldstone 2010

The right of Nancy Goldstone to be identified as the author of
this work has been asserted by her in accordance with the
Copyright, Designs and Patents Act 1988.

Maps by Jeffrey L. Ward

A CIP catalogue record for this book
is available from the British Library.

ISBN 978-0-7538-2684-3

Printed and bound in Great Britain by CPI, Mackays

The Orion Publishing Group's policy is to use papers that
are natural, renewable and recyclable products and
made from wood grown in sustainable forests. The logging
and manufacturing processes are expected to conform to
the environmental regulations of the country of origin.

www.orionbooks.co.uk

JOANNA'S ANGEVIN ANCESTORS AND THEIR RELATION TO THE CROWN OF FRANCE

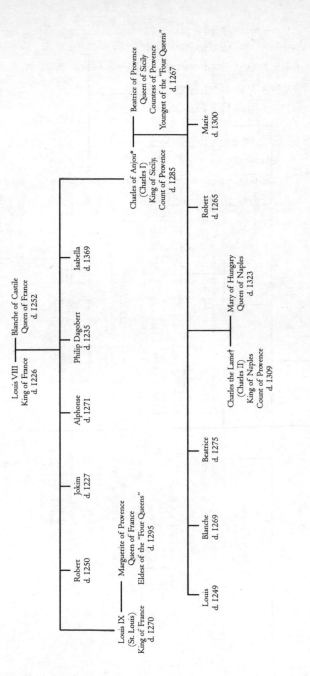

* Joanna's great-great-grandfather
† Joanna's great-grandfather

THE EXTENDED FAMILY OF ROBERT THE WISE

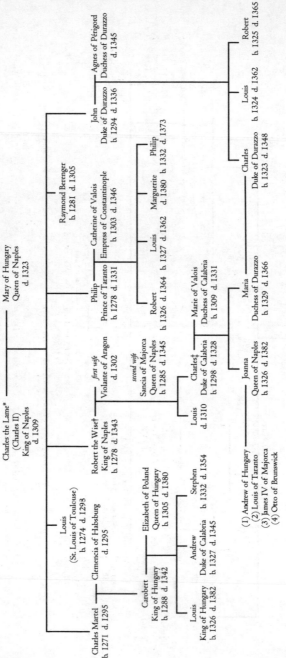

Charles the Lame* (Charles II) King of Naples d. 1309 — Mary of Hungary Queen of Naples d. 1323

Charles Martel b 1271 d. 1295

Louis (St. Louis of Toulouse) b 1274 d. 1293

Carobert — Clemencia of Habsburg d. 1295
Carobert King of Hungary b 1288 d. 1342 — Elizabeth of Poland Queen of Hungary b 1305 d. 1380

Louis King of Hungary b 1326 d. 1382

Andrew Duke of Calabria b 1327 d. 1345

Stephen b 1332 d. 1354

Robert the Wise† King of Naples b 1278 d. 1343
first wife Violante of Aragon d. 1302
second wife Sancia of Majorca Queen of Naples b 1285 d. 1345

Charles‡ Duke of Calabria b 1298 d. 1328 — Marie of Valois Duchess of Calabria b 1309 d. 1331

Louis d. 1310

Joanna Queen of Naples b 1326 d. 1382

(1) Andrew of Hungary
(2) Louis of Taranto
(3) James IV of Majorca
(4) Otto of Brunswick

Maria Duchess of Durazzo b 1329 d. 1366

Philip Prince of Taranto b 1278 d. 1331 — Catherine of Valois Empress of Constantinople b 1303 d. 1346

Robert b 1326 d. 1364

Louis b 1327 d. 1362

Marguerite d. 1380

Philip b 1332 d. 1373

Raymond Berenger b 1281 d. 1305

John Duke of Durazzo b 1294 d. 1336 — Agnes of Périgord Duchess of Durazzo d. 1345

Charles Duke of Durazzo b 1323 d. 1348

Louis b 1324 d. 1362

Robert b 1325 d. 1365

* Joanna's great-grandfather
† Joanna's grandfather
‡ Joanna's father
Robert the Wise also had another three brothers and five sisters but, as they do not play an active role in the narrative, they were omitted from this chart.

THE VALOIS DYNASTY AND ITS RELATIONSHIP TO FRANCE AND NAPLES

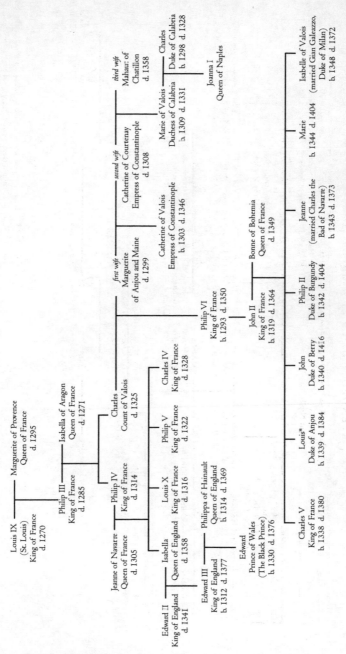

* Joanna's adopted heir, who tried to rescue her from Charles of Durazzo.

THE MARRIAGES AND CHILDREN OF JOANNA, HER SISTER MARIA, AND THEIR FIRST COUSINS

Louis the Great
King of Hungary
b 1326 d. 1382

— Elizabeth of Bosnia
Queen of Hungary
d. 1387

Catherine
b 1370 d. 1378

Mary
b 1371 d. 1395

Hedwig
b 1374 d. 1399

Joanna I
Queen of Naples
b 1326 d. 1382

first husband — Andrew
Prince of Hungary
b 1327 d. 1345

second husband — Louis
Prince of Taranto
King of Naples
b 1327 d. 1362

third husband — James IV
King of Majorca
b 1336 d. 1375

fourth husband — Otto of Brunswick
b 1320 d. 1398

Charles Martel
b 1345 d. 1348

Catherine
b 1348 d. 1349 b 1350 d. 1352

Françoise
b 1350 d. 1352

Maria
Duchess of Durazzo
b 1329 d. 1366

first husband — Charles
Duke of Durazzo
b 1323 d. 1348

second husband — Robert del Balzo
d. 1353

third husband — Philip
Prince of Taranto
b 1332 d. 1373

Jeanne
b 1344 d. 1387

Agnes
b 1345 d. 1388

Clementia
b 1346 d. 1363

Margherita
b 1348 d. 1412

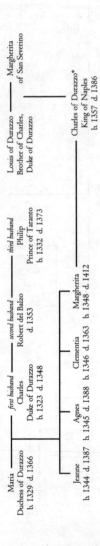

Louis of Durazzo
Brother of Charles,
Duke of Durazzo

— Margherita
of San Severino

Charles of Durazzo*
King of Naples
b 1357 d. 1386

*This is the Charles of Durazzo, formerly Joanna's heir, who invaded Naples in 1381, took the queen prisoner, and had her murdered in 1382.

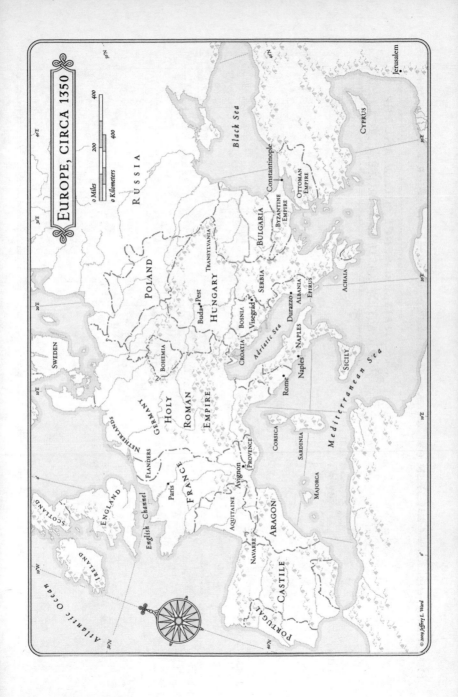

EUROPE, CIRCA 1350

0 Miles   200   400
0 Kilometers   400

Atlantic Ocean

SCOTLAND
IRELAND
ENGLAND
English Channel
NETHERLANDS
FLANDERS
Paris •
FRANCE
AQUITAINE
Avignon •
PROVENCE
NAVARRE
ARAGON
CASTILE
PORTUGAL
MAJORCA
SARDINIA
CORSICA
SWEDEN
GERMANY
HOLY ROMAN EMPIRE
BOHEMIA
POLAND
RUSSIA
HUNGARY
Buda • • Pest
TRANSYLVANIA
CROATIA
BOSNIA
Visegrád •
SERBIA
BULGARIA
Rome •
Naples •
NAPLES
Durazzo •
ALBANIA
EPIRUS
ACHAIA
SICILY
Adriatic Sea
Mediterranean Sea
Black Sea
Constantinople •
BYZANTINE EMPIRE
OTTOMAN EMPIRE
CYPRUS
Jerusalem •

© 2009 Jeffrey L. Ward

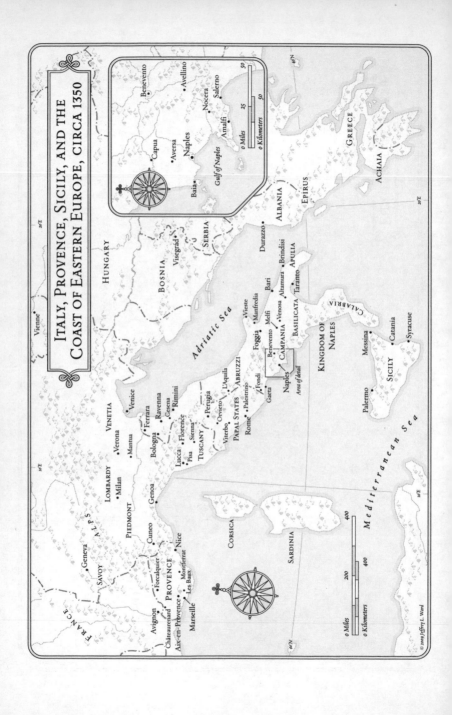

ITALY, PROVENCE, SICILY, AND THE COAST OF EASTERN EUROPE, CIRCA 1350

© 2009 Jeffrey L. Ward

Inset map (Gulf of Naples area):

Benevento · Avellino · Nocera · Salerno · Capua · Aversa · Naples · Amalfi · Baia · Gulf of Naples

0 Miles 25 50
0 Kilometers 50

Main map labels:

FRANCE · Avignon · Chateaurenard · Aix-en-Provence · Forcalquier · Montferrat · Les Baux · Marseille · Nice · PROVENCE · Geneva · SAVOY · ALPS · Cuneo · PIEDMONT · Genoa · Vienne · LOMBARDY · Milan · VENETIA · Verona · Mantua · Venice · Ferrara · Bologna · Ravenna · Cesena · Rimini · Lucca · Florence · Pisa · Siena · TUSCANY · Perugia · Orvieto · Viterbo · L'Aquila · ABRUZZI · PAPAL STATES · Rome · Palestrino · Fondi · Gaeta · Naples · CAMPANIA · Benevento · Foggia · Manfredia · Vieste · Melfi · Bari · Venosa · Altamura · Brindisi · Taranto · APULIA · BASILICATA · KINGDOM OF NAPLES · CALABRIA · Messina · Palermo · SICILY · Catania · Syracuse · Area of detail

HUNGARY · Visegrad · BOSNIA · SERBIA · ALBANIA · Durazzo · EPIRUS · GREECE · ACHAIA

CORSICA · SARDINIA · Adriatic Sea · Mediterranean Sea

0 Miles 200 400
0 Kilometers 400

ENGLAND, FRANCE, AND SPAIN, CIRCA 1350

SCOTLAND

IRELAND

ENGLAND

London

Calais

Boulogne

Crécy-en-Ponthieu

English Channel

FLANDERS

Atlantic Ocean

Caen

NORMANDY

Rheims

Paris

Vannes

ANJOU

Chartres

KINGDOM
OF FRANCE

HOLY
ROMAN
EMPIRE

VIENNE

Poitiers

Bordeaux

AQUITAINE

GASCONY

Bayonne

ARMAGNAC

PÉRIGORD

Avignon

Najera

PROVENCE

KINGDOM OF
NAVARRE

Soria

PORTUGAL

KINGDOM OF
ARAGON

KINGDOM OF
CASTILE

MAJORCA

Mediterranean Sea

10°W

0°

50°N

40°N

0°

0 Miles   100   200

0 Kilometers   200

© 2009 Jeffrey L. Ward

The Trial

THE PAPAL COURT at Avignon, March 15, 1348—On this
day, more than six hundred and fifty years ago, Joanna I, queen
of Naples, Sicily, and Jerusalem and countess of Provence, stood
trial for her life.

The entrance of the queen's party into the old city earlier that
morning had been marked by suspicion and fear. For the previous
two months, Avignon had writhed in the grip of the Black Death,
a pestilence so relentless and infernal that it has no modern equivalent. Thousands upon thousands had perished in agony; in the end,
the city would lose half its population. The symptoms were terrifying. Victims maintained a high fever, spat blood, and developed
painful inflammations under the arms and around the groin, which
turned black—hence the name. There was no hope for the stricken.
In almost every instance, those suffering from the disease died
within five days. "The plague began with us in January and lasted
seven months," wrote Guy de Chauliac, a scholar and eyewitness.
"[It] was extremely contagious . . . so that one caught it from
another, not only through close proximity but also through receiving
a glance from another. As a consequence, people died without assistance and were buried without priests." The number of corpses was

overwhelming. In desperation, the pope purchased a nearby field for burial, but even this measure was insufficient, and the pontiff was forced to sanctify the Rhône for this function. Joanna and her entourage were greeted that early-spring morning by the macabre vision of decomposing human remains floating with the current.

A crisis this severe naturally prompted speculation as to the source of the epidemic. The prevailing opinion, not unreasonably, was that it represented a punishment from God. The pope himself had admitted as much in a sermon where he had affirmed that the plague was evidence of the sinful state of the world. The populace tried to make amends; long lines of penitents, barefoot and dressed in sackcloth, paraded through the streets flagellating themselves. The pope held a special mass and distributed indulgences. Nothing worked. As the sickness continued to rage, some whispered that, rather than the general sinfulness of the world, one sin in particular was responsible for the Black Death. These rumors were given weight by Louis Sanctus of Beringen, chaplain to Cardinal Giovanni Colonna. In a treatise titled *Tractatus de Pestilentia*, the cleric suggested Avignon was being penalized as a result of the actions of Joanna, queen of Naples, who had violated the word of God by murdering her husband, Prince Andrew of Hungary.

As a result, not even the plague could prevent the lower classes from spilling out into the narrow streets of the old city, jostling among themselves for a glimpse of the woman accused of one of the most infamous crimes in history. Nor was the tumult limited to commoners. From every balcony, incongruously strewn with flowers and draped in rich tapestries as befitted the occasion of a visiting monarch, peered the wary eyes of Avignon's aristocracy, each nobleman and woman dressed as elaborately as lineage and circumstance could afford.

The crowds were not disappointed. In the Middle Ages, royalty understood the need for spectacle, both as a distraction from the cares of everyday life and as a means of reinforcing authority.

Because of the rumors, the queen's need to impress took on even greater urgency. A battery of thirty knights on horseback, wearing highly polished chain mail and armed with lances and brightly colored pennants emblazoned with their families' coat of arms, clattered down the streets. They were followed by Joanna's ladies-in-waiting, some reclining in litters, others sitting upright in side chairs, their ornate headdresses fashionably embellished with braided ropes of false hair made of yellow silk, the exaggerated points of their shoes just visible beneath the hems of their gowns.

Medieval protocol dictated the order of procession, and so Joanna, seated on a purebred white mare, led her entourage through the crooked passageways of the city. The queen wore a magnificent cloak of purple velvet trimmed in ermine and meticulously woven with gold thread in a recurring pattern of fleur-de-lis, symbol of the French crown from which she traced her lineage. Her horse was similarly attired in purple and fleur-de-lis, with a bridle and stirrups of gold. Although Joanna was an accomplished equestrian, on this occasion her mount was led by two grooms, as the queen needed her hands free to carry her orb and scepter, insignia of her royal status. Over her head was stretched a canopy of purple silk fringed in gold thread held aloft by four of her vassals.

The queen's party had been met at the outskirts of the city by an official delegation of senior church officials and government functionaries. Such was the gravity of the occasion that all eighteen cardinals of the Sacred College, formally attired in their traditional red hats and robes, appeared to escort her procession to the vast courtyard adjoining the Palace of the pope.

This was the queen of Naples's first glimpse of the great stone fortress designed to glorify the majesty of the church on earth. Still under construction, it was four times the size of any existing cathedral, dwarfing the Louvre in Paris and the Tower in London. Its vaulted ceilings rose two stories into the air, its towers, supplemented by spires, pierced to yet another story. The overall effect was one of soaring celestial grace combined with a monumental secular power. Here was a building constructed specifically to awe, to intimidate, to unnerve.

Joanna was offered the traditional refreshment of wine and pastry and then led inside the palace to the great hall of the consistory, the ceremonial public room on the ground floor customarily used by the pope to greet visiting royalty. It was a long room, very grand. One entire wall was masked by magnificent, life-size frescoes portraying the story of John the Baptist. These were the vivid creation of Matteo Giovannetti of Viterbo, the *pictor papae* (pope's painter), a master artist imported from Italy. At the far end of the room was a two-tiered dais with two velvet-and-gold thrones placed at the center of the top tier. The pope, wearing his tiara and white robes, sat upon one of the thrones. The other remained empty. The lower tier of the dais was occupied by the cardinals, who were arrayed in a semicircle. Together with the pope they represented judge and jury.

Joanna, her mantle held by two pages, walked the long length of the hall until she reached the dais. The room was filled with spectators. "From the upper end of the spacious hall to the entrance appeared prelates, princes, nobles, and ambassadors of every European power," wrote seventeenth-century church scholar Louis Maimbourg. Following protocol, the queen knelt on a cushion before the pope and kissed the gold cross embroidered on his slipper. Afterward he raised her up, kissed her on the mouth, and motioned for her to sit on the empty throne beside him. The pope then said a prayer and the room fell silent. The trial began.

The charges against the queen of Naples were read aloud in Latin, the only language recognized by the papal court. Joanna stood accused of conspiracy to commit murder. Her principal adversary, the powerful king of Hungary, brother of Prince Andrew, the victim, had earlier sent a squadron of ambassadors and lawyers to the pope to present Hungarian demands and evidence against the queen. It was common knowledge, they had argued, that Joanna and her husband had been estranged, and that her barons had tried to thwart his rule while he was alive. Additionally, the murder had taken place at one of the queen's own palaces, and very nearly in her presence; worse, she had not shown the proper level of remorse and had been so slow to investigate the crime that it remained unsolved. Lastly, she had been recently married again, to a man rumored to have been her lover, without prior dispensation from the pope, as was required by papal law. For these great sins the king of Hungary insisted that justice be done—that Joanna be deposed as ruler of Naples in his favor and that she be sentenced to death for her crimes.

The pope and cardinals listened to the evidence and then turned to the woman seated on the throne. Joanna had brought with her two highly educated, extremely experienced advocates, the brilliant statesman Niccolò Acciaiuoli and his cousin the bishop of Florence. But the queen of Naples had previously asked for, and received, papal approval to address the court on her own behalf, a highly unusual proceeding, particularly as it meant speaking in Latin.

Joanna was under no illusions as to the magnitude of the forces working against her. At stake was her crown, her kingdom, and her head. She rose from her throne and began to answer the charges.

She was twenty-two years old.

Joanna, queen of Sicily and Jerusalem, is more renowned than any
other woman of her time for lineage, power, and character.

—GIOVANNI BOCCACCIO
Famous Women, 1362

Giovanna Regina,
Grassa né magra, bella el viso tondo,
Dotata bene de la virtù divina,
D'Animo grato, benigno, giocondo.

(*Queen Joanna,*
Neither fat nor thin, her face an oval of harmonious art,
Well-favored with all of the divine virtues,
A gentle, gracious soul, generous and light of heart.)

—UNKNOWN FOURTEENTH-CENTURY POET
Archivo Storico per le Province Napoletane

CHAPTER I

✦

The Kingdom *of* Naples

*This city [Naples] . . . is joyful, peaceful, rich, magnificent, and under a single
ruler; and these are qualities (if I know you at all well) which are very
pleasing to you.*

GIOVANNI BOCCACCIO
The Elegy of Lady Fiammetta, 1344

JOANNA I was born in 1326, eldest child of the heir to the
Angevin kingdom of Naples, the largest and most prestigious sovereign entity in Italy. At its northernmost point, the realm jutted up
past the great forests of Abruzzi and into the central mountain range
of the Appenines. Its long eastern shore boasted an enviable number
of ports, including Vieste and Brindisi, from which fast boats ran
cargo, passengers, and armies across the Adriatic as a first stop toward
such distant destinations as Hungary and wealthy, exotic Byzantium.
At its western toe the important duchy of Calabria, on the Mediterranean, offered quick access to the lucrative trading posts on the
island of Sicily. The kingdom took its name from its capital city of
Naples, which housed the royal court, but this was a relatively recent
designation. In 1266, when Joanna's great-great-grandfather Charles
of Anjou (from whence the name Angevin derived) first established
the family's claim to sovereignty by wresting the realm away from its
former ruler, the domain had included the island of Sicily, and for
this reason had originally been called the kingdom of Sicily. But in
1282, in an incident famously known as "The Sicilian Vespers" for
having occurred at Easter, the people of Sicily rebelled against
Charles's harshly autocratic rule and instead invited the king of

7

Aragon to reign in his place. Charles of Anjou's descendants never accepted this diminution of their authority, however, and strove mightily to retake the island through both military and diplomatic means. As a result, during Joanna's lifetime, the kingdom of Naples was still known, variously and confusingly, as the kingdom of Sicily, or, sometimes, as the kingdom of the Two Sicilies.

Charles of Anjou, a man of little scruple and great ambition, was venerated as the founding patriarch of Joanna's family, and his legacy and vision informed its every movement in the century after his death in 1285. He was the youngest brother of Louis IX, king of France, later Saint Louis. As a member of the French royal family, Charles had the opportunity to make an extremely fortuitous marriage. Joanna's great-great-grandmother was Beatrice, countess of Provence, the youngest of a family of four sisters famous in their day for having all become queens. Charles then used his wife's aid and resources to conquer his Italian realm so that thereafter the kingdom of Naples and the county of Provence were inextricably linked. Joanna was therefore destined at birth to inherit the prestigious title "countess of Provence" and to rule over this strategically important region as well.

Most men would have been content with administering these two domains, but Charles was fueled by the need to become more respected and powerful than his older brother Louis IX, in whose shadow he had lived the majority of his life. Supremely confident of his abilities, Charles dreamed of an empire that would rival that of the kingdom of France. Conveniently, one seemed to be available—the Byzantine Empire to the east, which incorporated the storied city of Constantinople, had been weakened by a series of incompetent rulers. Charles moved quickly to transform aspiration into reality. In May of 1267 he contracted to acquire the legal right to the principia of Achaia, on the western coast of Greece, as a stepping-stone toward invasion. Although he did not realize this ambition during his lifetime, he never relinquished his goal, and the scale of his desire may be measured by his subsequent purchase, on March 18, 1277, of the title to the kingdom of Jerusalem, an honor for which he paid a thousand pounds of gold outright and an additional stipend of four thousand *livres tournois* annually. Charles was not a man to pay good money for an empty title; he believed himself or his descendants capable of capitalizing on this opportunity. Henceforth, all the Angevin sovereigns of Naples, including Joanna, were therefore also styled king (or queen) of Jerusalem, a durable reminder of their benefactor's expectations.

Dreams of empire aside, the southern Italian kingdom conquered by Joanna's great-great-grandfather was a place of profound physical beauty. A land of spectacular white cliffs and mysterious sea caves, of inviting beaches, fertile plains, and ancient forests, Naples was universally acclaimed for its scenery. A sixteenth-century notary referred to it as "an earthly paradise" in an official government report. The kingdom was also famous as the home of the baths of Baia, the most fashionable spa on the continent, a vacation spot that traced its celebrity back to the giddy days of Julius Caesar and the Roman Empire. "My lady, as you know, just the other side of Mount Falerno . . . lies the rocky coast of Baia high above the seashore, and no sight under the sun is more beautiful or more pleasant than this," wrote Giovanni Boccaccio, a brilliant author and haunting storyteller from the period who knew Naples well. "It is surrounded by the most lovely mountains thick with trees and vineyards; in the valleys any game that can be hunted is available; . . . and for amusements, not far away . . . are the oracles of the Cumaean Sibyl . . . and the amphitheater where the ancient games convened." Even Francesco Petrarch, the most important scholar of the fourteenth century, and a man who ordinarily scorned the pursuit of frivolous pleasure, was impressed by Baia.* "I saw Baia . . . and do

---

* It was Petrarch who labeled the papal residency at Avignon, known for its profligacy, with the withering sobriquet "The Babylonian Captivity," an unusually apt turn of phrase that stuck through the ages.

not recall a happier day in my life," he wrote to his friend Cardinal Giovanni Colonna in a letter dated November 23, 1345. "I saw . . . everywhere mountains full of perforations and suspended on marble vaults gleaming with brilliant whiteness, and sculpted figures indicating with pointing hands what water is most appropriate for each part of the body. The appearance of the place and the labor devoted to its development caused me to marvel."

But for all its natural beauty, the chief allure of Naples was the royal court, which supported a thriving metropolis. The many and varied personages traditionally drawn by the glow of princely wealth—solicitors and supplicants, ambassadors and architects, financiers, silk merchants, poets and pickpockets—gravitated to the capital city, swelling the number of its inhabitants to capacity. In 1326, the year of Joanna's birth, only four cities in Europe could claim a population of one hundred thousand: Paris, Venice, Milan—and Naples. London, by contrast, was home to only about sixty thousand people.

Although Venice and Milan, and even Florence, with a population of eighty thousand, might rival Naples in terms of size, they could not match it in distinction, for Naples was the only kingdom in Italy. This meant that, among the various heads of state, only Joanna's family hailed from royalty, and in the lineage-conscious fourteenth century, this made a very great difference indeed. Venice, with its monopoly on shipping lanes, was stronger economically, but it was administered by a large council, some of whose members were not even noble. Florence might be the acknowledged seat of European banking, but it was governed by an ever-changing group of middle-class burghers. The self-styled lords of Milan, the Visconti family, were members of the minor provincial nobility, ruthless parvenus who tried to buy their way to social and political legitimacy. Milan wouldn't even become a duchy until the very end of the century.

Joanna's ancestral credentials, on the other hand, were impeccable.

Her father was Charles, duke of Calabria, only son and heir of her grandfather, Robert, king of Naples, by his first wife, Violante. Violante had been a princess of the house of Aragon before her marriage. Joanna's mother was the exceedingly lovely Marie of Valois, daughter of the powerful Charles III of Valois, a younger son of the crown of France. On her father's side, Joanna's French ancestry was even more impressive: she was directly related, through Charles of Anjou, to Louis IX, the most revered king in living memory. Louis had been canonized in 1298, but he was not the only saint in the family. Joanna's great uncle Louis of Toulouse had also been beatified, and she was distantly related to the famous thirteenth-century Saint Elizabeth of Hungary. Even her father's tutor, Elzear, count of Ariano, would eventually be sainted. The blood of great men and women flowed through Joanna's veins, of kings and queens crowned by representatives of the pope and thereby invested with the heavy authority of the church. Hers was a legacy of stirring deeds, courage in battle, wisdom in ruling, piety, chivalry, and honor, the very best that the medieval world had to offer.

Almost from the moment she drew breath, Joanna was fated to be the victim, through her father and grandfather, of the unremitting capriciousness that constituted the politics of Europe, and especially of Italy, in the fourteenth century.

Italy existed only as a geographic designation, not as a political entity, in the Middle Ages. What we recognize today as the country of Italy was simply a string of independent, warring cities, anchored to the south by the Papal States and the kingdom of Naples. As a result, an individual living during Joanna's lifetime would not have considered himself or herself to be an Italian, but, rather, a Florentine or a Venetian, a Pisan or a Roman.

The exception to this rule was a small intellectual circle of which

Francesco Petrarch was the undoubted focal point. Petrarch, who devoted his life to recapturing the lost knowledge of the ancients, was enamored of the idea of a united Italy under the rule of a wise, benevolent emperor as a first step toward reinstituting the greatness of the Roman Empire. Actually, there was an emperor in Europe, the Holy Roman Emperor, but he lived in Germany, which was all that remained of Julius Caesar's vast dominions by the fourteenth century. The German emperor did have a great number of supporters among the people of Italy, who saw his influence as a counterweight to that of the church. This did not mean that those who upheld the emperor's authority were not religious, only that they did not want their particular town or city to become a fief of the papacy, which required conforming to whatever the pope mandated, like paying more money to the church or allowing one of his legates to adjudicate litigation. It was a secular, political issue, not a spiritual one. Members of the faction who favored the emperor were called Ghibellines. For the most part, the Holy Roman Emperor was so well-occupied by German affairs that he had neither the time nor the inclination to raise an army and venture into Italy in order to unify it benevolently or otherwise (although occasionally this did occur). In his absence, the Ghibellines functioned as the medieval equivalent of a modern-day political party, concerned with all the aspects of governing, from potholes to tax statutes.

Challenging the Ghibellines for local control of the major cities and towns in Italy was the other national political party, the Guelph, or papal party. Like the Ghibellines, Guelph supporters were in every part of Italy, although they were stronger in the south (closer to Rome) just as the Ghibellines were stronger in the north (closer to Germany). Assigning too much ideological emphasis to these designations would be a mistake, however. Party loyalties were often corrupted by petty personal concerns. If a Guelph businessman cheated his partner, then the aggrieved party might take his revenge by transferring his loyalty to the Ghibellines. Similarly, if a young

Ghibelline woman chose one lover over another, the spurned suitor and his family might become Guelphs. The concept of sharing local political authority between factions did not exist in the fourteenth century. When a division of the Guelph party, known as the "Black" Guelphs, seized control of Florence in 1301, for example, its members secured their victory by exiling all their political opponents (known as the "White" Guelphs) and appropriating their property. This, naturally enough, infuriated the Whites, who went over to the side of the emperor, and from their new homes in cities with sympathetic Ghibelline governments, they plotted the overthrow of the Black Guelphs.

As though conditions were not volatile enough, the power struggle for control of Italy was further exacerbated by the removal of the papal court to Avignon in 1305. This abandonment was unprecedented in church history. Except for the east-west schism created by Constantine a millennium before, and some temporary absences, a pope had resided in Italy since the days of Saint Peter. At the beginning of the fourteenth century, however, the papal court, which had heretofore withstood the fall of Rome, the invasion of Attila the Hun, the alien barbarity of the Goths, the advent of Charlemagne, and the abject humiliation of several of its pontiffs at the hands of the powerful German emperors, took fright at the hostility evidenced by its own unruly subjects and fled. The last pope to try to live in Italy had been Boniface VIII, who had run afoul of both the French king and the powerful Colonna family of Rome. Boniface was very nearly murdered in his own castle at Anagni. Although saved by supporters at the last minute, Boniface never again acted independently and died a broken man in 1303. This treatment had rather discouraged Boniface's successors, who were all closely allied with the French anyway, from taking the risk of setting up residence in the city of which they were, at least nominally, the bishop. Avignon, conveniently situated on the Rhône, with its pleasant climate, docile population, and excellent wines, seemed a much more attractive option.

However, just because the pope was no longer in Rome did not mean that he did not wish to control Italy. In the Middle Ages, popes did not limit their activities to matters of religion and the spirit. They considered themselves princes in the fullest sense of the term, and aspired to own and administer a large domain, maintain fiefdoms, acquire new provinces to increase their secular power, and raise the armies necessary to achieve these goals, exactly as would a king of France or England. Managing Guelph affairs from faraway Provence was unwieldy but not unworkable; the pope simply used surrogates. Often he sent ambassadors or papal legates to coax or bully local legislators into carrying out his instructions. But he also relied heavily on his most important vassal to shepherd Guelph interests in the region: the king of Naples.

Naples had been a fief of the church ever since Charles of Anjou had conquered the kingdom using papal funds and encouragement. By a contract dated November 1265, Charles had agreed to pay the pope eight thousand ounces of gold annually (later reduced to seven thousand) plus one white horse every three years in exchange for the privilege of ruling the realm. Moreover, also by virtue of this remarkable document, Charles had maintained the right to pass on the kingdom to his heirs, provided that they, too, kept to the terms of the agreement and did homage to the pope. As a result of this arrangement, unique in Christendom, over time cooperation between Naples and the papacy had deepened to the point where it approached the status of a partnership. The rest of Italy was of course aware of the Angevins' special relationship with the pope, and that was why, when Guelph Florence was threatened by Ghibelline interests in 1326, the Florentines turned for help to the son of the king of Naples, Joanna's father, Charles, duke of Calabria.

Charles of Calabria was twenty-eight years old and already a sea-soned warrior when he accepted the Florentines' offer of two hun-dred thousand gold florins and unilateral control of their government in exchange for defending the city against the hostile advances of Castruccio Castracani, the Ghibelline lord of neigh-boring Lucca. Charles was the obvious choice; his father, King Robert, was aging and Charles seemed well suited to the military. As a teenager he had demonstrated such high spirits that his father had felt the need to employ a tutor, the saintly Elzear, to moderate his son's behavior, but by his early twenties Charles was sufficiently responsible to come into his inheritance and be named duke of Cal-abria. In 1322 his father entrusted him with the difficult task of dislodging the entrenched Aragonese ruler of Sicily and returning the island to Neapolitan rule, an undertaking King Robert himself had tried and failed many times during his long career. Charles was no more successful than the king at achieving this goal, but he evidently acquitted himself with honor on the battlefield, and his reputation as an able military commander was firmly established.

King Robert adored Charles, his only legitimate child, and had high expectations for him. Charles's first marriage was to the daugh-ter of the Holy Roman Emperor. When she died prematurely and childless in 1323, Charles's father quickly arranged for his engage-ment to Marie of Valois, and even sent Elzear to France to ensure that this prestigious alliance with the French royal family came to fruition. Elzear died in Paris but not before accomplishing his mis-sion, and fifteen-year-old Marie married twenty-six-year-old Charles the following year.

Charles was clearly aware of his father's regard and had no trouble speaking his mind to his parent. The acclaimed nineteenth-century Italian scholar Matteo Camera recounted the story of how, when the great convent of Santa Chiara, a highly ambitious project that was initiated in 1310 at the beginning of Robert's reign and took more than twenty years to build, was almost completed, the king took his son for a tour of the new facility. "Robert ... asked him how he liked the sacred temple. To this question Charles replied that the great nave made it seem like a stable and the side chapels were like so many horse-stalls. Robert ... replied, 'May it please God, my son, that you not be the first to feed in this stable!'"

The duke of Calabria rode into Florence on July 30, 1326, accompanied by his new young wife, Marie, assorted members of the royal court, and a large army—"a thousand horse," according to Niccolo Machiavelli, who wrote about the incident two centuries later in his *History of Florence*. Charles's administration seems to have received mixed reviews. Although Machiavelli admitted that "his army prevented further pillage of the Florentine territory by Castruccio," the scribe claimed that the Florentines chafed under the rule of their new master because "the Signory [the city elders] could not do anything without the consent of the duke of Calabria, who ... drew from the people 400,000 florins, although by the agreement entered into with him, the sum was not to exceed 200,000." However, the Florentine chronicler Giovanni Villani, a contemporary of Charles's, presented a much more positive view of his regime. Although conceding the 400,000 florin figure, Villani asserted that this sum was more than offset by the increase in business associated with the transference of the royal court, which attracted large numbers of well-heeled aristocrats.

Certainly, the arrival of the duke and duchess and their many attendants, all of whom were young and sociable and used to spending significant sums of money on gifts and clothes and lavish entertainments, was a novelty in merchant-oriented Florence. (To ensure that the royal party was sufficiently provisioned during its stay in the Florentine palace assigned to their use, six thousand sheep, three thousand pigs, and two thousand calves had been sent on ahead in March.) The Florentine patriarchs, who had clawed their way to power through business acumen, were used to saving and reinvesting their money. They frowned on careless expenditure, especially on

fripperies, and had gone so far as to pass strict sumptuary laws forbidding the wearing of certain expensive articles of dress, a strata-
gem they managed to maintain until their wives caught a glimpse
of their new duchess and the chic fashions of Naples. Marie soon
proved herself an asset to her husband's government by embracing
her female subjects' perspective and defending their right to wear
what they could afford, a progressive stance that won the hearts of the
Florentine gentlewomen. "In the year 1326, in the month of
December, the duke of Calabria, at the petition which the ladies of
Florence made to the duchess his wife, restored to the said ladies a
certain unbecoming and disreputable ornament of thick tresses of
white and yellow silk which they wore about their faces instead of
their hair, which ornament, because displeasing to the Florentine
men . . . they had forbidden to the ladies, and made laws against this
and other unreasonable ornaments," wrote a disapproving Villani.

Joanna's birth, which occurred some time during the first half
of 1326, coincided with her father's Florentine commission. The
date was not recorded, but the chronicler Donato Acciaiuoli stated
that she was born in Florence; possibly he meant en route. Her older
sister, Louise, born the year before, had died that January, so Joanna's
birth would have greatly cheered her mother. In April 1327, Marie
gave birth to her third child, a son, Charles Martel, to great rejoicing, but he lived only eight days, so Joanna remained her father's
heir. According to Villani, when the couple returned to Naples in
1328, the duke of Calabria had "two female children, one born,
and another of which the duchess was pregnant" (Marie's fourth
child, Joanna's younger sister, Maria, born in 1329), again indicating
that Joanna was with her parents during their sojourn in Florence.

The duke and duchess's stay in Florence was cut off by the ominous prospect of imperial invasion. The Ghibellines, worried that
the duke of Calabria's presence signaled a new offensive on the part
of the Guelphs, appealed to the emperor for support, and this time,
unexpectedly, he answered their summons.

The emperor, Louis of Bavaria, had been plagued from the start of his reign by an extended quarrel with the papacy. Custom dictated that, in order to be recognized as Holy Roman Emperor, a candidate first had to be elected king of the Romans, which was the title the Germans gave to their monarch (yet another holdover from the days of Caesar), and then crowned emperor in Rome by the pope or one of his representatives. But Louis took the title king of the Romans by force after his election was disputed by an opposition candidate who had won an equal number of votes. This action provoked the ire of Pope John XXII, who claimed the right to mediate, and who further argued that nobody could be emperor without his approval. Just to make certain that his position on this matter was absolutely clear, the pope excommunicated Louis and placed all his constituents under interdict.

Louis still hungered for an imperial coronation, however, so when his Ghibelline supporters in Italy begged him to raise an army to come to their defense, he decided to use this occasion to get himself crowned in Rome, pope or no pope. Additionally, to punish King Robert for sending his son to Florence and upsetting the balance of power in the region, and to further needle his papal antagonist by adding Guelph territory to his dominions, Louis decided to attack the kingdom of Naples. To this end, he made an alliance with the Neapolitans' most feared enemy, Frederick III of Aragon, king of Sicily. Their plan was to encircle and then invade Naples, Louis with the imperial army from the north by land, and Frederick with his Sicilian forces from the west, by sea.

The Neapolitans knew their proximity to hostile Sicily made them vulnerable to a two-front war and had long dreaded precisely this type of assault. Robert in Naples and Charles in Florence carefully followed Louis' progress through Italy. Understanding that his primary target was Naples, many northern Italian towns were happy to pay Louis a tribute to leave them alone. The Ghibelline cities of Milan, Verona, Ferrara, and Mantua threw open their gates to the emperor, and their leaders were rewarded with imperial titles. The Florentines' bitter enemy, Castruccio Castracani, who had started all the trouble in the first place, was elevated to duke of Lucca by allying himself with the emperor and helping his forces to take Pisa away from the Guelphs. In January 1328, Louis triumphantly entered Rome, where he satisfied his ambition by being crowned Holy Roman Emperor by one of his supporters. "In this manner was Louis the Bavarian crowned Emperor by the people of Rome, to the great disgrace and offence of the Pope and the Holy Church," wrote Giovanni Villani in his chronicle. "What presumption in the accursed Bavarian! Nowhere in history do we find that an Emperor, however hostile to the Pope he may have been before, or may afterwards have become, ever allowed himself to be crowned by anyone but the Pope or his legates, with the single exception of this Bavarian; and the fact excited great astonishment."

At this point Robert judged the situation sufficiently dire to recall Charles home to prepare for the expected invasion. The duke of Calabria, together with his pregnant wife and two-year-old daughter and all their court, rode out of Florence, leaving the city under the protection of a viceroy and a standing army of a hundred thousand soldiers, and headed grimly for Naples, resigned to war.

But as so often happened in the Middle Ages, a mixture of politics, vanity, and accident intervened. The pope, hearing of Louis' Roman coronation, repaid the insult by issuing a bull from Avignon deposing him as emperor. In retaliation, Louis signed a proclamation deposing the pope and set up a new one of his own choosing in Rome. Then, instead of marching out of the city to join forces with the Sicilians, Louis, perhaps responding to the criticism voiced by Villani, stayed in Rome in order to organize a second coronation for himself, this time by his puppet pope. The festivities surrounding this second coronation so depleted the emperor's financial resources that he was no longer able to pay his army, and so, when the citizens of Rome finally rebelled against him in August 1328, he was forced to retreat to Germany. His pope fled to Pisa before falling into enemy hands and spent his remaining days in captivity in France. Ghibelline prospects in the region were further damaged by the sudden death of Castruccio and by the failure of the Sicilians to organize an offensive in time to coordinate with imperial forces. By 1330, Naples was no longer threatened, Rome had once again consented to the absentee leadership of the pope in Avignon, and everything was as it had been before. The Florentine elders even reinstated the sumptuary laws.

The ignominious retreat of the emperor would have been regarded as an unqualified triumph for the Neapolitans had it not been marred by tragedy: the premature death of the duke of Calabria upon his return to Naples. Joanna's father died on November 9, 1328, not of an ambush by enemies in the rushed journey home, nor of a wound or fall sustained in preparing for war, but of a fever contracted from overexerting himself in the heat at his favorite sport, falconry. The crown prince was laid to rest in a tomb at the church of Santa Chiara in one of the "horse stalls" he had earlier ridiculed. To his father's great grief—"The crown has fallen from my head," Robert is reputed to have mourned—the witty rejoinder Robert had made to his son had come to pass, or perhaps the chroniclers, as sometimes happened, supplied this prophetic response after the fact.

When their mother, Marie of Valois, died three years later and was laid to rest in yet another of the stalls of Santa Chiara, Joanna and her younger sister, Maria, found themselves orphaned. As a result, the children were brought up at the magnificent court of their paternal grandfather, Robert, king of Naples, and his second wife, Sancia of Majorca.

~☙~

CHAPTER II

The Court *of* Robert *the* Wise

N

O INFLUENCE IN Joanna's life matched that of her grand-parents King Robert and Queen Sancia. From the vulnerable age of five, Joanna lived with these two potent, charismatic, but utterly dissimilar personalities and their extended court at the grand pleasure palace of the Castel Nuovo. Everything that the future queen of Naples would come to believe about love, life, deportment, education, literature, religion, piety, and especially, the responsibilities of royalty and the role of the sovereign in society, was shaped during this period, either through direct instruction on the part of her grandparents or through observation of their behavior. No school could have offered a more thorough preparation for majesty than the royal court of Naples. The dazzling spectrum of medieval inconsistency was on display during the years of Joanna's youth. At once opulent and austere, secular and saintly, voluptuous and celi-bate, honorable and treacherous, the characters of Robert and San-cia embodied these seemingly irreconcilable contradictions.

Robert was a man of illustrious reputation, much admired throughout Europe for his devotion to learning, his prowess at expanding his dominions at his neighbors' (and the emperor's) expense, and his ability to manage such far-flung and diverse territories as Naples and Provence. He was universally referred to as "Robert the Wise," a sobriquet acquired not out of respect for his judgment, but rather for his ability to compose and deliver some three hundred sermons in Latin, a talent that eluded his counterparts on the other thrones of Europe. Ironically, Boccaccio reported that, as a child, Robert much preferred to throw stones than to study. A contemporary who knew the family went so far as to call him a dullard. Robert refused to learn to read until someone in the household hit upon the idea of teaching him, not with the pious psalms of an ordinary psalter, which was how most medieval children learned their letters, but with the inspired merriment of Aesop's *Fables.* The scheme worked; Robert learned to read and, eventually, to love books. During his reign he amassed a great library and was known for his patronage of scholars and writers. "Who in Italy and indeed throughout Europe is more outstanding than Robert?" wrote Petrarch to a friend in 1339.

Robert's life had been changed forever when his father, Charles the Lame (later King Charles II of Naples), eldest son of family patriarch Charles of Anjou, lost a battle for Sicily and was captured by the king of Aragon. Wishing to extricate himself from captivity, Charles the Lame arranged in 1288 for three of his younger sons— Louis, age fourteen, Robert, age ten, and Raymond Berenger, age seven—to take his place in prison until a treaty could be arranged.

The boys were trucked off to Cuirana, a lonely fortress high on a hill in Aragon. (Charles's eldest son, Charles Martel, heir to the throne of Naples, and another son, Philip, later prince of Taranto, were spared this ordeal.) The children were watched by armed guards day and night. Expenses for the boys' food and clothing fell to Charles, who frequently forgot to send their allowance. The warden of the castle in which they were confined, a cold, unfeeling man, did his duty without pity. "He seems to have tried to frighten the children by telling them if the king of Aragon ordered that they should be thrown down from the rock of Cuirana he would willingly carry out the command, a grim jest that strikes one as being a piece of unnecessary cruelty." The brothers would remain in this place, under these conditions, for seven years, prompting "the tears and terrors of Robert and Raymond Berenger, and especially . . . those of the former who, of the three boys, appears to have felt their captivity in Aragon the most keenly."

For solace, Robert turned to his older brother Louis and the one adult who showed him kindness, a Franciscan friar by the name of Francis le Brun, who had been the children's tutor since early childhood and had compassionately accompanied them to their prison in Aragon to take charge of their schooling. Friar Francis was a member of an extremist sect of the Franciscan brotherhood called the Spirituals, mystics who took their vows of poverty much more seriously than did the rest of their order. After seven years of Francis's tutelage, Robert's older brother Louis developed a tendency for lying on the cold floor all night in a paroxysm of ecstatic prayer and was secretly tonsured and ordained a priest. While not prepared to go that far, Robert maintained an affection for the Spirituals that survived his Aragon imprisonment. This is also, undoubtedly, where he learned the Latin for all those sermons.

In 1295, with the help of the papacy, a settlement was finally hammered out between Naples and Aragon. Charles the Lame was recognized and crowned king of Sicily by the pope, and the island was formally returned to Angevin rule. The king of Aragon, James II, was compensated for his loss by the annexation of Sardinia and Corsica, a consolation prize from the church. To cement the deal and discourage future aggression, a double wedding, admirable in its symmetry, was arranged: James II would marry Robert's sister Blanche, and Robert's older brother Louis would marry James II's sister, Violante. Upon the execution of these two marriages, the hostages would be released.

Charles the Lame himself led his daughter Blanche's wedding party to Spain, where he discovered that, while in captivity, Louis had taken a vow of celibacy and had developed such an aversion to women that he could not eat in their presence and would not even kiss his mother after an absence of seven years. Charles was forced to make a last-minute switch in the wedding arrangements and reluctantly sent Robert to the altar in his brother's place. There was nothing to do about it; *somebody* had to marry Violante.

Robert returned to Naples in the company of his father, brothers, and Violante. There was great joy on their arrival, but much had changed during Robert's absence. His younger brother Philip, closest to him in age, had grown to manhood, and the brothers had to become reacquainted. Spared the trauma of imprisonment, Philip had managed to impress his father as an able soldier and statesman, and as a reward, Charles had named him prince of Taranto and vicar-general of Sicily. Nor was Philip the only sibling with whom Robert had to contend. His parents had greatly expanded the family during his captivity; Robert now had three new brothers as well as three new sisters.

Tragedy had also struck the family. Both his eldest brother, Charles Martel, the heir to the throne, and his brother's wife, Clemencia, had died of illness six months before Robert's return. By right of primogeniture, which stated that inheritance was passed through the firstborn, Charles Martel's eldest son, Carobert, should have been acknowledged as the new crown prince of Naples upon the death of his father. But the orphaned Carobert was only seven years old when his father died, and Charles the Lame worried that Naples needed a strong adult ruler to succeed to the throne. Already the Sicilians, who had not been consulted during the negotiations between Naples and Aragon, had rebelled against the terms of the treaty and had elected James II's younger brother Frederick III as their king. Frederick, tickled at this blow to his older brother's prestige, had accepted the honor, raised an army, and was in the process of consolidating his hold on the island. Charles the Lame had not gone through two decades of painstaking negotiation to hand Sicily over to a renegade branch of the Aragonese crown. Frederick III's challenge to Neapolitan authority had to be met, and not by a seven-year-old.

As the second-born son, Louis was the natural candidate to become his father's heir, but the deeply religious Louis would have none of it. Charles ordered him to dress in the rich fabrics and gorgeous raiment of state; Louis wore a plain white friar's robe with a hood. His father insisted he ride, though Spiritual Franciscans were supposed to walk barefoot; Louis obstinately chose as his mount a lowly mule instead of a horse. When Louis absolutely refused to eat off the silver plates used during banquets, Charles finally gave up. In a ceremony at the Castel Nuovo in 1296, Louis publicly renounced his rights of inheritance in favor of Robert and soon afterward was accepted into the church. To get the inconvenient Carobert out of the way, Charles assigned him the lesser kingdom of Hungary, which was part of the dowry Charles's wife, Mary, had brought with her, and hustled him off to grow up and govern his new realm in the company of a small army. The pope's approval further legitimized what might otherwise have been construed as an unscrupulous usurpation of Carobert's rights, and that was how Robert, the little stone thrower, got to be heir to the throne of Naples.

Of course, this bending of the rules of primogeniture did not go unnoticed by Robert's brothers, and later, by Robert's brothers' wives. For if a third son could be king, why shouldn't a fourth or fifth son, or even a sixth, aspire to the position as well?

~⋇~

The other powerful personality at the court of Naples during Joanna's formative years was her step-grandmother, Robert's second wife, Sancia of Majorca. Violante had died in 1302 after only five years of marriage (the wedding had been contracted in 1295 but the ceremony hadn't taken place until 1297). Despite her short tenure, Violante nevertheless fulfilled the obligation for which she had been conscripted by leaving her husband two sons as potential heirs: Louis, who died in 1310, and Charles, future father of Joanna. Immediately after Violante's death, Charles the Lame sought a new wife for Robert and settled on Sancia. His decision was heavily influenced (as, indeed, were most of his decisions) by his obsession to retake Sicily from Frederick III. Sancia was the eldest daughter of the king of Majorca, uncle of the king of Aragon. By affiancing Robert to Sancia, Charles the Lame enlisted a fresh accomplice in the struggle for Sicily. Ideally, he expected that, at some unspecified time in the future, Robert and his new father-in-law would launch a two-pronged assault against Frederick, Naples from the east and Majorca from the west. Robert was duly married to Sancia in 1304, and when Charles the Lame died in 1309, the pair were crowned king and queen of Naples, Jerusalem, and Sicily, with the full support of the pope in Avignon.

Very early into his second marriage, the new king must have realized that, while the Angevins had no doubt gained a military ally, and Naples a queen, he, Robert, had not truly secured a wife. Sancia's most obvious and overpowering character trait was her extreme piety. The new queen of Naples hailed from a family that had been infected by the same strain of infatuation for the Spiritual Franciscans as had Robert's older brother Louis. To the great chagrin of the king of Majorca, three of Sancia's four brothers would eventually renounce their rights to his crown in order to join the mendicant friars.*

Like her brothers, Sancia embraced the cause of the Spiritual Franciscans and, because she was a woman, that of their sister order,

---

* This idea was evidently acquired by Sancia's eldest brother and passed on to the rest of the family as a result of a brief conversation with Robert's saintly brother Louis on his way home from prison in 1295.

the Poor Clares, a religious movement founded in 1253 by Saint Clare of Assisi. Poor Clares were nuns who completely withdrew from society, devoting themselves to a life of poverty, denial, and sacrifice. The sisters owned no property, relying on what sustenance their brother friars could beg. Poor Clares wore their hair short and wore coarse gray robes and sandals in imitation of Saint Francis; they fasted regularly and never ate meat; they lived shut off from the world in high-walled convents. Most prohibitive was the strict rule regarding conversation. The women who entered a Clarissan convent took a vow of silence. Speaking was allowed for only one hour a day, and never on Fridays or at meals.

Sancia made no secret of her attraction to the order. She petitioned the pope as early as 1312 to be allowed to surround herself with Clarisses in the inner sanctum of her rooms at the Castel Nuovo. The pope wrote back granting her two such attendants, later raised to three. Penetrating this human barrier of sanctity for the purposes of procreation must have been daunting. Robert might just as well have married the king of Majorca for all the conjugal bliss he got out of his relationship with his wife. The situation did not improve with time. In 1316, Sancia asked the pope for a divorce so that she could herself become a Poor Clare and retire to a convent. She reiterated the request the following year, at which time, to augment her case, she accused Robert of cheating on her. The pope wrote back twice denying her suit and admonishing her to pay more attention to her husband. He also chastised Robert for his infidelity. It came as no surprise to anyone in Naples that the couple had no children.

In place of offspring, Sancia devoted herself to the Spiritual Franciscans, referring to them as her "sons" and herself as their "mother." She conceived of herself as their protector and sought to establish Naples as a refuge for the movement. Her first act on becoming queen was to persuade Robert to begin work on Santa Chiara, the church Joanna's father, Charles, would later denigrate as a horse stable. Sancia designed Santa Chiara to house a double convent, one for the Franciscans (or the Friars Minor, as they were called) and one for the Poor Clares.

The Spirituals certainly needed the help, as their uncompromising stance on poverty had run afoul of official church policy, which was to accumulate as much wealth as possible in the shortest time. This was particularly true of Pope John XXII, whose reign coincided with the first twenty years of Sancia's. Notorious for taxing his flock unmercifully, selling papal offices to the highest bidder, and distributing high honors, including cardinalships, to family members, John slept on a pillow trimmed in fur and threw enormous, expensive parties, accounts of which have been preserved in the annals of the period. For the marriage of one of Pope John's great-nieces, for example, the guests dined on "4,012 loaves of bread, 8¾ oxen, 55¼ sheep, 8 pigs, 4 boars, a large quantity of different kinds of fish, 200 capons, 690 chickens, 580 partridges, 270 rabbits, 40 plovers, 37 ducks, 50 pigeons, 4 cranes, 2 pheasants, 2 peacocks, 292 small birds, 3 cwt. 2lbs. of cheese, 3,000 eggs, a mere 2,000 apples, pears and other fruits; they drank 11 barrels of wine."

Clearly, the Spirituals' spartan lifestyle and insistence that Christ had meant for the apostles (and by implication the church) to live in poverty was unacceptable. To John, their movement was not only embarrassing but also dangerous. Others were beginning to look askance at the papal lifestyle and were joining their voices in the call for reform. To squelch this opposition, John XXII issued a number of bulls insisting that Christ and the apostles were not against the owning of property and proclaiming it heretical to believe otherwise. Then, to emphasize his position, John had four Spiritual Franciscans who refused to recant their beliefs burned at the stake in Marseille in May 1318.

The pope's actions had the opposite effect: rather than suppressing the Spiritual movement, he hardened the will of its leaders and increased the calls for reform. Devout Franciscans flocked to Naples; the Castel Nuovo was filled with friars; Sancia's own confessor was one of the heads of the movement. The queen's eldest brother, James of Majorca, dressed in his ragged habit, could often be seen begging on the streets of the old city. There was even some talk within Sancia's circle of deposing John XXII in favor of her brother James. Encouraged by her followers, Sancia aggressively inserted herself into the reform debate, writing letters to both the pope and the Franciscan general minister. Robert, strongly influenced by Friar Francis's beliefs during his youthful captivity, with a revered brother who would be sainted for embodying Spiritual Franciscan values, supported his wife's program.

Although certainly sincere in her beliefs, an undeniable whiff of ambition pervades Sancia's frenetic activity on behalf of the Spirituals. Very likely, the queen aspired to sainthood. A hint of this is found in one of her letters to the Franciscan general minister, in which she urged the order to adopt the Spiritual interpretation of poverty. "I . . . consider it the greatest grace if God causes me to die and to be a martyr for this cause," Sancia wrote. A few lines later she went even further and implied divine inspiration, which might, in a pinch, stand in for the miracle that the queen knew was a necessary requirement for sanctification. "On Thursday, the eighteenth of April, I entered the small chapel next to my chamber in the Castel Nuovo in Naples where well through three candles before daybreak, with the door closed, alone with the body of Christ, which was upon the altar, I commended myself to him and afterward began to write as the Lord directed me, without any counsel, human or earthly . . . written in my own hand on the aforesaid day in the Castel Nuovo . . . in the year 1331."

Sancia assumed responsibility for the education of Joanna and her younger sister upon the death of their parents. Between having to sit through three hundred of her grandfather's sermons and the extreme spiritual indoctrination promoted by her grandmother, it is not surprising that Joanna developed a familiarity with the Latin tongue. The wonder would have been if she had not learned it.

~⊛~

Despite her grandmother's best efforts, however, Joanna's formative years were anything but sheltered. Other potent influences were at work at the court of Naples, which, even as a child, Joanna would not have been able to ignore. For competing with the climate of rigid asceticism fostered by Sancia was the all-too-material and decidedly less virtuous world of the royal entourage. Princely courts were extended-family affairs in the fourteenth century, and Naples was no exception. Of the many relatives who chose to avail themselves of the glittering social whirl of the capital, one stood out: Joanna's aunt, Catherine of Valois, widow of Robert the Wise's younger brother Philip, prince of Taranto.

Catherine was Joanna's mother's older half-sister (both were fathered by Charles of Valois). Catherine had married Philip in 1313, when Philip was thirty-five and she just ten. Catherine was Philip's second wife. He had divorced his first on a trumped-up charge of adultery after fifteen years of marriage and six children in order to wed Catherine, who had something he wanted. She was the sole heir to the title of empress of Constantinople.

How a ten-year-old French girl came to inherit the legal claim to this city in Greek Byzantium, possibly the most desired metropolis in history, manifests a peculiarly medieval contrivance. A century before, in 1204, the army of the Fourth Crusade, en route to the Holy Land to liberate Jerusalem for Rome, instead sacked Constantinople, even though it was a Christian city and the Greeks were in fact staunch allies of the pope in the struggle against the Muslims. Within three days the crusading defenders of Christianity had managed to destroy centuries' worth of the most precious art the civilized world had to offer. An eyewitness to the carnage, Nicetas

Choniates, described the crusaders' rampage: "They smashed the holy images and hurled the sacred relics of the Martyrs into places I am ashamed to mention, scattering everywhere the body and blood of the Saviour. These heralds of Anti-Christ seized the chalices and the patens, tore out the jewels and used them as drinking cups ... And they brought horses and mules into the Church, the better to carry off the holy vessels and the engraved silver and gold that they had torn from the throne, and the pulpit, and the doors, and the furniture wherever it was to be found; and when some of these beasts slipped and fell, they ran them through with their swords, fouling the Church with their blood and ordure." When they had finished vandalizing the city, the crusading knights, many of them younger sons of noble families from France, decided to stay and rule. They elected one of their company as emperor and then parceled out the territory west and south of the capital to themselves in order of rank. That was how the Latin Empire of Byzantium, so called for the official language of the western church, was founded.

The Greeks took nearly sixty years to recapture Constantinople, but they finally succeeded in 1261, forcing the last Latin emperor, Baldwin II, to flee the city in such a hurry that he left behind his luggage. Making his way to Italy, Baldwin II struck a bargain with Joanna's great-great-grandfather Charles of Anjou, in which the ousted crusader ceded the principality of Achaia, on the western coast of Byzantium, to Charles in exchange for Charles's help in regaining his empire. Although the planned invasion never came off—Charles's fleet was destroyed by a particularly violent storm on the eve of the attack—Achaia nonetheless remained in Angevin hands. In 1294, Charles the Lame awarded the territory to his son Philip, prince of Taranto. The Achaia legacy carried with it the unspoken expectation that Philip would expand the family's holdings to the east; this he had done by raising an army and conquering the important city of Durazzo, on the western coast of

Albania. A bustling fortified port, Durazzo was the starting point for the Via Egnatia, the principal east-west route in Byzantium, which led directly to Constantinople. "Now we come to speak of Albania, which, on its southern side, is right next to Greece," wrote a European chronicler, probably a member of the Dominican order, in 1308 in a journal titled *An Anonymous Description of Eastern Europe*:

> They do have one city called Duracium [Durazzo] which belongs to the Latins and from which they get textiles and other necessities. The Prince of Taranto, son of the King of Sicily [Charles II], now holds sway over part of this kingdom... From Apulia and the city of Brindisi one may cross over to Durazzo in one night, and from Durazzo one may travel on through Albania to Greece and to Constantinople much more easily and without all the road difficulties and perils of the sea. The Roman emperors of ancient times used this route for it is excessively tedious to transport a large army in such a period of time by sea and by such long roads.

By singling out Durazzo, Philip made plain his ambition to retake the capital of the Latin empire.

But Philip of Taranto had a rival. Charles of Valois, the powerful younger brother of Philip IV, king of France, had no kingdom of his own and wanted one desperately. Charles had muscled several other suitors out of the way in 1301 in order to marry Baldwin II's granddaughter, who had inherited the old emperor's claim to Constantinople. Unfortunately, in 1308, just as Charles was in the process of preparing for an invasion of Greece, his wife died, and the title of empress passed to their eldest daughter, Catherine. Even so prominent and influential a member of the French royal family as Charles could not hope to obtain a papal dispensation to marry his own daughter, and so he had reluctantly surrendered his dream of empire to Philip of Taranto, upon whom he had bestowed Catherine's ten-year-old hand in 1313.

Catherine was twenty-eight years old, recently widowed, and a force to be reckoned with when the newly orphaned Joanna and her sister, Maria, first knew her at the Castel Nuovo in 1331. Shrewd, highly intelligent, and vital, Catherine was supremely conscious of her exalted ancestry and wore her title of empress of Constantinople as though it were a rare gem of mythic origin. Even the death of her husband, Philip, in 1331 had not dissuaded her from persisting in her efforts to reclaim the Latin Empire for herself and her three young sons: Robert, Louis, and Philip. A series of shockingly inept leaders had left the Byzantine Empire vulnerable to attack from the west, and this state of affairs was well known in Italy. Moreover, Catherine was used to getting her way. Her splendid household, near the Castel Nuovo, constituted a court-within-a-court, a rival hub radiating energy of a distinctly worldly nature. Not for Catherine was the spiritual life of denial and chastity embraced by Queen Sancia. The empress of Constantinople was a devotee of earthly pleasures. She dressed royally, as befit her position, and even her objects of devotion were brilliant in their ornamentation. A penchant for luxury was not her only vice. Catherine enjoyed the company of men and made no secret of her dalliances. Less than a year after her husband died, she was already carrying on quite publicly with a twenty-three-year-old phenomenon by the name of Niccolò Acciaiuoli.

Niccolò, a Florentine, had arrived in Naples with his father to help represent his family's financial interests. The Acciaiuolis owned the third-largest commercial enterprise in Italy—one of the supercompanies, as they would eventually become known—which made it the third-largest business concern in the world. The family's interests were highly diversified: commodity dealing, shipping (the Acciaiuolis were one of three select firms contracted to manage the kingdom of Naples's virtual monopoly on grain and grain exports), banking and corporate finance, manufacturing, merchandising, the operation of retail outlets, multinational trading, including the wholesaling of fine art and rare spices from the Far East—the list went on and on. The Acciaiuolis maintained branch offices in nearly every kingdom in Europe, including the papal court at Avignon, and the company's senior executives whispered advice on tax collection and account balancing into the ears of every medieval monarch. The royal court of Naples was an especially choice assignment for a younger member of the Acciaiuoli clan like Niccolò, seeking to establish himself in the world. Robert the Wise, who needed ever-increasing loans to cover the skyrocketing expenses brought about by his repeated attempts to recover Sicily, was the family's most valued client.

In those days, representatives of the super-companies, particularly those dealing with royalty, were called on to provide a full range of services, including but not limited to making loans, tracking down exotic luxuries that had caught the fancy of a favored mistress, ferreting out confidential information, and playing the dangerous game of informant. Even by these standards, Niccolò was exceptional. Filippo Villani, who knew him, called Niccolò "very handsome . . . a marvelously fluent man." When Niccolò first arrived in Naples, Villani continued, he "kept a shop, not full of trash but of valuable merchandise brought from many places, and he was planning to do much business." Catherine of Valois, whom he met through his contacts at court, was one of his most prized clients. Intent upon her plans for empire, Catherine was involved in a particularly complex transaction with her brother-in-law John (another younger brother of Robert the Wise). John had agreed to cede his right to the principality of Achaia, which he had bought earlier for ten thousand ounces of gold from her late husband, Philip, to Catherine's eldest son, Robert, in return for a cash settlement. Acting as Catherine's agent, Niccolò managed the negotiation brilliantly. He bargained John down to five thousand ounces of gold from ten by sweetening the pot with the offer of the duchy of Durazzo in lieu of cash, and then secured the empress's further admiration by loaning her the entire five thousand from the Acciaiuoli banking concern. His handling of this affair so impressed Catherine that she made him her principal counselor, and even appointed him tutor to her young sons.

> He [Niccolò] began to frequent the court of the Empress of Constantinople. And since his affable wisdom greatly pleased that most prudent lady, he came to enjoy such high and honorable favor with her that she entrusted to him her entire family and freely committed to him the charge of her household. On his part, recognizing the importance of the duties imposed upon him he took it upon himself to instruct the children, previously neglected, as is the custom in Naples, with regard to the manners, habits and discretion suitable to their royal station.

Apparently, Catherine did not limit Niccolò's domestic responsibilities to the needs of her sons. "It was said openly that [Catherine] included Niccolò Acciaiuoli among her other lovers . . . and made him rich and powerful," Villani asserted bluntly.

Catherine's freewheeling lifestyle and generally conceited demeanor excited the jealousy and resentment of another cadet branch of the family—that of John, now styled duke of Durazzo as a result of the recent transaction with his sister-in-law. John had also taken a French girl, Agnes of Périgord, as a second wife after his first, a princess of Achaia, had refused to consummate the marriage and been imprisoned for her temerity. Agnes came from very good stock—not quite as grand as Catherine's, but still very distinguished and aristocratic—and she resented her sister-in-law's unquestioned air of superiority. The rivalry between the two women only deepened when John died in 1336 and his lands and titles devolved upon Agnes's eldest son, Charles of Durazzo, who was thirteen at the time of his father's death. Agnes was devoted to Charles and very ambitious for his advancement. She knew that

Catherine's sons held a slight advantage in rank over hers, owing to their father's having been older and therefore closer to the throne. But Agnes, while less flamboyant than Catherine, was every bit a match for the empress of Constantinople in terms of enterprise and calculation.

~⚬~

One other person occupied a position of importance in Joanna's life during her childhood years—her nurse, Philippa the Catanian.

Philippa had served Joanna's family for nearly three decades. She had originally been hired by Joanna's grandmother Violante, when, accompanying Robert the Wise in 1298 on one of his futile attempts to retake Sicily, Violante had discovered she was pregnant. An armed military camp not being the most convenient place to give birth, Violante recruited additional female household staff from the indigenous population. Catania, a port city on the eastern coast of Sicily, was nearby, and Philippa, "the daughter of a poor fisherman," who was nonetheless "attractive in manner and appearance" (according to Boccaccio, who knew her later in life), was employed as a wet nurse even though "only a few days before she had been washing the clothes of the foreigners."

Thrilled to have escaped the laundry room for the boudoir, Philippa applied herself to her new duties with diligence and competence. By turns charming, ingratiating, and soothing, Philippa soon made herself indispensable, so much so that when the military campaign ended, and Robert was forced (as usual) to retreat, Violante brought her new wet nurse back with her to Naples where Philippa "remained among the other servants."

Once ensconced in Naples, Philippa's life was to take the sort of preposterous turn more commonly associated with Shakespearean drama than with reality. At the same time Philippa was impressing Violante with her capabilities, an Ethiopian kitchen slave christened Raymond of Campagno (after the chief cook at the palace, who had purchased the African from some pirates) was similarly catching the eye of his employer, Violante's father-in-law, Charles the Lame. Raymond did such a good job at the royal banquets ("to him almost all the duties of the kitchen were assigned") that he ended up earning his freedom and replacing his namesake as head chef. From there, Raymond somehow made the leap from the kitchen to the royal household and was appointed guard of the king's wardrobe, at which time "he began to attract the favor of the King and the nobles and to amass wealth." Raymond turned from administrator to soldier, from soldier to commander. Cognizant of Raymond's obvious abilities, and seeking to further reward this exemplary manservant, King Charles thought to provide him with a wife, just as Violante, also seeking to reward a favored domestic (or perhaps apprehensive of Philippa's physical charms), was looking to provide Philippa with a husband. Such a happy convergence of royal interests was not to be ignored and so, without bothering to consult the principals, the marriage was arranged with admirable efficiency. Very soon, as Boccaccio observed, "the African soldier joined the bed of the Sicilian washerwoman."

Although brought together in this unconventional manner at the impulse of their sovereigns, Philippa and Raymond each nonetheless recognized and appreciated the resourcefulness of the other, and the opportunities afforded them by their union. In Raymond, Philippa obtained a spouse as industrious in his husbandry as he was ferocious on the battlefield. As victory after victory came his way, and he was raised to ever-higher commands, Raymond never failed to demand and collect his reward. Ever mindful of the poverty and concurrent helplessness of his youth, the Ethiopian kept a sharp eye on his assets and invested wisely. Philippa soon found herself mistress of a vast holding, which included "towns, estates, villas, horses, numerous servants, rich clothes, and all goods in abundance," noted Boccaccio.

For his part, Raymond acquired in Philippa an intelligent, attractive wife who gave him three sons and a daughter, and whose political acumen and connections helped him to advance his career. After Violante died, Philippa returned to the Castel Nuovo (thus lending credence to the notion that her marriage had been arranged because Violante feared a rival) to offer her services to Robert the Wise's new queen, Sancia, and to Joanna's mother, Marie of Valois. Again, Philippa proved herself invaluable to her royal mistresses. "She [Philippa] helped them, served them, and showed herself ever ready for their commands. She prepared and took care of their ornaments and various lotions and demonstrated that she was a perfect mistress . . . She exceeded in age the other women in the court . . . and it seemed by long habit she had learned the customs of the court." With Philippa's influence, Raymond was made royal seneschal, a chief adviser to the king himself. "What a ridiculous thing to see an African from a slave prison, from the vapor of the kitchen, standing before Robert, the King, performing royal service for the young nobleman, governing the court and making laws for those in power!" Boccaccio wrote.

When her husband became seneschal, Philippa too was rewarded with a promotion and appointed by Marie of Valois to be guardian to her daughter Joanna, the heir to the throne. In 1331, after Marie died, "Philippa was honored as Joanna's mother." While again unorthodox, the choice of Philippa as surrogate parent was perhaps, given the circumstances, the most compassionate. To five-year-old Joanna, bewildered by the loss of both parents and the concept of death, Philippa represented continuity and comfort. The older woman was someone Joanna had known from birth. She was familiar with her childish routine and could coax her, when necessary, through her duties. Emotionally, Philippa provided the warmth and love of which Joanna's step-grandmother, Sancia, was incapable, and Joanna clung to her accordingly.

Socially and politically, however, the elevation of the former laundress to so powerful an office as mother to the heir to the throne was more problematic. Already Philippa's rise, and that of her husband, was viewed with suspicion and jealousy by the nobility. The couple made no attempt to hide their good fortune and flaunted their wealth, particularly through their children, for Philippa, too, had sons for whom she was ambitious. "You would think they were the children of a king rather than of a slave," Boccaccio complained. Through the years of Joanna's childhood and young adulthood, Philippa's influence at court remained unparalleled. According to Boccaccio, "nothing serious, arduous, or great was accomplished unless it was approved by Robert, Philippa, and Sancia."

※

This, then, was the politically charged environment into which Joanna and her sister, Maria, were thrust. And just when it seemed impossible for the situation in Naples to become more complex, or for the competing ambitions at court (already unhealthily focused on Joanna as a conduit to the throne) to become more volatile, in 1333 a new, powerful, and highly dangerous player suddenly propelled himself into the mix.

Carobert, king of Hungary, forgotten eldest son of Charles Martel, the original heir to the throne of Naples, had decided to retrieve his birthright.

~⚓~

CHAPTER III

The Kingdom *of* Hungary

S URELY ONE OF history's wittier little mischiefs is that
Carobert, who had been summarily dismissed from Naples on
the grounds of youth, should turn out to be the family's most successful warrior. Arriving with his small band of knights in Hungary
in 1301, thirteen-year-old Carobert had been crowned king with a
makeshift diadem by a local archbishop. The new king's reign had
been immediately contested by some of the realm's most powerful
barons, who elected their own candidate, twelve-year-old Wenceslas,
son of the king of Bohemia, in his place. Carobert and his supporters were forced to retreat to southern Hungary, where they mar-
shaled new allies and engaged in a guerrilla war against the
pro-Wenceslas party.

Luckily for Carobert, his mother, Clemencia, had been a Habsburg and the daughter of the Holy Roman Emperor. Carobert
appealed to this powerful branch of the family for aid against his
enemies. By 1304, two of his mother's brothers, the king of Germany and the duke of Austria, had entered the fray on the side of
their nephew, at which point Wenceslas, who was never much of a
king anyway ("The barons did not concede him a single castle, nor
any sort of power or office, not even a parcel of royal authority," a

Hungarian chronicler sniffed), called for his father to come and get him and withdrew to Bohemia, taking his crown with him. When Carobert and his uncle, the king of Germany, pursued his former rival into Bohemia in 1305, Wenceslas hastily renounced the crown and his rights to Hungary in favor of his cousin Otto. Otto in turn went to Transylvania, at the outskirts of his new realm, as far away from Carobert and his army as possible, and had himself crowned king.

Carobert continued to make inroads into central Hungary, and by 1307 he was clearly the victor. Still, Carobert could not officially be crowned king because the Hungarians insisted that only the "Holy Crown" could be used for coronations, and Otto had the Holy Crown. It took several years to get it back, as Otto had himself lost it to another Transylvanian baron. Eventually the crown was tracked down and returned, and Carobert was proclaimed the legitimate king of Hungary "with great solemnity and joy" on August 27, 1310.

The rite of the Holy Crown only took the new king so far, however, and Carobert soon discovered that the task of subduing the kingdom over which he was now the legitimate sovereign was far from over. The twenty-two-year-old king faced stout opposition from Hungary's landed aristocracy, some of whom had grown so powerful that they functioned effectively as independent monarchs. One by one, with methodical determination, Carobert attacked these men and their families, besieging, expropriating, and then redistributing their vast estates and castles to himself and a rival set of barons, thereby creating a new ruling class loyal to the crown. His authority would not be consolidated for a further ten years, but at the end of that period, Carobert found himself the undisputed ruler of a realm that stretched from Bosnia and northern Croatia on the bank of the Adriatic Sea in the west, to Wallachia and Moldavia on the Black Sea in the east, and to Transylvania and the Carpathian Mountains in the north. Having been deprived of his birthright because it was feared he could not take Sicily, Carobert controlled an area approximately three times the size of the kingdom of Naples by the 1330s.

Fortune would favor Carobert beyond even these considerable military triumphs. For no sooner did he establish his prerogative in Hungary than gold was discovered in Slovakia, northwest of Budapest. The Hungarians had found gold before, most notably in Transylvania, but not like this. Suddenly, Carobert found himself sitting on the world's largest supply of the world's most precious metal. It is estimated that, starting in the 1320s, Hungary mined between two thousand and three thousand pounds of gold a year, or "one third of the total production of the world as then known, and five times as much as any other European state." Almost immediately, the kingdom entered an era of prosperity that even today is called, without irony, its golden age. Carobert levied taxes on his mining operations so that nearly 40 percent of the profits were diverted to the crown, and the royal income soared. There was at once enough gold for the kingdom to mint its own coins, which made procuring luxury goods and agreeable trading partners much easier. Even more to Carobert's interests, he now had enough gold to fund an army sufficient to carry out his expansionist plans and to intimidate his neighbors. Though the new king's tax policies were more demanding and oppressive than those of any previous monarch in Hungarian history, the populace neither rebelled nor took offense. That much gold excused a great many sins.

Despite the many years away from the land of his birth, and through all his trials and successes, Carobert never lost sight of his ancestry. Politically and culturally his ambitions and tastes were distinctly Angevin, not Hungarian. His improvements at court were Western European in nature. He organized his army along the sort of chivalric feudal lines familiar to his French forebears but strange to his Hungarian vassals. Similarly, his sweeping interpretation of the power of the monarchy, his contempt for the Hungarians' representative public assemblies known as Diets, and his "habit of granting privileges 'out of his special grace' (*de speciali gratia*), with no regard to the customs of the realm . . . probably derived from the political traditions of the kingdom of Sicily [Naples]." Carobert's administrative system, his attitude toward property (unless specifically deeded to an avid supporter or the church, it was his), and his insistence on recording documents in written registers came straight from a blueprint originally formulated by his great-grandfather Charles of Anjou seventy years before. When Carobert issued his first silver coin—conveniently they'd found silver mixed in with all the gold in the mines—the royal minters copied the style of those struck in Naples by his uncle Robert the Wise. Even Western European sporting preferences were foisted on his subjects: in 1318, the Hungarians were introduced to their first-ever competitive jousting tournament, a spectacle that was thereafter held annually.

When it came to matrimony, however, the king of Hungary wedded for tactical advantage, not lineage, as is evidenced by his marriage to Elizabeth of Poland in 1320. Elizabeth, Carobert's fourth and last wife, was the daughter of Wladyslaw I, king of Poland, known as Wladyslaw the Elbow-High. The king of Hungary had been an early champion of the diminutive Wladyslaw and by this marriage cemented their relationship, thereby achieving regional hegemony and presenting a formidable combination to opponents.

Elizabeth was fifteen to Carobert's thirty-two when the pair married. Her three predecessors had died young and childless, and the new queen of Hungary knew she was expected to provide her husband with an heir. To her and her husband's great joy and relief, Elizabeth fulfilled this obligation, giving birth to five sons, three of whom survived: Louis, born in 1326; Andrew, in 1327; and Stephen, in 1332.

With Elizabeth, Carobert acquired an exceptionally determined and energetic partner—manipulative, capable, and eager for power. The queen maintained her own household and senior advisers (another monarchical custom borrowed from Western Europe) and managed several important Hungarian estates and townships in her own name. Elizabeth did not shrink from adversity and was not inclined toward leniency. In 1330, her brother Casimir had deflowered one of her ladies-in-waiting, a naive young woman named Claire, during a visit to his sister's court. Distraught, Claire's father, Felician Záh, a minor baron, had barged into the royal dining room at supper time, sword drawn, to exact revenge for his daughter's stolen honor. He was pierced through by some alert guards, but not before he managed to stab Elizabeth through the hand. In the months following this incident, the queen showed neither mercy to her assailant nor sympathy for her former attendant. Felician's body was severed of its various appendages and then dispersed throughout the kingdom as a grim reminder of the perils of failed assassination attempts. "His head was sent to Buda, and his two legs and two arms to other towns," reported John, the Franciscan minister provincial of Hungary at the time. The baron's wife and children, including the hapless Claire, were rounded up and gruesomely tortured before being put to death, as were all their relatives "within the third degree of kinship." The crown's handling of this affair made quite an impression on the citizenry: neither Elizabeth nor any member of her family was ever bothered by a disgruntled subject in this fashion again. The queen seems to have accepted this outcome as a vindication of her methods.

Carobert had never resigned himself to the usurpation of his rights of primogeniture in southern Italy. From the day he had been shunted off to Hungary, he had continued to protest, both to Robert the Wise and to the pope, the 1309 decree expediently consigning the sovereignty of the kingdom of Naples to his uncle rather than himself. During his adolescence and early manhood, while the outcome of the Hungarian campaign remained in doubt, Carobert's protestations had not carried much weight in Naples or Avignon. In 1317, the king of Hungary had tested the waters by sending his brother-in-law, the dauphin of Vienne, to Naples, charged with reclaiming the principality of Salerno as a precursor to larger demands, but even this modest proposal was rebuffed. However, as time progressed and his situation improved, Carobert's complaints became more difficult to ignore. By the early 1330s, between his fortunate alliance with Poland through his wife, Elizabeth, and his immense financial resources, the advantage had swung undeniably in the king of Hungary's direction.

Suddenly John XXII, who had managed to ignore completely Carobert's pleas for justice for the previous fifteen years, took it upon himself to write to Robert the Wise to urge him to recognize the king of Hungary's claims and find a way to make satisfactory restitution. Deducing the reasons for the pope's abrupt solicitude for Carobert's cause is not difficult. Despite his unsuccessful Italian campaign, the Holy Roman Emperor, Louis of Bavaria, remained a threat to papal interests. To John XXII's great annoyance, the emperor was using the safety of his court to harbor outspoken theologians who held views on apostolic poverty and other spiritual matters antithetical to those of the pope. Since the emperor's theologians were decidedly more erudite than John XXII himself, support for their positions was gaining throughout Europe. Carobert, on the other hand, was viewed as a loyal servant of the church, having already demonstrated his allegiance to papal orthodoxy by enforcing all of John's edicts within his domain. (Unlike Robert the Wise and Sancia, the king of Hungary unmercifully persecuted the Spiritual Franciscans, driving them from the realm.) John XXII hoped Carobert would use his influence to counteract that of Louis of Bavaria in Eastern Europe. In addition, just at this time, John was also busy intriguing with the king of Bohemia against the emperor for control of northern Italy, and this could not be accomplished without Carobert's approval, or at least his willingness to sign a nonaggression pact.

Moreover, if there was ever a pope who appreciated the value of a gold florin, that pope was John XXII. Under his administration all sorts of new taxes and fines were levied, and the pontifical income rose accordingly. Though the pope was a reputed miser, his clerks were astounded by the treasure of gold plate, precious gems, and coins that were found in the papal vaults upon his death. John had regularly to remind Robert the Wise that the king was in arrears on the annual payment of seven thousand ounces of gold due the papacy according to the terms of the original agreement with Charles of Anjou. The extravagant wealth of the king of Hungary would not have gone unnoticed by John XXII.

For these reasons, then, the pope began pushing hard for reconciliation between Naples and Hungary. John knew that Robert would never have accommodated his nephew Carobert's demands while his own son and heir, Charles of Calabria, was still alive. But Charles had died in 1328. In his place was a little girl, only four years old on November 4, 1330, the day Robert had formally declared Joanna heir to all his lands in a public ceremony at the Castel Nuovo. And therein lay the pope's opportunity. He wasted no time in capitalizing on it. In a letter to Sancia dated December 15, 1330, John XXII proposed his solution to the problem: marry Joanna to one of Carobert's sons and let the eldest child of their union inherit Naples. To John, this arrangement must have seemed ideal—a clever plan to appease the king of Hungary without ever having to admit wrongdoing in the first place. For only in this way could Carobert's grievance be rectified without compromising the integrity of the kingdom of Naples or Robert's rule.

Evidence exists, however, that members of the Neapolitan royal family, already jostling for position within the kingdom as early as 1330, were far less enthusiastic about this matrimonial project than was its author. Ominously, Robert's brother Philip, the prince of Taranto, and his wife, Catherine, the empress of Constantinople, had refused to attend the November 30 ceremony investing Joanna with the rights of inheritance to the kingdom and so had not sworn the oath of fealty to his granddaughter demanded by Robert at that time. It took several months and much persuasion on the part of the pope to bring Philip to terms with his brother's decision, and even then the prince of Taranto refused to take the oath himself, claiming a bad case of gout. A hastily deputized subordinate was sent to the Castel Nuovo on March 3, 1331, as a substitute. Philip's truculence provoked the antagonism of Robert's other brother John, and his wife, Agnes of Périgord, who had dutifully sworn obeisance to Joanna, perhaps to win Robert's approval and improve the chances for a marriage between this valued granddaughter and one of their own sons. Already deeply in competition with each other, neither of these branches of Robert's line was willing to admit the rights of their Hungarian nephew.

Even Philip of Taranto's death in December 1331 did not stop Catherine from intriguing to place one of her sons on the throne of Naples. Aware of the pope's proposal, she appealed to her brother Philip of Valois, the powerful king of France, to secure marriage alliances between her sons, Robert and Louis, and Joanna and Maria. Philip intervened mildly, indicating approval for his sister's request, but the pope seems to have been prepared for this maneuver. In a March 1332 letter, John advised the French king that, unfortunately, Joanna and Maria had already been promised to their Hungarian cousins. Then, just to make sure there was no lingering doubt in anyone's mind as to where the church stood on this question, John issued a bull dated June 30, 1332, officially decreeing that Joanna and Maria marry the sons of the king of Hungary.

Robert and Sancia capitulated. In June 1332, they acceded to papal pressure and came to terms with Carobert. The diplomatic initiative eventually agreed to by both parties specified yet another double marriage. The first would be between Joanna and Carobert's second son, Andrew. Andrew would become duke of Calabria, effective immediately upon his betrothal, and upon reaching his majority (Andrew was only five), he would be crowned king of Naples. The eldest male child of this union, or eldest surviving daughter if the couple produced no sons, would inherit the throne and rule the kingdom.

The second marriage, meant to further tighten the bonds between the two kingdoms, would be between Joanna's younger sister, Maria, and Carobert's eldest son, Crown Prince Louis. Upon Louis' ascension to the throne, Maria would be crowned queen of Hungary, and the eldest surviving child of their union would inherit and rule the kingdom. This engagement would not take place immediately, however, because the treaty also stipulated that if Joanna died before her marriage was consummated, Andrew would marry Maria instead. "Maria was bound to wed one or the other . . . in view of mishap to her sister [Joanna], to whom she was heiress-presumptive, she was . . . looked upon as a reserve claim for Hungary in rebinding itself to the House of Naples."

Ironically, the precise and comprehensive nature of this alliance, which was clearly intended to anticipate every contingency, disguised a deep flaw in communication between the Hungarians and the Neapolitans. Although Robert the Wise agreed to have Andrew crowned king when he was older, he meant as consort to the queen only. Robert never intended Andrew to rule or participate in the Neapolitan government; that responsibility would reside solely with Joanna, whom Robert had already designated his legitimate heir. This distinction was very important to the king of Naples, for it touched on the old complaint that he had stolen the realm from his nephew. If Robert admitted Andrew's right to rule, he admitted guilt, which was out of the question. From the Neapolitan point of view, then, Andrew's future coronation was conceived as an empty honor, designed to raise the Hungarian prince to his wife's rank as a courtesy, nothing more.

Although the Hungarians later claimed to have been ignorant of Robert's true intent, Carobert likely *did* understand that the agreement with Naples was intended to redress his rights through the medium of the next generation and not the current one—that it would be the king of Hungary's grandchild, and not his son, who would rule. Carobert may well have chosen to gloss over this condition, knowing that, for the moment, this was the best deal he was likely to get. Whatever his reasoning, he accepted his uncle's terms without hesitation.

As a further expression of his good will and sincerity, Robert then graciously invited the king of Hungary to be his guest at the Castel Nuovo to celebrate the marriage of six-year-old Andrew to seven-year-old Joanna in a spirit of family unity and amicability.

Carobert and Andrew left Hungary for Naples in June 1333 accompanied by an impressively vast retinue of high-ranking Hungarian barons and churchmen. The queen and her eldest son, Crown Prince Louis, remained at home. Elizabeth's father, Wladyslaw, had just died, and Carobert needed his wife at home to help support her brother Casimir's ascension to the throne of Poland.

Arrangements for the journey were managed by Carobert's Florentine bankers, the Bardi and Peruzzi families, who, with their rivals the Acciaiuolis, comprised the richest and most successful super-companies in Italy. No expense was spared to ensure appropriately luxurious conveyances and provisions. The royal entourage traveled through Croatia to the Adriatic and crossed by ship. Having no choice but to submit to this compromise, the empress of Constantinople made the best of it by lending one of her fleetest vessels, a galley equipped with 120 oarsmen, to help ferry the king and his party across the sea. The royal luggage, which included more than two hundred horses, came by separate passage. "Truly the Angevins traveled more handsomely than emperors," observed a later scholar.

Carobert and Andrew landed at the port city of Vieste, on the eastern coast of the kingdom of Naples, on July 31, 1333. There they were greeted by John, duke of Durazzo, the most senior prince at court, along with a party of suitably eminent Neapolitan nobles whom Robert the Wise had commissioned to escort the Hungarians to the western coast of the kingdom. To mark the seriousness and splendor of the occasion, in a gesture of exceptional hospitality, the king of Naples himself rode out to meet his nephew and great-nephew halfway, near Melfi, to accompany them personally to the capital. The procession, Neapolitan and Hungarian alike, swept majestically into Naples on September 18, 1333, to the delight of the crowds that had gathered to get a glimpse of the two sovereigns and their magnificent trains.

The king of Hungary no doubt retained fond memories of his childhood in southern Italy, but nothing could have prepared his son or his retainers for the grandeur, opulence, and sophistication that was the kingdom of Naples under Robert the Wise. "Italy, as always, presents a somewhat distinct case since she was in essence the fashion leader of the world and the model for luxurious style." The teeming metropolis was filled with merchants and diplomats from what must have seemed to be every quarter of the known world. The heady scent of exotic spices like clove and nutmeg hung in the air, and the banquet tables proffered unfamiliar foods like figs and eel. An astonishing array of riches was on display: precious jewels glittering in ornate Byzantine settings; ivory combs imported from Alexandria and carved by Parisian masters; exquisite white soap produced with olive oil from Castile; the rarest Chinese silks, damasks, linens, and brocades, brilliantly multicolored and gorgeously patterned in intricate designs depicting flowers and birds, and embroidered with gold and silver thread such as "could only be afforded by emperors, kings, popes and their courtiers, or by bishops and princes." The kingdom of Hungary was geographically larger than the kingdom of Naples, but it was far from established shipping routes and no match for its counterpart in terms of population. The number of people living in the twin towns of Buda and Pest, which during the fourteenth century represented the two largest metropolitan boroughs in Hungary (they would not be consolidated into a single entity for centuries), would not reach twenty thousand for another hundred years. Moreover, the leading members of the Hungarian aristocracy spent the majority of their time on remote estates carved out of forests. To walk suddenly into a magnificent capital of one hundred thousand souls, the cultural and mercantile crossroads of east and west, north and south, must have been bewildering.

Carobert's barons were further dazzled by the elegant manners and carefree lifestyle of the Neapolitan court. Robert's extravagant establishment at the Castel Nuovo boasted nearly four hundred domestics. One hundred and four horsemen were on hand to accompany the king on his processions and twelve mule drivers saw to his luggage and other supplies. Forty-two valets and twenty-two demi-valets were on hand to see to the sovereign's every need. The kitchen was crowded with sauciers, pastry cooks, a green grocer, and porters for wood and water. Two servants watched over the tablecloths, and the henhouse had its own keeper. The household staff included carpenters, cleaners, doctors, chamber men and women, copyists of manuscripts and translators of Greek. Twenty-four chaplains and clerics oversaw the King's Chapel, and a lion tamer helped out at the menagerie. During their stay, the Hungarians were feted in a manner commensurate to the loftiness of the occasion, but which very probably seemed to them scandalously decadent. Boccaccio was at the court and left detailed descriptions of the entertainments and diversions in which the grand knights and ladies of Naples indulged during the long summer days. Of society life at Baia, for example, a favorite spot of the nobility during the hot weather, Boccaccio wrote:

> There more than anywhere else even the most chaste women forget their feminine modesty and seem to take more liberties

on all occasions ... For the most part, time is spent in idleness, and when it is spent more actively, women, either alone or in the company of young men, speak of love; there people consume nothing but delicacies, and the finest old vintage wines strong enough not only to excite the sleeping Venus but also, if she were dead, to bring her back to life inside every man, and those who have tried the power of the baths know to what extent their beneficial effects also contribute to this. There the beaches, the lovely gardens, and every other place always resound with festivities, novel games, most graceful dances, music, and love songs composed, sung, and played by young men and by young women as well ... In some places an extremely desirable sight appeared before the young men's eyes: beautiful women covered by sheer, silky tunics, barefooted, and with bare arms, walking in the water, picking sea shells from the hard rock, and as they bent in their task they revealed the hidden delights of their ripe bosoms.

The Neapolitan aristocracy, particularly members of the royal family like Catherine of Valois and Agnes of Périgord, although forced to accept the arrangement with Hungary, were distinctly displeased by it, and not only because it prevented one of their own sons from marrying Joanna. An ugly ethnic prejudice also colored their opposition to this marriage. Andrew was only a second son, and his mother was the daughter of a Polish king. Many of the future king's attendants were native Hungarians who dressed differently, behaved differently, even smelled differently. Their appearance and general unfamiliarity with the formal customs and refined manners of their hosts put the Hungarians at a disadvantage in that haughty society; privately, Andrew and his retinue were patronizingly dismissed as barbarians. That all of Eastern Europe was stereotyped in this manner by the cultural and political elite of Italy and France is underscored by a letter from Petrarch to the archbishop of Prague, in which the Italian scholar referred to a visit he had once made to the imperial court in Bohemia. "I recall," wrote Petrarch, "how courteously you [the archbishop] repeatedly said to me, 'I pity you, O friend, for having come among barbarians.'" Likely in recognition of these deep cultural divisions, Robert asked Carobert to leave Andrew in Naples after the signing of the engagement papers, to be brought up with Joanna at the royal court. This seems to have been an attempt to ameliorate the problem by familiarizing the young prince with the habits of the kingdom.

The marriage ceremony, coupled with the investiture of Andrew with the duchy of Calabria and the principality of Salerno (formerly denied to his father), took place on September 27, 1333. The magnitude of the interests at stake was reflected in the heightened degree of pomp and splendor that accompanied this affair. The actual event was preceded by days of stirring jousts and sumptuous feasts. Ambassadors from all over Italy were invited; Florence alone sent 150 of its most prominent citizens to the exalted proceedings. Unlike his 1330 assembly naming Joanna heir to the throne, Robert the Wise made sure that this time each and every member of the royal family along with the whole of Neapolitan elite society were on hand to witness his granddaughter's marriage to the king of Hungary's son. The illustrious guests arrived on jeweled caparisoned horses, attired in the finest costumes that the wealth of the kingdom could afford, and the great hall of the Castel Nuovo was filled with a riot of silks, gold, and precious gems. Robert and Sancia appeared in gorgeous robes of azure emblazoned with fleur-de-lis. There was in this deliberately elaborate spectacle an element of intimidation. If doubt, ambition, and disloyalty could be stamped out by a show of prodigious ornamentation, Robert would do it.

At the center of this stunning tableau stood a little boy and girl of six and seven, respectively. Perhaps Andrew had some small idea of what it meant to be a knight and thought that was what was happening when he knelt before this strange man, the king of Naples, and did homage for his lands; but if so, he confused the ceremony in which he was so intimately involved. Similarly Joanna, a bejeweled gold diadem formerly belonging to her step-grandmother perched atop her head in imitation of her elders (for which Sancia had been reimbursed with 450 ounces of gold by Robert), was still too young to fully comprehend the role she played as she did obeisance before that august assembly and listened to her grandfather sermonize on the sanctity of the marriage rite. They could not know, this childish pair, that when, during the ceremony, they exchanged vows and a chaste kiss, as they were instructed to do by their relatives, they had committed themselves to each other for the rest of their lives. They were innocent of the motives for the solemn occasion to which they had been invited; innocent of the hope for the future they represented to Robert and Carobert; innocent, too, of the bitterness and jealousy their union inspired within their families.

Trust was hardly the prevailing emotion at work among the hard-eyed spectators appraising this scene, however. The sixteenth-century Italian historian, Angelo de Costanzo, one of the earliest scholars of these events, reported that the empress of Constantinople and her sons, the princes of Taranto, and John and Agnes, duke and duchess of Durazzo, and their sons, in conformity with their sovereign's wishes, made an especially impressive appearance at the betrothal. But their magnificence created the opposite effect to that which Robert had intended. It was interpreted as a form of aggression, a statement of social superiority, and a show of the veiled power attendant on their high rank. They knew well that six years would pass before this marriage could even be consummated, and at least another eight before Joanna would be old enough to rule. They could afford to wait.

And so the oligarchs of Taranto and Durazzo observed the ceremony they had been required to attend and participated in the ritual banquet following the formalities. They were present as well to bid their royal visitor Carobert farewell on his journey home. The succession crisis in Poland demanded his immediate attention, obliging the king of Hungary to set off soon after the rite had ended and the papers were signed, leaving the care of his son, the future king consort, to his Neapolitan relations.

❧

CHAPTER IV

A Royal Apprenticeship

C AROBERT'S ABRUPT departure in October 1333 signaled an end to the wedding festivities. The houses of Taranto and Durazzo resumed their sharp negotiations over the ownership of Achaia. Catherine, especially, seems to have subordinated her opposition to her niece's arranged marriage in order to focus once again on the acquisition of an eastern empire. Andrew, now duke of Calabria, and his impressive household staff, composed of nearly sixty people, including his childhood nurse, Isabelle the Hungarian, settled without incident into rooms at the Castel Nuovo.

Joanna's upbringing proceeded unhindered by either her marriage or her new title (formerly her mother's) of duchess of Calabria. She continued to share a household and rooms with her younger sister, Maria, as she had before Andrew's arrival. Sancia persisted in her efforts to inculcate the future queen of Naples with the precepts of her own religious vision. Joanna arose each morning, washed her face and hands, and attended Mass along with Maria in the Castel Nuovo's private chapel. At some point during the day, the young duchess received religious instruction in the company of her grandmother and her confessor; presumably, this is also where she learned her letters by reading a psalter, the preferred manner of instruction in the Middle Ages. Her grandmother instilled in her a deep spirituality as well as a lifelong devotion to charity. Even as a little girl, Joanna was known for her concern for the poor, generously distributing handfuls of coins whenever she traveled through the city to visit her parents' tombs at the church of Santa Chiara and, together with Sancia, washing the feet of beggars at the Feast of Maundy during Holy Week.

But religious training was only one aspect of Joanna's life at court. As befit her station, the future queen of Naples grew up wrapped in the luxurious trappings of royalty, surrounded by courtiers and servants. It was expected that the daughters of all the highest-born Neapolitan families would be attached to the royal court, and so Joanna and Maria between them shared some twenty-four ladies-in-waiting. The two little girls also had their own kitchen staff, including a sommelier, a servant each for the sauce and the soup, and even a special valet specifically assigned to the orchard—the new duchess was apparently very fond of quince jam. When she rode out in procession, Joanna was accompanied by two guards on horseback and a page in livery. She slept on a bed covered in red and green satin, and her saddle was overlaid in red velvet brocaded with peacocks and her parents' coat-of-arms. Even as a young child, the future queen wore velvet gowns of deep purple stitched with fleur-de-lis of silver thread, which identified her instantly, even from a distance, as royalty.

For recreation, she gave herself up to the pleasures of the court. The Castel Nuovo was renowned for its gardens, and Joanna and Maria played in the shade of the trees and amid the profusion of flowers and fountains. The children learned to ride early. When Joanna was a toddler, her grandfather had given her a wonderful wooden horse carved in imitation of an Arab steed, complete with a saddle similar in fashion to those used by Saracen princes. Later, she and Maria had a stable of their own mounts. Hunting was popular in Naples, even among ladies, who used bows and arrows in addition to hunting dogs and falcons. Once cornered, the game was ensnared by nets. In hot weather Joanna, her sister, their cousins, and other children of the nobility went for boat rides and picnics. The culture of Naples worshipped youth and beauty. Winsome Joanna made an appealing impression on her subjects. Boccaccio was much taken with the royal family and the delights of aristocratic life in Naples during Joanna's youth, and left detailed descriptions of their days:

> It often happened that because of the very hot weather brought by the season many women . . . took to the sea on a very swift galley in order to pass the time more pleasantly; we plowed through the waves, singing and playing musical instruments, searching for remote rocks and caverns naturally carved into the mountains and most inviting with their shade and fresh air . . . When we reached the place we were seeking and occupied a broad stretch for our amusement, following our own desires, we went to look around, now at one group of young men and young women and then at another, because every little rock or beach even slightly protected from the sun by the mountain's shadow was full of them . . . In many places around there one would see the whitest of tables spread so beautifully and so preciously decorated that the mere sight of them could arouse appetite even in the most indifferent person, and elsewhere people could be seen having their morning meal, since it was already that time, and we or anyone else passing by were cheerfully invited to join their pleasure.

Evenings were spent at banquets with music and dancing. Robert the Wise patronized artists of all types: painters, musicians, troubadours, and storytellers were constant presences at the Castel Nuovo. The royal court showed a taste for theater—the records show that in June 1335 the king paid a group of Apulian actors six tarins (small gold coins) to put on a play. As she got older, Joanna participated in these amusements. The only real difference the duchess's marriage made in her life was that now she and Maria sometimes had to include this strange boy, her cousin and husband, Andrew, in their games and various diversions.

Andrew's situation was very different from his wife's. A child of six, he had been left with strangers, far from his family. Instead of affection and intimacy, Andrew had luxury. His rooms were sumptuously appointed and hung with banners depicting his family's coat of arms, and he had his own household staff, even grander than Joanna's; his father had made sure of that before heading back to Hungary. When Andrew rode out, he was accompanied by eighteen horsemen. He had three sommeliers, a furrier, a doctor, a surgeon, and a large and impressively costly kitchen staff—but no parents, siblings, or friends. As a mark of respect for his rank, Robert assigned a number of high-ranking Neapolitan and Provençal barons to help supervise and advise the new duke of Calabria, but since Andrew spoke neither Italian nor Provençal, it is not clear how much use they were to him. Occasionally Joanna or one of her younger cousins played marbles with him (they must have gambled on the outcome, because the accounts mention that one month he owed Joanna three tarins in compensation) but in general Andrew felt out of place.

His discomfort led to surliness and rudeness of behavior, the not-unnatural response of a misunderstood and unhappy little boy. His private suite did no better. The native Neapolitans did not hide their general disdain for the Hungarians, who reacted by holding themselves aloof and withdrawing into their own small society. The court soon realized it needed a strategy for assimilating the duke of Calabria to his new surroundings. To this end, a special tutor and confessor, paid at the goodly rate of four ounces of gold a year, was attached to Andrew's household in 1336. Since responsibility for Andrew's education, like that of Joanna and Maria, fell to Sancia, it was she who made the appointment. Not surprisingly, the queen assigned a Spiritual Franciscan by the name of Friar Robert to the position.

While there is no question that the majority of the mendicants of Naples who embraced poverty in defiance of the pope did so for the purest of motives, Friar Robert was not among them. Cunning and manipulative, Andrew's new tutor quickly perceived an opportunity for personal profit. Hiding his desire for power and wealth behind a façade of humble sanctity, the Franciscan, who had the advantage of being well acquainted with the subtleties of the competing interests at court, quickly gained ascendancy in Andrew's household. Petrarch, who knew him later, was scathing in his description of the man. "Alas, what a shame, what a monster! May God remove this kind of plague from Italian skies!" the scholar wrote to his friend Cardinal Giovanni Colonna in a letter dated November 29, 1343. "I saw a terrible three footed beast [an allusion to the friar], with its feet naked, with its head bare, arrogant about its poverty, dripping with pleasures. I saw a little man plucked and ruddy, with plump haunches scarcely covered by a worn mantle and with a good portion of his body purposely uncovered. In this condition he disdains most haughtily not only your words but also those of the Pope as if from the lofty tower of his purity. Nor was I astonished that he carries his arrogance rooted in gold. As is widely known, his money boxes and his robes do not agree."

To become a figure of intimidation and power, all Friar Robert had to do was win the confidence of the lonely, frightened, isolated boy who was married to the heir to the throne.

~<del></del>~

These years of Joanna's later childhood and adolescence were critical to her future political development. By this time, she was old enough to understand that she would one day be queen. Like many medieval heirs to the throne, she learned her trade through the daily observation of her grandfather's administration. Joanna's apprenticeship was unusual, however. Because the Neapolitan line of succession had been forced to skip a generation, she was absorbing the lessons of an old man's rule.

In fact, from a high point in 1317, at which time Robert the Wise's realm extended throughout Guelphic Italy—when the king of Naples held the simultaneous titles of senator of Rome, imperial vicar of Romagna, and vice-general of Tuscany and the lordships of Genoa, Piedmont, and Lombardy—Robert's influence had been in steady decline. Once, his ambition had been to rule all of Italy. In a 1314 letter to the pope, Robert had argued against the election of a German emperor as obsolete. "Who of sane mind doubts— who does not plainly perceive, that all temporal dominions, in the vicissitudes of time, undergo continual change? How senseless, then, is this idea of perpetuating a universal domination! Where is now the lordship of the Chaldeans, the despotism of the Persian, the command of the Egyptian and Hebrew peoples, the craft and wisdom of the Greek, the force and energy of the Trojans? Where, above all, the unique monarchy of the Roman, which, from worldwide dominion, is contracted to a mere handful of earth?" he wrote before advocating the selection of an Italian leader—himself—in the German's place.

By Joanna's childhood, however, the king of Naples had lived to see his dominions much reduced. John XXII's death in 1334 had resulted in the election of a new pontiff who preferred to keep the governance of Rome and Campania in his own hands. By 1335, King Robert's control over Genoa, Piedmont, and Lombardy had eroded as well.

Much of the blame for this shrinkage was attributable to Sancia. The Angevin system of government was predicated on the king's having access to a large pool of high-ranking generals and diplomats from within his own family who could be trusted to act as surrogates of the crown throughout Italy. Until Sancia's ascension to the

throne, the royal family had had no trouble fulfilling this requirement. Robert's father, Charles the Lame, had been one of seven children, four of whom were sons. Robert himself had been one of
fourteen children, nine of whom were male. In the early days of his
reign, Robert had been used to sending his brothers Philip, prince
of Taranto, and John, duke of Durazzo, into Tuscany and northern
Italy to ensure that his sovereignty and interests were protected, and
because they were of the same bloodline as the king, his brothers
were unhesitatingly accepted and respected as his intermediaries.
The Florentines had offered Charles of Calabria the lordship of
their commune when they needed protection from the Ghibellines
because he was the king of Naples's son. Similarly, Robert had designated Joanna's father to be his general in the ongoing war with
Sicily when the king had become too old to lead his own troops
into battle.

All this changed in the waning years of Robert's reign, and there
is no escaping that responsibility for the scarcity of descendants
was directly attributable to Sancia's decision to devote herself to
securing a place of honor in the next world, and not to the carnal
labors of this one. That it was Sancia who rejected her husband's
sexual overtures, and not the other way around, may be deduced
from the pope's response to the queen's 1317 request for a divorce,
in which he exhorted her to be nicer to her husband. The king of
Naples, on the other hand, seems to have tried to gain access to
Sancia's boudoir, but only made it as far as one of her ladies-in-
waiting, by whom he had an illegitimate son, Charles of Artois.

By 1335, Robert was fifty-seven, and his wife was fifty. His son
was dead, as were all but one of his brothers—the last, John, Agnes
of Périgord's husband, would succumb the following year. If he
hadn't capitulated to Carobert and the pope, Robert might one day
have utilized the empress of Constantinople's sons. Having been
rebuffed in her efforts to acquire the Neapolitan throne for one of
her progeny, Catherine of Valois had made other plans. In 1338,

the empress of Constantinople mustered a fleet, and, gathering together her entire household, sailed for Achaia, intent on fomenting revolt against the local Byzantine despot and establishing her rule in Greece.

Robert the Wise was aware of the decline in his fortunes and sought to achieve one last victory in the hopes of recovering past glory. Since the inception of his reign a quarter century before, the king of Naples's primary ambition—to overthrow Peter of Aragon, king of Sicily—had remained maddeningly unfulfilled. To this end, Robert now committed what resources were left to him. He assembled armadas three times in a four-year period. The first attack, in 1338, was commanded by his nephew Charles of Durazzo, Agnes of Périgord's eldest son, for Agnes wished to curry favor with the royal family. No sooner had the Neapolitans made camp in Sicily, however, than typhus set in among the infantry and they were forced to retreat. Charles of Durazzo, fifteen at the time, was lucky to escape with his life. The next year, the king's illegitimate son, Charles of Artois, had somewhat more success; he managed to capture Messina for a short period before withdrawing. The last attempt, for which Andrew was appointed titular commander, came after the king of Sicily's death in 1342. Although Peter of Aragon left only a helpless child as heir, Robert was unable to capitalize on this opportunity, and the island remained stubbornly beyond his control. The only tangible result of this expenditure of life, equipment, supplies, and effort was the accumulation of a large debt. By the end of this period, Robert owed one hundred thousand florins to both the Bardi and Peruzzi companies.

Reduced influence abroad and an inability to retake Sicily were not the only signs of Robert's growing impotence. Domestically, too, the king felt his authority wane. Despite numerous proclamations mandating respect for the law, crime increased dramatically during the years of Joanna's adolescence. Representatives of the super-companies complained of Neapolitan banditry to the new pope, Benedict XII, who sent emissaries to try to strengthen the king's hand, but their efforts were equally ineffectual. There was simply too little protection available to ward off the inevitable poaching.

Even more serious was the Neapolitan aristocracy's tendency toward violence. The wealth of Naples was concentrated in the hands of the royal family and a smattering of favored courtiers. The majority of the kingdom, subject to high taxes and the backbreaking labor associated with farming in hilly, arid terrain, was impoverished. For the peasants working the land during the reign of Robert the Wise, life was harsh, and for their masters, the local noble property owners, it was not much better. Fueled by scarcity, petty arguments between neighboring landed families over territory and privileges were pursued with a passion out of proportion to the original offense. Bands of armed noblemen roamed the countryside, striking out against perceived enemies and other hapless bystanders. These bands were then themselves struck down by the frenzied relatives of their victims, and by degrees developed a form of entrenched retribution which is still known today, seven centuries later, as the vendetta.

Robert's response to this domestic disorder seems to have been mixed. When an outbreak of violence between noblemen of the capital city and those of Capua and Nido occurred in the 1330s, he attempted to mediate and issued a firm decree "that men of the city may not disturb its tranquility, nor carry prohibited weapons by day or night, nor congregate in crowds, nor march through a piazza with weapons, nor commit violence on peers or inferiors, openly or stealthily, in public or private places." But his strict pronouncements against gang warfare were not supported often or quickly enough by military intervention, and by the end of the decade, his administration was openly accused of corruption. Giovanni Villani left a detailed description in his chronicle of a prolonged, particularly destructive display of domestic Neapolitan violence involving the count of Minerbino and his siblings, known as the Pipini brothers:

> In 1338 there began in the kingdom of Naples, ruled by King Robert, a great disturbance and nuisance in the city of Sulmona, and also in the cities of Aquila, Gaeta, Salerno and Barletta. In each of these places factions were created, and they fought against each other, with one faction driving out the other. These towns and their environs were devastated, and consequently the countryside filled up with robbers and brigands, who robbed everywhere. Many barons of the kingdom had a hand in these disturbances, supporting one side or the other . . . One faction was led by the Marra family, and with them was the count of San Severino and all his followers; in the other faction was the Gatti family and the count of Minerbino, called "the Paladin," and his followers . . . The king was much criticized on account of these disturbances . . . because of his tolerance of the devastation of his kingdom, out of his personal greed for the fines and compositions that would be paid as a result of these misdeeds . . . Then, only when the towns were well ruined, did the king send his troops to besiege Minerbino and the count; and the count's brothers came to Naples and threw themselves on the king's mercy. All of their property was confiscated to the crown and then sold, and they were held prisoner in Naples.

Frustrated in his attempts to govern, the king retreated to his sermons and books and in so doing ironically provided his administration with its one genuine achievement: the establishment of a vibrant community of scholars dedicated to the preservation and promotion of knowledge. The University of Naples, one of the oldest in Europe, was renowned for the study of law, as that of Paris was celebrated for theology, Oxford for math and science, and Salerno for medicine. Throughout his administration, Robert the

Wise protected and encouraged this important center of learning and made extensive use of its faculty. Its masters filled high positions in Neapolitan government, helped codify the laws of the kingdom, and provided the extensive legal arguments on which rested the king's sweeping interpretation of the royal prerogative.

In 1332, to promote further scholarship, Robert, with Sancia's approval, hired the accomplished scholar Paolo of Perugia to be keeper of the King's Library, at the munificent remuneration of 225 gold florins a year, and charged him with acquiring an extensive collection of manuscripts. Hard-to-find works by Seneca, Livy, Saint Jerome, and Saint Augustine, as well as many other volumes, were salvaged by this effort, and university clerks were employed to make copies for ease of research. "All the important additions of King Robert's reign in the fields of history, law, and medicine, occurred during the period of his [Paolo of Perugia's] librarianship." The king's interest in the Far East is confirmed by the trouble and expense he took to obtain and magnificently illuminate a copy of a relatively new work, De Mirabilibus Magni Canis (About the Extraordinary Things in the Country of the Great Khan), which described the adventures of a Venetian explorer named Marco Polo. This royal emphasis on recovering and consolidating knowledge set Naples apart from the rest of Italy and added greatly to the eminence of the kingdom. A library of more than one hundred volumes—substantial for the period—was soon amassed in the years following the appointment of Paolo. "Naples therefore in his reign became a famous emporium of learning, centered by the Castel Nuovo, a royal mine of wisdom and 'a place of the understanding.'"

The availability of these works, in combination with the patronage of the king, drew some of the most talented scholars in Europe to Robert's court in the latter years of his reign, and their energy and intercourse greatly enhanced interest in academic achievement. That Naples was the acknowledged center of classical study by

1340 is confirmed by Petrarch, who, having been given the choice of being crowned poet laureate under the sponsorship of King Robert or accepting an important teaching position at the University of Paris, chose to be laureate. In a letter to Cardinal Giovanni Colonna, dated September 1, 1340, Petrarch described his dilemma. "I find myself at a difficult crossroads, and do not know the best path to take," he wrote. "It is an extraordinary but brief story. On this very day, almost at the third hour, a letter was delivered to me from the [Roman] Senate, in which I was in a most vigorous and persuasive manner invited to receive the poetic laureate at Rome. On the same day at about the tenth hour a messenger came to me with a letter from an illustrious man, the chancellor of the University of Paris, a fellow citizen of mine and well acquainted with my activities. He, with the most delightful of reasons, urges me to go to Paris. I ask you, who could ever have guessed that anything like this could possibly have happened? . . . The one letter calls me East, the other West; you will see with what powerful arguments I am pressed hither and yon. . . . The fact that in Italy there is the king of Sicily [Robert the Wise], whom among all mortals I accept as a judge of my talents, turns the scales in one direction." Petrarch accepted Robert's invitation to come to Naples prior to his official coronation at Rome so the king could publicly certify that the renowned scholar satisfied the qualifications for the office of poet laureate.

The examination of Petrarch, which took place in March 1341 at the Castel Nuovo, was perhaps the greatest cultural event of the century, an extravagant exhibition of erudition. For three full days, before a packed audience which included members of the court, faculty and students of the university, the ruling council, and leading members of the citizenry, Robert the Wise, dressed in full regalia, queried Europe's leading intellectual on his knowledge of the works of biblical scholars and various Roman writers like Virgil and Seneca. The fact that Petrarch's mastery of the subject matter far exceeded that of his interrogator, so that he had no difficulty what-soever answering the king's questions, took nothing away from the exhilaration of the proceedings. The local scholars were awed at the presence of so great an intellect within their midst and elated by the exaltation he brought to their profession. The illustrious man of letters himself was exceedingly gratified to have his achievements recognized in so public a manner by so august a personage as the sovereign of Naples. The king was delighted to have his own intel-lectual pursuits confirmed by an outside authority. The rest of the populace, while probably not following much of the actual content, nonetheless received a smattering of an education in a highly enter-taining fashion. When, at the end of the third day, the poet had convinced the king of the merits of verse, there was a moment of high drama when Robert, who was too old to travel to Rome for Petrarch's official coronation, shrugged out of his ceremonial robe and, offering it to his guest as a mark of respect, requested that he wear it when receiving the honor of the laurel. The king also named him his chaplain, a title that entailed no official duties but much honor. Armed with letters patent signed by Robert attesting to his credentials, Petrarch then went on to Rome to receive his crown. On April 8, 1341, while wearing the king of Naples's royal mantle, Petrarch was crowned with the laurel to the sound of trumpets. "The King's [Robert the Wise's] hand was absent, though not his authority nor his majesty; his presence was felt not only by me but by all who were there," Petrarch later wrote to the Neapolitan royal secretary. To Robert himself he wrote: "How much the study of the liberal and humane arts owe you, O oh glory of kings."

Joanna was fifteen when she watched her grandfather sit in cere-monial judgment of Europe's leading savant. The spectacle was unique and memorable; nothing like this had ever happened before. Other than his coronation as king of Naples by the pope thirty-two years before, this was the moment of Robert's supreme glory, the zenith of his long trajectory, when his sovereign might was for once used for something other than territorial gain. For Joanna, there would have been great pride in being the granddaughter of such a man, and heir to such a legacy.

Nor was the achievement inconsequential. In this flicker of curiosity for the forgotten knowledge of the past, ignited by Petrarch, nourished at Naples, and later guarded by a devoted band of followers, lay the nascent sparks of the humanist movement, which a hundred years later would catch fire and astonish the world with the Renaissance.

~❦~

Unfortunately, this enlightened tribute to medieval scholarship, however significant in the long term, represented but a fleeting diversion from the cares of an increasingly perilous political and economic reality. The state of continental affairs was especially distressing. The first volleys in the Anglo-French conflagration, which would eventually be known as the Hundred Years' War, had been hurled by Edward III of England. In danger of losing Gascony, which was all that remained of England's once-extensive possessions in France, Edward had begun a deliberate campaign in 1337 to woo allies with the intention of isolating and encircling the French. In 1338, he traveled in great state to Flanders, where, "by fair speeches, promises, and a bountiful distribution of money," he secured not only Flemish support, but that of Germany and the Low Countries through the favor of the Holy Roman Emperor. Buoyed by these diplomatic successes, in 1340, Edward, who asserted a claim to the French throne through his mother, began publicly referring to himself as the king of England *and* France, as a provocation to the reigning king of France, Philip VI, Catherine of Valois' brother. The following year, he landed a military force in the duchy of Brittany, traditionally a vassal state of France. To counter, Philip relied on Naples and the papacy, for the pope, although publicly offering to negotiate a peace, overwhelmingly favored the French, not least because, by 1341, a full 60 percent of the papal income emanated from France.

The Florentine super-companies were torn, however. The great Neapolitan grain trade, so important in past decades to their financial well-being, had metamorphosed from a boon to a burden. By the 1330s, the three super-companies that shared the grain monopoly—those of the Bardi, the Peruzzi, and the Acciaiuoli families—had developed a vast and highly specialized organization designed to manage every aspect of the market, from harvest to mill. Their senior partners negotiated with officials from Robert's government on contracts to purchase all the kingdom's grain on a yearly basis, "and they did not hestitate to approach the king with complaints whenever they encountered difficulties with them [the Neapolitan officials]." They not only purchased the grain; they collected the cereal at its source, brought it to port, and shipped it on galleys rented from Venice and Genoa to clients up and down the Mediterranean and the Adriatic. To reach inland customers such as those in Bologna, they transported the grain by barge up the Po River; to reach Florence, they went overland by cart. Their position and influence in the kingdom of Naples was unprecedented. In addition to the grain trade, the super-companies formed a syndicate that "collected taxes, transported cash, paid bureaucrats' salaries and troops' wages, and managed military stores."

Despite these assiduous attempts to orchestrate every phase of the market, however, the super-companies' business was exposed to many risks, chief among which was an unfavorable change in weather conditions. Grain, as the primary component of the Mediterranean diet, and thus a necessity of life, was a politically charged commodity. Too much or too little rain could produce scarcity, even famine, which in turn invited governmental price regulation. This was particularly true of the super-companies' home state of Florence, which relied heavily on the importation of

Neapolitan grain to feed its citizens. Fearful of public unrest if the cost of bread rose too high, the ruling council of Florence frequently imposed price restraints on the super-companies' sales of grain, which resulted in a series of losses in the early 1330s. Additionally, beginning in 1333, King Robert, who needed money to finance his wars with Sicily, began imposing an export tax on wheat, which further degraded the super-companies' profit margins. Debts went unpaid, and capitalization was threatened; investors were losing confidence and demanding the return of their deposits.

In desperation, the super-companies sought new sources of revenue and settled on the English wool trade as the only market large enough to return the firms to their former levels of prosperity. English wool was considered the finest in the world. Access to this market meant that Florentine manufacturers could process high-grade luxury woolen cloth for sale in Naples in adequate quantities to offset company losses on grain. The Bardi and Peruzzi families seized on this opportunity as a way out of their problems and made their first large loans to Edward III in 1336, secured by licenses to import wool. By 1341 they were lending heavily to the English king, who used Florentine money to finance his rapidly expanding and extremely expensive military and diplomatic campaigns. The pope expressed his displeasure at the companies rendering such valuable assistance to an enemy combatant, but by this time the Bardi and Peruzzi families could not get out of the business even if they wanted to—Edward owed them too much money.

A further cause for worry, particularly in Italy and Avignon, was the advanced age of the king of Naples. Robert the Wise was noticeably failing. The Neapolitan succession that had been so carefully arranged would be tested upon his demise, and it was by no means assured that it would hold. If there was one consistent rule in medieval politics, it was that the death of a sovereign inevitably provoked uncertainty, and in uncertainty lay opportunity. Nothing bespeaks the veracity of this maxim, or the generally worsening conditions, than the hasty return of Catherine of Valois and her family to Naples from Achaia in August of 1341.

~❧~

The empress of Constantinople's expedition to Greece had been reasonably successful. Just before her departure three years earlier, Catherine had been the beneficiary of a stroke of luck: members of the opposition party to the Byzantine emperor's rule in neighboring Epirus had fomented an uprising. To this end, they had kidnapped the ten-year-old son of their former ruler from his mother's care, intending to use him as a rallying point. Catherine, recognizing that this situation could be exploited to her advantage, had had the child smuggled across the Adriatic to her court in Naples for safekeeping and then conveyed him, along with the rest of her family, to Achaia when she sailed in the fall of 1338. Through a deft combination of her fleet's ominous presence just off the coast and Niccolò Acciaiuoli's discreet payoffs, Catherine managed to establish her rule in Achaia fairly quickly. She then turned her attention to Epirus and by early 1339 had successfully promoted a rebellion against an unpopular governor, substituting her pawn, the boy, as ruler in his place. Her influence didn't last—the child surrendered to the Byzantine emperor, who arrived with an army the following year—but the scheme demonstrated Catherine's penchant for intrigue and her willingness to use unorthodox methods when necessary.

She was no doubt guided in her tactics by Niccolò's sage advice. Based on his remuneration, Acciaiuoli seems to have proven himself invaluable to the empress in Greece. He was granted large estates in Achaia and was allowed to establish a banking office there that would turn out to be extremely useful for keeping family funds out of the hands of grasping depositors and creditors in mainland Italy. So much did Catherine come to rely on the Acciaiuolis that when she decided events in Naples demanded her return in 1341, the empress appointed one of Niccolò's cousins to govern in her absence. Although many of the indigenous aristocracy objected to this arrangement, even appealing to the Byzantine emperor to over-throw Catherine's rule, the cousin proved difficult to displace. By remaining loyal to its Neapolitan sponsors, Niccolò's family would go on to increase its holdings and influence significantly in Achaia—so much so that one Acciaiuoli after another governed Achaia con-tinuously until into the next century.

Joanna was fifteen at the time of her reunion with her aunt, the empress of Constantinople, and her first cousins Robert, Louis, and Philip. She must have changed greatly during their three-year absence; no longer a child, by all accounts Joanna had matured into a radiant young woman, by nature playful, sunny, and full of life. Even the chronicler Domenico da Gravina, a contemporary of Joanna's who lived in the kingdom and who was in no way sympa-thetic to her, was forced to admit that both Joanna and her sister, Maria, were endowed with a "wonderful" beauty. Her newly returned cousins had also grown up and were apparently equally attractive. Already, Robert, also fifteen, and Louis, fourteen, were tall and blond and handsome, particularly Louis; they were athletes who had seen Greece and were supremely conscious of the figures they cut in society. Boccaccio, who knew the princes of Taranto well, was as infatuated with this pair as the rest of Naples. He immortalized them in his *Elegy of Lady Fiammetta*, written sometime between 1343 and 1345 when they were a little older:

> Our princes [Robert and Louis of Taranto] arrive on horses which run not only faster than any other animal but so fast that in running they would leave behind even those very winds believed to be the fastest; and the princes' youth, their remark-able beauty, and their notable excellence makes them exceed-ingly pretty to those who look at them. They appear on caparisoned horses, dressed in crimson or in garments woven

by native hands with designs of different colors and inter-
woven threads of gold and also garnished with pearls and precious stones; their long blond hair falling onto their extremely
white shoulders is tied onto their head with a gold ringlet . . .
Furthermore, their left hand is armed with a very light shield
and their right one with a lance, and at the sound of the summoning trumpets, one after the other and followed by many
others all wearing the same costume, they begin their jousting
for the ladies.

The contrast between these two paragons of Neapolitan young
adulthood and Joanna's own lord and master (for that is what husbands were called in the Middle Ages) was apparently obvious and
disheartening. At fourteen, Andrew had yet to display the physical
attributes that might have won him favor in the eyes of his female
subjects. Given his ancestry, he was likely short for his age—his
grandfather on his mother's side had, after all, been nicknamed "the
elbow-high." Despite the lack of a surviving description of Andrew,
Baddeley, who researched and wrote extensively about the kingdom
of Naples during this period, nonetheless hypothesized that
Andrew was "indolent; prefers food to anything else, and is likely
always so to do; heavy-jawed, dull of eye, and, compared to Neapolitan boys, clumsy of figure." This seems harsh, particularly as Andrew
was still so young. It also conflicts, not unnaturally, with Hungarian
assertions as to Andrew's appearance and personal habits that proclaimed, "The young prince . . . as he grew in years, prepossessed
everyone in his favor save his future bride."

In the absence of more solid evidence, the art of the period may
perhaps present a small clue as to the disparity between Andrew's
culture and physical appearance and that of Joanna and her cousins.
One of Andrew's books, an illustrated codex depicting the lives of
Hungarian saints, which his parents commissioned for their son's
education, survives. In it, most of the male figures are portrayed as

swarthy and unkempt, with a profusion of facial hair. This is very different from the Neapolitan manuscript art of the period, as represented by a treatise on music by Boethius that was illustrated for King Robert; it portrays men and women alike as delicate and graceful, with carefully arranged hair and elegant dress. These two books existed side by side and yet their aesthetics are so antithetical that it seems as though each emerged from a different, wholly incompatible world, and this, likely, approximates Andrew's predicament in Naples.

Andrew might have compensated for his less-than-imposing physical presence by force of manner or intellectual ability, but unfortunately these qualities, too, seem to have been lacking. His mental and emotional development is reported to have lagged behind that of his prospective queen. There is evidence that, being unsure of himself, he relied heavily on the advice and companionship of his confessor, Friar Robert, whose obvious influence over his Hungarian charge was noted at court. "He [Andrew] was manifestly no suitable partner for his consort." Again, given his youth, this was not quite fair. Certainly it is the rare adolescent boy whose demeanor is such that it impresses those around him.

Although clearly this was not a love match—being married to Andrew must have been a little like being wed to an annoying younger brother—Joanna accepted her circumstances. She was by this time keenly aware of critics' accusations that her grandfather had usurped the throne from his nephew and that by her marriage and, most important, the production of an heir, these allegations might be forever silenced. There is every indication that Joanna greatly admired Robert the Wise and sought to emulate his policies throughout her life, and that she was willing to sacrifice personal happiness toward this goal.

And yet, by the summer of 1342, Joanna's marriage remained unconsummated. Since at sixteen the duchess of Calabria was already well past the age of consent—in the Middle Ages, marital relations were sanctioned once the bride turned thirteen—the delay must have been attributable to her husband's immaturity (thereby buttressing the argument that at fifteen Andrew was still somewhat backward in terms of mental and physical development). The expedition to Sicily for which the duke of Calabria had been named commander was clearly intended by Robert as a means for Andrew to prove his manhood. Although originally scheduled to depart in the early spring of 1342, the invasion was delayed several times, seemingly due to its leader's reluctance to leave. (In fact, it never came off, even though the men and materials were in place.) To prod Andrew into undertaking this military service, the king announced that, after returning from Sicily at Easter of the following year (1343), the duke of Calabria would be formally knighted and his marriage finally consummated.

More than Andrew's slow development caused the delay, however. On July 16, 1342, a death intervened, that of Carobert, the king of Hungary. His widow, Elizabeth, in an effort to ensure a stable and orderly transition of power, lost no time in crowning her eldest son, Louis, Andrew's older brother, king in her husband's place. The coronation occurred on July 21, less than a week after Carobert's death.

Louis was only sixteen when he assumed his father's place on the throne. Very few teenagers ruled in the Middle Ages; instead, a regent or council of advisers, chosen from among the kingdom's most powerful noblemen, was usually appointed to take control of the realm until the sovereign came of age. But this did not occur in Hungary after Carobert's death, because the native baronage knew they did not have to worry about their sovereign's lack of experience. A shrewd political tactician, highly proficient at management, still held tight to the reins of government: Louis' most trusted and influential adviser, his mother, Elizabeth.

The queen mother's authority extended into every particular of the royal prerogative, but nowhere was her presence felt more powerfully than in the arena of international affairs. Elizabeth's policies were entirely focused on expanding Hungarian influence in Eastern Europe and on maintaining strong ties with her native Poland. As far as the queen mother was concerned, Hungarian rule in Naples was already established in the person of her younger son, who she fully expected would be crowned king upon the death of Robert the Wise. There was therefore no need, in her mind, to adhere to the second stage of the original treaty, which stipulated that her eldest son, Louis, wed Joanna's younger sister, Maria. To throw away Louis' marriage prospects on the younger granddaughter of the king of faraway Naples, when he could be making a much more attractive regional alliance, represented a wasted opportunity and a violation of Hungarian interests. Even before her husband's death, the queen mother had advocated that Louis be engaged instead to the daughter of the heir to the Bohemian throne. At Elizabeth's insistence then, in the fall of 1342, Louis married Margaret, the seven-year-old princess of Bohemia.

Robert the Wise took this rejection of his granddaughter Maria as a direct slap at Angevin pride. On January 16, 1343, visibly near the end of his days and too weak to arise from his bed, but nonetheless "sound of mind and able to speak," the king dictated his last will and testament. In the presence of witnesses he reconfirmed Joanna as his successor and sole heir to the throne of Naples, as well as to the rest of his far-flung empire (*"Rex ... instituit sibi haeredem universalem Joannam, ducissam Calabriae, meptem ejus primogenitam"*), which the king of Naples listed as the countship of Provence, the sovereignty of Sicily, and the inherited title to Jerusalem, as well as overlordships in Piedmont and Forcalquier. If Joanna died childless, this immense inheritance went directly to Maria, bypassing Andrew altogether. There was no mention of Andrew's being crowned king, not even in an honorary fashion as consort. By this will, then, Andrew was very publicly excluded from rule or indeed from playing any role whatever in his wife's government.

To further punish the Hungarians, Robert the Wise also improved Maria's standing at court. Should the long-contracted marriage between Joanna's younger sister and Louis of Hungary fail to take place (an allusion to the union with Margaret of Bohemia), Maria was instead specifically instructed to wed the heir to the French throne, or, if he were not available, a younger brother of the French royal family. In recognition that the accomplishment of so brilliant an alliance as a match with the crown of France was likely to require further inducement, Robert made provision for Maria's estate to be increased by a handsome bequest of lands, castles, men, and vassals estimated at a value of ten thousand florins in addition to a dowry of thirty thousand florins in cash, to be paid at the time of her marriage. By this will, then, Maria was made an heiress.

Special attention was also paid to Joanna's position as a minor. The document called for the establishment of a special council, chaired by Sancia, to rule in the young queen's place until she reached the age of her majority, which Robert the Wise denoted as twenty-five. Andrew and Maria were also considered minors, which meant they could not enter into legal contracts without the express permission of the special council, until this age. Since Naples was a fief of the papacy, and Joanna its vassal, the document made plain that the special council recognized the authority of the pope and commended the heir to the throne and the kingdom to his protection, a bid for the continuation of a foreign policy that relied heavily on the cultivation of an exceptionally close relationship with the Holy See as the source of Angevin Guelphic authority throughout Italy.

Finally, to ensure that none of the principals involved later challenged his instructions or deviated in any way from the strictures imposed by this will, Robert the Wise included the following codicil: "The before mentioned duke and duchess and the duchess' sister Maria, affirming themselves adult, and such from their appearance it is manifest they are, have promised and sworn by cor-

poreal touch of the Holy Gospel, in the presence of ourself, the
ruler and King [Robert], and of our judge, notary, and the under-
signed witnesses, to keep firmly and inviolably [the terms of this
will], and at no time whatsoever, by themselves or by means of
others, to do or act contrary to any of the aforesaid bequests and
conditions."*

And so was undone in a matter of hours the work of nearly a
decade. Nor was there time to thoroughly digest the implications
of this royal thunderbolt, nor to appeal to the elderly king's better
judgment, nor plead with him for restitution or reinstatement. For
by January 20, 1343, four days after the disclosure of this remarkable document, Robert the Wise was dead.

---

* "Item, praefatus dominus dux ac domina ducissa et Maria, soror ejus, puberes se affermantes, et sic ex
eorum aspectu apparebat, in praesentia domini Regis nostrumque, judicis, notarii et testium suprascripto-
rum, promiserunt et juraverunt ad sancta Dei Evangelia corporaliter tacta praemissa omnia et singular
tenaciter et inviolabiliter observare et nullo unquam tempore per se vel alium quovismodo contra facere
vel tenere, recipiens sibi adinvicem ipsam promissionem et sacramentum preadictum."

CHAPTER V

⭒⭒⭒

The Foolish Legacy *of* Robert *the* Wise

Fᴏʀ ᴊᴏᴀɴɴᴀ, confronting the loss of the only father figure she had ever known must have been devastating. Robert the Wise had been her earliest and most devoted champion, shielding her from the dark aims of those who would use her position for their own purposes. From her earliest days he had demonstrated faith in her ability to shoulder the demands of sovereignty. His presence had dominated the great arched hall of the Castel Nuovo for her as it had for the rest of his subjects.

Although with almost his last breath Robert the Wise had ensured that Andrew would have no influence over the government of the kingdom, the king must have nonetheless also left verbal instructions that Joanna's husband be raised to knighthood and her marriage consummated immediately. On January 22, just two days after Robert's death, while the king's body, surrounded by candles, still lay in state at the church of Santa Chiara, Andrew was hastily knighted in a private ceremony at the Castel Nuovo. Only three people witnessed the duke of Calabria's induction into manhood, all senior members of the ruling council. One was a notary, and one was the vice-seneschal Raymond of Catania, one of Philippa's sons. Since the court was officially in mourning, Andrew was denied the feasts and lavish public celebration that ordinarily would have accompanied the dubbing, but evidently even this scaled-down rite of passage served its purpose. For "on the day of Wednesday, the 22nd of the month of January [1343], as the lately deceased King Robert had dictated . . . Andrew . . . appeared lawfully at [Joanna's] door at the Castel Nuovo, despoiled her, and knew her carnally," reported the *Chronicle of Parthénope*, one of the official records of the period. That the members of the ruling committee and Joanna in particular acquiesced to this obligation of office so soon after Robert's death is a strong indication that all of those involved were in fact simply carrying out the old king's last commands.

Joanna's grief and affection for her grandfather may be measured in the size and splendor of the tomb she had built for him. At the young queen's behest, two Florentine master sculptors were engaged to erect the massive marble sepulcher, which still survives today in the church of Santa Chiara. Three stories high, the monument was larger and grander than any other reliquary in the vast church. Carved in imitation of the crypt of an emperor or a pope, the tomb depicted Robert surrounded by his family, including Joanna, who is represented as seated on a throne in the second niche, the whole "devised to silence doubts that Robert had been a usurper." Robert is himself presented to God on this statuary by two figures representing Saint Francis and Clare of Assisi, a reference not only to his lifelong commitment to the Franciscan order but also to his own preeminence on earth. In this way did Joanna successfully ensure that her grandfather's renown survived his death: "The altarpiece's significance to the Angevins never was forgotten in Naples." The scale of the commission also served as an announcement of Joanna's intention to build in the grand tradition of her ancestors, to leave her own imprint on the kingdom through the erection of important monuments. An attention to and pride in civic building and decoration, she knew, was part of the Angevin legacy of sovereignty.

But her grief at the loss of her grandfather did not blind Joanna to the risks to which his last will and testament exposed her and her kingdom. There was no way to judge the political and military ramifications of openly denying Andrew a say in the government of Naples. King Louis and his mother, Elizabeth, would undoubtedly protest the decision to the pope, and would perhaps even try to convince the papacy to substitute Louis' claim to the kingdom, as the eldest child of Carobert, for Joanna's. The specter of invasion, too, hung over the kingdom of Naples if Andrew's family did not have their way. The Hungarians could raise an impressive army at any time, and Louis was able-bodied and trained for warfare.

Joanna, by contrast, was severely handicapped by her sex and the requirement that the committee established to rule during her minority be consulted on every issue. For even if the committee agreed to her request for troops, who then would lead them into battle? Joanna could not do it herself, and there was no king. Without Andrew, she had no champion, no general who could force the hostile and competing factions within her family to ally together to face the threat. Nor could she procure a warrior by marriage, as she was already married. By his last will and testament then, Robert the Wise undermined from its first days Joanna's reign and made her vulnerable to attack.

That both Joanna and the ruling committee were aware of the tenuous position in which her grandfather had placed her is evidenced by the speed with which she named one of her most prestigious vassals, Hugo del Balzo, the count of Avellino, as her ambassador to the papal court. Protocol demanded that the new queen of Naples do formal obeisance to the pope for her kingdom, and Joanna invested the count with the authority to act as her surrogate at the ceremony. She also specifically instructed Hugo to petition the pontiff, Clement VI, to permit Andrew to be crowned king.

By asking for this coronation, Joanna did not mean to grant her husband rule of the kingdom or to share power with him, but merely to offer him the face-saving honor of a rank commensurate with her own. Moreover, the timing of this petition—Hugo del Balzo was dispatched to Avignon on January 25, only five days after Robert's demise, with the full approval of Sancia and the ruling council—would indicate that this bargain had been hammered out in advance of the king's death. It is difficult to believe that Andrew would have voluntarily sworn to abide by the conditions of the will had the prince and his counselors not been privy to secret assurances of some kind.

Unfortunately, Joanna's rational attempt at diplomacy—designed to reinstate the former status quo and thereby preempt any possible protests on the part of Andrew's family—was by no means the only scheme emanating out of Naples that found its way to the treacherous milieu of the papal court.

***

Throughout the long years of King Robert's deterioration, Agnes of Périgord had never surrendered her ambition to see her eldest son, Charles, duke of Durazzo, invested with the sovereignty of Naples. For this reason, Agnes had maintained close ties to the crown, helpfully offering Charles's services to Robert for one of his annual doomed attacks on Sicily and working to insinuate herself into the confidence of Sancia and the two young princesses. Although outwardly her efforts came to naught—the old king failed to reward her son or to legitimize his interest in the throne in any way—Agnes was nonetheless quick to recognize that by naming Maria as an alternate heir, Robert the Wise had left open the possibility of a new route to power. If Joanna should die childless, or be deposed by the pope or the Hungarians, Maria would inherit the kingdom. This made Joanna's fourteen-year-old sister, who by the same will was now also extremely wealthy in her own right, a highly attractive candidate for marriage. Robert had decreed that his second granddaughter should wed the heir to the French throne, but Agnes was as desperate to prevent this match as she was to advance her eldest son's career. Philip VI, the king of France, was Catherine of Valois' brother. Inevitably, then, a marriage between Maria and a scion of France would overwhelmingly favor the interests of the house of Taranto over those of the Durazzo.

Letters indicate that some initial negotiations with the French had taken place, but the details of so important an alliance would, Agnes knew, take time. While Maria's fate remained in this unsettled state, it might still be possible to independently petition the papacy for the princess's hand in marriage. This could only be accomplished by someone with close ties to the Sacred College, someone with the ability to call on a powerful advocate who was on such intimate relations with the new pope (Benedict XII had died the previous spring) that he could persuade the pontiff to act in the interested party's favor. Happily, Agnes was connected to just such an advocate: her brother Cardinal Talleyrand of Périgord.

A venerated ancestor of the Talleyrand of Périgord, who four centuries later would be famously associated with both the French Revolution and Napoleon, Agnes's brother was one of the most influential cardinals at the papal court at Avignon. Petrarch wrote of the cardinal, "He himself denies it, but everyone affirms that he has made two pontiffs in a row." One of these was the new pope, Clement VI, whose election the previous year, expertly steered by Talleyrand, had taken only four days to secure. Cardinal Périgord owed his eminent position in life both to his mother, who had caught the eye of an earlier pope, Clement V ("for it was openly said that he had as mistress the countess of Périgord, a most beautiful lady," the chronicler Giovanni Villani reported), and to his family's determined allegiance to the French. The county of Périgord represented a front line in the theater of the Hundred Years' War. It was located in that part of the kingdom over which both Edward III and Philip VI claimed sovereignty. The king of France knew that he could not afford to lose the loyalty of a vassal who fought so consistently against encroachment by his enemy, and so he made efforts to reward the family through grants of new property and other signs of royal favor, including the demonstrable promotion of the cardinal's career. "It was probably this close association with the French crown which explains Talleyrand's prominence in the College of Cardinals from the very outset, and his growing reputation as a leader of the French party in the College which was in such a majority."

Confident of her brother's leverage at the papal court, Agnes proceeded with her plot to circumvent King Robert's instructions. In this, she seems to have gained a willing accomplice in the prospective bride herself. Maria was likely never enthusiastic about having to leave her childhood home in Naples in order to marry the faraway king of Hungary, nor, at fourteen, was she happy to wait indefinitely for an offer, which might never come, from the French royal family. Her cousin Charles had gone out of his way to make himself agreeable to the young princess, and his efforts seem to have met with success. From Maria's point of view, it was certainly better to stay in Naples and marry someone she had known and grown up with than to trust her fate to a complete stranger.

Sancia's support for the match—Agnes took King Robert's widow into her confidence as well—is also understandable. The dowager queen disliked and distrusted the haughty Catherine, and much preferred the company of the duchess of Durazzo, with whom she was intimate. Later, Sancia would name Agnes and her sons among the executors of her will, an honor conspicuously withheld from the members of the house of Taranto. A marriage between Maria and Charles of Durazzo would demote the empress's power within the kingdom, and Sancia was apparently willing to risk the ire of her Taranto relatives in order to accomplish this end.

With Sancia and Maria in favor of the match, it was not difficult for Agnes to convince Joanna as well of its worth. The young queen's acceptance of this arrangement, attributed by the chronicler Domenico da Gravina to Sancia's influence, is also a clear indication that, far from being forced into marriage, Maria actively expressed a desire to wed Charles. Joanna and Maria were very close. They were almost the same age and had been orphaned together. They had been each other's playmate for as long as either could remember; they had been brought up in the same castle, eaten the same meals, listened to the same church services. During the first few months after Robert's death, the accounts show that Joanna made an effort to please her sister, hosting a feast in her honor and gambling at hazards with her. Joanna was unlikely to have added her approval of a union with the house of Durazzo, knowing the likely reaction of the house of Taranto, if Maria had not wished for it.

Having secured the surreptitious assent of both queens (although not that of the ruling council), Agnes hurried to translate the promise of success into reality. The duchess of Durazzo proved herself an extremely adept conspirator. She understood that the empress of Constantinople, through her brother the king of France, was fully capable of preventing any alliance that ran counter to the interests of her sons, even one which boasted the approval of the pope. The dispensation for Maria's marriage therefore had to be worded carefully so as to allow Agnes complete freedom of movement and the ability to act unilaterally if necessary. Such favors did not come without a price, so in her appeal to her brother, the duchess of Durazzo did not rely simply upon family feeling. Instead, she offered Talleyrand twenty-two thousand florins—the whole of the dowry still due her in connection with her marriage—if he would arrange matters to ensure her son's wedding.

As it happened, Talleyrand of Périgord nourished his own aspirations as regards the Curia. Agnes's bribe aside, the cardinal no doubt reflected that having one of his nephews placed as a possible successor to the powerful throne of Naples might prove extremely useful the next time the Sacred College was called upon to elect a pope, and he promptly spoke to Clement VI about accommodating his sister's request.

Clement had a well-deserved reputation for high living, aristocratic taste, and easy generosity (which had no doubt served him well among his fellows in the recent papal election). The new pope's two favorite sayings were "No one should go out from the prince's presence discontented" and "A pontiff should make his subjects happy." Clement was acutely aware of his obligation to the cardinal and saw no reason not to accede to his wishes. On February 26, 1343, he signed a bull that allowed Agnes's son Charles to wed any woman he liked, as long as her relationship to the duke did not fall within the normally proscribed bounds of consanguinity. In this way was the marriage to Maria sanctioned by the church without the pope's actually having to reveal the name of the intended bride, a detail that might have proved awkward in later conversations with the kings of France and Hungary, who were bound to be somewhat put out by this appropriation of a valuable asset. This bull was made public in Naples.

Not made public were two additional dispensations addressed to the house of Durazzo, which were also signed by the pope on February 26. The first of these invested Agnes and her progeny with the power to consult their own desires when choosing a priest and declared that these priests would be allowed to administer any or all of the sacraments at the location of the Durazzos' choice, "even in prohibited places of worship." The second secret bull, which was directed to Agnes alone, contained a blanket permission for the duchess of Durazzo to retreat at any time to any convent she liked.

Once again, the rapid manner in which these papal documents were obtained—they were issued less than six weeks after Robert's death—is a strong indication that the conspiracy predated the king's passing. And clearly Agnes, at least, was well aware of the provocation this marriage would represent to her adversary, the empress of Constantinople, and the likely violence of Catherine's response. The business about retiring into a convent was in the nature of an escape clause.

In due course, Charles's vague but nonetheless official papal dispensation for the marriage to his cousin arrived in Naples, and Joanna and Sancia hosted the formal celebration of Maria's engagement on March 26, 1343, at the Castel Nuovo. The speed with which the pope had sanctioned this union would naturally have been interpreted as a sign of papal favor and must have encouraged Joanna and Sancia to believe this was an appropriate step to take to both resolve Maria's future and stabilize the order of succession. In yet another stab at legitimacy, all the members of the ruling council, having previously been informed of the bull's contents, were present to witness the ceremony. But even the authority of this delegation could not disguise the atmosphere of menace created by the pointed absence of the empress of Constantinople and her brood. In fact, Catherine was livid at having been outmaneuvered in this fashion and protested the betrothal in the strongest possible terms to both her niece Joanna and the pope; and just as the duchess of Durazzo had predicted, she called upon the king of France to intervene on her behalf in Avignon to have the dispensation rescinded.

But Agnes, having anticipated this response, was ready for it. Two days later, on March 28, the house of Durazzo launched the second, covert half of its plan. One of Maria's ladies-in-waiting, a young woman by the name of Margherita di Ceccano, herself the niece of a cardinal, was an accomplice to the plot. With Margherita's help, Charles of Durazzo quietly lured his young fiancée into the west garden of the Castel Nuovo, which abutted the grounds of his family's estate. According to Domenico da Gravina, from there he "abducted" her to his castle, where a sympathetic priest was waiting. This priest, by the power invested in him in accordance with one of the secret bulls signed by the pope, then hurriedly and secretly married the couple. But the performance of so unorthodox a nuptial sacrament was not enough to assure Charles of his bride. So just to make certain that there was no going back, as soon as the priest was finished, the duke of Durazzo took the precaution of consummating the marriage. Or, as Domenico da Gravina, relaying information that was obviously common knowledge at the time, reported, "having intercourse, it is said, and keeping her in his own palace."

Even an environment as sexually permissive as court life in Naples apparently had its limits. Charles's and Maria's behavior scandalized the kingdom. Worse, it goaded the house of Taranto to drop its diplomatic effort in favor of a strategy centered on armed conflict. Louis, Catherine's second son, who excelled at warfare, organized a small force of friends and their retainers for the purpose of striking back at his cousin Charles. They captured one of the duke of Durazzo's outlying castles and some of his other property and made plain their intention to continue hostilities. This necessarily prompted Charles and his mother, Agnes, to band together a group of their vassals for the purpose of defense. Within weeks, Naples stood on the brink of civil war.

If she did not realize her mistake in permitting her sister's engagement to Charles before, Joanna knew it now. She refused to recognize the sham wedding, denied her sister her dowry, and wrote at length to the pope, complaining bitterly about Agnes's and Charles's conduct and the insult they had perpetrated on her family. She insisted that the papacy reverse its earlier decision and annul the marriage. She remonstrated vehemently with her sister, and when Charles and Maria remained defiant, switched her allegiance to Catherine. The king of France, too, wrote to Clement VI demanding an explanation and seeking compensation for the damage to his sister's interests in Naples. Even the queen mother of Hungary, hedging her bets, weighed in with a letter expressing her extreme displeasure that a dispensation had been issued in direct contradiction to her kingdom's original, papal-approved marriage contract with Naples—after all, by that document, if Joanna died, Maria was obligated to marry Andrew in her place.

Under the circumstances, Clement's two dicta about always making everybody happy were put to the test. The pontiff did his best to placate the various parties involved, chiefly by telling a different story to each. On May 29, 1343, he wrote angrily to Sancia and Joanna that he was annoyed with their response to Maria's marriage since "we have granted a dispensation for this union on account of the benefit to be expected from it." Ten days later, in reaction to yet another irate letter from Joanna, he softened his language significantly and, in an obvious attempt to achieve a paternal tone, asked her to forgive Charles and Maria, referring to the marriage as an impetuous action undertaken "by reason of their tender years." (Charles was twenty.) The pope continued to Joanna: "You, as her only sister, nourished and educated beneath the same roof, should palliate these things so imprudently done and guide her [Maria] back to the path of honor and favor." To Maria he wrote: "The marriage did please and does please us, but it would please us more but for these sinister occurrences. Appease Joanna advisedly." Elizabeth of Hungary received a disingenuous epistle (a variation of which was also dispatched to Philip VI of France): "As to the arrangement of king Robert that his two granddaughters should be united to two of your sons, we have never counteracted it; but we did concede to Charles, duke of Durazzo, a dispensation of a general sort, by which he could marry any noble lady . . . no especial person, however, being named therein. Under this dispensation, we being entirely unaware [of the duke of Durazzo's intention], he married the second daughter of Charles, duke of Calabria [Maria]."

In the end, Cardinal Talleyrand was forced to send his own chamberlain to Naples, charging him with the dual task of settling the controversy in his nephew's favor and securing from his sister the promised bribe of twenty-two thousand florins. The chamberlain, aided by the fact that Maria was by this time noticeably pregnant, so Joanna really had no choice but to recognize the marriage, succeeded admirably in both instances. On July 14, 1343, an agreement was reached whereby Charles, in exchange for settling some of his own lands on his bride, was officially accepted as Maria's husband by Joanna's government. Maria's position as successor to the throne in the event that Joanna died childless was also formally reaffirmed by the royal court at this time. Catherine and her family were compensated for being outmaneuvered by a substantial cash settlement to Robert of Taranto drawn from funds in the royal treasury. Similarly, Joanna consented to pay Maria's considerable dowry, although in fact the queen of Naples held up the payment of this money to her sister for years, an indication, perhaps, of the deep distrust she had developed for her new brother-in-law and his family. Agnes, by contrast, having emerged the victor in this contest of wills, paid her brother's courier promptly and included in her return package to Talleyrand a long, highly flattering letter, thanking him profusely for the many services he had provided to her family.

Agnes's success did not come without a further price, however. Whatever goodwill the duchess of Durazzo had built up with the new queen before this incident was destroyed by her perfidy. After the agreement in July, Joanna began a policy of deliberately embracing counselors outside the Durazzo circle, particularly Robert of Cabannis, another of Philippa the Catanian's sons, and Charles of Artois, Robert the Wise's illegitimate son. Both men were promoted and rewarded with large salary increases in order to ensure their loyalty to the queen. The Durazzos found themselves shunned from the avenues of power by these new political favorites, and even Agnes's old ally Sancia could not provide them their former access. Although Joanna did not blame her grandmother for the debacle of Maria's marriage as she did Agnes, the outcome did teach the younger woman not to rely on Sancia's political acumen.

Having to navigate the dark waters of internecine rivalry, international intrigue, and near civil war in the first year of one's reign would have taxed the resources of any new ruler, let alone one who was only seventeen. But Maria's marriage, for all its deeper political implications, turned out to be just the warm-up. Less than two weeks after Joanna's formal recognition of Maria's marriage, a challenge of even greater magnitude abruptly materialized in Naples. On July 25, 1343, a procession of some four hundred Hungarian noblemen, knights, and courtiers, accompanied by their respective equipment and retainers, paraded solemnly into the capital city. At the head of this formidable assembly sat Joanna's mother-in-law, Elizabeth, dowager queen of Hungary.

Elizabeth's sudden descent upon her son and daughter-in-law had been prompted by disturbing reports of the deteriorating political climate in southern Italy. The pope had yet to revise the terms of Robert's will in Andrew's favor despite strong pressure from Hungary to do so. The queen mother was aware that this hesitation, coupled with the obvious influence of Cardinal Talleyrand, as reflected by the marriage of Maria to Charles of Durazzo, was an indication that her son's coronation was by no means assured. Members of Andrew's household had also apprised the dowager queen of the many factions jostling for power at the Neapolitan court and the inferiority of her son's position relative to that of his wife. Frustrated by the failure of her agents to reverse these disquieting trends, Andrew's mother had come to Naples determined to evaluate firsthand the nuances of the political climate and to alleviate the obstacles to her son's ascension to power. An experienced professional, Elizabeth made no secret of the manner in which she proposed to accomplish her ends. More intimidating than her entourage was the arsenal of specie accompanying the queen mother on her journey. According to the Hungarian chronicler Thuróczy, Elizabeth had taken the precaution of bringing along "for her expenses" some twenty-seven thousand marks in silver and a further twenty-one thousand marks in gold ("corresponding to 1,449,000 florins but presumably in bars"), not to mention a wagon half full of florins. From the astounding quantity of this potential bribe, estimated to represent some two or three years' worth of Hungarian mining output, it may be inferred that Elizabeth had some idea of what she was up against.

Almost from the moment she set foot on Italian soil at the port of Manfredia on the Adriatic, the queen mother of Hungary was aware of the awkward status her son occupied in his adopted kingdom. When, as a matter of courtesy, Andrew had ridden out to Benevento to escort his mother to her guest quarters at the Castel Nuovo, he was pointedly not accompanied by his wife. Instead, Joanna, dressed formally in her robes of state and wearing her crown as befit a sovereign welcoming an official foreign dignitary, received her mother-in-law several days later at Somma, just outside the capital city. These arrangements were entirely reflective of the royal couple's everyday existence. Except for important state ceremonies and religious holidays, Andrew almost never saw his wife. They took separate holidays—if he went to Salerno, she went to Resina, for example—prayed at separate churches, rode out with different people. Even when family obligation demanded a joint visit, as when Robert of Taranto had fallen ill at the beginning of the summer, Andrew inquired solicitously after his cousin's health on June 26 while Joanna waited until June 30. There are no records of the number of nights the couple spent together, but it seems likely that, after the initial consummation, Joanna felt that she had done her duty and contrived to keep her lord and master at arm's length in this activity, as in all others, as much as possible. Evidence indicates that Andrew had to ask permission to enter his wife's bedroom.

Nor was a lack of intimacy the only peculiar aspect of their relationship. Although everyone in Naples, including Joanna, referred to Andrew as "the king" (a gimmick designed to gull the Hungarians into believing that all was as it should be), it was clear that he was, in fact, no such thing. He had never been officially crowned, nor by this time did it seem likely that he would be. He had no connection with the government and did not seem to have been burdened with any responsibilities, even in the matter of expenses. Joanna paid for the upkeep of his household, right down to the purchase of knives for the kitchen and roses to perfume the soap. She bought him his shirts and doublets and paid for his trips to the seashore. He owed her for the silver he carried in his purse and had to account for his spending whenever he went over his allowance. And yet, before his mother's arrival, there is no record of Andrew's objecting to this arrangement, and it is not difficult to see why. He was, after all, only fifteen years old. He had leisure, fine clothes, and fast horses; he lived in a kingdom with many avenues for amusement. He had grown up in Joanna's shadow, and by this time was used to it.

His mother, however, had come to Naples to improve his position. She first sought to work through Sancia, but Sancia was ill that summer and deferred in favor of her granddaughter the queen. Joanna listened patiently to her mother-in-law's lectures and did not trouble to disagree with her, hoping to weather the visit by diplomacy. Elizabeth's arguments, as later employed by her envoys at Avignon, have survived:

> There would be no downside in asking the Holy Father that her [Joanna's] husband be officially granted the title of King, a title she already used for him. Didn't she [Joanna] also agree that, for the good of the kingdom as well as for her own peace of mind, it would be preferable that her husband assist her in sharing the burden of power? Without even considering the question of marital harmony, there exist issues that their subjects would prefer to see a man tackle rather than a woman; and in the event foes had to be pushed back, this would be a matter for the husband more than for the wife. In the end, she [Joanna] risked nothing in inviting her husband to lead

the kingdom. All that would be needed would be to set limits that he should not infringe upon, and to obtain the necessary guaranties regarding this.

Joanna's outward show of consideration did not, however, fool her mother-in-law. The dowager queen understood that her son's wife very much approved the current arrangement and would do nothing to expand her husband's authority in the kingdom. Nor could Elizabeth find the means of circumventing Joanna's purpose by negotiating with one of the other branches of her family. The queen mother of Hungary soon came to the conclusion that bribing either the Taranto or Durazzo family (or both) was a waste of time, as the one branch was certain to oppose whatever the other supported no matter how attractive the financial incentive. But in short order Elizabeth identified an alternative. The dowager queen dispatched her cash wagons and sacks of gold to a place where she knew she could get value for her money: the papal court at Avignon. The bribe was accompanied by a prestigious delegation that included a bishop, a high-ranking Hungarian count, and Andrew's cousin the dauphin of Vienne, all charged by Elizabeth with the task of convincing the pope to crown her son king and to vest him with at least some of the powers of sovereignty. Then, having satisfied herself that she had done all she could to promote Andrew's interests in Naples, the queen mother and the remainder of her entourage took off to Rome for a few months' sojourn.

The timing of this intercession could not have been more unfortunate. The Hungarian delegation appeared at Avignon with their money, complaints, and demands just as Clement VI, finding the volume of correspondence directed at him from Naples since the death of King Robert to be wearily copious, was weighing the advantages of assigning a legate to the kingdom. The appeal of having a representative on the scene, empowered to act in the pontiff's name and so save Clement from having to respond personally to the entreaties of the various Neapolitan parties, was obvious. With the arrival of Elizabeth's emissaries, it became irresistible. Here was yet another faction clamoring to be heard, crowding the halls of the already overcrowded papal palace, demanding an audience, pouring forth a litany of grievances, all of which had to be duly recorded and investigated, and the various principals by degrees cajoled, flattered, or reprimanded according to circumstance or temperament. Clement consigned the Hungarians to his cardinals and made known his intention to procure a legate for Naples.

This news was communicated rapidly to Joanna's court. The specter of having her reign and kingdom compromised by the introduction of a papal legate who would rule in her place was repugnant. Aside from the humiliation of being publicly stripped of her legitimate sovereign authority by the pope, there was the very real threat that the legate, whoever he might be, would tip the fragile balance of power that currently existed at the Neapolitan court away from Joanna's family and toward her husband's. Even if this did not occur, at the very least, Joanna and her subjects knew that the assignment of a legate would result in wide-ranging and significant financial hardship. Papal representatives had a well-deserved reputation for siphoning off as much of a kingdom's wealth as possible for their own personal use and that of the church. Indeed, this was often the unofficial motive for their appointment. For this reason, legates were abhorred and their rules resisted throughout Italy. Accordingly, on September 5, 1343, after a hurried consultation with the ruling council, Joanna addressed an official petition to the pope, which was presented at the Holy See by Hugo del Balzo, supplemented by a party of Neapolitan advisers, which included two counts and a doctor of civil law, formally protesting the appointment of a legate to her realm on the grounds that it violated the original 1265 agreement between Charles of Anjou and the papacy. This reliance on legal precedent was entirely in keeping with the policies of the previous administration. Joanna knew that, had Robert been presented with a similar imperilment to his rule, he would have handled the situation in precisely the same way.

Unfortunately, the legality of a position in the Middle Ages, however well established, was often undermined by mitigating factors, a category under which Elizabeth's lucrative offering to the pope unquestionably fell. Nor could Joanna have predicted just how influential Hungarian wealth would be in the coming months. Superstition dictates that misfortune, when it occurs, manifests itself in groups of three. In Joanna's case, this condition was satisfied in October, when the super-companies began, one by one, to fail.

⊷

CHAPTER VI

Papal Politics

T HE LAWS OF money are as immutable as the laws of nature. Maintaining a successful commercial venture, be it conducted in the twenty-first century or the fourteenth, is a function of the profitability of its underlying business, the ability of management to adapt to changing conditions, and the continued confidence of its investors or depositors, with the first two criteria necessarily influencing the third. The largest of the super-companies, forced by the losses they sustained in the Neapolitan grain trade to diversify into English wool, found themselves trapped by Edward III's ever-increasing need for funds to prosecute his war with France. Senior management at these firms, whose partners represented the most sophisticated financial talent the world had yet known, tried desperately to limit their exposure to the English king. Their loans were actually advances against monies due them in trade, or from the taxes or fees assigned them from the royal exchequer. But it took far more time for the super-companies to collect the taxes and fees owed them by the crown than it did for Edward to spend their loans, and once the loans were spent, he wanted more.

The vacillating policies of the Florentine government during the critical period of 1340 to 1343 had only added to the super-companies' difficulties. Jealous of the emerging economic strength of the neighboring town of Pisa, the commune of Florence had elected to try to solve the problem by declaring war on the city, an expensive undertaking that the Bardi, Peruzzi, and Acciaiuoli partners were obliged to help underwrite. When, in 1341, the war turned against them, the Florentines had solicited Robert the Wise for help, but the old king, preoccupied with the proposed invasion of Sicily under Andrew's questionable leadership, had failed to send the necessary troops. This had prompted the government of Florence, which until this point had always stood firmly with Naples and the papacy against the Ghibbelines, to appeal to the emperor for military aid in the spring of 1342. Furious, Robert had retaliated by seizing the Neapolitan assets of the super-companies. The pope had followed suit by directing church business routinely handled by the Bardi, Peruzzi, and Acciaiuoli families to other, smaller companies whose politics were reliably pro-Guelph. Although Florence hurried to correct its mistake by canceling its imperial embassy and electing a new leader with unimpeachable Guelphic credentials, the damage was done. Those who had placed deposits with the super-companies clamored to have their money back.

In the fall of 1342, the new leader of Florence, who had been elected "dictator for life," sought protection for the firms by declaring a three-year moratorium on payments, hoping to buy the time necessary to collect the monies due the companies in England and so maintain their solvency. But rather than pay, Edward III instead launched a series of audits intended to minimize his obligations to his Florentine creditors, at which point it became clear that the super-companies would sustain major losses. This was the final blow. The government of the dictator for life fell on August 3, 1343, and a full-scale panic ensued.

To protect the kingdom's interests, Joanna and Sancia together signed a letter on August 25 to the government of Florence, reminding the commune of the close relationship that had always existed between the Angevin kingdom and their city, and demanding that Neapolitan claims be given preference in the distribution of assets. But in truth there was nothing to be done. The Peruzzi and Acciaiuoli families declared bankruptcy in October 1343; the Bardi limped on before finally shutting down in April 1346. Payouts to creditors were less than 50 percent of the asset base, and the small size of the settlement was not entirely the result of losses. The partners of these firms were evidently as adroit at hiding their money as they had once been at making it. "Most of the shareholders appear to have fled the city and arranged to shift property into safer hands. Such action seems to have been standard practice in Florence at the time."

Businesses had failed before in the Middle Ages, but not like this. Due to advances in transportation and education, the size and scope of the super-companies' dealings were unprecedented. Giovanni Villani estimated that the super-companies' demand for skilled labor was so great that 1,200 Florentines had been taught to read and write in the vernacular and to use an abacus. The Bardi family alone employed a workforce of between 120 and 150 people spread across Europe, an administrative network second only to the Curia. These firms represented the first truly modern multinational corporations, and when they failed, they touched off the first truly modern multinational recession. Wages fell, businesses closed, and unemployment rose all over Europe; people lost their life savings, and credit, which had been so easily obtained in the past, was no longer forthcoming. Governments as well as individuals were affected. Because nothing like this had ever happened before, royal treasuries were not equipped to handle the crisis, the ideas of coordinated central bank intervention and government bailouts being still six hundred years away from conception.

Every economy in Western Europe was impaired, but nowhere was the damage inflicted as severe as it was in Naples, where for decades the super-companies had effectively functioned as the financing arm of the royal government. The entire wealth of the kingdom was based on these firms purchasing the enormous output of grain, which in a good year achieved a level of 45,000 tons. The revenues associated with the super-companies paid for all the finished goods that flooded the Neapolitan marketplace, including the luxury items—the silks, the jewels, the multicolored, gold-threaded cloth from the Far East, the exotic eatables, the spices, the perfumed soap. They financed the building of the impressive castles and churches commissioned by Charles the Lame and Robert the Wise and his queen and paid for their decoration by the finest artists in France and Italy. The great grain trade was the motor that allowed a succession of Angevin rulers to run up, year after year, the huge military expenses associated with the fruitless campaign to retake the island of Sicily and to deliver the seven thousand ounces of gold (and probably the white horse as well) for the annual tribute every Angevin monarch, male or female, was obligated to pay the papacy without fail.

Of course, no one living in 1343 could have guessed how long and how deep the downturn would be, or its implications for Naples over time. The court must have expected that the super-companies would recapitalize at some future date and the kingdom return to its previous condition of affluence. But in fact, the prosperity associated with King Robert had been the product of luck and unsustainable economic realities, and not good government. "The Angevins remained dependent on the merchants as they embarked on a spending spree, rebuilding Naples and indulging themselves in prestige-enhancing conspicuous consumption. Thus, the lucrative grain trade . . . became transformed into a long-term quasi-monopoly for them [the super-companies], as a result of subsequent Angevin profligacy." By rights a realignment of the grain trade ought to have taken place in the previous decade. Only the extreme competence of the managing directors of the Bardi,

Peruzzi, and Acciaiuoli families had put off the bust until the beginning of Joanna's reign. But no one understood that at the time, and the new queen was blamed for it.

Blame was the least of Joanna's problems. Although Robert the Wise had left a substantial surplus in the royal treasury at his death, he had also encumbered his estate with a number of bequests and conditions, which Joanna, as his heir, was legally required to honor. Mostly these had to do with earmarking funds for another attempt on Sicily as well as ensuring that many of the old king's favorites—including his illegitimate son, Charles of Artois, and certain members of Philippa the Catanian's family—were protected and promoted. Unfortunately, however, payment of these stipends had the effect of draining the kingdom's resources at an accelerated pace. Nor could Joanna apply, as had her grandfather, for easy credit when this money ran out; her bankers, even those who had managed to escape town or jail, were no longer in business. The days of unlimited Angevin spending were over.

Even the weather turned against the kingdom. For the next two years the average rainfall rose precipitously, drowning the grain fields, reducing crop yields, and adding greatly to the general atmosphere of anxiety and foreboding.

❧

While Joanna and her counselors struggled to limit the kingdom's losses in the face of this financial crisis, the court was distracted by the arrival of yet another visiting dignitary. On October 11, 1343, Francesco Petrarch, the poet laureate, rode into Naples. His was not a social visit. The great scholar was acting in an official capacity as a personal emissary on behalf of his good friend Cardinal Giovanni Colonna, a member of Rome's powerful Colonna family. The cardinal was a rising force at the papal court in Avignon (and, as such, a rival of Cardinal Talleyrand of Périgord). Petrarch had been charged by his friend with obtaining the freedom of the imprisoned brothers of the Pipini family.

The three Pipini brothers, led by the eldest brother, Giovanni, count of Minerbino, had been jailed by Robert the Wise for their criminal participation in the civil unrest of 1338. So little concern for the rule of law or the general populace had the brothers displayed while pursuing a vendetta against their enemies that they had been nicknamed "the scourge of Apulia." A small army had been required to force them to capitulate, but they were eventually brought to trial in 1341 and subsequently convicted in a court of law of murder, rape, pillage, arson, treason, "kindling civil war," and other assorted capital crimes. They had originally been slated for execution, but their mother had pleaded successfully with Sancia to have the sentence commuted to life imprisonment, and so the three young men were currently spending their days in fetters in the dungeon of one of the royal castles. After Robert's death, their mother had had the sudden inspiration to send a heartfelt appeal, supplemented by a substantial bribe, to Cardinal Colonna, a distant family relation, to secure their release. After all, it had worked for Agnes.

The cardinal had obliged by sending Petrarch, who was assumed to have influence at the royal court because of his earlier visit to Naples. Petrarch was a famous poet and a revered scholar, but he was an inexperienced diplomat, and his attitudes toward politics were at once naive and self-serving. His errand was viewed with marked disfavor by Joanna and her court, and his entreaties for clemency on behalf of his clients were met with resistance. The prisoners' property, appropriated at the time of their conviction by Robert and subsequently reassigned to political favorites, including Raymond del Balzo, a relative of Hugo, would have to be returned if they were pardoned. Raymond, a member of the ruling council, was naturally reluctant to do this. But dwarfing this objection was the royal court's fear of the known characters of the men involved.

They were arrogant, unrepentant killers, and their release was sure to visit fresh calamity upon the kingdom.

Not wishing to offend so distinguished and respected an emissary, or his patron, however, rather than simply denying Petrarch's request, Joanna, Sancia, and the ruling council stalled and equivocated. Joanna granted the poet several private interviews at which she apparently discussed, not the liberation of the Pipini brothers, but literature. On November 25 she signed letters patent appointing him her domestic chaplain, the same esteemed scholarly position he had occupied under her grandfather's regime. Sancia (herself a beneficiary of Pipini property, some of the brothers' most valuable horses having found their way into her stable) also granted an audience to Petrarch at which she commiserated with him over his and his clients' plight. "The elder queen, formerly the royal spouse, now the most wretched of widows, has compassion, as she says, affirming that she can do nothing more," Petrarch observed to Cardinal Colonna in a letter written from Naples soon after his arrival. "Cleopatra [by which he means Joanna] with her Ptolemy [Andrew] could also show compassion if Photinus [Friar Robert] and Achilles [Raymond del Balzo] would allow it." The two queens' sympathy was, in this case, feigned. Joanna later explained her position in a letter to the pope, which she asked Petrarch to deliver. "Letting the Pipini go free would be incentive to emulate them," she wrote to Clement VI. "These prisoners could not presume to speak of innocence when no one is unaware of the extraordinary abuse they perpetrated in the time of King Robert; devastation, plunder, arson, murders and abuse of all kinds; when no one is unaware, too, of their open rebellion and insane stubbornness, and how, despite the King's summons and threats, they continued to disturb the peace and quiet of the realm, and were so bold as to hold out against the royal troops and fight them with their gang of outlaws, knaves and other such criminals . . . By the letter of the law they deserved to be sentenced to death."

The scholar attributed the thwarting of his mission, not to a genuine concern for the safety of the kingdom and its inhabitants, but rather to the "seductive band of courtiers" surrounding the two queens, particularly the odious Friar Robert, whom he claimed exerted undue influence over the rest of the council. "Relying not as much on eloquence as on silence and on arrogance, he [Friar Robert] wanders through the courtyards of the queens, and, supported by a staff, he pushes aside the more humble, he tramples upon justice, and he defiles whatever remains of divine or human rights," he wrote, which is to say that the friar, too, opposed the release of the Pipini. "I have no hopes, except from the intervention of some superior power, as my dependence on the clemency of the council is out of the question," Petrarch reported gloomily to Cardinal Colonna.

Frustrated and disappointed, the unhappy ambassador sent a number of letters to Avignon complaining of the corrupt and dissolute state of the kingdom. He seems to have been prejudiced against Naples even before his arrival, for he had written to his friend Barbato da Sulmona at the time of Robert the Wise's death some nine months before, "I am really alarmed about the youthfulness of the young queen, and of the new king, about the age and intent of the other queen, about the talents and ways of the courtiers. I wish that I could be a lying prophet about these things, but I see two lambs entrusted to the care of a multitude of wolves, and I see a kingdom without a king. How can I call someone a king who is ruled by another and who is exposed to the greed of so many and (I sadly add) to the cruelty of so many?" Nor was Petrarch likely to view Joanna's rule with enthusiasm. "I consider what Plautus says in his Aulularia much closer to the truth: 'There is no excellent woman; one is really worse than another,'" he once wrote, and, "A single law governs all females: they desire silly things, and they dread things of small account."

Through the letters with which Petrarch peppered Cardinal

Colonna, the papal court at Avignon was treated to a litany of grievances and the discouraging image of a realm in utter chaos. "Perhaps last night I might have obtained the courtesy even of rejection had the Council not adjourned because of the approaching darkness, and had not the incurable disease of the city compelled everyone to return home early. Though very famous for many reasons, the city possesses one particularly dark, repulsive, and inveterate evil: to travel in it by night, as in a jungle, is dangerous and full of hazards because the streets are beset by armed young nobles whose dissoluteness cannot be controlled by the discipline of their parents, the authority of their teachers, or by the majesty and command of kings," he wrote bitterly to the cardinal, seemingly oblivious to that fact that his purpose in Naples was to apply pressure for Joanna and her court to put three of the worst of these offenders back on the streets.

Lawlessness was by no means specific to Joanna's reign. During this very same period, the English town of Ipswich, for example, was so beset by criminal bands who roamed the countryside, and so helpless against feloniousness, that the ruffians felt comfortable enough to amuse themselves by taking over the regional courthouses. They pretended to hold trials at which they fined their hapless victims and deposed the local authorities "in mockery of the King's justices and ministers in his service," as a legal complaint in the year 1344 read. Ironically, the same conditions Petrarch now deplored had existed during the emissary's previous visit in 1341, when the Pipini brothers were still at large and wreaking havoc on the populace—but at that time the poet had evidently been so gratified by the honor conferred on him that he hadn't noticed. Instead, Petrarch attributed the city's criminality to the barbarity of the gladiatorial tournaments with which aristocratic Naples entertained itself. "Here human blood flows like the blood of cattle, and often amidst the applause of the insane spectators, unfortunate sons are killed under the very eyes of their wretched parents," he wrote indignantly to the cardinal. "I have already wasted many words speaking of it with the obstinate citizens. Indeed we should hardly be astonished that your friends [the Pipini brothers], offering as they do such a prize for greed, should be prisoners in that city where killing men is considered a game, a city which Virgil indeed does call the most delightful of all, but as it stands now would not be considered unequal to Thrace in infamy." Petrarch was well aware of the influence his words would wield in Avignon, and so he made a point of ensuring that his opinions would be broadcast at the curia. "And you will have to share some of the blame if from the information that I sent at some length in other more confidential letters you do not keep the Roman Pontiff better informed," he warned his correspondent grimly.

The Hungarian party recognized its opportunity. Elizabeth's ambassadors in Avignon reported on Cardinal Colonna's interest in the Pipini brothers and Petrarch's description of the intractability of the Neapolitan court to the queen mother, who was not only still in Italy but was actually staying as a guest of the Colonna family in Rome. The result of this exchange was that Andrew suddenly took up the Pipini cause in Naples. The prince promised to do what he could to free the brothers, an advocacy position for which both Petrarch and his sponsor Cardinal Colonna were extremely grateful.

This action on the part of the Hungarians, in combination with their considerable financial resources and a letter-writing campaign initiated by Elizabeth, by which every prince, priest and prelate over whom the queen mother exercised influence inundated the Sacred College with correspondence demanding that Andrew be crowned and Naples assigned a legate, finally succeeded in shifting the balance of power at Avignon away from Joanna and toward her husband. Petrarch's damaging reports, as presented by Cardinal Colonna, provided Clement VI with the justification he needed to subvert Robert the Wise's will. On November 28, 1343, the pope announced in the preamble to an official bull that "the age of the queen [Joanna] rendering her still incapable of governing, since the temperament of children is inconstant and easily influenced"—that must have gone down well at the Castel Nuovo—he was dissolving the ruling council and prohibiting Joanna from exercising her sovereign right as queen. The pope then named Cardinal Aimeric de Châtelus to act as legate, investing him, as the papal surrogate, with full powers to rule the kingdom of Naples.

The publication of this decree in Naples marked the commencement of a new, highly charged, dangerously desperate period at the royal court. From this point on, no policy, action, initiative, program, or plot was undertaken by any of the various interested parties in Naples without an eye to, or a reciprocal maneuver planned by, the interested parties at the Holy See in Avignon, and vice versa. It was as if the two courts, separated though they were by three hundred miles and the Mediterranean, nonetheless operated as parallel, mirror universes, two partners in a long-distance dance so attuned to each other's rhythm that the slightest motion by one set off a reaction in the other. Outwardly, the struggle between the Neapolitans and the Hungarians had all the hallmarks of the usual medieval diplomatic wrangling, but this was a sham: both sides understood that no mediating solution could be imposed by an external authority. It was a winner-take-all situation, and was fought as such.

Joanna lost no time in responding to this dismaying turn of events through both official and unofficial channels. She dashed off a letter to Clement, which was presented at the papal court on December 19 by Hugo del Balzo, in which the queen of Naples indignantly protested the abrogation of her rightfully held powers and warned the pontiff against interference, "praying him to treat no further with the Hungarian envoys concerning the coronation of Andrew and the administration of her kingdom." Nor did Joanna allow past grievances to prevent her from making use of every political advantage. Two days later, she dispatched a second, private letter to Avignon, this one addressed to her former nemesis, Cardinal Talleyrand, rival of her present adversary, Cardinal Colonna, in which she implored Talleyrand's help in reversing Clement's decision. "Pleading with confidence for your protection in our difficult situation," she wrote, "we beg affectionately of you to prevent the dispatch of the legate by whatever means you deem necessary." By now quite familiar with the cardinal's preferred methods of operation, she included in her correspondence the intelligence that she was sending by separate courier "certain things, which you would not find displeasing."

Joanna's ties to Talleyrand deepened in January 1344, when her sister, Maria, gave birth to a son who lived only a few hours. Pity and grief for the young duchess of Durazzo's loss reconciled whatever lingering grievances existed between the sisters, and Joanna moved sufficiently closer to her brother-in-law's family to send Charles of Durazzo's younger brother Louis to Avignon to support Cardinal Talleyrand in his efforts to quash the Hungarian campaign to have Andrew crowned and a legate appointed. But the new year also brought the resignation of a valuable ally when Sancia abruptly decided to abandon the cares of political office in order to enter the Clarissan convent of Santa Croce.

The older queen had made no secret of her desire to retire from society and take up religious vows in the past, but her permanent withdrawal on January 21, 1344, almost a year to the day after the death of her husband, represented a victory for the Hungarian party and a validation of their methods. Clement VI's assignment of a legate to administer the kingdom she and her husband had ruled absolutely since 1309 was a blow from which Sancia did not recover. As there is no evidence of a falling out between Joanna and her grandmother, Sancia likely considered that the matter had been taken out of her hands by the pope's dissolution of the ruling council. At fifty-eight and failing, Sancia understandably wished to devote herself fully to matters of the spirit; however, in doing so, she left her granddaughter alone to manage a particularly complex and dangerous situation. After Sancia's withdrawal, among Joanna's nearest advisers, only her surrogate mother, Philippa the Catanian, remained of the triumvirate that had once ruled Naples.

If the Hungarians thought that the removal of one of their Neapolitan adversaries would weaken the young queen's resolve, they were soon disabused of the notion. On January 24, just three days after Sancia entered the convent, Joanna addressed another letter to Clement in which she reaffirmed her position in the strongest possible terms. After advising the pope again to withdraw the legate and resist Hungarian demands to have Andrew crowned king at her expense, she asserted her conviction that she alone was best suited to manage both her husband and her kingdom. "Your Holiness will deign to call to mind kindly my steadfast and immutable purpose not to make over the administration [of the realm of Naples] to my revered lord and husband," she wrote, "for it must reasonably be understood that there is none living who will strive after his advantage and honor as I shall; and when I know how to arrange our respective affairs, that will be made manifest to all."

Persuaded by Joanna's letters and envoys, Clement compromised. Although he agreed to bestow the title of king on Andrew, promising him in a letter dated January 19, 1344, that he would be crowned along with his wife if both he and Joanna demonstrated true obedience to the legate, the honor was empty. Andrew was very deliberately not given a share in the government of the realm. Instead, on February 3, Clement specified in a letter to Joanna that, while her husband would be crowned with her, only her coronation would be considered blessed by God. The kingdom of Naples, the pope declared, unambiguously for once, belonged to Joanna alone as the rightful heir of King Robert "tanquam vir ejus" ("just as if she were a man"). Then, to ensure there was no confusion on the part of the Hungarians as to his true intent, on February 22 Clement penned a missive to Andrew's older brother, Louis, king of Hungary, in which the pope explained he was acceding to the Hungarian request that Andrew be crowned king but only in his capacity as Joanna's husband and under the strict understanding that should Joanna die before an heir was produced, the kingdom would pass to Maria.

Aware that this decision was a victory for Joanna, Clement sought to soften the blow to Andrew by singling him out for preferential treatment in matters of the spirit. Clement threw in a grab bag of religious favors: Andrew was now allowed to carry his own portable altar when he traveled; he had the right to celebrate mass before dawn if he so chose; he and a small party of followers were even permitted to enter the cloister of secluded nuns if ever the need to do so arose. Additionally, perhaps as a means of increasing the honorary king's popularity in his adopted realm, or at least providing a decent turnout at religious festivities, Clement decreed that any Neapolitan subject who attended a church ceremony at which Andrew was present would earn absolution for a year's worth of sins and an extra forty indulgences. As a final measure of Clement's desire to compensate the young king fully for the loss of his rule, Andrew, alone in the kingdom of Naples, was allowed to eat meat on fast days.

❧

The arrival of the letters acquainting the Neapolitan court with the official papal position on the all-important question of the role Joanna's husband would play in the royal government happened to coincide with the return of Andrew's mother to the capital. Having completed her tour of Italy, Elizabeth decided to see her son one last time before embarking on the sea voyage home. She could not have chosen a more inauspicious occasion for a return visit. The degree of animosity displayed by the native courtiers toward the Hungarian party, and her son in particular, took her aback. Everyone knew that, as a result of her interference, the royal government was about to be replaced by a legate, and that, further, the dowager queen and her eldest son were actively trying to put Andrew on the throne and had at least partially succeeded.

Elizabeth was able to experience personally the results of her handiwork when the Hungarian members of Andrew's household grimly informed her that they had uncovered evidence of plots and intrigues against her son's life. The queen mother wrote to the pope complaining of the danger and demanding action, but Clement had had enough of Hungarian disgruntlement by this time and likely considered Elizabeth's letter yet another thrust in her offensive to put her son in power, and so he ignored her warnings. Failing to achieve satisfaction from official channels, Elizabeth then determined once again to take matters into her own hands and announced that she was taking Andrew back to Hungary with her.

The dowager queen was only dissuaded from carrying through on this resolve by the combined appeals of Joanna, Agnes of Périgord, and Catherine of Valois, surely the first time in the history of the kingdom that these three women had agreed to act in concert on anything. The most likely explanation for this united front was the recognition that if Elizabeth succeeded in removing Andrew from Naples, he would certainly reappear later accompanied by his brother the king and a large Hungarian army, a situation to be avoided at all costs. Domenico da Gravina reported that Joanna was in tears during the interview, although he cast doubt on her motives and those of the empress; only Agnes was portrayed as honestly concerned with Andrew's rights and welfare.

Elizabeth's desire to remove Andrew suggests that he was still being treated as a child, though he would turn seventeen that year. Petrarch, while attributing to him a "lofty mind" (this was after

Andrew had sided with the poet in the controversy over the Pipini brothers), nonetheless referred to the prince as a "boy" in a letter to Cardinal Colonna, while Joanna was always denoted as "the Queen." Clement, too, made this distinction between them. In a later letter to Joanna, the pope, seeking to reconcile the queen of Naples to her husband, commended Andrew, but "his praise sounds like the praise that would be given a child, and shows that the pope considered Andrew as such, even though he was only about twenty months younger than his wife." At seventeen, Edward III of England had had the energy and presence to overthrow the government of his mother, Queen Isabella, and her consort Roger Mortimer. No one would have dared to suggest taking Edward home for his own good. This adds credence to the idea that Andrew was immature and somewhat backward for his age.

The Neapolitan strategy worked. Elizabeth allowed herself to be convinced of the court's good intentions regarding her son, and Andrew stayed. Since the queen mother was hardly a neophyte politically, it may be presumed that she judged Joanna's emotions and intentions to be genuine. Having secured her purpose, Joanna hastened Elizabeth on her way by commissioning three of her own galleys to take her mother-in-law and her entourage across the Adriatic on February 25, before the older woman had a chance to change her mind.

The dowager queen's tender concern for her son's welfare did not prevent her from continuing to demand that he share power with his wife. On the contrary, upon her return to Hungary, she and King Louis increased their efforts to pressure the pope to amend his decision regarding Andrew's right to govern Naples, even though Elizabeth was perfectly aware that it was this very policy that most put her son's life at risk.

~≫~

CHAPTER VII

Nest *of* Vipers

Two months later, the papal legate, Cardinal Aimeric de Châtelus, rode into Naples.

A career diplomat with a long history of dogged service and equally persistent failure in the employ of the church, Aimeric's principal utility seems to have been his willingness, at least initially, to be transferred into whatever locality or situation his superiors deemed necessary, however hopeless. His first appointment, more than two decades earlier, had been as rector of Romagna, a particularly turbulent region incorporating the cities of Ravenna and Rimini, where his subjects assiduously ignored his pronouncements and decrees. Aimeric had retaliated by complaining vociferously by letter to the curia, calling the province "vainglorious" and "always ripe for deceit . . . its inhabitants are . . . cunning . . . and in trickery, supreme in Italy." In the end, jurisdiction over the province had to be allocated instead to Robert the Wise. Aimeric's desultory performance did not deter his career; after Romagna, he was promoted to archbishop and, after a series of similarly inept postings, eventually to cardinal. He had been more successful at his most recent task, which was the relatively modest errand of returning to Rimini and Ravenna to wring from their citizens the proceeds of a tax previously imposed by the church. But this sort of bill collecting was hardly preparation for the complex demands of the royal court of Naples.

If the legate was under any illusions that the queen of Naples had reconciled herself to his presence, he was immediately disabused of the notion. Before he arrived, Joanna had sent a wave of emissaries of ever-increasing rank—first a court official, then two high-ranking members of the baronage, and finally a duke—to intercept Aimeric along his journey and prevent him from entering the kingdom and discharging his orders. Her ambassadors at Avignon, Louis of Durazzo and Cardinal Talleyrand, had given her reason to believe that the legate's term of office would be fixed to six months, and Joanna wanted Aimeric to delay his arrival until this negotiation had been finalized. But the legate, who had already been accused by the pope of tardiness in possessing himself of his new posting, journeyed so quickly in an effort to clear himself of this charge that he eluded all the queen's intermediaries. He was at the border in early May, where he took the precaution of tacking a copy of the papal bull officially announcing his appointment to the door of the cathedral at Rieti; by May 12 he was in Capua. Joanna, informed of Aimeric's imminent arrival only at the last minute, had to scramble to mobilize a welcoming ceremony of sufficient dignity to satisfy protocol. The streets of Capua were hastily hung with silk banners and the usual ornaments, and a makeshift dais knocked together at which the entire royal family, roused from their respective castles and rushed to the city, were sullenly assembled to greet the cardinal. Andrew rode out to meet him at Aversa, and on May 20, 1344, Joanna herself accompanied Aimeric to the monastery of Saint Antonio, just outside the capital city, where permanent lodgings had been prepared for him.

Taming the powerful factions of the royal court of Naples would have taxed the resources of the most skilled administrator. The situation cried out for the appointment of an individual equipped with imagination, keen judgment, subtlety of manner, and the ability to adapt quickly to fluctuating conditions. Aimeric was patently none of these. He had a functionary's horror of criticism; his greatest fear was of making a mistake and earning the censure of his superior. Accordingly, he fell back on caution and delay, and a rigid adherence to rules and instructions. The day after his arrival, Joanna came to see him, intending to take privately the odious vow of obedience that the pope had decreed a condition of her vassalage. But Aimeric refused to accept her pledge on the grounds that he had not yet communicated his presence in Naples to the Curia, nor received specific orders regarding his assignment. Frustrated, Joanna returned many times over the next two weeks to try to fulfill this requirement, but "he persists in his inflexibility," she observed icily in a letter to the pope. Eventually, Aimeric forced both Joanna and Andrew to take the oath of obedience in a very public ceremony in front of the whole court, and even then did not accept their submission until a precise written account of the proceedings had been filled out and sent to Clement for approval. Beginning in this fashion did nothing to improve relations, already strained, between the papal representative and his host kingdom, and Aimeric was made to feel the court's hostility. Joanna's family was very good at making other people uncomfortable. In no time at all, Aimeric was writing to the pope begging to be transferred.

But Clement consoled his legate with forty florins a day, in addition to the ability to draw on Joanna's treasury for whatever amounts Aimeric deemed necessary to maintain a lifestyle appropriately opulent to his position. The pope also gave the cardinal the right to raise taxes on the clergy and to increase his personal income further by selling temporal and spiritual favors as he saw fit, and Aimeric resigned himself to his task. The next step in the elaborate ritual governing the transition of power from Joanna to the cardinal was for Aimeric to accept the queen's oath of homage to the church, at which point she would in turn officially recognize church authority over her realm, and the government of Naples would formally pass to the legate. But Joanna fell seriously ill that summer, and the ceremony had to be postponed until August. This delay added to the confusion and unrest in the kingdom, as no one was quite sure who was in charge. The ruling council had been disbanded by the pope's bull of the previous November; the legate stubbornly refused to take responsibility for Naples until the queen had formally made him an oath of homage; and Joanna herself was incapacitated. During the approximately two-month period of her illness, then, the kingdom effectively functioned without a government.

That the vacuum created by these conditions would inevitably lend itself to opportunism by the various parties jockeying for power was predictable; that it would be Andrew who would step forward and seize the initiative was not. Nonetheless, on June 24, Andrew took advantage of the unsettled state of the government to order the release of the three incarcerated Pipini brothers, and then, on the afternoon of their liberation, personally knighted them.

If he had let Genghis Khan out of prison and knighted him, Andrew could not have caused greater controversy. The already delicate balance of power between the varying Neapolitan court factions disappeared completely as members of the nobility who had been recipients of the brothers' property rushed to ally themselves with other like-minded families against the Pipini. For their part, the Hungarian party instantly gained three intimidating warriors, not to mention all their family members, known associates, and servants as allies. "Being puffed up with triumph, they [the Pipini brothers] began to live luxuriously, riding in royal state, holding jousts, and appearing in the presence of the Queen and Andrew with loftier banners than their own," Domenico da Gravina observed. Buoyed by his success, Andrew made it clear that those who opposed his coronation could expect retribution. "Sometimes toward the Queen and sometimes toward the magnates he employed threats, which contributed, with other causes, to hasten his cruel and violent death," Villani observed.

During this atmosphere of turmoil, Joanna recovered sufficiently to take her oath of homage. On August 28, at a ceremony conducted at the church of Santa Chiara and witnessed by the whole court, Aimeric formally recognized Joanna alone as heir to the kingdom and then accepted command of her government according to his instructions.

~≈~

As galling as it must have been for Joanna to lose her rule in so demeaning a fashion, she surely must have taken some satisfaction in watching Aimeric fail so convincingly in her former position. The legate's first acts were to remove from authority all the members of the ruling council and other respected and powerful courtiers belonging to the old regime, as well as to replace each of the governors of the various provinces in the kingdom with new officials. The old appointees immediately protested their respective demotions; the countryside rebelled against the new nominees; large numbers of citizens used the resulting chaos as an excuse to avoid payment of their taxes; revenues fell; civil salaries went unpaid; violence broke out; banditry increased; the crime rate soared. Open opposition to the legate in the form of letters and complaints censuring Aimeric's policies flooded the court. The cardinal rebuked transgressors and ordered reprisals, but no one carried out his orders. Joanna herself used the legate's rule as grounds to refuse to render the pope the yearly Angevin tribute of seven thousand gold florins, claiming, that, as she was no longer in possession of her kingdom, she was no longer under the obligation to pay according to the original contract. This turned out to be an extremely effective argument.

Between the complaints against Aimeric emanating from Naples, the withholding of the tribute, the continued pressure by Cardinal Talleyrand and Louis of Durazzo to limit the intervention to six months, and the legate's own increasingly demanding, heartfelt supplications to be recalled, Clement began to think that he might have made a mistake. When Philip VI of France added his objections to those of the Neapolitans, the decision was made. On November 19, 1344, the pope wrote a letter to Joanna in which he announced that, because she had demonstrated the proper humility and had by her obedience profited and matured greatly under Aimeric's instruction, the young queen no longer required the services of the legate, whose talents were, in any event, required elsewhere. Accordingly, the pontiff was returning the rule of the kingdom of Naples to its eighteen-year-old sovereign. In place of the legate, Clement decided to send Joanna a nuncio, but in an advisory position only; this new papal representative could neither make law nor interfere in her government.

The recall of the legate promised Joanna complete freedom of action for the first time. Ironically, by his interference, initially justified by her youth and inexperience, Clement had released Joanna from the moderating influence of the ruling council, which had been established by Robert's will and anchored by Sancia, an experienced monarch. Where the old king had tried to shelter his granddaughter from the heavy responsibility of absolute rule until she had reached the more mature age of twenty-five, the pope now handed it to her while she was still in her teens. The only detail marring this serendipity was that Aimeric, in the absence of specific orders, stubbornly refused to leave his post until his replacement, the nuncio, had arrived. Since the nuncio was held up until the following May, the legate remained in Naples for another six months. During this time Aimeric gradually relinquished his legislative activities but did not officially return complete control of the government to the queen until just before he left.

Once in receipt of Clement's letter of November 19, however,

Joanna no longer felt herself constrained by the cardinal's stern admonitions and pronouncements or the absence of an official ceremony, duly recorded in writing and forwarded to the pope, denoting the transference of power. The court of Naples had degenerated dangerously into warring factions during Aimeric's short tenure, and the queen moved quickly to protect herself. The pope had legally affirmed her sole right to rule, but this was not enough to secure her office in the present unstable political environment. The alliance between Andrew and the Pipini brothers, in particular, had damaged her position. She recognized that, now that he had such potent support within the kingdom, her husband's promised coronation presented a real threat to her sovereignty. Once Andrew was crowned in a public ceremony, he would be unlikely to adhere to the restrictions imposed by the pontiff. Her subjects could not be expected to distinguish between the niceties of an honorary title and genuine authority; if Andrew gave orders, he would be obeyed. Moreover, she foresaw that, now that Andrew was maturing, it would be increasingly difficult for her to control him as she had in the past. The best way to stop her husband from acquiring power, then, would be to prevent the investiture ceremony from occurring in the first place. So she refused to set a date and asked Louis of Durazzo and Cardinal Talleyrand to focus their efforts on persuading Clement to rescind the promise of a double coronation to Andrew.

At the same time, she moved to build up her own power base within the kingdom. Recognizing that she needed to surround herself with counselors and barons who could be counted on to remain loyal to her and to resist the slightest incursion into her authority by her husband's party, Joanna issued a series of edicts granting monies, property, and promotion to certain key members of the aristocracy who were already disposed to distrust and oppose Andrew and the Pipini brothers. These included, among others, the extended family of her adopted mother, Philippa the Catanian; Robert the Wise's illegitimate son, Charles of Artois; and the house of Taranto. In particular, she showed marked favor to one of Philippa's sons, Robert of Cabannis, bestowing on him the countship of Eboli and raising him to grand seneschal of the kingdom.

Since Joanna and Andrew were known to be quarreling—to use the pope's term—not surprisingly, the chroniclers began reporting around this time certain rumors regarding Joanna's sexual behavior. (Like any euphemism, "quarreling" does not do justice to the young couple's relationship; apparently, he was threatening her and she was taunting him.) Domenico da Gravina accused Catherine of arranging for her second son, Louis of Taranto, to slip into Joanna's bed, while Boccaccio suggested that in fact the queen's lover was Robert of Cabannis, whom Joanna had just promoted to a position of power. "For Joanna was given in marriage to Andrew . . . and when King Robert died, Sancia, the queen, went into a convent," Boccaccio wrote in his biography of Philippa the Catanian.

> Disputes arose between Joanna and Andrew by the wicked urging of certain persons. Andrew was despised, for the nobles of the kingdom had sworn oaths to Joanna when Robert was alive. By Joanna, Robert [of Cabannis] from being the Seneschal of the Court, was made Great Seneschal of the Kingdom, and Sancia, his niece [Philippa's granddaughter] was married to Charles, Count of Marcone.
>
> These extraordinary successes came to these Africans, however, not without some spots on their honor. Though it may not be right to believe it, it was said that the pandering of Philippa was responsible for putting Joanna into Robert's embraces. This crime requires a lot of faith for . . . no others except these [Philippa, Joanna and Robert] must have known Joanna's secret.

There is no way to tell if any or all of this was true. Certainly, Joanna was never caught in the act of engaging in an extramarital affair. The existence of two distinct paramours, rather than a single lover, and the differing stories would seem to cast doubt on the chroniclers' knowledge. (Giovanni Villani claimed that Joanna also took as her lover Charles of Artois' son, Bertrand, and several other nobles including Louis' older brother, Robert of Taranto. But Villani, imprisoned at the time for his participation in one of the failed Florentine banking concerns whose assets Joanna and Sancia had seized, was perhaps not the most reliable observer.) As Boccaccio himself admitted, "When there is the least familiarity of any sort with a man, disgrace easily stains the most honorable woman."

Reports of Joanna's licentious nature must also be balanced against her deep spirituality and commitment to religion, an eye-witness account of which Petrarch recorded in a letter to Cardinal Colonna after a particularly violent storm the year before. "Good God! When was anything like this ever heard of? . . . The entire shore line was covered with torn and still living bodies: someone's brains floated by here, someone else's bowels floated there. In the midst of such sights the yelling of men and wailing of women were so loud that they overcame the sounds of the seas and the heavens . . . Meanwhile the younger queen [Joanna], bare-footed and uncombed, and accompanied by a large group of women, departed from the royal palace unconcerned about modesty in the face of great danger, and they all hastened to the Church of the Virgin Queen praying for her grace amidst such dangers." To leave the relative safety of the castle and brave a frightening storm in order to pray for her people is entirely reflective of Sancia's training and renders the reports of easy adultery somewhat less credible. Still, Joanna would not have been the first eighteen-year-old to flirt with other suitors, particularly when her own husband was so difficult.

Aimeric made haste to transmit Joanna's activities to the pope, dwelling particularly on the queen's generous grants of property and income to her favorites, which profligacy the cardinal warned, not without justification, was in danger of draining the royal treasury.

The church's interests and income in Naples were threatened by her extravagance, Aimeric continued. (There was no little hypocrisy in this, as, between them, Joanna and the Neapolitan clergy were ultimately forced to pay the legate nineteen thousand gold florins for services rendered during his brief tenure.) Also, the courtiers surrounding the queen were openly hostile to Andrew and were encouraging the rift between husband and wife, Aimeric noted.

Clement might have vacillated on awarding power and privileges, but when it came to protecting church income, he acted quickly and decisively. On January 30, 1345, he dashed off a bull striking down every grant of money and property made by either Joanna or Sancia since Robert the Wise's death on the grounds that they constituted alienation of the realm. "Since all power over these States belongs to the Holy See, including goods, rights and honors pertaining to the estate, we order you to revoke all handovers, gifts, and relinquishments of land, towns, fiefdoms, privileges and income granted by her for whichever reason, since the death of the late King," Clement wrote to Aimeric. "The beneficiaries of these gifts will have to return them without delay, or face excommunication." This proclamation was followed on February 5 with another decree in which the pope published a list of twelve persons who were cited for provoking mischief between Joanna and her lord and master, and were consequently forbidden from social intercourse with the queen. Chief among this group were Philippa the Catanian and her family, including her two sons, Robert of Cabannis and Raymond of Catania, and her granddaughter Sancia of Cabannis, in addition to "certain others whom we do not at present name," by which the pope almost assuredly meant Charles of Artois and Catherine of Valois and her sons.

The boldness of Clement's action—after all, he was challenging gifts of land and lordships made to persons of very high birth, including members of the empress of Constantinople's family, who were likely to react with violence to their invalidation—was somewhat compromised by the surreptitious note to Aimeric that accompanied these documents. "If you deem either untimely or unwise the publication of these minutes while still inside the Kingdom," the pope wrote confidentially to his legate, "do so upon your departure, in a sufficiently sizable township close to the border." Consequently, although the papal bull revoking the queen's grants of property was issued in January, the queen and her court remained in ignorance of the repeal until Aimeric's departure in May. It must have been a great relief to Aimeric not to have to bear the responsibility of breaking this unpleasant news until his replacement, the nuncio, had arrived and the legate could honor his instructions while well on his way out of the kingdom.

The reprimand prohibiting Joanna from the society of Philippa's family and other of the queen's intimates was made public in February, however, and the courtiers judged it politic to appear to be conforming to the pope's wishes. Joanna herself felt pressure in the aftermath of these injunctions to conciliate her husband and his party, at least nominally, for fear of further reprisals. Aimeric was still in Naples and the queen was aware that the cardinal was spying on her. Not wishing to give the pope an excuse to extend the legate's stay, she resumed an attitude of conjugal normalcy with Andrew. This domestic détente between husband and wife in turn gave rise to an event that once again shattered the fragile equilibrium at court. For in April, it became generally known that the queen of Naples was pregnant.

The expectation of an heir to the throne abruptly introduced a new and disruptive element to the political status quo. Its immediate effect was to reshuffle the hierarchy of those close to the seat of power. Despite the rumors of infidelity, there seems to have been no question that the child was Andrew's, and so the primary beneficiary of the political re-ranking was the prospective father. Andrew was now more than simply Joanna's liege lord; he was sire to the future heir to the throne, with responsibility for the infant's welfare and upbringing. Overnight, it became much more difficult to deny him the coronation previously promised by the pope. Similarly, the great losers in these altered circumstances were unquestionably Charles of Durazzo and his mother, Agnes of Périgord. The existence of Joanna's unborn child all but extinguished any hope harbored by the duke of Durazzo to one day rule Naples through his wife, since Maria could only inherit if Joanna died childless. Even if this baby died, Joanna was young; there would be others. Already excluded from the queen's inner circle—for, although Joanna worked with the Durazzos because of their connection to Cardinal Talleyrand, she had never forgiven either Charles or Agnes for the shameful seduction of her sister—Charles and Agnes found their access to the halls of power further diminished by this event.

As for Joanna, the pregnancy legitimized her position within the kingdom far more effectively than could any declaration by the pope. She had proved she was not barren, an issue of paramount importance to the realm. More than this, once she gave birth, she would establish a hereditary line of succession that would put to rest forever the destructive whispers of her grandfather's, and by extension her own, usurpation. The unborn child was both a rebuke to the Durazzos and a vindication of her marriage to her in-laws. Andrew's child would inherit the kingdom as had been stipulated in the original contract between Naples and Hungary, and that should by rights put an end to the complaints of her husband's mother and elder brother.

But the expectation of an heir only served to incite Elizabeth and Louis of Hungary to intensify their efforts to propel Andrew into power. Louis dispatched a series of bishops and lawyers to Naples to advise his younger brother on ways to undermine his wife's authority and encroach on her sovereignty. Elizabeth's ambassadors at Avignon renewed their appeals to Clement, arguing that it was unseemly for the father of the future sovereign of Naples to be of lower rank than his child. Andrew must not only be crowned, the Hungarians again insisted, but also must share power with his wife. To demonstrate the seriousness with which the crown of Hungary regarded this issue, King Louis instituted a special tax, the proceeds of which found their way to the papal court.

There is no reliable record of the magnitude of the sum the Hungarians used to cajole the pope this time. One chronicler estimated the bribe to be eighty thousand gold florins; another, forty-four thousand marks; later historians put it as high as one hundred thousand florins. Whatever the amount, Clement judged it sufficiently munificent to prompt an immediate reassessment of Andrew's future role in the government of Naples. On June 10, 1345, the pope wrote to Joanna, chastising her for trying to delay the double coronation and, in a complete reversal of his former position, ordered her to give her husband "an honorable role" in the administration of the realm.

This new papal imperative turned out to be one directive too many. Joanna had only just rid herself and her kingdom of Aimeric. Clement's nuncio had finally arrived in mid-May, and on May 19 the legate had formally returned the rule of Naples to its queen. Five days later the cardinal had departed the capital. But no sooner had the legate left than Joanna discovered that, before he had entirely quitted the kingdom, Aimeric had stopped at a town near the border to post a papal bull revoking all gifts of money, property, and title that had been granted since the death of Robert the Wise and ordering their return on pain of excommunication. Exasperated by the disclosure of this first bull, kept secret by Aimeric since January, Joanna was in no mood to entertain additional papal interference, particularly as she was well aware that her husband's family was behind it. She was nineteen, pregnant with the heir to the throne, and had already been officially anointed by the church (as represented by Aimeric, standing in for the pope) as the sole sovereign of Naples. The nuncio Clement had sent her was only a bishop and, as such, was not of sufficient rank to challenge a member of royalty in full possession of her government. In response, Joanna asserted her prerogative in a letter to Clement in which she reminded him sharply that he was exceeding the limits to his authority as outlined in the original contract between the papacy and Charles of Anjou. She and the rest of her court then proceeded to ignore the pope's instructions.

But word of Clement's espousal of the Hungarian cause won Andrew an influential new partisan within the kingdom. According to Domenico da Gravina, Charles, duke of Durazzo, began openly supporting the Hungarian's right to be crowned and share power. This assured the duke of a measure of influence within the government should Joanna's husband succeed. Emboldened by the pope's decree, and seeking to put pressure on Joanna and her advisers, Andrew conducted himself as though his coronation and rule were now assured. Domenico da Gravina reported that around this time Andrew began carrying a new banner, expressly made to his specifications, depicting not the Hungarian coat of arms, but an ax and a stake, a grim indication of what those who opposed the king might expect upon his ascension to power. The existence of the banner goes far toward explaining the stubborn resistance in Naples to Andrew's rule.

The issue was still unresolved when Sancia, who had been in failing health for some time, died on July 28. Her body was laid to rest behind the altar at Santa Croce, the same position her husband's corpse occupied at the church of Santa Chiara. Joanna was at her summer palace at Castellamare when she was given the news of her grandmother's passing, and she ordered the construction of a prominent carved tomb commemorating Sancia's life, as she had for Robert the Wise.

Even so poignant an event as the old queen's demise was sacrificed to the harsh political realities of Naples that summer. Although in her will Sancia had left a large portion of her estate to a number of monasteries, including her cherished Santa Croce and Santa Chiara, Joanna, hoping to subdue tensions and appease the warring factions within her family, distributed this property instead to Charles of Durazzo and Robert of Taranto. This caused fresh controversy at the Curia, which subjected Joanna to renewed accusations of profligacy and pillage, followed again by demands that she revoke the bequests. Annoyed at the recalcitrance of the queen, Clement ordered his nuncio in an August 21 letter to arrange for a double coronation over Joanna's objections. But even this announcement, as inflammatory as it was, was eclipsed by the news of the sudden death, under what were deemed to be highly suspicious circumstances, of Agnes of Périgord.

The dowager duchess of Durazzo, committed to the advancement of her family, had not ceased in her efforts to place all her children in as advantageous a position as possible. Her latest intrigue had been to try to marry her second son, Louis of Durazzo, to the empress of Constantinople's daughter, Marguerite, and thereby cleave the united front heretofore displayed against her family by the house of Taranto. Catherine opposed the match, but Agnes, no doubt emboldened by her previous success at surreptitious matchmaking, and apparently following much the same strategy, did not back down in the face of the empress of Constantinople's resistance. Instead, in late 1344 she had begun to pressure Clement into granting permission for the match, working as usual through her brother Cardinal Talleyrand.

But it was best to be at the peak of one's abilities when taking on an enemy of Catherine's caliber, and Agnes had the misfortune to fall ill in May and was still bedridden by August. Domenico da Gravina is the sole source for the chronology of events which transpired in the days immediately preceding her death. "Madame the duchess of Durazzo was ... gravely ill," the chronicler related, when a very prominent medical doctor named master Giovanni da Penne . . . arrived in Naples. Hearing of his arrival, the duke of Durazzo asked him to come and examine his mother . . . The doctor took the duchess' pulse and reassured her, as well as her son, as to her health. Also present in the room were madame Maria, her daughter-in-law, madame Margherita di Ceccano and her daughter, madame Sancia, and several other ladies and maids-in-waiting.

It just so happened that at that time, duchess Agnes was not on good terms with her son and his wife; good relations had returned between the duke and his brothers . . . but all disagreements had not been fully resolved between the women. The doctor required that the sick woman's urine be collected at daybreak and given to him in the morning so that he could draw his diagnosis. Exhorted by the Empress and the Queen, malevolent women arranged to have madame Sancia [who was pregnant] sleep near the patient that night. They collected the duchess' early morning urine, but then threw it out, replaced it with Sancia's, and showed that to the doctor when he arrived.

As soon as he saw it, the doctor realized it was that of a pregnant woman. He blushed and was shaken to the point of stammering; then, taking the duke outside, he told him in secret that his mother's urine revealed that she was expecting a child. The duke, equally angry and astounded, did not know what to say. He could not believe that his mother would be in that state. The doctor had the urine brought to him and explained the signs that allowed him to conclude that it was that of a pregnant woman. He was right, of course, but uncovering the betrayal of the duchess was beyond his science.

In ignorance of the trap set for his poor mother, and having carefully avoided this topic with his brothers, the duke was most troubled and lost interest in his mother's welfare. Those women who were in charge of her poisoned her with a potion in which they had added a toxic substance. A few days later, she died in Christ, free of the sin she was blamed for.

There is no way to tell how much of this story is true. Agnes had indeed recently made herself unpopular with Joanna by frequently siding with Aimeric during the legate's tenure in an attempt to curry favor with Avignon. Sancia of Cabannis, Joanna's nearest friend and one of her ladies-in-waiting, was pregnant during Agnes's illness, and the queen's own pregnancy might have given Joanna the idea for this plot. Moreover, poison was unquestionably the instrument of choice among women for dispensing with an unwanted rival.

On the other hand, the credulity of the men involved, particularly Charles of Durazzo, is not quite believable. Even if the duke was weary of his mother's interference, he would not have condoned this stain on the family honor. Nor was poison necessarily required to finish off Agnes, for although the doctor might have been able to detect pregnancy in urine, the state of medicine in the Middle Ages was not such that he could have acquired the means to cure a serious disease, which, from the length of the dowager duchess's illness, it is evident she had. Poisoning was the suspected cause of death for many who died of illness in the Middle Ages, as it made for much more interesting gossip than death by an ordinary malady. The rumor had circulated sufficiently for a chronicler who was not a member of the royal court to be familiar with it, yet no member of Agnes's family complained to either Talleyrand or the pope of these suspicions, or called for an investigation into the dowager duchess's death. This last is especially telling, for if Charles of Durazzo could have proved Joanna's complicity in his mother's death, he could have had her deposed, and Maria would have then inherited the kingdom. This inevitably leads to the possibility that the dowager duchess, weakened by a long illness, simply succumbed to an opportunistic bacterium in the stifling heat of a southern Italian summer.

What can be said with certainty is that even those outside the royal court perceived an alliance of interest between the queen, the family of Philippa the Catanian, and the house of Taranto against the advancement to power of the Durazzo branch of the royal family, which had consequently allied itself with the Hungarian party. The death of Agnes of Périgord exacerbated this competition and contributed greatly to the atmosphere of desperation and treachery that permeated the realm that fateful summer. The nuncio's subsequent announcement that Andrew would be crowned with Joanna in a formal ceremony on September 20 did nothing to dispel the general recognition that events were spiraling out of control.

⊷⊷

After Agnes's death, the royal court moved once again, this time to the summer residence at Aversa, a twelfth-century castle favored at this time of year for its proximity to the extensive grounds and cool, pleasant gardens belonging to the adjacent Celestine monastery. Joanna and Andrew rode out to the palace together, arriving on September 7, intending to stay in Aversa until the morning of the 19th, at which point they and their households would make the short journey back to Naples for the coronation ceremony on the 20th. The queen was by this time in her sixth month of pregnancy and looked to prolong her respite from the late-summer heat of the capital city until the last possible moment.

Just as Joanna and Andrew were setting out for Aversa, Cardinal Aimeric, who had been held up in Rome trying unsuccessfully to settle differences between the Colonna family and their archrivals, the Orsinis, finally returned to Avignon. On September 5, the pope honored the legate for his service in Naples and the next day began a series of extended debriefings with the cardinal, at which Aimeric reported his impressions and eyewitness accounts of the powerful political forces at odds within the kingdom. During these conversations, the former legate of Naples learned of Clement's June 10 dictate that Andrew be crowned and share power with Joanna, and of the subsequent decision to impose the double coronation over her protests.

Aimeric might have been incompetent, but he wasn't stupid. His year in Naples had taught him the danger inherent in raising Andrew to the throne, and he apparently communicated this forcefully to Clement. The upshot of these discussions was that the pope reversed himself again. A new series of papal letters, dated September 20 and September 21, were dictated to Joanna and Andrew. The queen was once again recognized as the sole heir to the throne, according to the conventions that had existed since the original contract between the church and Charles of Anjou. Andrew was chastised for his immature behavior. His coronation was once again made conditional upon his recognizing Joanna's sovereignty. He was expressly forbidden, upon pain of excommunication, to interfere with his wife's authority and prerogative after the ceremony.

While Clement and Aimeric were thus in the process of revising, yet again, the official church position toward the sovereignty of Naples, Joanna and Andrew were ensconced at their castle in Aversa. Joanna continued to administer her government and saw delegations from the capital nearly every day. On September 15, she renewed the rights of the convent of Santa Chiara and forbade the prostitutes of Aversa from conducting business too close to the castle. On September 17, she drew up papers recommending special privileges for merchants in the town of Gaeta, nominated a distinguished jurist to an official position in Provence, and received a deputation of apothecaries angling for commercial advancement within the kingdom.

For Andrew, the sojourn to Aversa was in the nature of a holiday, and he took advantage of the country surroundings to enjoy himself. On September 18, after the midday meal, the soon-to-be-crowned king spent the afternoon watching, and frequently joining, the dances that were being performed on the main road outside the castle, and evidently continued to participate in the general merriment until long after dark. As the couple were intending to leave the next morning for Naples, Joanna retired early that evening, without waiting for her husband to return to their rooms. She and Andrew slept in separate bedrooms but shared a common living room and a gallery overlooking the garden. By her own account, Joanna was already asleep when Andrew finally returned to their apartment.

The king was in the act of disrobing for bed when he was notified that a courier bearing important papers requiring his immediate attention, possibly having to do with his coronation, had just arrived from Naples. Andrew dressed hastily and followed one of his household out of the room and to the gallery, but instead of a messenger he found a group of armed men. Before he could move, he was seized and the door was shut and bolted behind him to prevent his escaping back into his quarters. There was a struggle, but Andrew, half-clothed and without a weapon, was easily subdued. The men had brought a rope, which they used to strangle the teenager; they dragged him to the end of the balcony and hung him over the side, while other assassins, stationed in the garden below, proceeded to pull on his legs to accelerate the process of asphyxiation. "Immediately he [Andrew] was summoned by them, he went into the gallery or promenade which is before the chamber. Certain ones placed their hands over his mouth, so that he could not cry out, and in this act they so pressed the iron gauntlets that their print and character were manifest after death. Others placed a rope around his neck, in order to strangle him, and this likewise left its mark," read the official report of the crime filed later at Avignon. "Others tore out his hair, dragged him, and threw him into the garden. Some say that with the rope with which they had strangled him they swung him, as if hanging, over the garden. Some [also] got him under their knees and we heard that this likewise left external traces."

The conspirators' next move was to dispose of their victim's body and so hide the evidence of their crime. Intending to bury Andrew in the garden, they cut the rope by which the young king was suspended over the balcony. But the thud of the corpse hitting the ground awakened Andrew's nurse, Isabelle the Hungarian, who had been in charge of the king since he was a child. Hurrying to investigate, Isabelle surprised the assailants before they had time to conceal the body. At the sound of her screams, they scattered and disappeared into the darkness of the night. "It was further related to us that they intended to throw him [Andrew] into a deep well (even as St. Jeremy was thrown into a pit), and thereafter to give it out he had left the kingdom by counsel of some of those who were loyal to him, who had resolved to kidnap him and send him to the king of Hungary . . . and this they would have carried out had not his nurse quickly come upon the scene," Clement himself concluded in a document addressed to one of his cardinals.

The rest of the castle, alerted to the crime by Isabelle, conducted a search of the grounds but only succeeded in recovering Andrew's body. At this point the queen of Naples was awakened by her ladies-in-waiting and informed that her husband, Andrew of Hungary, was dead.

Two days later, the papal letters rescinding Andrew's share in the government of the kingdom, which might have saved his life, were issued in Avignon.

~☙~

CHAPTER VIII

Under Siege

T HE HEINOUS NATURE of Andrew's assassination, given
substance by the underlying political context, instantly created
an atmosphere of sensationalism around which misinformation,
exaggeration, and rumor swirled. The number of ordinarily reliable
chroniclers who on this occasion eschewed any pretension of objec-
tivity is material. Some of this is attributable to a deliberate campaign
by the Hungarians to paint the conspiracy as broadly as possible for
political purposes. Giovanni Villani, for example, who was in Florence that fateful September, relied for his information upon the testimony of Isabelle's son Nicholas the Hungarian, who was
dispatched to Visegrád to inform the royal family of the circumstances of the crime and who stopped in the Italian city just long
enough to regale the populace with his version of the atrocity. But
the Hungarian offensive, which would not begin in earnest for several
months, cannot be held wholly responsible for the numerous errors
and propaganda that sprang up in the wake of Andrew's demise. The
murder was much more compelling if told from the perspective of
a grand conspiracy, and was made even more shocking if the queen
herself played a leading role, and this was not an insignificant inducement to embellishment. The chroniclers were, in the end, storytellers.

And so Domenico da Gravina asserted that, once informed of the murder by Isabelle the Hungarian and the other royal ladies-in-waiting, the queen was so struck by shame and guilt that she lay immobilized in bed, unable to meet the gaze of any of those around her until far into the next morning. She was accused by another chronicler of having neglected her husband's corpse for three days before a canon of the cathedral of Naples finally took it upon himself to inter Andrew's remains, while a third source, Giovanni da Bazzano, asserted that, on the contrary, Andrew's body was laid out and posthumously crowned by a cardinal sent by Clement for this purpose. But undoubtedly it was Giovanni Villani's account (as supplied by Nicholas the Hungarian) of the day immediately following the murder that captured the imagination of succeeding generations:

When morning came, the entire population of Aversa went to the queen's residence to find out who had perpetrated such a crime, and to exact retribution. The queen suddenly blushed, and, as if transfixed, kept her head down and her tearless eyes averted. Leaving her dead husband behind, she went without delay to another residence and prolonged her stay there, as if in her guilt she feared that the people might kill her. Meanwhile, the news of the duke's [Andrew's] death had reached Naples at sunrise. The duke of Durazzo, his brothers, and the prince of Taranto, along with Bertrand del Balzo, several other counts and barons of the kingdom, and almost all of the knights, squires, and citizens of Naples immediately took to the road to Aversa in an uproar of cries of pain and sorrow and with great anger in their soul: each of these mighty lords was surrounded by a well-armed retinue.

They reached Aversa and came upon a throng in tears, then went to the body of the unfortunate duke, lowered their heads, and cried. They then attempted to inquire as to the circumstances of the murder, but no one knew either its cause or its perpetrators.

In fact, the queen did not flee Aversa on September 19, eyes averted and fearing for her life, as Villani reported, but stayed at the castle for at least four days, as letters written under her seal attest. Nor did she leave her husband's body neglected and exposed to the elements. On the contrary, both the official journals of the period, the *Chronique of Parthénope* and the *Chronicon Siculum*, record that Andrew was "honorably interred" (but not crowned) on September 20, the day after the murder, in the cathedral of Naples, an important Gothic church built by Charles the Lame to house the relics of the royal family. Andrew's battered corpse was buried in the chapel of Saint Louis, next to the remains of his paternal grandfather, Charles Martel (Robert the Wise's eldest brother), and grandmother, Clemencia of Habsburg, just as it should have been. Joanna further ordered a mass to be celebrated daily in the chapel in her husband's memory, and she appointed and paid a specific clergyman for the rite. Lastly, the murder investigation could not have been quite as fruitless or inexplicable as Villani claimed, since within forty-eight hours of the slaying, on the same day Andrew was buried in Naples, one of his assailants was apprehended in Aversa. The culprit's name was Tommaso Mambriccio, and he had been Andrew's chamberlain, which meant he served in the bedroom.

Tommaso was the son of a nobleman who had been bankrupted by the collapse of the super-companies. The chamberlain apparently was one of those whom Andrew had threatened to execute after his coronation, and in his desperation to avoid this fate had undertaken to preemptively rid himself of his persecutor. Tommaso seems also to have been paid to participate, which obviously implied additional, wealthier and more high-ranking conspirators. He was captured (or more likely given up) on September 20 and, in typical medieval fashion, promptly tortured. To demonstrate the crown's commitment to catching and punishing Andrew's murderers, his interrogators, Charles of Artois and his close friend and ally the count of Terlizzi, both associated with the anti-Pipini faction at court, put Tommaso in a cart and rolled him through the streets of Aversa, all the while tormenting him with red-hot pincers in an effort to extract information from him regarding the details of the plot. While Tommaso's well-documented agony, which ended in his death, no doubt satisfied the public lust for retribution, it was unfortunately of limited practical utility, as his overseers had taken the prior precaution of cutting out their victim's tongue. "Tommaso was prevented from divulging his accomplices and abettors," the *Chronicon Siculum* reported, among whom Charles of Artois and the count of Terlizzi were generally assumed to number.

This was Joanna's dilemma. Tommaso was undeniably guilty of taking part in Andrew's assassination, but it was equally clear that he had neither instigated the homicide nor acted alone. To the end of her life, the queen steadfastly and vehemently maintained her innocence of the crime of murdering, or of conspiring to murder, her husband. The best efforts of her many enemies to associate her with the plot, which included the use of forged letters, propaganda, torture, bribery and intimidation, all failed to yield the slightest proof of her guilt. More than this, Joanna's one goal in the almost three years since her grandfather's death had been to hold on to her kingdom against Hungarian encroachment. The scandalously crude and violent manner of Andrew's demise could only further degrade her family name and was almost guaranteed to provoke a military response on the part of her in-laws. Joanna had been sufficiently astute the previous February to recognize that Elizabeth's desire to take Andrew back to Hungary was part of a larger scheme to wrest Naples away from her by force, and to frustrate that attempt by prevailing upon the older woman to leave her son and by implication accept a political solution. It defies reason that the queen of Naples would suddenly decide, in a fit of naïveté, to all but invite the

Hungarians to invade by deliberately planning or condoning Andrew's murder.

And yet, a vigorous and thorough investigation into the matter would almost certainly lead to the incrimination of many of those within the queen's inner circle on whom she relied for protection. If she gave these people up to prosecution, she would be left defenseless against her enemies. Moreover, once she admitted the possibility of a larger conspiracy, her adversaries could use the acknowledgment as a means of eliminating their political opposition. The innocent would be accused along with the guilty, and Joanna would not be able to separate those who should be punished from those who were blameless. There were no forensics in the Middle Ages: no DNA, no wiretaps, no listening devices. Guilt was established through confession, almost always torture-induced confession, a method that could be relied upon to produce a culprit, albeit not always a genuine one. Many of the people who would be named in a general conspiracy were dear to Joanna and might be innocent, or perhaps they simply looked the other way because they believed it to be in her best interest.

But the assassination of her husband could hardly have been more detrimental to the queen. There must have been many occasions when Joanna wished she could have rid herself of Andrew, but not *this* way. She was almost certainly aware that she would be held accountable for, and very likely accused of, his murder.

⁂

In the wake of the slaying, the distasteful task of informing the outside world of the tragedy fell to the queen. Joanna first dispatched messengers to the pope and the Hungarians, notifying each court of Andrew's slaying and registering her shock and horror at what had occurred at Aversa. She then communicated the news to other diplomatic partners and governments. Of the many missives she must have sent in those first few days after Andrew's murder, only one letter survives to give a clue to her state of mind. Dated September 22, it is addressed to "the nobles, statesmen, and Governing Council of the Republic of Florence," the kingdom's nearest ally:

An unutterable crime, a prodigious iniquity, a sin inexpiable, hateful to God and horrifying to mortality, perpetrated with inhuman ferocity and the shedding of innocent blood, by the hands of miscreants, has been committed on the person of our hitherto lord and husband.

On the 18th of this month, our lord and husband, late at the hour of retiring, would have gone down to a certain garden adjoining the gallery of our palace at Aversa, unwisely and unsuspecting, boy-like rather (as often, both there and elsewhere, at doubtful hours, he was wont to do), taking no advice, merely following the rash impulse of youth, not permitting a companion, but closing the door after him. We had been awaiting him, and owing to his too long delay, had been some time overtaken by sleep. His nurse, a good and respected woman, took a light to search anxiously [for him], and at length discovered him close to the wall of the said garden, strangled. It is impossible for us to describe our tribulation. And albeit from the vile perpetrator of this unheard-of crime is sought by stern justice done [already] whatever can be extracted or ascertained; nevertheless, viewing the atrocity of his deed, the severity must be considered mild ... He carried out his outlandish crime with the aid of a menial who is not yet caught. The villain adduced for motive of his setting on [Andrew], that he had brought upon himself the punishment of death by designing against our former lord and husband ... When, therefore, we find ourselves, in consequence of such a disaster, environed by perplexities, it is our trust, relying on

God, Holy Church, and our faithful subjects and allies, that
the guidance of divine mercy and the grace of God's pity will
not be lacking to us.

Dated at Aversa, on September 22, under our secret seal.

This was a diplomatic document, not a personal one, and must
be interpreted as such. Joanna's job was to prevent panic and present
the picture of a government in control of the situation. Only four
days had passed since her husband's murder, but she was already
able to reassure her principal trading partner that Andrew's assassin
had been caught and put to death, not before implicating a low-
level accomplice for whom investigators were still searching. It is
possible that, having been briefed by Charles of Artois, Joanna
believed—or more likely, wanted to believe—that this was actually
what had transpired, since it took a special papal investigation before
a more accurate description of the events of that evening were made
known. Still, she left a loophole—"environed by perplexities"—
should the inquiry lead to further accusations. The one key to her
emotional response, aside from her repugnance over what had
occurred, was her evident frustration that Andrew and the Hungarian guards assigned to protect him, who had been warned repeatedly
of the existence of plots against him, had not exercised more caution. Domenico da Gravina, who otherwise took the part of the
Hungarians against the queen, admitted as much when he wrote:
"They [Andrew and his guards] had supped gaily, which, in sooth,
was the cause of the profound grief of this realm." "Supped gaily"
is medieval for "got drunk."

Joanna's communications to her in-laws and the papacy are no
longer extant, but Clement's reply to her, written on October 10,
1345, would indicate that her notes to him took much the same
form as the one she sent to the Florentines. "We have received your
Majesty's letters containing expression of your intense grief at this
terrible occurrence, the diabolical death of King Andrew, your

husband, and to some extent describing the manner of it," the pope wrote. "Not without great bitterness of heart, while condoling with you, dearest daughter, we prepare to reply. Truly, we do not wonder that you bewail such a deplorable event, outrageous to God and shocking to the whole world." No doubt anticipating the Hungarian reaction to these tidings, Clement made sure to enunciate what a distinguished prince Andrew had been, "so inoffensive, so God-pleasing and agreeable to mankind." He then laid the blame squarely on the Neapolitan members of Andrew's household, perhaps a reference to Tommaso, but more likely a sweeping accusation fueled by Aimeric's intimate knowledge of Joanna's court: "Moreover, shall not reflection as to time, place, and manner of this awful crime excite amazement in the hearers, considering that where most safety might be relied on, the snare of death awaited him—even at the bloodthirsty hands of those by whom he was hoping to be protected from the plots of others.

"Nevertheless," Clement continued, "we do not write thus in order to re-picture the awful incident so as to re-arouse in you affliction which has not lightly distressed you, and which we believe still distresses; but rather we enlarge upon these things because of the regard borne by us to the said Prince; the enormity of the crime to be expiated, and the dread of disturbance in your dominion (which of necessity would agitate us), do not permit us to keep our grief within bounds. We further write to counsel you to take proper precautions regarding yourself and the one yet unborn (of whom you have made mention, and in consequence of whom we derive joy and consolation, even as you similarly should feel consoled). Also, be sedulously on your guard as to whom you trust, and whom you ought to avoid," the pope warned in conclusion.

This last admonition is telling. The viciousness of the crime, coupled with the understandable wrath of the victim's powerful relatives, demanded that justice be done and those responsible for the murder exposed and punished to the full extent of the law.

Neapolitan antagonism to Andrew's rule, particularly among the aristocracy, was too well established to allow retribution to be limited to the prosecution of an underling like Tommaso. The pope was painfully aware that his own ambivalence toward Andrew's reign might well be interpreted harshly by the dead man's relatives, and rushed to defend himself. "Your envoys will confirm that we had dispatched the bishop of Chartres to the kingdom to see to his [Andrew's] coronation well before we received the current unfortunate rumors about your brother," Clement wrote to the king of Hungary on October 9, neglecting to mention that, along with the bishop, the pope had also dispatched letters limiting Andrew's role in the government and forbidding him to challenge Joanna's rule.

Still, the Curia was resolved that Hungarian bitterness not be allowed to trespass into the realm of territorial ambition. There was far too much military posturing in Europe already, with Edward III of England raising men, arms, and allies for the obvious purpose of invading France, a cataclysm Clement was desperate to avoid. Hungary already leaned toward England in the conflict. To ensure a searching and impartial result, and therefore deprive King Louis and his mother of an excuse for armed intervention (as well as make up for any lingering suspicions that the church had been somehow lax in pursuing the dead man's coronation, and therefore tangentially responsible for his death), Clement announced to all the parties concerned that the Curia would bear the responsibility for the investigation of Andrew's assassination. On October 27, the consistory made good on this promise by naming two cardinals as special emissaries to Naples and by charging them with ferreting out all the conspirators, whoever they might be.

⁂

Joanna did not protest Clement's decision to assume control of the inquiry into Andrew's death, even though it meant the injection of skeptical outsiders into the confidential circle around her at court. In a sign that the queen was perhaps not quite sure of the loyalty or intentions of those close to her, and that the pope's warning— "be sedulously on your guard as to whom you trust, and whom you ought to avoid"—had resonated with her, at the beginning of November she suddenly made a strange request. Faced with her coming seclusion (the baby was due in late December), the nineteen-year-old begged Clement to send her maternal grandmother, Mahaut, countess of Valois (third wife of Charles of Valois), to be with her during her confinement. That Joanna sought out the company of a complete stranger—she had never met her mother's mother—at a time when she would most need comfort, and when she and her child would also, coincidentally, be most vulnerable (women very frequently died in childbirth during the Middle Ages), says something about her state of mind. When Mahaut was unable to make the journey to Naples, Joanna instead placed herself and her baby in the hands of Andrew's nurse, Isabelle the Hungarian, when her time came.

In fact, in those first few months after her husband's death, the queen gave every indication of a woman casting about for allies. As early as the beginning of November, she expressed her desire to marry again in her correspondence with the pope. Her request was in no way unusual for the period. Joanna was a beautiful young woman, with many years of childbearing ahead of her, who was also in sole possession of one of the most prestigious kingdoms in Europe. It was unthinkable that she would remain single, and Clement recognized this. If nothing else, she needed a partner who could act as commander-in-chief should Naples face a military threat from abroad. "[If] after the loss of such a consort, you feel your loneliness, and for the security of the realm you should desire to re-marry, be careful that the partner chosen be a personage suitable for the governance of the realm and devoted to the Church," the pope warned her in a letter dated November 13, 1345. The next month, an official petition arrived from the queen, formally requesting that the Curia provide a dispensation for her to marry her cousin Robert of Taranto, Catherine's eldest son. The pope received similar notification from Robert.

But Joanna's document was a sham. She loathed Robert, who had forced her to send the petition. She would later disavow it through emissaries. But her cousin had knights, and weapons, and men-at-arms, and she did not; owing to her condition, she could not even stir from the castle. Her petition is an indication of how little power the queen exercised in the final weeks of her pregnancy, as she wavered over whom she could trust. She must have known that she did not have much time to come to a decision. Robert's threats and aggressive claim to her hand only highlighted her weakness and taught her that she must remarry, and soon, if she wished to make her own choice.

Joanna was saved by the elephantine pace of papal administration; before Clement could act on her request, the queen went into labor. Early on the morning of December 25, 1345, in the presence of all the great officers and ladies of the court, Joanna delivered her firstborn, a healthy son, the one bright spot in an otherwise wretched year. The promise of stability, finally, lay ahead. The line of succession had been established; even better, the heir to the throne was male. To underscore that this was Andrew's child and appease her Hungarian in-laws for the loss of her husband, the next day, Joanna had the infant baptized Charles Martel by the bishop of Cavaillon, the chancellor of the realm. This deliberate reference to Robert the Wise's eldest brother was intended to heal the rift created not only by Andrew's murder, but also by the original Hungarian grievance that the kingdom had been stripped illegally from Carobert by Joanna's family. In a further gesture of good will, Joanna gave her son to Isabelle the Hungarian to raise and assigned a large staff at the Castel dell'Ovo for her use. The queen also appointed a high-ranking Neapolitan nobleman as Charles Martel's protector and convinced the pope to accept the office of godfather to her child.

As Andrew's son would one day rule Naples, the queen considered that she had upheld and satisfied the condition of her marriage contract. Accordingly, she sent emissaries to King Louis and the dowager queen Elizabeth charged with communicating the happy news of the birth of the child and negotiating for her release from certain remaining clauses in the nuptial treaty of 1333, so that she would be free to remarry.

The arrival of this embassy in Hungary had much the same effect on Louis and Elizabeth as if a siege-ball had been hurled across the Adriatic and landed on the family castle at Visegrád. For the first time, the Hungarians awoke to the possibility that they might have been outmaneuvered, and that if they did not act quickly, their hold on Naples, which only a few short months before had seemed assured, was in danger of slipping away. Knowing that Charles Martel would one day rule in Andrew's place was little consolation; to have their claims to the kingdom resolved by the next generation had never been satisfactory. In fury, the crown of Hungary recognized that, although the papacy had undertaken to investigate Andrew's death, no Neapolitan of rank had been charged with the murder for the simple reason that, owing to unforeseen delays, neither of the two cardinals assigned to the case had yet set foot in the kingdom. Justice had not been done; the conspirators against their kinsman were still at large; and now the queen of Naples was angling to marry a cousin from the house of Taranto, thus effectively cutting out Hungarian influence altogether.

A great howl of rage rose up out of Hungary and directed itself at the Holy See in Avignon in the form of a high-ranking delegation that included a duke and two counts. "My brother's infamous death occurred while Your Holiness was cradling us with hope," King Louis bitterly accused the pope in letters dated January 15, 1346, and entrusted to his emissaries, who did not arrive until March.

"Turning to you, most Holy and most Clement [a sarcastic play on the pope's name], who are by divine clemency the vicar of Christ most high; I beg of you, as your humble and devoted son, in your forgiving clemency, to call on all your heart, all your soul and all your thoughts so as to ensure revenge for this crime of lese-majesty; and so the felons covered in my brother's blood are deprived of all their rights to the kingdom of Sicily [this is what the Hungarians called Naples] and its dependencies." Since the Curia had yet to indict a single suspect, Louis and his mother helpfully supplied the pope with their own list of conspirators: "And these murderers are the aforementioned Joanna, husband-killer and widow of my brother; Madame Maria, her sister; Robert, prince of Taranto and his brothers; Charles, duke of Durazzo and his brothers; and all who aspire to and covertly aspire to the crown of the kingdom of Sicily," Louis wrote as a prelude to accusing some two hundred other supposed perpetrators, among whom Cardinal Talleyrand of Périgord's name was prominent. The dowager queen seconded her son's accusations, labeling Joanna as a "viricide," or man-killer, and demanding that the queen of Naples be stripped of her kingdom. Elizabeth also insisted that her grandson, Charles Martel, be torn from his mother and brought to Visegrád for his own safety and raised by his Hungarian relations before returning to rule Naples.

As to who would rule Naples while the kingdom waited for Charles Martel to come of age, King Louis, in the same letter, proposed his own solution: "Your Holiness knows it is established that I am the first born of the first born of the ancestral king of Sicily; and I once again call upon your Most Clement and Most Sublime Holiness and beg you, as your most humble and pious son, to show pitiful clemency and restore life to my embittered soul and warmth to my troubled heart, by deigning, in your kindliness and apostolic magnanimity, to entrust to me in full (along with my brother Stephen) and under the conditions set for the kings who preceded me, the kingdom of Sicily . . . as well as its estates." Then, knowing how business was transacted in Avignon, Louis added: "So that I can commit to our Most Holy Mother, the Roman Catholic Church [a reference to taking Clement's side, or at least remaining neutral, in the pope's struggles to resist the territorial ambitions of Edward III and the Holy Roman Emperor]; so that I can pay its dues [the annual tribute of seven thousand ounces of gold which Joanna had not paid the year before, owing to the legate's having taking over the administration of the kingdom]; and so that I may settle the same obligations as the previous kings [a commitment to ensure the payment of the tribute in the future], and even some larger ones [the expected bribe]," the king of Hungary hinted significantly.

This letter outlined clearly the Hungarian response, not to Andrew's murder, but to Joanna's proposed remarriage. No accusation against the queen of Naples had been levied by her husband's family in the more than three months since the assassination. Only after her daughter-in-law revealed her intention to marry outside the house of Hungary did Elizabeth discover her to be a murderess. Had Joanna consented to marry the third son, Stephen, the Hungarians would likely never have made the charge in the first place, but this Joanna had preemptively indicated she would not do by sending her envoys specifically to negotiate that she be released from the original contract. For the Hungarians to achieve their ambitions in Naples, which, as articulated in the January 15 letter to Clement, involved setting up Stephen in Joanna's place (Louis needed to reside in Hungary in order to maintain his power base) and taking Charles Martel away from his mother for the purpose of inculcating him with Hungarian values and ambitions, Joanna would have to be deposed. Hence the need to fling the web of guilt as widely as possible, and above all, to ensnare the queen in the net, for her culpability was the foundation on which all Hungarian hopes rested.

The delivery of a healthy child seems to have infused Joanna with new purpose, for soon after the birth of her son, the queen took action to protect herself by publicly renouncing Robert of Taranto's suit in favor of that of his younger brother Louis. Ironically, Joanna found the support she needed to reject Robert from within her cousin's own family. Louis was favored by both his mother, Catherine of Valois, and by her chancellor and chief adviser, Niccolò Acciaiuoli, both of whom had their own reasons for championing this match. Niccolò's sister was Charles of Artois' second wife, and both Charles and his son Bertrand were suspected of having participated in the conspiracy to murder Andrew. Niccolò was much closer to Louis than to Robert; Louis listened to him, whereas Robert did not. Also Robert, who was arrogant and overbearing, had quarreled openly with his mother. Catherine disliked him almost as much as Joanna did, and had appealed to her brother Philip of Valois to support Louis' suit over that of his elder brother. The French king agreed and intervened with the papacy on Louis' behalf.

Although Louis was Joanna's only real alternative—she needed a husband quickly, someone who understood the internal politics of Naples, which precluded obtaining a suitor from outside the kingdom, and after Agnes's betrayal, there was no chance of her turning to the Durazzo side of the family—there are indications that this match was more than simply a political arrangement. Louis was among those whose names had been romantically linked with Joanna's by the chroniclers. Like Andrew, Louis was a year younger than Joanna—nineteen to her twenty—but he was also strong, blond, and exceedingly handsome. Most important, Louis was known for his prowess at arms. He was a practiced warrior who could protect his wife, her infant son, the court, and the realm. Joanna wrote to the pope explaining that she had changed her mind for the good of the kingdom, based on the advice of the prelates and barons who were her counselors, but Clement didn't believe her.

In a letter to the king of France dated March 30, 1346, the pope revealed that Louis had been chosen over his brother because he had promised to shield the queen's favorites from prosecution for conspiring to kill Andrew. "If his marriage [to Joanna] is accomplished, those who are vulnerable for being suspected of participating in the criminally infamous death of the king are guaranteed by Louis to be declared safe from punishment," Clement wrote.

It does appear that, by this time, whatever doubts Joanna may have entertained initially regarding Philippa and her family's role in Andrew's murder had passed. The queen gave every indication of a woman convinced of the innocence of those with whom she was intimate, and she actively sought to protect them. Her attitude may have been a reaction to Robert's aggressive attempts to wed her, but it might also have been because Joanna understood that her courtiers were obvious targets. Although there are no extant descriptions of Raymond of Catania, Robert of Cabannis, and Sancia of Cabannis, they were the children and grandchildren of an African slave, and so it is likely they were black. Their racial heritage did not affect Joanna's judgment of their abilities, nor her affection for them, but others within the kingdom felt differently. When Boccaccio had written of Philippa's husband, "What a ridiculous thing to see an African from a slave prison, from the vapor of the kitchen, standing before Robert, the King, performing royal service for the young nobleman, governing the court and making laws for those in power!" he was probably expressing not simply his own feelings but an opinion generally held by the public, and which would then have also applied to the man's descendants. Louis may well have urged his suit against that of his brother Robert by promising to defend the queen's intimates from the mania of a witch hunt.

Robert had no intention of withdrawing gracefully from his engagement, however. The crown was within his grasp, and he was determined to possess it, with or without the consent of the bride. Louis was equally resolved to frustrate his brother's suit and marry

Joanna himself. There followed the sort of drama that served as fodder for the songs of the troubadours throughout the ages. Brother fell upon brother and army upon army, all battling for the hand of the queen. Civil war rent the kingdom.

Because his elder brother controlled the family estates, allowing Robert to call on his own vassals to provide men and arms for the struggle, Louis was forced to recruit the bulk of his army from outside the kingdom. Niccolò Acciaiuoli, who had strong ties to Florence (his cousin was bishop there), utilized two Florentine agents to scout among the available manpower in Tuscany and the surrounding area. Necessarily, they relied on mercenaries. The agents were not particularly selective about enlistment, with the result being that a large percentage of those who marched south to Louis' aid were Ghibellines who carried standards and banners identifying them as such. When these troops entered the capital city of Naples, it appeared to the populace as though the queen had appealed to the kingdom's most feared adversary, the emperor, for reinforcements against her Guelphic subjects.

Robert was quick to capitalize on this political weakness. He banded together with his cousin Charles of Durazzo, who was only too happy to participate in any activity that might result in the deposition of Joanna in favor of her sister, and the two portrayed themselves as stalwart defenders of the church. Since the Holy See had undertaken to expose and punish Andrew's executioners, in an adroit bit of partisan maneuvering, Robert and Charles suddenly embraced this cause as their own, announcing that they were not fighting Joanna because she had chosen to wed Louis over Robert, but because she and her lover were harboring the queen's favorites, who had murdered her husband. The fact that Andrew had by this time been dead for six months and neither man had thought to pursue his killers before Joanna announced that she was marrying Louis was conveniently forgotten.

The impetus for Robert's and Charles's newfound zeal to see

justice done may be traced to Hugo del Balzo, the count of Avellino and Joanna's seneschal in Provence, who was in this instance acting as a secret agent on behalf of the pope. Boccaccio wrote that Hugo "conspired with all of the princes" to investigate and then pass judgment on the alleged miscreants. Frustrated that the two cardinals originally chosen for this mission had been so long detained by other business, Clement sought in the count of Avellino the clandestine services of a less public emissary. Buttressing this theory is the fact that Hugo, who had been away on crusade for much of the previous year, returned to Avignon in time to meet with the pope on January 8, and by February 13 was on his way to Naples.

This new strategy on the part of the queen's antagonists had the added attraction of targeting precisely those wealthy and titled individuals who in the past had denied Charles's access to power and were currently resisting Robert's attaining the throne. If they could be proven to have conspired against Andrew, then not only would Robert's and Charles's political opposition be swept away in a single stroke, but all the culprits' considerable property would be declared forfeit and could be seized by the victors as spoils. This was such a good plan that Robert and Charles must have wondered why they had not thought of it themselves.

The long investigative delay into Andrew's murder had indeed served to weaken the queen's position. Although Joanna had only acceded to the pope's wishes by accepting church authority over the case, and was in fact waiting with everyone else in the kingdom for the arrival of the two cardinals charged with delving into the matter, the unpardonable tardiness of the papal investigators gave the queen the appearance of deliberately obstructing justice. A dreadful crime had been committed, and retribution ought to have been swift and terrible. When this did not occur, the atmosphere festered and the population first wondered, then grew restive. It was a relatively simple matter for Robert and Charles to coalesce popular opinion around their cause, particularly after the arrival of the Ghibelline mercenaries. Citizens from as far away as Salerno, Nido, and Capua poured into the capital to demand that the queen surrender her favorites. Robert, Charles, and Hugo del Balzo, with their supporters (by this time all the Durazzo brothers were involved), moved among the populace spreading the rumor that Joanna had been prevented from bringing Andrew's executioners to justice by her cronies. The vigilantes raised tempers in hopes of inciting a mob. They also obtained the discreet services of a noted cutthroat by the name of Fra Moriale.

Matters came to a head on March 6, 1346. To reduce the risk of violence to the general population, Raymond of Catania, in his position as seneschal of the court, issued a decree prohibiting the carrying of arms in public. When Raymond and a small party of knights bravely took to the streets of Naples to ensure that the order was enforced, they were ambushed by Fra Moriale and his men. A terrific fight ensued, and when it was all over, Fra Moriale had earned his pay. Raymond of Catania was taken prisoner.

His persecutors brought him first to a main public square, to be exhibited in front of the populace during torture, to satisfy the bloodlust of the mob. However, as it was important that just the right conspirators be named during interrogation, Robert and Charles left nothing to chance and had Raymond's tongue cut out, and all their questions accompanied by drum rolls, so that none of their audience could hear clearly. After that, they took their captive into Robert's castle and placed him on a balcony, so that Raymond's agony, if not his actual confession, was comprehensible to the crowds below. In this way they obtained the names of a satisfying (and expected) number of high-level conspirators: the marshal of the realm, the count of Terlizzi; the grand seneschal, Robert of Cabannis; Nicholas of Melizzano, a member of the royal household (who actually seems to have participated in the killing); Joanna's nurse, Philippa the Catanian; Philippa's granddaughter, Sancia; Charles of Artois and his son Bertrand; Tommaso Mambriccio's brother and sister; and a number of others associated with Joanna's circle. Such was the persuasiveness of Robert's and Charles's methods that Raymond of Catania himself confessed to the slaying, even though it had been established several months previously that the seneschal had been asleep in his room at the royal residence at Aversa at the time Andrew was killed.

When the identities of the accused were later revealed to the crowd by a public notary (Raymond of Catania, being unable to speak, was forced by his tormentors to nod his head after each name was read as verification), it caused a sensation. Under the leadership of Robert, Charles, and Hugo del Balzo, the mob was subsequently incited to frenzy, generously armed with cutlasses and spears, and then pointed in the direction of the Castel Nuovo. According to yet another chronicle of the period, the enraged citizens, carrying Guelphic banners identifying themselves as warriors for the church, shouted, "Death to the traitors!" "Death to the whore of a queen!" and "Surrender the traitors!" as they converged on the castle.

This show of force, while undoubtedly dramatic, was not particularly effective. Daggers and javelins are not much good against sturdy stone walls. The Ghibelline mercenaries hired to protect Joanna and her court merely locked the impregnable front door and rained ballistics down on the hordes below—arrows from the crossbows, rocks and other heavy projectiles, loose tiles, wood originally meant for the cookstoves, pots and pans, anything that came to hand.

In fact, Joanna was not even present at the Castel Nuovo during the attack. Unbeknownst to her persecutors, the queen had repaired to the Castel dell'Ovo, the most secure fortress in Naples and her family's traditional retreat for safety, to be with her child, as a much later letter dated August 28, 1347, attested. "Nobis absentibus abinde," Joanna wrote. "From me, who was away from there [the Castel Nuovo]."

The mob fell back but did not disband, and a new plan of action was hastily devised. It was decided to surround the castle, institute a state of siege, and wait for supplies to run out. This second strategy was far more successful, particularly as the Ghibelline mercenaries seemed to be as interested in looting their employers as they were in defending them. After three days the castle was forced to come to terms and surrender the accused.

Even then, those negotiating within the Castel Nuovo in the queen's name on behalf of the terrified courtiers did their best to protect their familiars from the vigilante justice of the mob. A deal was brokered through Hugo del Balzo whereby Hugo, Robert, and Charles pledged that the prisoners would be transferred unmolested to the Castel dell'Ovo for safekeeping until the chief justice of the kingdom could investigate to see if the charges against each suspect had merit. Only then would the law of the land be applied and capital punishment meted out if appropriate. To ensure further protection from the seething multitudes, Hugo offered to transport the captives from the Castel Nuovo to the Castel dell'Ovo, about a half mile up the coast, by sea in one of his own galleys. This proposal was accepted by the accused, which included the count of Terlizzi, Robert of Cabannis, Sancia of Cabannis, Philippa the Catanian, and Nicholas of Melizzano, among others. To the chagrin of the victors, Charles and Bertrand of Artois, father and son, had managed to escape the Castel Nuovo undetected and were later discovered to be under the protection of the empress of Constantinople at one of her castles outside the city.

The prudence of the Artois' decision to evade capture and take their chances with Catherine of Valois was soon made manifest. The vessel containing the prisoners never reached the Castel dell'Ovo. Instead, Hugo del Balzo, with a blithe disregard for the formalities of the just-concluded agreement, stopped his galley a little out to sea, about midway between the point of departure and the supposed destination, and much to the enjoyment of a large crowd of spectators on the beach, proceeded to torment his helpless passengers.

"In front of the whole city and upon the open sea—with the entire population watching—he [Hugo, count of Avellino] naturally tortured poor Philippa, Sancia and Robert [of Cabannis] upon a monstrous rack," reported *De Casibus*, a chronicle of the time. "Whoever was a friend of Avellino ... immediately tortured Sancia, the countess of Marcone," the *Chronicon Siculum* agreed.

When Hugo finished at sea, he took his anguished, mutilated captives (Philippa was in her sixties and Sancia was pregnant) to the duke of Durazzo's castle so as not to deprive his compatriots of the pleasure of interrogating their former political opponents. They then spent the night being further tortured by Charles of Durazzo in the secret recesses of his dungeon. Finally, an emissary sent by Joanna, who voiced the strongest protest at this treatment, managed to wrest the suspects away from the duke the next morning with the help of a guard of knights loyal to the queen. Even then the prisoners were not transferred to the Castel dell'Ovo, as originally agreed, but, more ominously, to the Castel Capuano, the same prison at which the convicted Pipini brothers had been detained.

The surrender of these courtiers, formerly among the most wealthy and influential nobles in the kingdom, marked a clear victory for the queen's antagonists. In the aftermath at the tumult, Louis of Taranto was forced to retreat north to Capua with what remained of his troops, leaving the capital city under the control of his rival. Over Joanna's vehement objections, Robert took advantage of his newfound power to move in with her at the Castel Nuovo and soon thereafter began publishing royal proclamations. His first edict, issued March 25, stipulated the arrest and expulsion of the mercenaries fighting on behalf of his brother. On April 4, this command was buttressed by a notice tacked up on the doors of all the principal buildings, including the cathedrals of Naples and Aversa, forbidding any citizen of the realm to obey an order given by Louis. At the same time, Robert urged the pope to issue the dispensations which would allow him to wed Joanna, arguing that the marriage had been made necessary by the recent civil unrest and other pressing matters of state.

The queen resisted her cousin's tactics tenaciously. She sent secret emissaries to the pope charged with communicating her adamant refusal to marry Robert. Conflicting edicts emerged from the Castel Nuovo as Joanna battled her unwanted suitor for power. On April 26, Robert had himself named captain general of the kingdom, the highest military position in the land. On April 30, the queen specifically assigned Louis of Taranto control of a large battalion attached to one of the royal castles. By a May 6 proclamation Robert took control of all public finances. On May 30, Joanna pointedly assigned Louis state revenues in the amount of six thousand ounces of gold.

Joanna's efforts on the part of her preferred lover were not in vain. Louis' actions in the wake of the initial defeat justified the queen's belief in his martial abilities. He stayed in Capua just long enough to regroup and then fought his way to Benevento, which surrendered to him; from Benevento he moved on toward Naples, gaining territory, supplies, and soldiers as he went. By June he and a strong force were ensconced on a hill northwest of the capital, close enough to look down on the city and for those in the buildings below to be aware of his looming presence, and there he sat, building strength, and waiting for an opportunity to strike.

And at almost exactly the same moment Louis took his position on the hill, word came that the Hungarians had assembled a prodigious army with the intention of invading Naples.

~⊰⊱~

CHAPTER IX

The World *at* War

THROUGHOUT THIS PERIOD, Clement VI had struggled, with conspicuously little success, to influence events in Naples. To be fair, this lack of progress was not entirely the pope's fault. Clement certainly meant to investigate Andrew's death and bring the real murderers to justice quickly but his administration was simply overwhelmed by the other pressing concerns demanding the Curia's attention. What with England's menacing France, and the territorial ambitions of the Holy Roman Emperor, legates were in short supply. The first two cardinals assigned to investigate Andrew's murder were redeployed to other trouble spots en route to Italy and so never arrived in Naples. When the pope finally settled on a new legate, Bertrand de Deux, the cardinal of Saint-Marks, to act as his representative in Naples (Aimeric adamantly refused to go back), the cardinal fell ill and his departure had to be delayed indefinitely.

Then, in early June 1346, the papacy received a disturbing letter from the queen mother of Hungary. In it, Elizabeth renewed all her previous demands regarding her daughter-in-law and the kingdom of Naples and now also insisted that Maria's marriage to Charles of Durazzo be annulled (by this time the pair had three children, all daughters) and that Joanna be refused permission to remarry for the rest of her life. The queen mother scoffed at the notion that any person of rank would be punished for Andrew's death if the matter were left to Neapolitan justice, and made clear Hungarian intentions to intervene as they saw fit. "This letter very closely resembled a declaration of war."

Elizabeth's missive was sufficiently alarming to spur Clement into action. He immediately dispatched an envoy to Visegrád to reason with the queen mother. The pope followed this with a letter dated July 17 in which he reassured Elizabeth that, regardless of rank, her son's executioners would be brought to severe justice. Nonetheless, he refused to yield to her demands and warned that if Hungary went through with an invasion, the kingdom would be denounced as an enemy of the church, a label that carried the threat of inter- diction.

The pope had already turned his attention to Naples. Forced to work through native surrogates, in a June 3 letter Clement author- ized the chief justice of the kingdom, Bertrand del Balzo (cousin of Hugo), to act for the church in carrying out the maximum sen- tence possible on those suspects convicted of murdering Andrew. On June 8, he wrote to Joanna, the empress of Constantinople, Robert and Louis of Taranto, and Charles of Durazzo, exhorting each member of the royal family to do everything in his or her power to aid the chief justice's efforts in meting out swift and sure pun- ishment to the killers. The pope's intention was clearly to appease the Hungarians by a very public show of law and vengeance—an obvious and extravagant bloodbath, undertaken and supported by the crown of Naples, being deemed the best way of eliminating the stated motive for invasion. However, mindful that the consequences of this sort of deliberate savagery were sometimes difficult to con- tain, particularly after the uncontrolled violence of March, Clement also communicated secretly to Bertrand del Balzo on June 4 to abstain from punishing any member of the royal family suspected of participating in the assassination. Instead, the chief justice was to refer the matter to Avignon. The pope reserved for himself the right to judge and inflict punishment on those of exalted rank.

Bertrand del Balzo set to his task and immediately ran into a formidable obstacle: the empress of Constantinople. Announcing grandly that, if punishment were necessary, reprisals would be meted out as she saw fit, Catherine refused to surrender either Charles or Bertrand of Artois to the chief justice's authority. Domenico da Gravina asserted that the empress was motivated by a desire to keep the Artois' considerable wealth, which would be forfeit upon a conviction of guilt, for herself rather than handing it over to the church. But there may have been other incentives for her unwillingness to cooperate with the official investigation. It seems very likely that Bertrand of Artois was in fact one of the primary architects of the crime, and there was no controlling the testimony of a man under torture. In the hysteria of the prosecution, accusation might have spread inconveniently to Catherine's own family and favorites, not to mention the matriarch herself, a situation she was keen to avoid. So for the time being, Charles and Bertrand of Artois remained sheltered behind the haughty disdain of the empress's defiance and the sturdy walls of her castle, which, coincidentally, was located only about ten miles from Aversa.

Those surrendered from the Castel Nuovo during the riots of March were not so fortunate. Through confessions obtained through torture or the threat of more torture, Bertrand del Balzo and the small committee of jurists assigned to aid him uncovered two additional plots against Andrew's life, one to poison the prospective king and the other to kill him through witchcraft. This was helpful as it allowed the investigators to judge all the suspects, even those who had clearly not been involved in the actual assassination, guilty of conspiracy to murder Andrew in one form or another. By July, all the influential courtiers who had formerly made up Joanna's circle of intimates had been condemned to death and stripped of their titles and fortunes. The chief justice himself appropriated one of Sancia of Cabannis's estates in Provence. The first executions began in early August (although two minor aristocrats, whose relatives swore they were innocent, but who had nonetheless been swept up in the general frenzy, died of illness and complications from torture while still in detention). On August 2, Robert of Cabannis and the count of Terlizzi were transported from the Castel Capuano to a dais that had been specially erected on the beach just outside the Castel dell'Ovo. "The prisoners were sentenced to death amidst the mob's insults," wrote Domenico da Gravina.

> The Chief Justice armed his guard; carts were prepared; forges were lit and loaded, and the executioners climbed aboard. In one cart was the count of Terlizzi, bound in iron chains, and in the other cart was the seneschal . . . The prisoners were . . . paraded through every street in Naples, flagellated repeatedly, their flesh mercilessly seared by the torturers' red hot irons; and the throng, from the most diminutive to the most sizable, shouted in unison: "Would all such traitors suffer the same fate and worse!" They were spat upon and stoned. When at length they arrived at the place where the pyre had been built (even though there was very little left of the prisoners to burn), Master Robert had already just passed away. The count of Terlizzi, however, was still alive. Both men were hauled off the carts, and placed upon the pyre. But at that point, the mob . . . ran to the pyre and removed the bodies which, dead or alive, were then cut into pieces and thrown back into the fire as so many logs. Some craftsman took bones with which to fashion dice and knife handles as keepsakes.

The frenzy did not end there. In imitation of a particularly notorious execution which had occurred in Florence previously, Boccaccio continued: "The semi-burned corpses were pulled from the flames and . . . some people tore out the hearts and lungs to eat them. Then hooks were jabbed in the bodies and they were dragged in the mud and the sewers throughout the town; and bits of these bodies remained here and there, torn to shreds." On August 7, this performance was repeated with Raymond of Catania and Nicolas of Melizzano. On the day of each courtier's execution, the victim's property was divided among his persecutors. Bertrand del Balzo, in particular, received a large share of the spoils.

After this first round of executions, the chief justice took a short break. During the interval, on August 26, 1346, a seismic event took place, one whose political repercussions were felt in every court in Europe and which, though occurring far from Naples, would nonetheless powerfully influence the fate of its queen. The site of this upheaval was a little town on the northern coast of France, very near the county of Flanders, by the name of Crécy.

In the five years leading up to the battle of Crécy, Edward III, king of England, had enjoyed some not inconsequential success in his campaign against the French. In 1342, Edward had taken sides against Philip VI of France in a succession dispute in Brittany, offering men and arms to the pro-English candidate. The king crossed the Channel and landed three battalions in support of his ally, one of which he led himself. In the subsequent fighting the English took the city of Vannes and much of the coastline before agreeing to a three-year truce with the French. Encouraged, King Edward and his sixteen-year-old son, Edward, Prince of Wales, landed an army in Normandy in the summer of 1346, sacked Caen, and marched north to Ponthieu, barely bypassing Paris. Philip VI hastened to counteract English momentum by raising an army several times the size of his opponent's. He, too, led his own forces, marching to intercept his foe. On the afternoon of August 26, these two armies met at Crécy.

Philip boasted overwhelming superiority of numbers—
approximately fifty thousand men to England's thirteen thousand—
but Edward had military discipline and, in the English longbow, a
weapon that had previously been used only against Scotland, a
crushing technological advantage. The French troops were tired, particularly their Genoese crossbow men, who had "marched on foot
that day six leagues [approximately fifteen miles], completely armed
and carrying their crossbows," as the famous fourteenth-century
French chronicler Jean Froissart observed. The English, who had
arrived the night before, were rested. Under Edward's leadership
they were formed into three battalions, placed strategically for tactical advantage, and then sat placidly awaiting the arrival of the
enemy. "There is no man, unless he had been present, that can imagine or describe truly the confusion of that day," Froissart wrote:

Especially the bad management and disorder of the French,
whose troops were out of number . . . The English, who, as I
have said, were drawn up in three divisions, and seated on the
ground, on seeing their enemies advance, rose up undauntedly
and fell into their ranks . . . You must know that the French
troops did not advance in any regular order, and that as soon
as their King came in sight of the English his blood began to
boil, and he cried out to his marshals, "Order the Genoese
forward and begin the battle in the name of God and St.
Denis" . . . The sun shone very bright; but the French had it
in their faces, and the English on their backs. When the
Genoese were somewhat in order they approached the English
and set up a loud shout in order to frighten them; but the
English remained quite quiet and did not seem to attend to
it. They then set up a second shout, and advanced a little forward; the English never moved. Still they hooted a third time,
advancing with their cross-bows presented, and began to
shoot. The English archers then advanced one step forward,

and shot their arrows with such force and quickness that it seemed as if it snowed. When the Genoese felt these arrows, which pierced their armor, some of them cut the strings of their cross-bows, others flung them to the ground, and all turned about and retreated quite discomfited.

Disorganization turned into rout. Furious at the retreat of the crossbow men, Philip VI ordered his cavalry forward with instructions to kill the Genoese if they got in the way; this did not improve morale. The ranks of the French cavalry were cut down by the arrows of the longbow men before the knights had a chance to engage their English counterparts. Still, the French fought bravely, surrounding the soldiers mobilized under the leadership of the Prince of Wales. When the son sent an emissary to his father to bring aid, Edward III refused saying, "return to those that sent you, and tell them from me not to send again for me this day, nor expect that I shall come, let what will happen, as long as my son has life; and say that I command them to let the boy win his spurs, for I am determined, if it please God, that all the glory of this day shall be given to him, and to those into whose care I have entrusted him." Fortunately for Edward, his son prevailed, and from this battle on was known as the Black Prince, so named both for the reputed color of his armor and the fear his ferocious warfare inspired in the French.

When, by the end of the day, the king of France was forced to flee the field with a mere handful of his barons, the English victory reverberated throughout Europe. Edward had lost only fifty knights, where Philip counted among his dead "11 princes, 1,200 knights, and about 30,000 common men," according to Froissart. "It was not merely a victory but one of the few classic fights of history. The overweening power of France, leader of the West, had been humiliated by an army . . . not more than a third the size." Worse, Edward moved immediately to capitalize on his success, marching his army north to Flanders in order to besiege the important coastal town of Calais. Suddenly, the English seemed unstoppable.

The outcome of the battle of Crécy caused considerable anxiety in Avignon. The Sacred College, dominated by French cardinals, did not even pretend to neutrality, and the pope himself lent Philip VI 592,000 gold florins in the wake of the disaster. An English chronicler of the period, John Erghome, wrote that Clement "always, inasmuch as he was able, was with the French against the English." The papacy understood that the balance of power, which had favored France and served Avignon so well in the past, was shifting ominously. Momentum now favored the English and their allies, among whom the Hungarians were predominant. "At this time, Pope Clement and the king of France . . . were leagued together; on the other side were the king of England, Louis of Bavaria [the Holy Roman Emperor], and the king of Hungary," reported an Italian chronicler. As early as March, Edward III had sent a letter by emissary to Louis of Hungary, encouraging the king to invade Naples, writing: "We will freely give both counsel and assistance towards avenging such a crime," referring to the murder of Andrew. France had already relinquished much of its western coast and was suddenly in danger of losing Calais and possibly Flanders; it could not afford to lose its close ally Naples. And yet the internecine warfare between Robert and Louis of Taranto had fractured the kingdom, which meant that the Hungarians were almost guaranteed a victory should King Louis decided to attack.

Desperate to prevent this eventuality, Clement redoubled his efforts to forestall a Hungarian invasion by implementing a policy of appeasement. The executions of the first round of supposed conspirators, savage and grisly as these were, had failed to satisfy Andrew's relatives, and so new, more stringent measures were called for. The pope demanded the enforcement of the death sentence for the remaining courtiers charged by the chief justice and threatened the empress of Constantinople with excommunication if she did not surrender Charles and Bertrand of Artois. At this time, too, Clement began to put forward the idea that the child Charles Martel should be taken from Joanna and brought, not to Hungary as Elizabeth had demanded, but to Avignon for safekeeping. If this represented a compromise measure, the pope acceded wholly to the dowager queen's will in a far more threatening way. On August 28 and then again on the 31st, Clement directly addressed Elizabeth's skepticism of the papacy's willingness to convict members of the Neapolitan royal family for the murder of her son, by conferring on his legate Cardinal Bertrand de Deux, who had finally recovered sufficiently from his illness to leave Avignon for Naples, the power to prosecute, pass sentence, and finally, to execute Joanna or any member of the royal family found guilty of conspiracy to murder Andrew.

⁂

Sovereigns did not keep diaries in the fourteenth century, nor publish their memoirs, nor confide their innermost worries and schemes to a favorite chronicler for posterity's sake. Motive must be deduced from action, an imprecise process. Yet even by this clumsy standard, Joanna seems to have experienced a turning point in the autumn of 1346.

She was twenty years old, a mother and widow, hunted by powerful adversaries, confronted with bitter divisions within her realm. She had been stripped of her closest counselors and forced to stand by helplessly while her former confidantes suffered torments. The woman she called mother languished, bloodied and wretched, in the dank chill of a dungeon along with her granddaughter, Joanna's intimate friend Sancia of Cabannis. Although the queen had managed thus far to shield the pair from the ultimate anguish, this was, she must have known, a matter of mere delay rather than commutation. The path of Joanna's own future was also equally, brutally clear:

without intervention she would lose first her child, then her kingdom (for she understood, if the pope did not, that nothing, save her deposition in their favor, would prevent her Hungarian in-laws from invading), and eventually, her life. Under the circumstances, paralyzing despair would not have been an unnatural reaction to the challenges that lay ahead.

But Joanna was sovereign during a period in history when that concept still meant something, and she took strength from it. A queen embodied courage—and this may well have been Joanna's defining trait—persistence, and above all, an unshakable belief in her own rights and abilities and office. As ruler, legal tools were yet available to her, and she used them. She seems finally to have recognized that she could not afford to let the papacy, or the Hungarians, or Robert of Taranto or Charles of Durazzo or even Louis of Taranto, dictate or impose policy on her. To safeguard her prerogative she had to take the initiative.

As there was no one she trusted left to guide her, she fell back on her original training in order to devise a plan. The security of both her child and the realm demanded that the kingdom, now fractured, be unified, and the Hungarians made to look like interlopers. In September she took the first step toward this goal by establishing the official line of succession at a ceremony in which the heir to the throne, Charles Martel, received the homage of the baronage and was formally invested duke of Calabria, just as Robert the Wise had legitimized her claim to the kingdom while she was still a child. To further her agenda, she proposed in a letter of September 18 to Clement that a marriage for her son be arranged with the crown of France to ensure the interest of that kingdom in Naples, and thereby gain a more active ally against Hungarian encroachment, promising to send by special messenger "certain quantities of silver, in compensation for these numerous dispensations."

These measures naturally inspired opposition from the queen's antagonists, of whom Charles, duke of Durazzo, now emerged as one of the most dangerous. The duke's initial collaboration with Robert of Taranto had always been convenient, a way of damaging Joanna's authority in the hope that she would be removed in favor of her sister. When this did not happen, and Charles began to realize that Joanna might actually marry one of his Taranto cousins and circumvent the Durazzo interests altogether, he turned traitor. Domenico da Gravina claims that the duke wrote to his Hungarian cousin King Louis as early as June, promising his support and that of the Neapolitan barons allied with him should the king decide to attack, but it seems likely that Charles did not actually invite the Hungarians to invade until after Charles Martel had been granted the duchy of Calabria, an honor the duke of Durazzo had himself demanded of the queen. In either case, it is reasonably certain that by September, Charles of Durazzo was in clandestine communication with the king of Hungary in an attempt to better his family's prospects in the event of an invasion. The duke had already earned Joanna's profound enmity for his role in the apprehension and torture of Philippa and Sancia; now she recognized him as jeopardizing not only her own welfare, but the kingdom's as well.

But there was nothing to be done until she could evade Robert's advances. Louis had been dissuaded from attacking his brother's forces in the capital at the last moment by the pope's holding out the promise of an approved marriage with Joanna. "If you attend to our admonitions, and obey them by refraining from creating these present disturbances, we will do as favorably for you as can be in those affairs concerning which Catherine, your august mother, has written to us," Clement had written. Although Robert could see that his mother's influence was working in his younger brother's favor, he remained determined to wed the queen. Despite the entreaties of both Joanna and the pope, who warned that his continued presence at the Castel Nuovo incensed the Hungarians, the elder prince of Taranto stubbornly refused to vacate the palace, and while Robert was there, Joanna had little hope of unifying the kingdom.

Then, on October 4, after an illness of only a few days' duration and within hours of being excommunicated for her refusal to surrender Charles and Bertrand of Artois to the authorities, the empress of Constantinople quite unexpectedly died. Although her conspiracy in the death of Andrew was never proven, her influence on the events succeeding the assassination was unmistakable. She and Niccolò Acciaiuoli together chose Andrew's eventual successor, protected at least one of his killers, and secured the fortunes of the Taranto family over those of the Durazzo. Ruthless, driven, and with a keen eye for political gain, Catherine's abilities dwarfed those of her sons. It was Acciaiuoli who assumed the mantle of family leadership after her death.

Her aunt's demise provided Joanna with the opportunity she had been seeking. By command of the queen, Catherine's funeral was to be celebrated at the church of San Domenico, in the heart of the old city of Naples, on October 8. When, as was expected, Robert of Taranto rode out of the Castel Nuovo to pay his last respects to his parent, Joanna was ready. According to both Domenico da Gravina and the *Chronicon Siculum,* she and her guard quickly evicted her cousin's retainers and then shut and locked the doors of the castle against him. When he returned in the evening, he was refused reentry. The queen had rid herself of one unwanted suitor.

But she did not then immediately embrace Robert's brother—to do so would only have further incited the Hungarians to hurry their attack, and Joanna needed time. Instead, she fell back on her grandmother's practice and petitioned Clement to be allowed to surround herself with four sisters from the nearby Clarissan convent, a request granted by the pope on October 30. When Cardinal Bertrand de Deux, the papal legate, finally arrived after an extended tour of Italy on November 20, he too moved into the Castel Nuovo. Let her mother-in-law complain about that.

Although the cardinal's first undertaking was supportive—on December 6 he reenacted the homage ceremony to Charles Martel, thereby providing official church sanction to the queen's policy and legitimizing her son as heir to the throne—Joanna understood that the legate's presence in Naples meant that she could no longer protect Philippa and Sancia from execution. The pair had been condemned, and Bertrand de Deux had his instructions. If the queen opposed his dictates, she risked alienating the Holy See at a time when the kingdom of Naples needed all the allies it could get. She had no choice but to sacrifice her adopted mother and one of her most intimate friends, despite the belief, well founded by the lack of evidence, that they were innocent of the crime of which they had been accused.

On December 29, Philippa the Catanian and Sancia of Cabannis were tortured and burned. Boccaccio reported that their naked bodies "bound to poles [were] in wagons led through the city," but Giovanni da Bazzano, another chronicler of the period, was more explicit. "Sancia, who had endured torture . . . yet had calmly and repeatedly denied the accusations, was brought to sea near Castel Nuovo. There, she was dangled from the crown of a galley's mast, sprayed with brimstone and boiling pitch, and then was dropped into the sea near the hull . . . Unable to resist such torture, she confessed." Philippa, mercifully, seems to have died from her wounds long before reaching the pyre, but Sancia, younger and more resilient, lived through the entire, excruciating process: "After that, she [Sancia] was paraded here and there, stretched out on red hot coals and tortured with pliers until her internal organs burned and she breathed her last," the chronicler concluded.

There is no record of Joanna's personal response to the agony endured on this day by those for whom she cared most in the world.

Despite repeated torment, neither woman ever named the queen as a conspirator in the death of her husband.

Events moved quickly after the arrival of the legate. As might have been expected, the execution of this latest round of condemned assassins in no way halted Hungarian aggression. In the weeks immediately following the futile deaths of Philippa and Sancia, Louis of Hungary and his younger brother Stephen arranged a war council with the Holy Roman Emperor, the king of Russia, the son of the king of Bohemia, and numerous other lords, counts, and barons. (The English were busy besieging the city of Calais.) At a meeting on January 24 and another later in February, those present formed an alliance for the purpose of avenging the death of Andrew. Each promised to return on April 22, the feast day of Saint George, accompanied by armed troops and supplies in anticipation of invading Naples. On March 27, Louis of Hungary sent a formal declaration of war against Joanna's kingdom to Avignon.

Clement reacted by putting more pressure on his legate to fulfill the twin tasks of taking Charles Martel away from his mother and of convicting and executing a member of the royal family, preferably Joanna, which the pope believed might yet dissuade the king of Hungary from his planned attack. Bertrand de Deux, whether through cowardice, weakness, incompetence, or a sincere unwillingness to persecute those whom he believed to be innocent, was unable to achieve these goals. Almost as soon as he arrived, the legate reported to Clement that "the Princes are innocent," but this failed to satisfy the pontiff, who suspected that the cardinal shrank from prosecuting the royal family in Naples for fear of reprisals. "It is most important that you lead an active and reliable investigation of the Queen and the Princes, in accordance with the letters we have sent you," Clement responded to his representative in a letter dated February 17, 1347. "Our intention certainly is not to endanger your life in any way. But if this business cannot be conducted safely or practically in the Palace, or in Naples, or at one of the Queen's estates, then it is absolutely necessary that you do this . . . where we trust your prudence will guide you." As to the legate's initial impression of the innocence of the queen and her family, Clement continued: "We are quite happy to hear this, but you should nevertheless not cease to investigate."

The cardinal was equally unsuccessful at convincing Joanna to surrender her child to the care of the church. The pope, evidently responding to information received earlier from the legate, who had sufficient time to observe Joanna with her son, tried to coax Bertrand de Deux into action, writing that if Charles Martel were removed from the kingdom, "nothing would lead to a suspicion of the Queen, who loves, cares for and raises her child with unusual maternal love."

The legate's failure to act decisively on his instructions kept Joanna in power and allowed her to prepare for the coming war. Knowing how violently her in-laws were against her marrying a second time and to give the appearance of complying with Hungarian demands, she asked Clement, through a private channel, not to sanction her union with Louis of Taranto just yet. She also supported the legate in his efforts to make the prince of Taranto, who had taken over his mother's position as jailer to Charles and Bertrand of Artois on her death, surrender Bertrand to the chief justice after Charles of Artois died of a long-standing case of gout on March 1. Bertrand, one of the foes whom Andrew with his banner had threatened with death as soon as he was made king, was turned over to the authorities later that month, and the man who actually seems to have both planned and participated in the assassination was himself finally executed for the crime. (The straightforward and excessively violent mode of the attack on Andrew was far more consistent with a hotheaded young man's temperament and abilities. A woman or elder statesman would have given more consideration to appearances and opted for the far subtler approach of poisoning.) Because Bertrand was of high birth, being a direct descendant (albeit illegitimate) of Robert the Wise, he was spared the agony and humiliation of a public execution and was instead put to death privately, for which reason some chroniclers believed that he evaded punishment altogether by escaping to Achaia with Niccolò Acciaiuoli's help. His death of course in no way satisfied the Hungarians.

The next phase of Joanna's policy was to sufficiently unite her realm to be able to at least make the effort of repelling an attack. To do this, it was vital that Charles of Durazzo be persuaded to fight on the side of the kingdom, and so she bribed him with her most valuable asset: her son. On June 18, Charles Martel was affianced to his cousin Jeanne, daughter of Charles of Durazzo and Joanna's sister, Maria. It was understood that Joanna would eventually marry Louis of Taranto and that the house of Taranto would rule in the present generation, but by this act a member of the Durazzo family would rule in the next, and this was sufficient to buy Charles's loyalty. On June 20, Louis of Taranto was named vicar-general of the realm; on June 23, Charles of Durazzo accepted the position of captain-general of the army. Niccolò Acciaiuoli was immediately dispatched to Florence with a letter from Joanna for the purpose of recruiting troops from this ally for the coming battle. This left only Robert of Taranto, who was soothed by a dispensation from the pope on July 4, 1347, to marry the wealthy Marie of Bourbon, widow of the king of Cyprus and daughter of one of the most influential families in France. Marie owned a great deal of property in Achaia and helped Robert, who had inherited the title of emperor of Constantinople upon his mother's death, to focus his attention on his eastern holdings.

No sooner had these painstaking negotiations with her family achieved the desired result than the queen was faced with the reality of conflict. In late June, word came to the capital that an advance guard of the Hungarian army had already arrived and was threatening the northeast corner of the kingdom. A battalion under the leadership of Charles of Durazzo was immediately dispatched to Abruzzi under orders to reconnoiter and hold back enemy advances until a more potent army could be raised.

The appearance of Hungarian troops on Neapolitan soil freed Joanna at last from having to pretend to accede to her in-laws' demands. On August 15, the legate moved out of the Castel Nuovo and Louis of Taranto moved in. A week later, Joanna married her cousin at the hour of vespers. There was no time to obtain official papal approval or the necessary dispensations for the wedding. The queen knew that Clement, still hoping to avoid war, would have sided with the Hungarians anyway and delayed or denied her permission to remarry as a gesture to Andrew's family, and this Joanna could not afford. The kingdom needed a committed general, and now she had one, the best available to her.

In September, Charles of Durazzo and his men returned to the capital to report on activity at the front. The news was grim. The advance guard of the Hungarian army had combined with some rebellious barons in the kingdom's northeast corner. Charles had made a stand at L'Aquila but had been forced to retreat in the face of superior numbers. The crisis was at hand.

Together, Louis and Robert of Taranto and Charles of Durazzo went about the business of raising an army by mustering their various vassals and subjects and distributing arms. Joanna directed a diplomatic offensive and succeeded in obtaining an agreement from the Sicilians to abstain from launching their own invasion of Naples while the kingdom was under threat from the Hungarians—a significant achievement, as the prospect of a coordinated action between these two adversaries would certainly have doomed the realm. But the news from Florence was disappointing. Despite the queen's entreaties and Niccolò Acciaiuoli's family's influence, the commune declined to send troops to fight beside those of its longtime ally. The Florentine elders, ever the practical businessmen, had already judged the likely outcome of the conflict and preferred to keep on friendly terms with King Louis of Hungary, who displayed no signs of extending the war beyond Neapolitan borders so long as no one stood in his way. Since Florentine territory was not at risk in this contest, the government concluded that there was no need to respond to the queen's summons.

The lack of Florentine support, while disheartening, was not crippling. According to Giovanni Villani, by working together, probably for the first time in their lives, Louis and Robert of Taranto, along with Charles of Durazzo, managed to raise an army of more than 2,500 knights, some from as far away as Provence, as well as the customary German mercenaries. In consultation with Niccolò Acciaiuoli, Louis determined that the best place to make a stand was at Capua. About twenty miles north of Naples, Capua was of vital strategic importance. Much of the kingdom of Naples was composed of marshes and wetlands; only the Via Appia, an ancient road leading from Rome to Taranto, was reliably firm enough to allow a large army, with all its attendant baggage, machinery, and supply wagons, to pass quickly without fear of becoming stuck in the mud, and Capua was on the Via Appia. The city had the additional advantage of being bordered on three sides by a cove in the Volturno River, which more or less gave it its own moat and made it much easier to defend. Capua had long ago been recognized as a crucial component of the kingdom's deterrent capabilities and as such had been well barricaded by successive rulers, so that the city resembled a fortress.

In December, Louis of Taranto, accompanied by his brother Robert and his cousin Charles of Durazzo, gathered his army together and marched to Capua, leaving Joanna, pregnant with his child, alone in Naples to await the coming storm.

CHAPTER X

❦

The Scales *of* Justice

Louis of hungary left Visegrád to invade Naples on November 11, 1347. Despite the promises of his earlier war councils, the king did not ride out accompanied by a massive army. Marching too many soldiers the long distance south would have been slow and unwieldy. Louis would have had to provide supplies, which meant lumbering carts over uncertain roads. Instead the king of Hungary, opting for speed, handpicked one thousand of his most ferocious and experienced knights and set off for northern Italy with only these elite troops, supplemented by an ample quantity of silver, expecting to hire mercenaries along the way.

Through strict discipline—he and his men rode methodically for six hours every day—the king of Hungary was in Cittadella, between Verona and Venice, by December 3; from there he went west to Vicenza and reached Verona by the 8th. These cities, predominantly Ghibelline, opened their gates immediately and enthusiastically to welcome a sovereign who was allied with the Holy Roman Emperor and who planned to invade Guelphic Naples. Louis' army swelled with recruits, including many German mercenaries eager for spoils. Edward Acciaiuoli reported that by the time he reached the outskirts of Joanna's kingdom, the king of Hungary was leading a battalion of five thousand knights and four thousand foot soldiers. Another chronicler set the figure as high as fifteen thousand cavalry. Louis met no resistance on his way south. Even Guelphic Florence, which had asked for and received military aid from Naples so often in the past, chose simply to get out of the invader's way, sending a fawning delegation to inform the king of the city's neutrality and even cravenly settling on him the honorary title of signore. By Christmas Eve, King Louis, accompanied by a now-formidable combat force, had met up with his advance guard at the town of L'Aquila in Abruzzi. But instead of immediately engaging Louis of Taranto, whom he knew to be at Capua, the king of Hungary, taking a roundabout route through the mountains, descended on Benevento, a minimally guarded city that he captured easily on January 11, 1348.

News of King Louis' victory over Benevento, and the size and strength of the Hungarian army, spread rapidly throughout the kingdom. There was great fear in Naples; Benevento was only a three-day march from the capital. In Capua, the Neapolitan princes held a war council, at which, according to Domenico da Gravina, Charles of Durazzo and Robert of Taranto decided to capitulate to their Hungarian cousin and do homage to him without a struggle in order to get into his good graces. Despite the repeated pleas of Louis of Taranto to stay and fight, these two princes returned to the capital to prepare for the king of Hungary's arrival. They took many barons and knights with them, a betrayal that left Joanna's husband, along with Niccolò Acciaiuoli and Louis of Taranto's first lieutenant, the loyal count of Altavilla, alone with a much reduced force to try to repel the invaders.

When Joanna saw the duke of Durazzo and Robert of Taranto and their attendant troops ride into Naples, she knew she had lost her kingdom and was in imminent danger of losing her life. If Louis of Hungary caught her, he would kill her, of that she had no doubt. Her only hope was to flee Naples for Provence, which remained under her jurisdiction. If she survived, she might yet organize a counteroffensive by calling on her Provençal subjects and the papacy and Louis of Taranto's uncle, the French king, for aid. She called together the members of her household and, in the interests of an orderly transition of government, appointed a committee of noblemen to administer the realm in her absence. To protect her people as much as possible from the wrath of the invaders, the queen formally released those present, and through them all her subjects, from the oath of loyalty they had taken to her until such time as she returned to Naples, and she advised her partisans, for their own safety, not to resist Louis of Hungary's entrance into the capital.

Then came the hardest part: leaving her son behind.

Joanna adored her child and must have wanted to take him with her. The queen had been given ample opportunity over the past year to deliver the boy to either Clement or the Hungarians and had steadfastly refused to do so, despite the ever-increasing pressure of her mother-in-law's threats and demands. But she was about to take an uncertain voyage on rough seas in the middle of winter, which might be dangerous for the toddler. Even should she have decided to hazard this, there was no way to spirit Charles Martel, who was under the strict eye of his governor and Isabelle the Hungarian, away from the Castel dell'Ovo without alerting them to her intentions. Joanna knew that no harm would come to the boy from the Hungarians if he remained in Naples. Andrew's child was precious to her in-laws. To take him away from his mother was one of the reasons King Louis had invaded in the first place, and so she could be confident that if Charles Martel remained behind, he would be cared for and protected, and the citizens of Naples spared, at least in some measure, the conqueror's ill humor and reprisals. Charles of Durazzo no doubt intended to offer up the heir to the throne immediately to his victorious cousin as a means of furthering his own interests and might well surrender her to the Hungarians along with her son. She could not take this risk; it is not known if she was even able to say goodbye. Her only hope of being with her child at some time in the future was to leave him now.

Taking as much specie from the royal treasury as she could manage for her expenses and the inevitable bribes she would need to buy support—she was, after all, going to Avignon—and accompanied by a small group of retainers that included her chamberlain Enrico Caracciolo, Joanna slipped away during the night of January 15, 1348, and, having previously arranged for three galleys to be waiting in the harbor, set sail for Provence.

❧

Whispers of the queen's midnight flight reached Capua early the next morning causing Louis of Taranto, accompanied by Niccolò Acciaiuoli, to hurry back to the capital, leaving the garrison under the command of the count of Altavilla. When the two men discovered that the rumors Joanna had escaped the city were true, Niccolò convinced the prince of Taranto to do the same. Louis of Taranto could not kneel to the king of Hungary as his older brother and cousin intended to do; as Joanna's husband, he would be executed if he fell into enemy hands. Like the queen, his only hope of success lay in securing outside reinforcements to replace those troops his older brother and Charles of Durazzo had so treacherously withdrawn from Capua at the last moment. Giovanni Villani reported that Louis and Niccolò tried to find an armed galley, in case they met resistance along the way, but there were none to be had. With the Hungarian army on the move and no time to spare, the pair hired the only vessel they could find, a narrow, flimsy fishing boat, and took off on the evening of January 16 in the middle of a driving winter storm in this small craft to try to convince the Florentines one last time to help.

❧

After resting and reorganizing his army at Benevento for six days, during which time he received delegations from throughout the kingdom offering surrender and homage in the hopes of preventing additional pillage and slaughter, Louis of Hungary had indeed begun marching his troops west toward Naples on January 16. The king did not attempt to take the capital immediately. Naples, with its crowded population and maze of narrow streets, would be a difficult city to quell if its citizens decided to resist. Instead, the Hungarian army bypassed the capital and headed north, a route that took them directly past Capua. At the approach of the enemy, the German mercenaries under the command of the count of Altavilla, seeing a large number of their compatriots in the body of the opposing army, deserted to the Hungarians. At this final defection, the count was reduced to hanging a Hungarian banner over the wall of the city in surrender. Louis of Hungary, having thus conquered the kingdom without having to engage in a single battle, arrived the next day at Aversa and occupied the city. As Joanna had anticipated, her brother-in-law's first act was to send an envoy to Naples to demand that Charles Martel be relinquished into Hungarian control, a transfer that was effected immediately. "In the same year, on the 19th day of the same month—it was Sir Amelio del Balzo who was taking care of the Lord Charles Martel—they assigned him [Charles Martel] to Count Ciccono of Hungary, who received him in the name of the king of Hungary, and they even assigned to him [Count Ciccono] the Castel dell'Ovo," reported the *Chronicon Siculum*.

Also on January 19, Charles of Durazzo and Robert of Taranto made a grand entry into Aversa, at the head of a long procession of the capital's highest-ranking aristocrats, to do formal obeisance to the victorious king of Hungary. Although the fact that King Louis chose the site of his brother's assassination as the setting in which to receive the homage of his Neapolitan relatives should have been a tip-off, the duke of Durazzo, in particular, was confident that at least he and his family—he had brought the younger of his two brothers, Robert, along on this diplomatic mission—would receive a warm reception from his cousin. Charles had, after all, befriended Louis' brother Andrew before his death; had led the relentlessly merciless offensive against the victim's killers that had resulted in the public torture and extermination of those closest to the queen; had urged his Hungarian relatives to invade the kingdom, promising his support and those of his vassals and allies in the event the attack took place. His nominal participation in the war effort mounted by Louis of Taranto, if it was known to the king of Hungary at all, would not, the duke of Durazzo must have reasoned, be held against him as Charles had laid down his arms peacefully and had convinced others to do so as well. The groundwork for this moment had been laid carefully through months of clandestine communication with his royal cousin, and so Charles rode into Aversa full of praise, humble servitude, and sympathetic family feeling for the new ruler of Naples.

And it all went just as Charles had expected. Louis of Hungary met the overtures of the Neapolitan delegation with a satisfying graciousness. He took a special interest in his cousins, inquiring of the whereabouts of even the younger members of the houses of Taranto and Durazzo. When informed that two of the male representatives of the family, Philip of Taranto and Louis of Durazzo, had stayed behind in the capital in order to arrange a magnificent welcoming ceremony for the king, Louis of Hungary insisted that they, too, come to Aversa and be present at a festive banquet he planned to host on January 22. Charles of Durazzo and Robert of Taranto made haste to inform their two younger siblings of the king's invitation, and so, on the evening of the appointed day, the male members of the entire family sat down together for a celebratory feast, the consummation of which was captured for posterity by Domenico da Gravina:

"The king greeted the princes graciously, conversed with them, left them in the great hall of the palace and went into his room with his advisors. After careful consideration, the counsel decided that the princes would be arrested at the end of the meal," recorded the chronicler. "The king left his room and came back to the company of his cousins; he discussed a thousand diverse topics with them, as well as with the lords and squires in attendance until dinner time. When dinner was ready, water for his hands was brought to the king, then to the duke and to the prince of Taranto [Robert], then to all the others, according to hierarchy.

"The duke, the prince and their brothers ate at a different table than that of the king's. [A nobleman] took advantage of this to say to the duke, as he was serving: 'Unfortunate Duke, you wouldn't believe me, but you came to your misfortune. You can still escape. Believe me, leave!' But the irritated duke glanced sharply at him and almost reported these words to the king; he contained himself, however, and said nothing . . . When dinner was over and the tables cleared, the king summoned the duke and the other princes. His smile was replaced by the harshest expression as he unveiled with terrible words the true feelings he had for the princes and that he had kept hidden until then:

> Duke of Durazzo, monster of iniquity, know that you are in our hands to suffer the consequences of your crimes and to pay for your treason with your life. But before you die, confess your betrayals against our Royal Majesty so that we do not have to call on other witnesses to inflict on you the punishment for your treason. Thus tell us, duke, why you ensured that your uncle, the duke of Périgord, delayed the crowning of our brother duke Andrew in the court of Rome, which enabled his ignominious death . . . Might you wish to refute that you are the author of this scheme? Here are the letters you wrote, under your seal.* You know full well that the will

---

* These letters have never been documented; it has been suggested they were forged.

of our great uncle king Robert gave us to marry his granddaughter Maria, whom you married fraudulently . . . After our
brother's death, you showed much zeal in pursuing his murderers and you exacted the harshest revenge. This might have
earned our forgiveness. You wrote to invite us to this kingdom,
and promised to bring us in with the help of the counts in
your party and to deliver the regicides into our hands. How
could you then dare, you traitor, on the order of Joanna your
queen, to lead an army [against us] at L'Aquila . . . Our armed
forces were to help you destroy Louis, Joanna and the other
princes, your cousins, and to banish them from this kingdom;
you would then have remained the sole power in this country
and you would have then plotted our death . . . But all these
fine plans have come to naught, as one cannot hope to play
us this way.

After this outburst, so reminiscent of the charges Louis of
Hungary and his mother had elaborated in their earlier letters to
the pope, all five men were arrested. Robert and Philip of Taranto
and Louis and Robert of Durazzo were deposited in the dungeon
under guard. Charles of Durazzo was hauled in front of a Hungarian tribunal, which quickly condemned him for the murder of
Andrew. At dawn the next morning, the prisoner was brought
back to the castle, where Louis of Hungary and a party of soldiers awaited him. The king demanded to know the exact location
of his brother's assassination. The duke had no choice but to comply with this request, and brought the king of Hungary and his
attendant guard to the terrace where Andrew had been hanged.
Upon being informed that this was the site of his brother's
ambush, Louis of Hungary coldly gave the command for his
cousin's execution. Charles of Durazzo was beheaded on the spot,
and the bloody trunk of his body thrown over the balcony railing
and into the garden below, there to lie as Andrew's corpse had

lain on that fateful September night some two years before.

Hours later, after the king had left the castle, friars from the adjacent monastery crept out and removed the remains of the once-feared duke of Durazzo and brought his headless body to a tomb at the church of San Lorenzo Maggiore in Naples, where it was discreetly interred.

⚘

Having revenged his brother's death in this convincing manner, Louis of Hungary left Aversa and marched his army to the capital city of Naples. The shocking news of the summary execution of the duke of Durazzo and the imprisonment of the other male members of the houses of Durazzo and Taranto had preceded the king, as had many of his soldiers, bent on looting. "A night of violence followed this tragic evening," Domenico da Gravina wrote. "Servants from [the princes'] escorts were hunted down and slaughtered in the streets of Aversa, and their homes in that town as well as in Naples were plundered." The Hungarian marauders converged on Charles's Neapolitan palace. "His wife [Maria] barely escaped this peasant revolt," the chronicler asserted. "She ran away in the middle of the night, half naked, her two young children in her arms, and took refuge in the nearby convent of Santa Croce." The duchess of Durazzo (who was pregnant again) and her children were soon joined at the convent by Robert of Taranto's new wife, Marie of Bourbon, in a similar state of privation. Joanna's sister was eventually smuggled out of Naples disguised as a friar; she and her children escaped to Tuscany and from there took a galley to Provence. Marie of Bourbon was similarly spirited away safely by sympathetic partisans to Florence.

Louis of Hungary arrived just as evening was falling. The city had been on the lookout for him all day. As soon as his army came into view, a mixed throng of commoners and aristocrats sallied out to meet him. As part of the grandiose welcoming ceremony (ironically arranged by Philip of Taranto and Louis of Durazzo, who were currently languishing in Hungarian captivity), the king was offered his choice of three magnificently ornamented canopies, specially designed for the occasion, to ride under as he entered the capital. The king refused them all, hardly an encouraging sign. Nor did his attitude toward his conquered subjects improve on further acquaintance. The Hungarian's first act, after taking over the Castel Nuovo, was to divide up the palaces, property, and possessions of the houses of Taranto and Durazzo and dispense these riches to himself and his generals. His second was to threaten the populace with a general sack if the citizenry did not raise an exorbitant sum in taxes to their new sovereign.

The rank and file of the capital, used to the more benevolent ways of a queen who fed the poor and dispensed alms with generous regularity, resisted their new sovereign's severe approach to administration, secretly electing eight leading citizens to act as an unofficial government and organizing themselves under these representatives into a voluntary militia. On the night of January 28, having put up with looting by mercenaries billeted in private homes all over the city for five days, and convinced a general sack was imminent, the city fought back. Digging up the streets, the townspeople erected makeshift barriers by heaping the cobblestones into piles. These bulwarks, in addition to blockading the entrance to roadways and private homes, provided the disgruntled citizenry with ammunition against the enemy. Under the command of their eight generals, the population kept watch in shifts all night. When a mercenary showed himself, his way was blocked, and he was immediately pelted with rocks from doorways and rooftops. Finding themselves under attack from all sides, Louis' soldiers retreated; many died and a large number surrendered. The king was forced to negotiate with the leaders of the ad hoc government and agreed to pay the mercenaries from his own cache of silver in order to reduce the risk of looting. If the male members of the Neapolitan royal family had shown one tenth the resilience and courage of the common inhabitants of the capital, they might have saved themselves the unpleasantness of death, despoliation, and a prolonged imprisonment, not to mention retaining the kingdom.

As it was, though, after the king of Hungary came to this new understanding with his metropolitan subjects, the incidents of armed resistance decreased. Louis, who now styled himself king of Jerusalem and Sicily, prince of Capua and Salerno, and king of Hungary, Dalmatia, Croatia, Serbia, and Bulgaria, among other titles, was soon able to fulfill the last and most coveted of his objectives. On February 2, under the guise of protecting the heir to the throne from phantom Neapolitan intrigues against his life, he dispatched two-year-old Charles Martel, along with his four captive royal cousins, home to Hungary as spoils of the campaign. The toddler, who had been raised in the warmth of southern Italy and had never known ice or snow, was surrounded by an entourage of Hungarian noblemen and nurses who transported him by litter to the eastern shore of Naples. From there, the procession crossed the Adriatic for the Dalmatian coast on February 12 as a prelude to the long, dangerous trip north, through the frigid mountains and furious gales of winter, to Visegrád.

This was the last anyone in Naples saw of Joanna's child. Charles Martel, weakened by the arduous journey, died soon after arriving in Hungary.

⚜

The queen's galleys made the voyage across the Mediterranean quickly. Joanna was able to land in Provence on January 20, just five days after fleeing Naples. She and her entourage traveled immediately to Marseille, where the queen knew she would be assured of a warm welcome. Years of preferential treatment had inspired in the inhabitants of the city a keen loyalty to the "Mistress of Marseille," as Joanna was called, for the Angevin rulers of Naples had recognized early the importance of this port as a conduit for trade, men, and arms between the various far-flung regions of the domain. On January 29, the queen was treated to a festive ceremony, accompanied by as much pomp and splendor as the town could arrange on short notice, at which she publicly pledged herself to maintain the welfare and interests of the city. In turn, her vassals promised to defend and support her in her time of need. Nearly the whole of the population crammed itself into the streets for this rare look at their sovereign.

Unfortunately, Marseille was not the seat of regional government—that dignity belonged to the capital city of Aix-en-Provence. Joanna's relationship with that municipality, or, more specifically, with the provincial nobility who lived there and governed in her name, was much more troubled than it was with her Marseille subjects. A number of grievances, dating from the time of Robert the Wise, had never been assuaged to parochial satisfaction, and the discontent had recently been amplified by the queen's having put forward Neapolitan candidates for administrative positions that the local magnates, jealous of their income and authority, felt should have gone to one of their number. These resentments, always present in some form between official Aix-en-Provence and Naples, had been fanned by Hungarian agents, chief among them Andrew's cousin the dauphin of Vienne, who frequently acted as an operative for the crown of Hungary in Provence. The extent of the native aristocracy's unhappiness, and of Hungarian inroads into her territory, were made plain to Joanna when, on her way to Aix from Marseille on February 2, she was accosted by a military guard, who arrested her chamberlain and the other Italians traveling in her suite on the charge of conspiracy in the murder of Andrew and imprisoned them in a nearby dungeon.

Joanna recognized this act for the bargaining ploy it was and not as a substantive threat to her rule. After all, if the dauphin of Vienne had truly convinced the governing elite of Provence to switch their allegiance to the king of Hungary, it was the queen herself who would have been arrested rather than her servants. So she continued on to the capital and ensconced herself in the ancestral palace to begin negotiations with the provincial government to resolve the troublesome issues. The luster of the royal presence in Aix, coupled with the beautiful young queen's sympathetic attention and evident willingness to accommodate their complaints, soothed the wounded feelings of her slighted administrators and led quickly to reconciliation. There was nothing the regional authorities could do about her entourage—because the church was responsible for investigating Andrew's assassination, only the pope had the power to free those charged in the case—but a compromise was arranged. Joanna swore by solemn oath at a public ceremony on February 19 to appoint only persons native to Provence to the government, and this gesture was immediately reciprocated by an oath of fealty from the local authorities and regional aristocracy, both to herself and to her son, Charles Martel. From this point on, Hungarian encroachment in this all-important region was effectively arrested. Provence remained loyal to the queen.

Had she wished to serve out the rest of her reign in comfortable exile, this would have been enough, but Joanna had come to Provence to fight, not to hide. To renew the struggle, the queen needed men and arms to launch a counterattack, which meant an infusion of new funds and the recruitment of allies. Four months' pregnant, she also required a papal dispensation to legitimize both her marriage and her unborn child in the eyes of the church. Mostly, though, she needed to publicly clear her name of the charge of conspiracy in the murder of her husband, as none of the former goals could be accomplished without the latter. Of all the rulers in Europe, only the pope was capable of granting these requests.

Yet she knew she could not take a chance of arriving uninvited in Avignon and perhaps enduring the humiliation of Clement's refusing to see her, or worse, of ordering her arrest. If she came to the papal palace, it had to be on her own terms: as a queen consenting to appear, a meeting between two equals, with all the dignity and respect due to visiting royalty. She could not afford surprises; the details of their interview had to be arranged in advance. More than this, Joanna understood that in order to gain the maximum benefit from the rendezvous, there had to be as many witnesses present as possible. If they met secretly, Clement could then simply deny the audience had ever taken place. She had to force the pope to receive her publicly. And so, beginning in February, the queen of Naples began a letter-writing campaign from her castle in Aix, lobbying the Holy See for an interview.

Clement was not pleased to hear from her. Joanna's sudden appearance in Provence had put the pope in an awkward position. Despite the king of Hungary's undeniable military success, the papacy still hoped to persuade him to withdraw voluntarily from Naples, and agreeing to meet with its fugitive queen would certainly antagonize Louis. At the very moment Joanna was pelting Clement with letters entreating his support, the pope was also contending with a party of ambassadors sent by King Louis, advising the Holy See of the Hungarian victory in Italy and aggressively forwarding their sovereign's demand that the queen (whom Louis knew to have escaped to Provence) be deposed and executed and he, the king of Hungary, be crowned in her place. Clement, who knew that he would have eventually to choose between the two rulers but who did not wish to choose just yet, resorted to his customary tactics of vacillation and delay. Ominously, in a February 16 letter, he refused Joanna's request for an audience, using as his excuse the hostile presence of the Hungarian delegation at the papal court, and recommended instead that the queen travel west to Châteaurenard, to be closer to Avignon, and there wait for his emissaries to contact her. Hoping to acquire through obedience that which had so far been denied her by diplomacy, Joanna took the pope's suggestion and removed to Châteaurenard on February 27 in the company of eighteen knights sent by the cardinals in recognition of her rank and position.

There is no way to tell how long she might have sat there waiting for Clement's agents—or worse, his inquisitors—if the queen's side in this political tug-of-war had not gotten an unexpected boost with the sudden arrival of Louis of Taranto and Niccolò Acciaiuoli in Provence.

~*~

They were lucky to be alive. Buffeted by high winds in the rain and cold, Joanna's husband and his chief adviser had somehow brought their small boat into the port of Siena. From there they had journeyed inland to one of the Acciaiuoli family estates just outside the walls of Florence. News of their arrival caused unease in the Guelphic city. Some of the inhabitants, remembering the aid Joanna's family had rendered to the commune so often in the past, spoke out in favor of assisting Louis of Taranto in his struggle against the Eastern European invaders, but the Florentine elders, fearful of the king of Hungary's proximity, overruled these partisans and locked the gates of the city against the Neapolitan prince. Only Niccolò's cousin, the bishop of Florence, was brave enough to defy the signory and leave the city in order to meet with Louis and Niccolò. Together, the three decided that the best course of action would be to apply to the pope for aid. Chartering a much sturdier boat, they embarked from Pisa, arriving in Aigues-Mortes, near Marseille, the second week in February. Hearing that the queen had landed safely, but that her entourage had been imprisoned by Hungarian supporters, the Acciaiuolis rode immediately to Avignon to begin a dialogue with the Holy See, while Louis of Taranto moved into a castle in Villeneuve-d'Avignon, the area of town where all the cardinals lived, just across the Rhône from the papal palace.

Faced with the oratory of two such forceful advocates as the Neapolitan banker and his cousin the bishop, not to mention the presence of the king of France's nephew just across the river, Clement agreed to receive Joanna. Niccolò Acciaiuoli, who clearly had a very high opinion of himself and a strong inclination toward self-promotion—he alone among the dignitaries of the period would think to ensure his place in history by penning an autobiography—would later take full credit for the success of these papal negotiations, and subsequent historians have uniformly taken him at his word. "When first the King of Hungary invaded this realm (Naples)," he wrote:

> It became expedient for the Queen and my Lord the King [Louis of Taranto], whose welfare I had clung to so steadfastly and hopefully, to quit the kingdom, both by reason (to speak politely) of the shiftiness of her own subjects, and because the princes, magnates, and almost all the people, were willing to obey the King of Hungary. I alone, relinquishing everything I possessed in the realm, which amounted to no small reckoning, followed their fortune ... In those times the ground would seem to quake at the mere mention of that King's name [Louis of Hungary's], as the Clementine and other Cardinals and courtiers well knew. The Queen was pregnant and still lacking Apostolic dispensation, while my master was young and inexperienced. It fell, then, to my lot, in default of any one better, to endeavor by every possible means to end the cruel disorder and destructive embroilment of their affairs.

However, while Niccolò no doubt played a role in bringing Joanna and the pope together and certainly handled the subsequent financial transactions resulting from their meeting, there were several other influences at work that led to Clement's decision to grant Joanna an audience. The king of France, who had by this time lost

Calais as well as Crécy to the English, wanted Joanna's marriage to Louis of Taranto sanctioned and the young couple supported in their efforts to repel the Hungarians, and had sent ambassadors to Avignon with instructions to achieve these results. Joanna's cousin James III, king of Majorca (Sancia's nephew), who had lost his kingdom to the crown of Aragon and was looking for papal assistance in securing his birthright, also happened to be in Avignon at this time, adding another champion to the queen's cause. With all due respect to Niccolò's diplomatic talents, it is likely that this pair of royal advocates had as much to do with Clement's capitulation as did the Acciaiuolis. Nor was the banker completely ingenuous about the selflessness of his motives in defending his sovereigns. Niccolò sacrificed nothing by fleeing with Joanna and Louis of Taranto. He well understood that his association as adviser to the queen and her second husband was public knowledge. If he had stayed behind, he would have been arrested and executed, and his lands and goods would have been confiscated by the Hungarians.

But perhaps the most significant factor in formulating papal policy with respect to Naples was the behavior of the king of Hungary himself. By this time, Joanna's sister, Maria, penniless and distraught, had also arrived in Provence with her children and made straight for the palace of her dead husband's powerful uncle, Cardinal Talleyrand of Périgord. With Maria came the dreadful news of Charles of Durazzo's execution at the hands of his Hungarian cousin, the imprisonment of the remaining Neapolitan princes, and the pillaging of the royal property.

This was too much for Clement, particularly as Louis of Hungary, through his ambassadors, persisted in accusing Cardinal Périgord of having masterminded his brother's assassination even after the pope had stoutly denied the allegation. Under Talleyrand's leadership, all the French cardinals, who made up the majority of the Sacred College, lobbied in favor of Joanna, and Clement, appalled by the indefensible mode of Hungarian vengeance (and worried that, in his eagerness to despoil his Neapolitan cousins, King Louis was absconding with property that belonged to the church), allowed himself to be persuaded to receive the queen. Word of his decision was dispatched to Joanna, who was waiting patiently at Château-renard. It must have taken no small amount of courage, with the plague at the height of its relentless force, to make the pilgrimage to Avignon at just this time, but Joanna did it without a murmur, arriving at the head of a grand procession escorted by a guard of thirty armed horsemen on March 15, 1348.

There is some confusion as to whether she proceeded directly to the papal palace on that date, or whether the pope received her a few days later. Giovanni Villani stated that Joanna stood before the consistory on March 27, but as Clement referred to his audience with the queen in a March 23 letter to the legate Bertrand de Deux, the Florentine chronicler seems to have been mistaken. Some historians believe the event took place on March 19 rather than the 15th, as the pope also penned a letter to the dauphin of Vienne on March 20 in which he wrote sympathetically of Joanna's plight in a manner indicating that a personal appeal by the queen had just taken place. That Joanna succeeded in her first goal of being greeted by the Holy See, not as a suspect or a refugee but as a visiting queen, with all the pomp and respect required on such an occasion, is without question. In a letter to a later legate, Guy of Boulogne, Clement observed that the interview had been conducted "according to the ceremonial protocol observed by the Church for the reception of Royalty."

But once inside the papal palace and having traversed the gauntlet of the great hall, Joanna still had to weather the hazards of an inquest. The queen could not ignore the fact of Andrew's murder or the charges of complicity that had clung to her in its wake any more than the pope, who had publicly undertaken to investigate the crime, could receive her without definitively addressing the question of her guilt or innocence. Nor was this audience, so eagerly sought on the one side and so reluctantly brooked on the other, a mere formality, hastily organized to disguise a foreordained conclusion. Joanna was well aware that she stood before a man who, stung by the dowager queen of Hungary's taunts that the church was incapable of confronting the royal family and administering justice in Naples, had sent a legate to her kingdom with specific instructions to convict her of the murder of her husband. "Consistory was . . . the supreme court of Christendom, and pope and cardinals together would sit in judgment, as they did on Joanna for Andrew of Hungary's murder."

With so much at stake, Joanna had asked for and obtained permission in advance to speak on her own behalf in order to refute the Hungarian accusations, a highly unusual occurrence. There is no record of what she said for the very good reason that Clement, hedging his bets as usual, did not wish to advertise this meeting to the king of Hungary, and so her inquest was not inscribed in the official church annals. This allowed the pope to write a year later to Louis of Hungary denying the rumors that he had granted an audience with the queen at this time with a clear conscience. Instead, to mollify the king, the pope reported that Joanna had been received by only a few cardinals and that, when told she must submit to an inquiry, she had quitted Avignon altogether without answering the charges against her. This letter was, of course, refuted by the much earlier missives Clement dispatched to both the dauphin and Bertrand de Deux, in which the pontifical inquest of the queen was expressly referred to, but then Clement was in no way the first of his profession to feel the need to sacrifice a little truth on the altar of diplomacy.

The report, then, of what did occur between the queen of Naples and the Holy See in the great hall of the papal palace on that March day in 1348 comes from the sixteenth-century Neapolitan annalist Angelo da Costanzo and the seventeenth-century Provençal historian Honoré Bouche, both working from sources contemporary to the period that are no longer extant. There is also a description of this event by the seventeenth-century church scholar Louis Maimbourg. All three of these accounts are in agreement. "Joanna arrived in Provence; since she had come not so much to protect herself against retaliation by the king of Hungary but rather to defend herself to the Holy Father Clement VI, she immediately went to see him in Avignon; she was welcomed with all the honor and pomp that a great Queen deserved in her own city and was received publicly by His Holiness with all the cardinals and ambassadors and agents of all the princes of Christendom in attendance," wrote Bouche.

And so Joanna faced her inquisitors and answered the charges brought against her. It seems clear that she beguiled her audience. The pope was something of a connoisseur of beautiful women—during his tenure, the papal palace served as the site of an array of glittering banquets attended by many glamorous noblewomen, including, according to Matteo Villani, the pope's special friend Cécile, the countess of Turenne. In the immediate aftermath of Joanna's rebuttal, Clement evinced great sympathy for the queen of Naples's plight. In a March 20 letter addressed to the dauphin of Vienne, the pope wrote, "You know of the wretched situation . . . our very dear daughter in Christ, the Queen of Sicily, finds herself in, and we believe you will be moved with a pious compassion for her, your cousin."

But charm alone would not have sufficed to win the queen her suit. Joanna needed not sympathy but support; not a judgment but an ally such as could only be obtained by a sweeping dismissal of the charges. She had to make her interrogators believe not only in her innocence but also in her fundamental right to rule, and most important, her ability to win back her kingdom. The image of majesty and lineage Joanna projected clearly influenced those judging her—she stood before them the granddaughter of Robert the Wise, the niece of the Valois king of France, the embodiment of a legacy long recognized in its legitimacy by the power of the church, an irresistible indictment against the Hungarian usurper. By her side were the twin pillars of her administration, evidence of the strength at her command by which she intended to recover her kingdom: her new husband, Louis, prince of Taranto, a warrior of unimpeachable credentials in the full flower of manhood, with an exalted ancestry to match her own; and Niccolò Acciaiuoli, a wily finance minister and statesman, with strong ties to Guelphic Florence.

The queen finished her recitation; the pope conferred with his cardinals; the judgment was handed down. "Not only innocent, but above the suspicion of guilt," reported Costanzo. "She spoke at length with such grace and eloquence, brought forth so many good reasons for her defense, that . . . His Holiness was compelled to declare her innocent of the crime and of the suspicion of the crime that she stood accused of," observed Bouche. "As far as the murder of her first husband Andrew of Hungary that many accused her of, she justified herself fully . . . both in that none of them [those already convicted and executed for the crime] ever implicated her in the horrific torture they endured, and by the eloquent defense she delivered herself in open consistory to the Pope Clement and the ambassadors of the Princes of Christendom with such strength and clarity that this Pontiff declared in an official act that not only was she innocent of this crime, she also could not be suspected of ever taking part in it," agreed Maimbourg. So taken was Clement with the queen of Naples and her new husband that on March 30, the pope presented the golden rose (a highly valuable ornament encrusted with pearls and garnets, with a sapphire at the center of its golden petals, traditionally bestowed on the fourth Sunday of Lent as a mark of special papal favor) not, as he had originally intended, to the king of Majorca, but to Joanna's champion, Louis of Taranto.

~∗~

CHAPTER XI

The Return *of the* Queen

T HE MAGNITUDE of the queen's achievement may be measured by the obvious and immediate boost the pope provided
to her position in the aftermath of her acquittal. On April 22,
Clement issued a bull legitimizing Joanna's marriage to Louis of
Taranto. On May 7, the pope sent a strongly worded letter to
Bertrand de Deux with instructions to deny Louis of Hungary's
demand to be crowned king of Naples. "However, and even though
in point of fact Queen Joanna had been dispossessed of her states,"
wrote Clement, "she could not be deprived of them legally as she
was neither convicted nor condemned of the crime of which she was
accused. Even if she had been, her kingdom would go to the child
Charles Martel rather than to her opponent. Finally . . . all civil and
religious laws concur that anyone who took over someone else's
property of his own accord and judgment, even if he had a remote
right to do so, must be dispossessed of them . . . We have nothing
to blame ourselves about, having done all we could both for
Andrew's coronation and for the punishment of his murderers. On
the other hand, the king of Hungary has committed multiple and
grievous offenses against the Holy Church. Charles Martel's capture
and transport away from the Kingdom trespassed on their rights

and the respect owed to them. Charles of Durazzo's execution was both an injustice, since this prince was innocent, and an illegality, since, had he been guilty, his judgment and punishment would be the domain of the Church; and he had been executed without any form of justice."

Whether Louis of Hungary was ever acquainted with this papal remonstrance is unclear. By the time the letter was written, Bertrand de Deux had escaped to Rome. Even if the legate had remained in Naples, he would not have been eager to forward its contents to the volatile conqueror. Not that the chiding would have made much difference to the king. Louis of Hungary was preoccupied with much more tangible obstacles, the majority of his own making. Soon after securing his hold on the capital city, the king of Hungary had begun a reign of terror in order to ferret out all possible accomplices in the death of his brother. The Hungarian troops were particularly brutal in their investigations. According to Domenico da Gravina, many innocent people had their hands and noses cut off during interrogation. "Nor was any mercy shown by the invaders for the people," lamented the chronicler, who previous to this had sided with Andrew and the Hungarians in his account of events. No one was immune from prosecution. Members of the highest nobility were threatened with death unless they produced suspects from within their own families. Louis of Hungary's methods were considered extreme, even by a populace inured to the effects of boiling oil and red-hot pincers. One aristocrat "was put to the question in the presence of the king, and confessed everything anyone wanted," Domenico da Gravina recounted. "Louis [of Hungary] chose for him a particularly refined punishment: the condemned man was placed above a wheel outfitted with razor-sharp blades, which as it turned tore him to pieces ... The business lasted from halfway through third mass until well past vespers ... Assuredly it was unheard-of and utterly cruel," the chronicler observed.

Not surprisingly, as a result of policies like these, Louis of

Hungary had difficulty winning over the native baronage, a necessary step toward consolidating his authority over the kingdom. He needed noble families like the Balzos and Sanseverinos as administrators, but the barons and lords of these houses, appalled by Hungarian excesses, refused to cooperate and instead plotted rebellion. (To give a sense of how little the king of Hungary understood his new subjects and their relationship to his late brother, he appropriated property belonging to the Pipini brothers and banished the elder sibling from Naples, a course of action that naturally resulted in the entire family going over to the opposition, where they made a potent contribution.) In the beginning, this rebellion took the form of noncompliance: when the king of Hungary demanded that a count or baron present himself at court and do obeisance to his new sovereign, Louis invariably received the polite reply that, unfortunately, illness prevented the vassal from appearing for an audience.

This excuse took on a new and far more menacing undertone at the end of April with the arrival in Naples of the plague. Boccaccio, who was in the kingdom during the Hungarian occupation, left a searing description of the Black Death in *The Decameron*: "The violence of this disease was such that the sick communicated it to the healthy who came near them, just as a fire catches anything dry or oily near it. And it even went further. To speak to or go near the sick brought infection and a common death to the living; and moreover, to touch the clothes or anything else the sick had touched or worn gave the disease to the person touching . . . Such fear and fanciful notions took possession of the living that almost all of them adopted the same cruel policy, which was entirely to avoid the sick and everything belonging to them . . . What is even worse and nearly incredible is that fathers and mothers refused to see and tend their children, as if they had not been theirs . . . In this way many people died who might have been saved if they had been looked after . . . Many ended their lives in the streets both at night and during the day; and many others who died in their houses were only known to be dead because the neighbors smelled their decaying bodies. Dead bodies filled every corner." It is estimated that within three months the kingdom of Naples lost nearly half its population.

Given these circumstances—a hostile citizenry, the lack of papal support, and the sudden appearance of a terrifying, uncontrollable, mortal disease—Louis of Hungary abruptly reconsidered his decision to remain in southern Italy. On May 24, 1348, accompanied by only a small retinue, he quietly slipped away by ship from the port of Barletta on the eastern coast, leaving the bulk of his army behind. So stealthily did the king retreat that it took nearly a week for many of his new subjects to realize that the invader had gone.

⁂

The news of Louis of Hungary's personal withdrawal, an unlooked-for piece of good fortune, reached Avignon almost as soon as it became widely known in Naples and infused Joanna and her now-legitimate husband with fresh purpose and a sense of immediacy. On May 31, Louis of Taranto dispatched a letter to Florence advising the city that he and the queen were preparing to return to Naples to reclaim the kingdom, and on June 3, Joanna issued a summons to her regional government to appear on June 15 in Aix-en-Provence in order to marshal support for a counteroffensive. But nothing could be done without money, and this was in short supply. Already, the queen had had to pawn all her most valuable possessions, including two velvet-and-gem studded saddles, her jewelry, several gold statuettes, one in the form of an eagle, and even the coronet she had worn to address the consistory, just to pay for her daily living expenses, and these together had brought her only eighteen thousand florins. She needed substantially more than that to mount a war effort.

There was only one way to quickly raise the sum she needed: to sell property. On June 6, the queen and her chief financial adviser, Niccolò Acciaiuoli (now, in recognition of his inestimable service to his sovereign, the new count of Terlizzi), entered into negotiations with the papacy to transfer the city of Avignon to the authority of the church. Clement, who had no intention of returning to Rome, and who had already invested a great deal of money in the papal palace as the new permanent seat of his court, had apparently coveted this consignment for some time. Voluntary alienation of a segment of her realm was not part of Joanna's upbringing; the queen clearly took this step reluctantly and only as a last resort. She intended the transaction to be temporary; she pawned the city as she had pawned her jewels, a standard practice in the Middle Ages. In three subsequent letters the queen made reference to verbal promises the pope had made to her, in the presence of at least one cardinal, that she would be able to redeem Avignon at any time upon repayment of the sum advanced. With this condition agreed to, it took only three days to complete the deal. On June 9, a contract was signed whereby Joanna received eighty thousand gold florins in exchange for delivery of the city of Avignon. Eighteen thousand of this went to redeem the queen's valuables. She wasn't going back to Naples without her crown.

Once these funds were obtained, preparations for Joanna and Louis' departure proceeded at an accelerated pace. On June 11, the queen sent letters to Naples enlisting various high-ranking members of the aristocracy, including members of the Sanseverino and Balzo families and a former admiral of the navy, in the struggle to recover the kingdom. Four days later, the representative assembly at Aix-en-Provence volunteered two hundred knights toward the war effort. And on June 23, Clement issued a bull granting the queen a tenth of all annual church income in Provence, which ordinarily should have been reserved for the prosecution of a crusade, to be used instead to win back her realm. Twelve galleys and an armored vessel were then engaged to carry Joanna and Louis and their forces to

Naples. At this time Joanna also lent the king of Majorca an additional fleet of Provençal ships to assist him in the reclamation of his kingdom, a strong indication that her royal cousin had indeed been of aid to her in her pursuit of papal support.

Encouraging tidings from within the kingdom of Naples arrived in Provence. On June 18, the admiral, in combination with a party of noblemen, forced a confrontation with the enemy and won the engagement; and Niccolò Acciaiuoli's son, Lorenzo, held Melfi, in the very center of the kingdom, against a prolonged siege by the invader. Emboldened by these military successes, the queen's banner had been raised in the capital city of Naples and a delegation sent to Avignon urging Joanna to return to the realm as quickly as possible. It had only taken a few months of Hungarian rule to convince the native aristocracy of the merits of their former sovereign's administration.

The queen was in the final weeks of pregnancy and could not risk a sea voyage, but she sent Niccolò, armed with a quantity of specie and promoted to grand seneschal of the kingdom, ahead to Tuscany to recruit mercenaries and allies. On June 30, she gave birth to a daughter, Catherine, and on July 3 she and Louis of Taranto formally solicited Clement's protection for the child. The next day, the pope made a point of sending letters and emissaries to Joanna's supporters in Naples, encouraging the baronage and church officials to continue in their efforts to resist the Hungarians and advising them to remain loyal to the queen.

By the end of the month, Joanna was ready to travel. She and Louis, together with their fleet, embarked from Nice on August 1; by the 17th they had arrived on the shore just outside Naples. "Since the castles of Naples ... [and] the harbor and the armory were in the hands of the king of Hungary's men, they [Joanna and Louis] could not land at the harbor or in its vicinity; but rather outside of Naples ... where they came ashore," reported Matteo Villani. "Then they went to the church of Notre-Dame to wait for the barons and the ambassadors of Naples, who were to let them into the city." As soon as it was made known that they had landed, a great procession, led by members of the Sanseverino and Balzo families flaunting "ostentatious outfits, with great celebration and joy," arrived to welcome the queen and her husband. The chronicles are unanimous in their descriptions of the rapturous reception with which Joanna and Louis were greeted. "The Florentine, Sienese and Luccan merchants, the Genovese, Provençal and other foreigners were grouped by country of origin, dressed in sumptuous velvet, silk and wool robes and followed by a throng with all sorts of musical instruments," Matteo Villani declared. The *Chronicon Siculum* reported that the whole of the capital city was illuminated in celebration of the homecoming that evening.

While Joanna must have rejoiced at this outpouring of affection, she was under no illusions as to the enormity of the task ahead. The vast majority of the Hungarian army remained in Naples. Louis of Hungary's soldiers held important castles in all the major cities and provinces, including Campania, Aversa, Capua, and Abruzzi. In the capital city itself the enemy held both the Castel Nuovo and the Castel dell'Ovo, and these strongholds were so well supplied and fortified that they were capable of resisting a siege for months, possibly even a year. The queen still had to take back her kingdom.

~❧~

At first, fueled by the momentum of her homecoming, Joanna's side in this conflict made great progress. The castle at Capua was recovered within a month. The army split up in order to cover the maximum possible territory. Louis of Taranto took three thousand mercenaries and fifteen hundred horsemen to Apulia; by December 1 he had retaken Calabria. Joanna stayed behind to besiege the capital with a strong force and was rewarded with the recapture of both the Castel Nuovo and the Castel dell'Ovo when their disgruntled Hungarian occupiers, by now several months in arrears on their salaries, surrendered on January 17, 1349.

But medieval warfare was rarely characterized by a string of unbroken successes, and the reclamation of the kingdom proved to be no exception. Louis of Hungary, hearing of the return of the queen and of Louis of Taranto's victories, made plans to return to Naples with reinforcements. The Hungarian army, buoyed by this information, regrouped at Foggia and beat back the queen's forces. Louis of Taranto, frustrated and bitter, particularly at a lack of promised support from Florence, was forced to retreat to the capital. He arrived in February, at which point the war entered a new and distinctly less promising stage.

The decline in military fortunes was accompanied by a similar and far more ominous deterioration in the conjugal relations between the queen and her champion. Their daughter, Catherine, died about this time, and this would have added an extra strain to their intimacy. But even given the adverse conditions in Naples during the spring of 1349, the speed with which Joanna's marriage collapsed is breathtaking. Within two months of Louis of Taranto's return to the capital, Joanna and her husband were engaged in a fierce struggle for power marked by the arrest of her chamberlain Enrico Caracciolo on a trumped-up charge of having engaged in adulterous relations with the queen.

The accusations against Joanna and Enrico were clearly false; this was a coup d'état by Louis of Taranto orchestrated by Niccolò Acciaiuoli and his cousin the bishop of Florence, now keeper of the royal seal. Enrico, one of those members of Joanna's household who had fled the capital with her only to be detained in Provence under suspicion of complicity in Andrew's murder, had been freed along with the rest of Joanna's household by Clement after her acquittal in consistory. He had then accompanied his sovereign on her return to Naples the previous August. Enrico made a very convenient pawn; in just this way had Louis of Taranto's father, Philip of Taranto, rid himself of his first wife in order to marry the empress of Constantinople. Likely, Joanna's second husband never cared for her and had seen the marriage only as a conduit to power, a salient truth that the pope, who instantly took the queen's side in this affair, did not fail to note. In a letter dated September 4, 1349, Clement wrote to Louis:

> Although of royal birth, you were by inheritance poorly off. By your union with the Queen, who openly honored you with preference above your kindred, you have become possessed of abundance and an exalted position. We were not unnaturally hopeful that in return you would prove grateful to her, and show her the affection which is not only her due, but would benefit your own honor. You, however, as is a matter of common report (and we are sadly surprised to hear it), forgetful of all of this, not merely do not treat her as behooves a wife and a Queen, but scornfully curtailing the area of her prerogative, you have caused her to be reckoned rather a slave than a spouse. It is further reported that, ruled by the promptings of advisers (at whose mere nod you make and unmake the administration of the kingdom, to which she so affectionately admitted you), you have deprived her of the society and audience of her trusted servants, so that without your permission and that of the aforesaid advisers, no one is given speech of her. Moreover, you have taken the royal seal and handed it over to the Bishop of Florence and certain others, who, it is said, in the face of the Queen's protest, and greatly to her prejudice, impudently seal letters of state concerning all things, both important and unimportant, under her name and title . . . For the rest, since, as we understand, the Queen, conscious of her innocence, fears for her good fame on account of the imprisonment of Enrico Caracciolo . . . we exhort you,

out of consideration for her ... to act with clemency and defer to her wishes.

Joanna hotly defended herself against the charge of adultery in a subsequent letter to Clement, written on November 12, which demonstrates that the queen was well aware of what was said of her and how the strategy of adding new insinuations to those for which she already stood accused was being employed deliberately to undermine public confidence in her ability to rule.

Most blessed Father (in Christ), your letters touching ... my husband and privately certain of my affairs, have been respectfully received ... I proffer a humble oblation of thanks to the Holy Father, and trust that it may be agreeable to him that the investigation should lie with him ... For I call God to witness (nor do I misdoubt the testimony of my lord and husband himself) that I have never licentiously done anything derogatory to his honor, or forgotten either due respect or submission to him. If, however, occasionally, in domestic confidence (as between man and wife is wont to occur), I am accused of annoying unthinkingly, there was no aversion, nor does there exist any (far be such), but rather (it was intended) to stimulate the force of stronger love ... I admit that I preferred him in marriage to all the princes; and still I prefer him to all other men to the degree that I trust no other but him ... I shall none the less strive to comfort myself that the truth of my words will more and more become confirmed. Verily, what with those things alleged to the weight of my transgression, concerning my impatience with my former husband [Andrew], and my annoyance arising out of the arrest of Enrico Caracciolo ... I am vexed beyond measure; now this and now that, heaped up or over-colored by repetition, these greater actions are put down to a predilection for disorder, those lesser, to unlawful lapses of the passions. But indeed it shall be my consolation to make manifest my innocence, to preserve indifference to the tongues of slander, and to submit myself as a daughter to the judgment of your Holiness, whose integrity is infallible.

Relations between husband and wife did not improve, even though by the time the queen wrote this letter, she was pregnant again, clearly by Louis as Enrico had been in captivity for the previous seven months. Joanna was forced to cede power to her husband, upon whom she had generously bestowed the title of count of Provence while the couple were still in Avignon. Now Louis of Taranto used this position to countermand orders and appointments the queen had made previously. The situation was only made worse by her sister Maria, who, having been left destitute by the assassination of Charles of Durazzo, had returned to Naples to demand the remainder of her substantial dowry from the queen. Since by now the king of Hungary had also returned to the kingdom, accompanied by yet another large army, and the crown obviously needed every florin to prosecute the war, the time was hardly convenient to pay out a large sum. When Joanna denied her sister's request, a wrathful Maria moved into the Castel dell'Ovo with her children by her side and treachery in her heart.

The arrival of Joanna's third child, disappointingly another daughter, Françoise, in March of the following year, provoked a crisis. Enrico Caracciolo had by this time been executed, and Louis of Taranto had Joanna under virtual house arrest, where he further menaced the queen with threats of death or life imprisonment. No one was allowed to speak with Joanna unless her husband was present, and rumors abounded that Louis of Taranto intended to kill her. The queen did her best to circumvent her persecutor by smuggling a secret emissary to Avignon with instructions to convey the perilous nature of her position to the pope. This, clearly, her ambassador did, as on April 17, Clement, who by this time had learned to listen to death threats emanating out of Naples, wrote to the doge of Genoa: "The quarrel between Louis and the queen, if one reads all of their letters, puts the life of Joanna in danger. Protect her!" Genoa, which had promised ships to Louis of Hungary, retracted them and from this point on supported the queen's side in the war. The papacy then directed a steady stream of letters to Naples instructing all parties, including the Acciaiuolis, to restore peaceful relations between husband and wife.

By June, Louis of Hungary and his army had arrived outside the gates of Aversa, which were closed to the invader, and had begun a siege of the city. The nearness of the king prompted a new subterfuge involving Joanna's sister, Maria. Louis of Hungary's young wife, Margaret of Bohemia, had died the previous year, fueling speculation that the situation in Naples might now be resolved through matrimony rather than warfare. The captive princes of the houses of Taranto and Durazzo, who despite the papacy's best efforts were still being held prisoner in Visegrád, put forward Maria's name as a possible candidate as an inducement toward their liberation, even though the king of Hungary had been responsible for murdering Charles of Durazzo and causing his widow to flee for her life. Astoundingly, Maria was receptive to the idea of marrying her husband's assassin. The widowed duchess of Durazzo quietly dispatched one of her own household, an emissary named Marino Rumbo, to meet with the king at the small village of Trentola outside Aversa to negotiate the terms of the marriage contract. According to the *Chronique of Parthénope*, "After deliberation with the royal family who remained prisoner in Hungary, the king of Hungary made a secret accord with Madame Maria to make a marriage with her which dictated that the king would receive the dominion of the realm of Sicily [Naples] while Queen Joanna would remain countess of Provence." A document to this effect was actually drawn up and sealed by both parties.

But, as futile as the situation might appear, Joanna was far from helpless. By her performance in consistory, the queen had made a powerful ally of the pope, and she still retained many faithful subjects in Provence who were angry that Louis of Taranto had usurped power from Robert the Wise's legitimate heir. These supporters now came to her aid. The pope dispatched Hugo del Balzo, the count of Avellino—the same Hugo del Balzo whom Clement had sent in the aftermath of Andrew's murder to prosecute Joanna's favorites—and a nuncio, the bishop of Saint-Omer, to Naples to intervene on the queen's behalf. Suspecting that a show of force might be necessary, Hugo took the precaution of recruiting a squadron of loyalists, mostly from Marseille, before embarking for the kingdom.

Thus, on or around July 20, 1350, the people of Naples awoke to find a fleet of six galleys filled with armed men from Marseille and flying the banners of the church and the queen of Naples (but not, significantly, those of Louis of Taranto) anchored off the coast between the Castel Nuovo and the Castel dell'Ovo. Louis sent representatives to discover the count of Avellino's intentions, to whom Hugo replied that he was in Naples at the request of the pope, who had instructed him to ensure the reestablishment of harmonious relations between Joanna and her husband. The bishop of Saint-Omer then requested a private audience with the queen, which Louis dared not forbid. This was the first time in nearly a year that Joanna had been allowed to speak to an ally without her husband's being present. There is no record of what the pair discussed. When he emerged, the bishop merely said that he was happy to find the queen in such good spirits and then left for Aversa to meet with the king of Hungary, leaving Hugo to rescue the queen.

This the count of Avellino did quite effectively by enlisting the aid of the Neapolitan population against Louis of Taranto, a strategy with which the courtier had some experience. He began by spreading the rumor that Joanna's husband was trying to poison her, and announced that he would use his men and ships to besiege the Castel Nuovo in order to save her. He further threatened that if Louis of Taranto continued to resist the pope's authority, and the people of Naples did not take measures to help reinstate their legitimate sovereign, the queen, then the pope (as represented by Hugo) would side with the king of Hungary and use his fleet to conquer the city. However, if the citizenry obeyed the instructions of the church and helped convince Louis of Taranto to surrender power to his wife, then Hugo promised to force the Hungarian army to retreat and to establish a lasting peace with its king. According to the *Chronicon Siculum*, during the two weeks or so that the count of Avellino was delivering this message, the sailors on board the galleys would regularly chant "Long Live the Pope! Long Live the Queen! Down with Louis of Taranto!," just in case any of the general population were in doubt as to the official church position on this matter.

Faced with the implacable resistance of the pope, and a growing resentment among his fellow countrymen, Louis of Taranto abruptly capitulated. By August he had drafted and signed an official edict acknowledging the queen as the sole ruler of Provence and had accepted Clement's decision, as stipulated in a July 20 letter from the papal court, that as Joanna's consort he could be crowned king if he desired but in name only; under no circumstances would he have a say in her government nor in any way trespass upon her prerogative. On August 17, in recognition of the reestablishment of her authority, Joanna immediately named a new seneschal of Provence, replacing her husband's former appointment, and two days later she sent a letter to Clement, thanking him profusely for his intervention. Nor did the queen forget her true deliverers: on September 2, she sent a special emissary to Provence with a letter conveying her "best love" to the people of Marseille.

While this drama was unfolding in the capital, the bishop of Saint-Omer was busy negotiating a truce with Louis of Hungary, which went into effect in September. According to the *Chronicon Siculum*, the king of Hungary formally agreed to a suspension of all

Robert the Wise (kneeling) being crowned by his older brother, St. Louis – a famous scene which never occurred since Louis died in 1297, twelve years before Robert was crowned by Clement V.

The coronation of Pope Clement VII, 1378.

A view of Naples
in the Middle Ages
including the Castel
dell'Ovo on the
bay and the Castel
Sant'Elmo on the
hill.

Illustration from
a Hungarian book
of saints, called
a Legendary,
commissioned by
Carobert in 1333 and
most likely presented
to Andrew to further
his education while
in Naples.

An example of
manuscript art
created at the court
of Naples during the
reign of King Robert,
a very different
aesthetic to Andrew's
Hungarian Legendary.

Distribution of grain in Florence during the famine of 1335. Losses incurred at this time forced the super-companies to look to Edward III and the English wool market for new profits.

Burying victims of plague in 1349.

The Battle of Crécy, 1346.

King John the Good surrenders to the Black Prince in 1356 at the Battle of Poitiers, in an illustration from the *Chronicles* of Jean Froissart.

Two scenes from *The Sacrament of Marriage*, commissioned by Joanna to ornament the church of Santa Maria Incoronata in the early 1360s. The frescoes were painted by Roberto Oderisio, a disciple of Giotto and Joanna's court painter.

An illustration of knights jousting for Queen Joanna and the ladies of Naples, from a manuscript produced for Louis of Taranto in the 1350s.

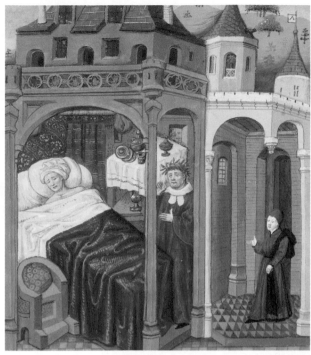

Petrarch appearing to Boccaccio in his sleep.

The *Via Veritatis*, or Way of Salvation. Joanna, crowned with blonde hair, is kneeling, third to the inside; beside her is Catherine of Sweden, with Lapa Acciaiuoli on the end in profile. St. Bridget of Sweden is behind her daughter in black.

Joanna, crowned, on her knees and wearing her robe of state (golden Angevin lilies on a blue background), praying to the Madonna and Child for an heir, one of only two surviving images of the queen painted during her lifetime.

Detail of Joanna I.

hostilities for a period of six months, or until April 1351, with the caveat that each opposing force held its territorial gains. This meant that the Hungarian army, which had just taken Aversa after a prolonged siege, would remain in that city, while the queen's forces stayed in Naples. During the truce, as a gesture to the Hungarians, the papacy agreed to try Joanna again for the murder of her husband. If she was found guilty, she would lose her kingdom, which would then go to Maria. (Since the king of Hungary expected to marry Maria, a scheme that the bishop of Saint-Omer had been told to encourage for the time being, this condition was considered acceptable.) If Joanna was found innocent, however, Louis of Hungary would give up his claim to the kingdom and forfeit all the land and castles he occupied in Naples, which would then be returned to the queen. To sweeten the deal, no matter what the outcome of this second inquest, Joanna was also required to pay her adversary three hundred thousand florins, ostensibly to ransom the captured members of the royal family but in reality to pay off the king of Hungary to accept the terms of the treaty. Lastly, during the six-month period of the truce, while the outcome of the criminal proceedings remained in doubt, all the principal combatants—the king of Hungary, Joanna, and Louis of Taranto—were required to leave the kingdom.

There are many reasons why Louis of Hungary, despite his initial military successes, decided to accept this deal. The citizens of Aversa had put up significantly more resistance this time than they had previously, and the king had sustained a serious leg wound as a result of the hostilities. Matteo Villani reported: "The king of Hungary had attacked Aversa at length with strong forces and despite its weak defenses and scant fortifications, had failed to conquer the town by either assault or siege; he thought the other, larger and stronger cities would prove even more strenuous to conquer as they were in the hands of his enemies and his difficulties in conquering Aversa would increase their resistance. Also, his barons had completed the military service they owed him; to keep them to help him conquer the kingdom meant to pay them, and he had little money and could not get more from a country that had been ravaged by war. He saw that Louis of Taranto, his vassals and supporters were prepared to defend their walls. Thus he changed his mind easily, ready to agree to a compromise that would allow him to leave the kingdom without losing face."

For their part, Joanna and Louis of Taranto, having tried to reclaim the kingdom with mixed results, were also amenable to this arrangement. "As for Louis of Taranto," Matteo Villani continued, "he was reduced to being unable not only to resist the enemy, but even to face the most basic expenses for survival. And if the Neapolitans had not agreed to defend him and the Queen, they couldn't have stayed. In this context, a few mediators meddled and easily obtained an agreement." To a warrior like Joanna's husband, however, the terms of the peace treaty hinted faintly of dishonor. To remedy the situation, he challenged his opponent to a duel, to be held for fairness in the presence of either the pope or the king of France. Louis of Hungary countered by agreeing to single combat only if it were adjudicated by the Holy Roman Emperor or the king of England. Since neither man was willing to fight on the other's turf, the proposed competition never materialized.

Joanna, having pleaded her case so successfully the first time, did not fear the outcome of a second inquest, so she raised no objection to this condition. The queen did, however, protest the magnitude of the ransom she would be required to pay, and she eventually convinced Clement to advance the funds for her, pending her guarantee that she would reimburse the church at a later date.

Both sides having formally accepted this agreement, the principals made good on their pledge to withdraw from the kingdom. On September 17, Louis of Hungary quit Aversa for Rome, leaving a force of five thousand knights under the direction of the voivode of Transylvania, the regional governor. Joanna appointed Francisco del Balzo, a relative of Hugo's, to govern Naples in her absence before she and Louis of Taranto also embarked for Rome on September 17. Hugo del Balzo graciously offered the royal couple his own vessel for the journey, and the queen and her husband sailed out of the harbor accompanied by three of the galleys from Marseille. The count of Avellino delayed his own departure, remaining behind with the other two ships, ostensibly to ensure a smooth transition in the queen's absence, although he promised to catch up with Joanna and her party before she reached Rome.

No sooner had the galleys left Naples, however, than Hugo del Balzo put into motion a plot that seems to have been concealed from both Joanna and Louis of Taranto. In a sign that Clement had had enough of Hungarian demands for sovereignty over Naples, and considered the negotiated peace settlement the last word on the subject, Hugo had remained behind specifically to marry his own son Robert, who had accompanied his father to Naples, to the widowed duchess of Durazzo. As the pope's instrument, Hugo would not have taken such a step without prior approval. But as the marriage represented a debasement for Maria—the Balzo family were not members of royalty—Joanna would have been expected to object to the match, and for this reason was not informed of the scheme. Neither, as it turned out, was Maria. This was a unilateral action taken both to thwart the duchess of Durazzo's secret compact with Louis of Hungary and as a reward to the count of Avellino for services rendered. As such, at least in Hugo's opinion, there was no need to consult the wishes of the prospective bride.

Accordingly, the chronicles, utilizing varying degrees of detail, report that Robert del Balzo, under orders and in the presence of his father, raped Maria in order to effect the desired nuptials. "On September 29," the *Chronicon Siculum* reported, "the count of Avellino entered the Castel dell'Ovo, took Madame Maria, the duchess of Durazzo, and married her to his son." "The count went to the castle with a small escort to visit Maria before leaving," Matteo

Villani agreed. "Unawares, the duchess asked that the doors be opened so that he could enter freely. He walked in with his two sons and his armed close counselors whom he ordered to guard the doors and the castle. When he [Hugo] arrived in the presence of the duchess, he said he wanted her to marry his son Robert, and had the marriage consummated by force."

Even setting aside the brutality of his action, the presumptuousness displayed by Hugo—in allying his son to Maria he put his family in line to one day possibly inherit the throne of Naples— was startling and resulted in his swift downfall. When Hugo, with Robert and Maria in tow, rendezvoused in Gaeta with Joanna on October 7, news of her sister's ordeal leaked out to the queen's party. Matteo Villani reported that Joanna was profoundly outraged at Hugo del Balzo's betrayal. Louis of Taranto, still smarting from the humiliation of having to cede power to his wife that had been imposed on him by the count of Avellino and aching to relieve his feelings, saw his opportunity. When the crew of Hugo del Balzo's ship took shore leave, they were bribed by Joanna's husband to remain on land and betray their master, who was still on deck recovering from an attack of gout. Louis then armed himself and, accompanied by a small party of warriors, boarded the count of Avellino's vessel and there stabbed Hugo repeatedly with his sword before throwing the corpse of his victim into the sea. Robert del Balzo was arrested; the liberated duchess of Durazzo came ashore and spent the winter in Gaeta with her sister and her sister's husband. The prisoner was eventually transported to a dungeon at the Castel dell'Ovo, where, despite Clement's plea in a letter of February 1, 1351, to Louis of Taranto to spare the son punishment for the sins of the father, Robert was executed. Matteo Villani affirmed that the duchess of Durazzo was herself responsible for Robert del Balzo's death. While Joanna, her husband, and the rest of the court were away on a holiday outside the capital city, Maria stole into the Castel dell'Ovo with four armed men she had hired for the purpose and had her former assailant hacked to pieces in her presence as an effective warning to those who would presume upon the dignity of a royal princess of the house of Anjou in the future.

~

The lurid termination of this episode marked the end of hostilities between the kingdoms of Naples and Hungary. By the end of October 1350, Louis of Hungary had left Rome for Visegrád, never to return. In February 1351, Louis of Taranto and Niccolò Acciaiuoli came back to the kingdom and liberated Aversa; Joanna and her sister traveled separately by sea. "At the end of the month of February, the king [Louis of Taranto], the queen, and the duchess of Durazzo, reentered the capital city of Naples," the *Chronicon Siculum* reported. Despite the clause in the peace treaty, there is no record of Clement's having convened a new tribunal in order to further investigate Joanna's role in her first husband's death. Certainly, she was not required to make an appearance in either Rome or Avignon in order to give evidence again. The Hungarians must have finally given up or lost interest, as the absence of the inquest did not affect the pace of reconciliation. By June 14, Niccolò Acciaiuoli was able to write: "The general accord between our masters and the king of Hungary has been accepted by both sides, the princes are being liberated, and we have peace." There remained the crippling obligation of the ransom, but even this issue was resolved in Naples's favor. When on December 28, 1351, after stalling for months, Joanna finally sent Clement the repayment guarantee he had demanded for agreeing to forward the three hundred thousand florins on her behalf, Louis of Hungary, in a burst of chivalry, surprised everyone by suddenly forgiving the debt, citing as his reason to the pope: "Because he did not go to war for greed, but to avenge the death of his brother," Matteo Villani explained.

The spring of 1352 was marked by joy and a new spirit of

cooperation between Joanna and her husband, an ebullience scheduled to culminate in May with the celebration of an elaborate double
coronation. In January, Louis of Taranto had formally agreed to all
the limitations to his kingship that Andrew's family had previously
rejected, including the recognition of his wife's prerogative. He was
to be crowned as king consort only; his children by Joanna could
inherit the throne (by this time it was known in Naples that little
Charles Martel had died) but recognition of his title would not survive her death: if Joanna died without heirs, the kingdom would go
to Maria. Robert the Wise's legitimacy as sovereign was finally fully
established, and the hierarchy of succession remained in principle
as delineated by his will.

Pleased by Louis of Taranto's new compliancy, Joanna actively
and enthusiastically embraced the notion of a double coronation
as a means of stabilizing her relationship with her husband and
ensuring the safety and welfare of her kingdom. What she had
wanted most was official recognition of her inherited right to rule,
and once that issue was resolved, she volunteered to work together
with Louis in the interests of reform and unity. There was both a
sense of fairness and practicality in this gesture. She must have recognized that, more than anyone else, Louis of Taranto was responsible for Joanna's regaining her birthright; he had led her armies and
made the conquest of the realm sufficiently difficult that her Hungarian brother-in-law saw fit to accept a negotiated settlement. And
the kingdom still needed him: there were yet castles in the hands of
enemy soldiers, and these men had to be encouraged to leave their
posts quietly. Criminal activity, such as looting and robbery, also
had to be inhibited and boundaries secured against future
aggressors.

The result of this unaccustomed political accord was a number
of forward-looking edicts issued in the names of both the queen
and the prospective king and bearing both their seals. One of the
most intelligent was the proclamation, on April 7, 1352, of a general

amnesty toward those of their subjects who had cooperated with or supported the Hungarians during the invasion. This decree included not only a full pardon but also the restitution of all goods confiscated by the crown during the war, a generous decision that won Joanna and Louis much support from their former opponents in the kingdom. However, the queen's newfound collaboration with her husband was not so trusting that she did not take measures to protect herself. Although she allowed the chancellor of the realm to retain possession of the grand seal, as was customary, she insisted on keeping her personal seal in her own chambers, so that it could not be used against her, an indication perhaps that Joanna had not forgotten, much less forgiven, Louis' earlier treachery.

The rest of April was taken up with preparations for the coronation. The event was conceived on a scale to rival the celebrations hosted by the court during the days of Robert the Wise, when spectacle was used deliberately as a means of establishing political legitimacy. Invitations were dispatched by courier to allies as far away as Provence, Siena, and Florence. Noble families from every corner of the kingdom were summoned. High-ranking syndics and churchmen were required to attend. The pope sent a special emissary to perform the ceremony in his name. Joanna and Louis had requested that a cardinal officiate, but Clement, fearful of provoking Hungarian ire again by a too-obvious favoritism toward Naples, sent the archbishop of Braga instead. Church approval was reflected in the speedy arrival of the ecclesiastic on the shores of Naples—for once the papal representative managed to arrive on time.

Finances were a problem—the royal treasury had been almost completely depleted by the war—but this did not deter the queen in her expenditure. The populace would expect opulence, and after years of hardship, Joanna was determined to give it to them. She spent lavishly—over five thousand florins for jewels alone—and solved the difficulty by sending the bill abroad. On April 26, the queen signed an official order for payment to her seneschal in

Provence: "In conjunction with our festive coronation to be celebrated on Pentecost [mid-May] ... we owe to two Florentine noblemen, in return for an advance of 4,371 florins and a three part share
of our other expenses listed below, namely: twenty-eight girdles
adorned with silver in diverse designs; a tunic of pearls and silk;
two silver swords, one a dagger; 115 strings of amber [rosary] beads
for Paternoster; ... two silver saddles for our horses; a goblet of
crystal and silver ... twelve barrels of beer with silver tankards; two
staffs of silver; ten pearls fastened in golden rings; four diamonds
fastened in golden rings; thirty-nine mother-of-pearl buttons
adorned with gold and precious stones; twelve brooches suitable for
wearing on the chest, from gold and silver; six red semi-precious
gems ... three rubies, six emeralds, seventeen sapphires and a pearl
and sapphire ring."

The ceremony, which was preceded for days by festive public
entertainments such as pageants, jousts, games, and other merry-
making, was held on May 27, 1352, the feast of Pentecost. As a
gesture to Louis, the coronation service was conducted inside the
ancestral palace of the house of Taranto. In front of the massed
assembly of the court and invited guests, the archbishop of Braga,
after an official benediction, placed crowns, first on the head of
Louis, then Joanna, and anointed both with holy oil. The religious
rite concluded, the king and queen seated themselves on their
respective thrones and proceeded to receive the homage of their
barons. Only Maria, who had come so close to ruling Naples herself
and was reduced by this ceremony and her sister's priority once again
to the nebulous condition of stand-in, refused to do obeisance to
her sister and brother-in-law. Since her return to Naples, she had
remained destitute, and Louis of Taranto, perhaps not unreasonably
given her attitude and past behavior, had worsened matters by ordering that she and her children be confined to the Castel dell'Ovo to
prevent further treason with Hungary. Clement eventually negotiated an accord whereby Maria won her release by agreeing to do

homage for her lands in a private ceremony conducted in October.

The rite of homage was followed by a triumphant procession through the streets of Naples, to allow the citizenry a view of the spectacle. According to Matteo Villani, an ominous incident occurred during the parade, which foreshadowed an even greater tragedy. The narrow streets of Naples were crowded with onlookers, which made the horses, whose jeweled bridles were held by grooms, jumpy. When a gentlewoman coquettishly threw a bouquet of flowers down to Louis of Taranto from the balcony where she was standing, the king's horse suddenly shied, and Louis was forced to leap from his saddle to avoid injury. In the act of saving himself, his crown flew off his head and broke into three pieces on the cobblestones. This was naturally taken by those who witnessed the accident as an evil omen, but Louis simply laughed it off and, calling for another horse, fitted the crown together as best he could, replaced it on his head, and continued to ride with Joanna until they had finished their rounds. But superstition won out nonetheless; throughout her life, the queen of Naples was fated never to experience joy unalleviated by grief. Weary but elated, Joanna, accompanied by her husband, finally returned home to the Castel Nuovo at the end of the evening only to find the household in devastated mourning: during her absence, two-year-old Françoise, her only surviving child and the heir to the throne, had been stricken with a fatal illness and died.

In the decade succeeding the death of her grandfather, Joanna had weathered murder, treason, civil unrest, the death by excruciating torture of her best friend and surrogate mother, exile, a trial for her life, plague, war, treachery, and finally, the anguishing loss of all three of her children. Her sacrifice was matched only by her determination to prevail. For all the sorrow, no monarch in Europe had fought harder for his kingdom than the queen of Naples, nor succeeded so convincingly in the face of such odds.

~⪧~

CHAPTER XII

Foreign *and* Domestic Relations

NOTHING IN JOANNA's background could have prepared her for the devastation that greeted her on her return to power. Plague, followed closely by the brutal invasion and the prolonged destruction of an extended war, had decimated the realm. The statistics are so dire that they defy imagination. In one three-month period, half the inhabitants of the capital city succumbed. Additionally, one third of the kingdom's towns and villages suddenly disappeared or were abandoned, particularly in the low-lying regions of Apulia and Abruzzi. Nor was Naples unique. The population of Florence dropped from eighty thousand to thirty thousand. Pisa, which began the century with fifty thousand citizens, recorded less than ten thousand still living in the town in 1428. The story was the same in every major city in Europe stricken by the Black Death. "Is it possible," wrote Petrarch after experiencing the plague in Avignon, "that posterity will believe these things? For we who have seen them can hardly do so."

Those who had managed to survive the onslaught wrought by nature had then to contend with the hardships inflicted by war. The Hungarian army had deliberately destroyed homes and fields both to punish loyalists and to deprive the opposition of food and supplies. "I found my Pouilles lands [in Apulia] in a pitiable state and poverty-stricken such that, far from being able to extract any harvest, I had to provide so that its inhabitants wouldn't abandon them for a better life elsewhere," Niccolò Acciaiuoli wrote in a letter to one of his Florentine relatives in 1352. "I must still have my castles watched carefully, so recent is the disease we just bore." Niccolò was wise to be vigilant. The plague would strike Italy again in 1362, and once more in 1373, further frightening the inhabitants and depressing birth rates. The capital city of Naples would not regain its former population level for 150 years.

Such poverty and desperation bred lawlessness on a scale that dwarfed former experience. With the advent of peace, the thousands of mercenaries who had been recruited by the Hungarians and the Neapolitans found themselves lacking employment. Accustomed to a life of pillage and threat in the cause of one monarch or another, they organized themselves into large groups and continued their former activities for their own benefit. The "free companies," as these criminal gangs became known, preyed upon the citizenry, extorting protection money from towns and villages and waylaying merchants and innocent travelers.

Economic recovery was impossible under these conditions, so one of the first steps Joanna took after her coronation was to appoint a new chief justice and provide him with the means and authority to vanquish the outlaws. "Followed by 400 horsemen," Matteo Villani reported, "he [the chief justice] rode across the kingdom, pursued criminals, brought barons and townships to compliance, insisted on collecting taxes and ensured that feudal services were carried out. Thanks to him, roads became free and safe." Boccaccio, writing in 1362 about Joanna in his treatise *Famous Women*, agreed: "If we examine her domain closely, our amazement will equal its fame, for it is a mighty realm of the sort not usually ruled by women. Yet far more admirable is the fact that Joanna's spirit is equal to its governance, so well has she preserved the luminous character of her ancestors. For example, after she was crowned with the royal diadem, Joanna bravely took action and cleansed not only the cities and inhabited areas but also the Alpine regions, remote valleys, forests and wild places from bands of outlaws ... and the siege of these places was not lifted until their strongholds had been captured and the accursed men inside executed. No previous king had been willing or able to do this."

Within two years of her coronation, Naples was able to begin producing grain again—not at the same heady levels that had once encouraged the growth of the super-companies, for the labor force available to achieve that goal no longer existed—but harvests sufficient to meet the kingdom's own needs and even a little for export.

This strong beginning was soon challenged by malevolent forces outside the queen's control, both at home and abroad. The first obstacle came upon the death, on December 6, 1352, of Clement VI.

***

With Clement's passing, from an internal rupture, Joanna and her kingdom lost an advocate whose power and influence rivaled that of her original sponsor, Robert the Wise. Just as important, because the queen had known the pontiff personally and was well acquainted with his manner and habits, she had been able to anticipate his response to any given situation. But suddenly, Clement was gone and in his place was an unfamiliar cardinal who had taken the name Innocent VI.

Innocent was a lawyer by training and an ascetic by temperament. His election, orchestrated in a mere forty-eight hours by Cardinal Talleyrand of Périgord, was designed to deflect the charges of corruption and high living that had tainted Clement's regime. Even so, Innocent was a compromise candidate. Originally, the cardinals had thought to elect the prior general of the Carthusian order, a man

renowned for piety, but were apparently talked out of it by Talleyrand. "My Lords Cardinal, you don't know what you're doing," Talleyrand retorted, according to an unnamed chronicler of the period.
"Surely you must realize that the Carthusian prior will be moved
by such justice, rigor, and righteousness, that if we elect him pope
he will certainly set us back in our old condition. Why, within four
months our mounts will be dragging horse-carts. He fears no one,
and in his zeal for Mother Church he has all the confidence of a
lion!" Whether this story is true is unclear; there were other objections, of a more practical political consideration, to the candidacy
of a Carthusian prior. Innocent's election, on the other hand, is
readily explained. He was already in his sixties, in poor health, and
was often swayed by the more powerful personalities surrounding
him. "No doubt the Sacred College hoped to mould him easily to
its wishes."

The new pope could not have been more different from his predecessor. Where Clement had been generous and expansive, spending lavishly and welcoming supplicants and their bribes to Avignon,
Innocent's first action was to require all beneficed priests to return
to their benefices, with disobedience punishable by excommunication. "In this way he emptied the Papal Palace of a crowd of useless
courtiers, whose only occupation was intrigue and money-making.
Naturally frugal . . . he banished all splendor from his Court . . . he
required the Cardinals, many of whom were given up to luxury and
had amassed great wealth, to follow his example." Already an old
man when he assumed his post, Innocent was inclined to be short-
tempered and querulous. He ate sparingly and was prone to many
physical ailments, which did not improve his mood. Nor did his
advanced age unduly affect or abbreviate his pontificate. He managed to hold on stubbornly for a full decade.

Aware that he owed his office to Talleyrand, Innocent followed
his benefactor's advice in most matters, especially during the early
years of his pontificate. And although the cardinal of Périgord had

in the past allied himself with the queen of Naples when her interests coincided with his own, this had not been the case for some time. Talleyrand was keenly interested in the welfare and advancement of his nephews, the younger princes of Durazzo, who had been held captive by the king of Hungary since the beginning of the war. He had opposed the double coronation of Joanna and Louis of Taranto as according too much power to the Taranto family over that of the Durazzo, but he had been overruled by Clement. With Clement dead and the hostages, freed by the peace treaty, on their way home to Naples, Talleyrand was determined to protect his family's birthright and ascendancy in the kingdom. Louis was equally resolved to maintain Taranto supremacy over that of his cousins, drawing the lines for confrontation.

In this atmosphere of disquiet, the captive princes, both Durazzo and Taranto, straggled home. If the king of Hungary had had any idea how much trouble they would cause, he would have let them out much earlier.

~⊹~

Robert of Taranto was the first to return to Naples, arriving in the spring of 1353, followed closely by his younger brother Philip. The new king of Naples restored enough of his family's former estate to his older brother to merit, if not his loyalty, at least his outward compliance. Philip's settlement was smaller, but Louis of Taranto made known his intention to safeguard his younger brother's interests by marrying him to Joanna's sister, Maria, who, having rid herself of her second husband, Robert del Balzo, in so convincing a manner, was once again unattached. Maria's opinion of this prospective arrangement was of no concern to Louis of Taranto. Despite having taking the oath of homage to Joanna and Louis, Maria was still viewed with suspicion. To ensure her good behavior, all four of her daughters, any one of whom might one day inherit the throne, had been placed under Joanna's guardianship, while the king of Naples kept control of their considerable assets himself. Still, as long as the duchess of Durazzo remained single, she posed a threat to the monarchy, as any potential husband could rally support from among the disaffected and make a claim to the throne of Naples through his wife. For this reason Louis of Taranto was determined to marry her safely to his brother Philip.

This arrangement provoked vociferous opposition from the two remaining Durazzo brothers, Louis and Robert. Upon his return to the kingdom in the summer of 1353, Louis of Durazzo, the oldest surviving member of Agnes of Périgord's brood, tried to recover both his ancestral estate and his nieces' property but was rebuffed. The youngest Durazzo brother, Robert, did not bother to return to the realm at all but went straight to the court of his powerful uncle in Avignon to see what could be done to improve his prospects. Robert of Durazzo was particularly hotheaded and pugnacious. Upon his release from captivity, not content with slipping away quietly like his brother, Robert had instead brazenly challenged Louis of Hungary to a duel, an unhelpful maneuver that exasperated the rest of the family and very nearly provoked renewed hostilities with that kingdom.

The cardinal of Périgord immediately took up his Durazzo nephews' cause, advising Innocent VI to prevent the marriage of Maria to Philip of Taranto and demanding that the pope try to force Joanna's husband to relinquish Maria's daughters' assets to the care of their uncle Louis of Durazzo. Talleyrand also took steps to secure Robert of Durazzo's fortune by engaging his young kinsman to a niece of the wealthy Giovanni Visconti of Milan, in the hopes that Robert could then use his wife's money and her family's military prowess to recover Naples for the Durazzos.

Joanna's official stance toward the Durazzos and her attitude in connection to the proposed marriage of her sister to Philip of Taranto is difficult to pinpoint, chiefly because her relationship with her own husband during this period was so pernicious. The death of their one remaining child, Françoise, had apparently shattered whatever fragile equilibrium existed between the couple in the months preceding their coronation. Although Louis of Taranto had promised in writing not to impinge on Joanna's sovereignty, he experienced no such qualms when it came to imposing his authority over her in their private lives. Matteo Villani put it bluntly: "He honored the Queen little; whether this was his fault (and his responsibility was great) or that of the Queen, he often beat her as one would a lowly woman, to the great shame of the Crown." Joanna herself complained in a letter to Innocent VI in December 1353 that she was "humiliated" and "anguished" in her relations with her husband. He cheated on her regularly and fathered at least three children by other women. Joanna, on the other hand, had no more pregnancies with Louis after Françoise. Although she clearly loathed him, this did not necessarily imply a severing of cohabitation. After he died, she refused to wed the king of France's son, another Valois, on the grounds that marrying too closely within the family led to "sterility in her times of fertility" and the early death of children, an indication that she had continued trying to conceive an heir with Louis but had been unsuccessful.

So whether she disapproved of Louis' promoting his family's interests over those of the Durazzos and was simply unable to control her husband's actions, or whether she hated him but in general approved these policies, is difficult to say. What is known is that she cared for her sister's children as though they were her own, particularly her youngest niece, Margherita, the baby born in Avignon after Maria fled there on the death of Charles of Durazzo. The most likely scenario was that she recognized Maria represented a threat to her rule and approved of her husband's remedy, even if she disagreed with his methods.

The irony of this situation was that the king and queen of Naples, while personally incompatible, were nonetheless united in their goals for the realm. Both desired stability and peace within the kingdom and the reestablishment of their influence as the leader of the Guelphic party throughout Italy, just as it had been during the reign of King Robert. Right after his coronation, Louis of Taranto founded a new chivalric order that embodied all the lofty goals and ideals of empire originally espoused by Charles of Anjou, chief among which, as Niccolò Acciaiuoli wrote to his cousin the bishop of Florence, was to "recover the kingdom of Jerusalem after regaining Sicily." Nothing could have been closer to Joanna's own conception of the responsibilities of the monarchy or of her most cherished objectives for the realm. And so she seems to have endured her personal abasement as best she could in the interests of a larger cause.

She was rewarded for this effort almost immediately by a diplomatic coup. With the stability of the Neapolitan monarchy firmly established, and its reputation rising in Italy, one of the two warring factions in Sicily suddenly invited the king and queen of Naples to take over the island.

༺ঌ

As blighted as conditions in Joanna's kingdom in the years prior to her coronation had been, those in Sicily had been even worse. Plague had swept through the island in 1347, claiming as one of its victims the regent in charge of the ten-year-old king, Louis II, and his six-year-old brother, Frederick. With no adult leader at the helm, the island divided into two camps: the Catalan party, allied to Aragon; and the Latin faction, headed by two native clans, the Chiaramonte and Ventimiglia families. A protracted civil war with no clear victor ensued until an uprising in Messina in 1353 suddenly brought Louis II, still a minor, under the control of the Catalan party. Seeking to exploit this advantage to maximum benefit, the Catalan leaders made overtures to Aragon, offering to wed Louis to Constance, one of the king of Aragon's daughters, in exchange for help in subduing their rivals. Faced with this unexpected shift in the balance of power, the Latin faction was compelled to seek outside assistance as well. That they appealed to the island's decades-long enemy, the crown of Naples, was a sign of how respected Joanna's government was in the aftermath of the war with Hungary. In exchange for military aid, the Chiaramonte family, which controlled Palermo and Syracuse, offered to return the island to Angevin rule, provided that the Latin faction, working in conjunction with the royal court of Naples, controlled the local government. A document to this effect was drafted in Palermo on February 6, 1354, and transmitted to the queen by her grand seneschal, Niccolò Acciaiuoli.

There was no question the crown should act upon this opportunity; the problem was how to do so in the face of extremely limited resources. Naples was momentarily secure, but incursions by the free companies and the threat from the disgruntled princes of Durazzo demanded that the king and queen be prepared to act quickly. Neither Joanna nor Louis had the means to engage in a discretionary war, no matter how ardently desired. Later, in 1359, after the crown had achieved some small measure of financial stability, Louis would write: "I swear . . . that I have amassed this treasure myself with great effort; by practicing such harsh frugality that it was offensive for the monarchy; from a flock of nothings and crumbs fallen from a meager table; and with the aim of not being left without resources if faced with an urgent need to defend the realm: as I have been scalded by boiling liquid, I now fear a droplet of cold water." Defense of her native realm was Joanna's priority as well. The queen, who had been forced in the early days of her reign to give away much of the domain to favorites and family in order to buy loyalty, could no longer count on the rents and taxes associated with those demesnes. She never recovered the affluent standard of living that had characterized her youth. This reduction in the royal income has left Joanna vulnerable to the criticism of historians, who frequently cite her poverty as an example of the incompetence of her rule as compared with that of her grandfather. Yet Robert the Wise had not been required to contend with famine brought on by excessive rainfall and then the recession caused by the collapse of the super-companies, which later deepened to depression with the advent of the plague and the hostile occupation of the realm, all within a decade.

However, one person in the kingdom was wealthy enough to finance, if not full-scale war, at least a moderate effort: the grand seneschal. As a result of his service to the crown, Niccolò Acciaiuoli had been showered with titles and properties. By this time he owned, in addition to a number of other estates, the cities and surrounding areas of Corinth, Gozzo, Malta, Amalfi, Canosa, and Lucera, which made him richer than either of his suzerains. Conscious that his own rapidly growing reputation as a statesman, not to mention any future honors or treasure, were linked to the successful execution of the grand objectives of the Neapolitan regime, Niccolò undertook to finance a small fleet from his own pocket. According to Matteo Villani, the grand seneschal organized eight galleys of various sizes and then supplemented these vessels with a plethora of rowboats and dinghies, to ferry a force of one hundred knights and four hundred foot soldiers across the Mediterranean. To ensure that his army remained provisioned in case of siege, he also brought along three barges of grain and other necessities.

When Niccolò's somewhat motley squadron appeared in the harbor at Palermo, the city's Sicilian inhabitants, starved from the years of unrelenting civil war, which had destroyed the island's ability to grow food, were not so much frightened of its warriors as in awe of their supplies. The port surrendered without a struggle on April 17, 1354. When news spread through the countryside that the invaders had arrived with enough grain to fill three ships, two thirds of the rest of the population followed suit. The only holdouts were the cities of Messina and Catania, still firmly in the grasp of the

Catalan party. Niccolò, pressing his advantage, began a series of raids against these enemy strongholds but soon realized that he did not have the men or ships necessary to defeat them. He sent a series of envoys to the court at Naples urgently requesting reinforcements before the kingdom of Aragon could come to the aid of its allies. One of these, Zanobi da Strada, reported that he hounded Joanna and Louis with this request, refusing to "leave their side day or night, even when they were in bed."

But Joanna and Louis did not send more troops to Sicily, despite the continual badgering of Niccolò's surrogates. Instead, they recalled the grand seneschal, leaving the task of subduing the remainder of the island unfinished. The wisdom of the crown's retaining its own forces and resources in case of need was soon made manifest when the house of Durazzo, precluded from power by the court of Naples, provoked a crisis.

While Niccolò labored to subdue Sicily, the crown of Naples had continued to lobby the papacy for a dispensation to marry Louis of Taranto's younger brother, Philip, to Joanna's sister, Maria. To counteract Talleyrand of Périgord's influence, Joanna and Louis turned to Cardinal Guy of Boulogne, who over the next several years would advance to become Talleyrand's chief rival for influence within the Holy See. Guy had been one of Joanna's earliest supporters. Louis of Taranto had stayed with the cardinal at his palace in Villeneuve-d'Avignon when he and Niccolò had fled Naples at the start of the war with Hungary, and Guy had been among those who pressed Clement VI to receive Joanna and legitimize her marriage at that time. Later, Guy also sided with Clement against Talleyrand on the critical issue of the king and queen of Naples's double coronation. The cardinal now undertook to use his influence at the papal court to secure Philip of Taranto's marriage.

But Talleyrand was equally determined to prevent this alliance and to do what he could for his nephews, and for the moment, his interests prevailed. Innocent VI refused to issue the necessary dispensation for Philip's wedding but did authorize the marriage of Robert of Durazzo to the niece of Giovanni Visconti of Milan; the pope also demanded that Louis of Taranto surrender the property of Maria's daughters to Louis of Durazzo, a directive with which the king of Naples adamantly refused to comply. Antagonism between Avignon and Naples deepened over the course of the summer as the stalemate persisted.

In this poisoned atmosphere, any perceived weakness on one side was destined to provoke opportunism on the part of the other. Robert of Durazzo, having secured the approval of the pope for his marriage, left Avignon for Milan at the end of June. Along the way he was lured to the court of the count of Savoy, ostensibly to discuss inheritance rights in Achaia but actually because the count's wife, Sybil del Balzo, aunt of Robert del Balzo (who had been so dramatically executed by Maria), in an excess of family feeling, sought to avenge the murder of her nephew. Why the countess chose to focus her revenge on Robert, who had had nothing to do with it, is unclear; most likely his proximity—he was the only Durazzo she could get her hands on—provoked her fury. In any event, on July 12, 1354, she had him arrested and Robert found himself for the second time in six years confined to a dungeon.

The countess of Savoy's action caught the Durazzo alliance off guard, and the Tarantos, sensing their advantage, struck. In autumn, still lacking papal approval, Philip of Taranto married Maria in the hopes that, like his brother before him, the pope would accede to a fait accompli and legitimize the union after the fact. But Innocent VI was not one to yield to pressure. Incensed by this flagrant repudiation of his wishes, and noticing also that the king and queen of Naples, due to their straitened financial circumstances, were in dereliction of the annual tribute, in January

1355, the pope excommunicated both Joanna and Louis of Taranto and placed the kingdom under interdict.

The advantage immediately swung back to the Durazzos. By March 18, 1355, Innocent and Talleyrand, working together, had secured the release of Robert of Durazzo from his Savoyard prison. Seething, the youngest Durazzo returned to his uncle's court spoiling for a fight. That spring, in a coordinated action, the Durazzos retaliated. On the evening of April 6, in Provence, Robert scaled a castle belonging to the Balzo family and began wreaking havoc on Joanna's subjects in the surrounding area of Les Baux, using the captured fortress as his base of operations. He particularly soothed his wounded feelings by capturing Anthony del Balzo, provost of Marseilles and relative of Sybil, and throwing *him* into a dungeon. At almost the same time, Louis of Durazzo joined forces with the eldest Pipini brother, who had survived the war with Hungary and found a home with one of the free companies. The pair infiltrated the kingdom of Naples, leading their army of ex-mercenaries and hardened criminals in a revolt against the crown. In an attempt to capitalize on the sentence of interdict, the huge gang—"twenty-five hundred well-armed, well-mounted barbarians, a large number of horsemen and looters on old horses and beasts of burden, one thousand scoundrels and crooks and courtesans and a motley crew of six thousand men in all," according to Matteo Villani—marched south carrying banners emblazoned with the insignia of the church, so that it appeared that they had been sent by the pope as a punishment relating to the interdict. The rebels set up a base camp in Apulia and began terrorizing the countryside.

Whether Joanna had originally supported her husband's plan to disinherit the Durazzos and marry his brother to Maria, or whether she had been forced to comply with his wishes because he threatened her physically, was suddenly no longer relevant; the danger to her kingdom drove the queen instantly into the Taranto camp. Philip of Taranto was immediately dispatched to Guy of Boulogne in

Avignon to report on the crisis and see what could be done to improve Innocent VI's relations with the royal court at Naples. Lacking ready money, Philip was authorized to offer Jeanne of Durazzo, Maria's eldest daughter,* "possibly the richest heiress in south Italy," in marriage to Guy of Boulogne's brother, Godfrey, in an attempt to ensure the cardinal's good will and best efforts. This proposal was accepted by the cardinal, who immediately went to work on behalf of the Tarantos. Additionally, the queen sent Niccolò Acciaiuoli, who had returned from Sicily to help manage the crisis, to Florence and Tuscany to raise troops for a counterattack against the enemy stronghold in Apulia.

Guy of Boulogne's efforts to convince the pope to intervene on the side of the Tarantos were aided enormously by Innocent's displeasure with the antics of the Durazzos. Talleyrand tried to mediate, but his nephews did not listen to him and his influence waned accordingly. The pontiff demanded that Robert of Durazzo release his hostage and surrender his stolen castle, and when the malcontent refused, Innocent began excommunication proceedings against him on May 2. The pope also condemned Louis of Durazzo's insurrection and on May 20 lifted the interdict against Naples, thereby robbing the rebels of any lingering public credulity that the free company was operating under the approved auspices of the church. When Joanna and Louis of Taranto issued a proclamation asking the seneschal of Provence to rally their forces and take arms against Robert of Durazzo, the pope made a point of condoning their action by sending a personal representative to Les Baux to participate in the siege. It took two months, but the Provençal forces eventually recaptured Les Baux and delivered Robert of Durazzo

---

* Jeanne was originally engaged to Joanna's son, Charles Martel, in 1347, to buy Charles of Durazzo's loyalty. Because Jeanne was promised to the heir to the throne, an inheritance fit for a queen, consisting of much of Maria's legacy from Robert the Wise, was bestowed on her at that time. This explains why Louis of Taranto was so vehement in his refusal to surrender her assets to the Durazzos.

to Avignon. As his prospects for advancement had dwindled significantly, he left almost immediately for Paris, to see what could be done to improve his lot by putting his martial abilities in the service of the king of France.

After trying unsuccessfully to raise troops through Niccolò, Joanna and Louis began negotiations with the insurgents and the following year arranged a compromise. The king and queen promised to transfer the property of Maria's daughters, first to her husband, Philip of Taranto, and then later from Philip to Louis of Durazzo. They also agreed to pay the free company a monetary settlement to leave the kingdom peacefully. At the end of July 1356, the crisis averted, the mob filed out from behind its stronghold and slowly departed the kingdom.

But it did not go very far. By August, the free company had found new employment raiding the countryside of Cesena in central Italy, only a few days' ride from the kingdom of Naples, under the surreptitious sponsorship of the ruthlessly ambitious Visconti family of Milan.

≈⊀≈

CHAPTER XIII

Queen *of* Sicily

A S S O O N A S the threat posed by Louis of Durazzo and the
free company passed, the recapture of the island of Sicily once
more became the chief focus of Joanna's government. In September
1356, Niccolò, determined this time to complete the conquest he
had been forced to suspend previously, sailed his small fleet directly
to the port of Messina, still under the control of the Catalans. As
the grand seneschal remembered to bring along three more barges
full of grain, he had no trouble capturing the city, which by November had opened its doors to the invaders and their provisions.

In fact, the Catalan party was in disarray even before the re-
appearance of the Neapolitan warships. During Niccolò's absence,
plague had struck the island again, this time smiting both the head
of the Catalan party and the young king of Sicily, Louis II. The
succession had passed to Louis' fourteen-year-old brother, Frederick
III, later known as Frederick the Simple, a moniker that more or
less summarized the Catalans' problem. Lacking a strong leader, the
Catalan party had degenerated into warring factions, which seriously
impeded their military and political effectiveness.

The grand seneschal's reputation as a warrior and statesman, on
the other hand, had swelled while he was away. Five years later, in

1361, Niccolò would write: "The Sicilians had such an impression of me (and I wish I could live up to it) that, when they saw me appear in person in Messina, they became more terrified of this impression than of reality." When the Neapolitans entered the city, they discovered that their Catalan antagonists had departed in such haste that they had left behind Frederick III's two sisters, whom Niccolò then took into "courteous custody" at the royal castle. So convincing was the Neapolitan victory, and so firm their hold over their enemy's former citadel, that Louis of Taranto felt safe enough to visit Messina secretly the next month. Having determined that Sicily was indeed secure, the king of Naples then dramatically revealed his identity to the native inhabitants, and even trolled the coastline for an hour or so, waving ceremoniously to his new subjects from the front deck of the royal galley to general acclamation.

Thus was the stage set for one of the great triumphs of Joanna's long career. In December, the queen of Naples herself sailed to Sicily. On December 24, 1356, she and Louis of Taranto, together with their court, entered Messina, and the very next day the pair were officially installed as king and queen of Sicily. Afterward, the new sovereigns received the homage of the native aristocracy, the vast majority associated with their allies from within the Latin faction, although one of Frederick III's own cousins changed parties and did obeisance to Joanna and Louis.

The planned incorporation of Sicily into the kingdom of Naples, painstakingly negotiated in the months preceding the coronation ceremony, demonstrated acute political sophistication by both sides. Despite having endured more than half a century of conflict, Joanna's government had the good sense to treat its former enemy with respect and generosity. The Sicilians, as represented by the Latin faction, had asked that Joanna and Louis return to Sicily every three years in order to have a presence on the island, and also that leading members of the Latin party be brought in as counselors to the kingdom of Naples, so that the island would become integrated into the realm and not remain simply an appendage. The crown acceded to these stipulations, asking only, on Niccolò's recommendation, that the court at Naples reserve the right to appoint officials to rule the island in their stead, as the royal seneschal did in Provence. The Latin party agreed to this condition provided that all administrators were chosen from within its ranks. This left the Catalan faction effectively disenfranchised, which ensured its perpetual opposition, but to expect otherwise was asking for a significantly more enlightened perspective than the governments of the Middle Ages were generally capable of exercising.

On Christmas Day of 1356, Joanna achieved the long-desired reclamation of the island of Sicily, the cherished goal that had eluded her father, her grandfather, and her great-grandfather before her. Only Charles of Anjou, the esteemed patriarch of the family, had stood where Joanna now stood, had received the homage of the native population as the queen did now, was acknowledged sovereign as she was so acknowledged. Despite enormous outlays of money and troops, no one else in her family had even come close. On a personal level, the magnitude of the triumph must have been overwhelming, for there was no better way to justify both her reign and her grandfather's faith in her than by having brought Sicily back into the kingdom.

Moreover, this victory for the queen of Naples stood in sharp contrast to other, similarly momentous, events of that year. At almost exactly the same time that Joanna was recovering Sicily, her cousin, the Valois king of France, was undertaking his own military campaign against his habitual enemy, the king of England, with considerably less gratifying results.

～✲～

Philip VI, Catherine of Valois' brother, had died in 1350 and was succeeded by his son, John II, known, inexplicably, since neither his temper nor his administration justified the sobriquet, as "the Good." King John was already thirty-one and married with five children when he ascended the throne, which ought to have introduced an element of stability to the royal transition; unfortunately, John's feeble judgment belied his maturity. In the first months of his reign, the new king took a number of questionable initiatives, including rashly executing the constable of France in order to replace him with one of his own favorites, and devaluing the money supply in an attempt to restock the royal coffers—policies that did not endear him to his subjects.

Still, he might have muddled through were it not for his cousin, Charles, king of Navarre, whose nickname, "the Bad," was, by contrast, perfectly apt. Charles was young, charming, talented, and ambitious, but he was also cunning, volatile, and treacherous. As a direct descendant of Philip IV, he had a claim to the French throne and considered the Valois to be usurpers. Not satisfied with his own relatively insignificant domain, Charles made no secret of his desire to replace his cousin as king of France, or, failing that, to increase his own possessions and prestige as much as possible at John's expense. John tried to buy him off in 1351 by marrying his eight-year-old daughter Jeanne to the nineteen-year-old Charles, but the king of Navarre interpreted John's policy of appeasement as weakness and moved to confront him more directly. In 1354, Charles the Bad openly rebelled by brazenly murdering John's new constable of France, Charles of Spain. "Know that it was I who, with the help of God, had Charles of Spain killed," he wrote coolly to an astonished Pope Innocent VI. When John retaliated by claiming the king of Navarre's estates forfeit, Charles the Bad invited Edward III of England to raise an army and meet him in Normandy, promising to augment the English military effort with his own troops and to use his Norman castles as a base of operations in order to strike a blow against John "as he shall never recover from."

England was only too happy to answer Charles's summons. In

1355, two expeditions sailed for the western coast of France. The first, led by the king's son Edward, the Black Prince, landed at Bordeaux that summer with a thousand knights and two thousand longbowmen; the second, commanded by the duke of Lancaster, made for Normandy some months later with three thousand cavalry and two thousand archers. On and off for the better part of a year the Black Prince terrorized the civilian population, ravaging towns and villages and looting everything in sight. "My lord, as to news from these parts," wrote Sir John Wingfield, who accompanied Edward on this campaign, in a December 23, 1355, letter to the bishop of Winchester, "you will be glad to know that my lord [the Black Prince] has raided the county of Armagnac and taken several walled towns there, burning and destroying them, except for certain towns which he garrisoned. Then he went into the viscounty of Rivière, and took a good town called Plaisance, the chief town of the area, and burnt it and laid waste the surrounding countryside. Then he went into the county of Astarac, and took several towns and had them burnt and destroyed, and the countryside likewise ... Then he entered the county of Lisle and took some of the walled towns and had a good number of good towns through which he passed burnt and destroyed."

Such extreme provocation could not be ignored. In April 1356, King John finally had Charles the Bad arrested and thrown in prison. John then readied himself for war. "He gathered all the forces of the kingdom of France; there was neither duke nor count nor baron of note whom he did not summon, and all assembled at Chartres. He brought together a noble army; according to the list he had more than ten thousand," wrote Chandos Herald, a chronicler of the period. By now thoroughly alarmed, Innocent VI dispatched his two most experienced and powerful cardinals, Talleyrand of Périgord and Guy of Boulogne, to intercept the antagonists, negotiate a truce, and so prevent war. The French army marched south from Chartres; Edward and his men moved north from Bordeaux; the cardinals hurried west from Avignon. On September 18, 1356, these three groups met at Poitiers.

The papal emissaries did the best they could, particularly the cardinal of Périgord, who convinced the belligerents to postpone battle "out of reverence for holy Church and in order to save the shedding of Christian blood," according to the English chronicler Geoffrey le Baker. Talleyrand then used the agreed-upon hiatus to engage in some last-minute diplomacy, riding back and forth between the French and English camps. "The battle that day was stopped by the Cardinal of Périgord," wrote the chronicler Jean Froissart, "who earnestly endeavored to bring about a peace, but in vain, for neither party desired it." Instead, both sides used the recess to prepare more thoroughly for conflict: the English army obtaining a much-needed rest, while "the French army increased by a thousand men at arms and many more common people."

The next day, peace negotiations having failed, the battle was joined. Conditions were similar to those at Crécy in 1346. Again, the English forces were overwhelmingly outnumbered. "The whole army of the prince, including everyone, did not amount to 8,000; while the French, counting all sorts of persons, were upward of 60,000 combatants, among whom were more than 3,000 knights," asserted Froissart (although in reality the overall number of French soldiers was probably closer to 16,000). Again, the English, in the instrument of the longbow, held the technological advantage, a superiority evidently recognized by Edward, who made a special point of addressing his archers separately from the main body of the army. "Occasion, time, and dangers maketh of fearefull men very strong and stoute, and doth many times of dull witted men make wittie: honour also, and love of the countrey, and the desire of the rich spoyle of the Frenchmen, doth stirre you up," cried the Black Prince in an attempt to rouse this critical unit to the task at hand. Again, the English army fought with discipline and coherence while the French king deployed his troops chaotically, which allowed

Edward's men to ambush and pick off the enemy in a piecemeal fashion, thereby effectively negating the numerical superiority of King John's forces.

Still, both sides battled valiantly, and no one showed more courage than the king of France, who, with his youngest son at his side, remained in the thick of the fighting throughout. Finally, after some seven hours of struggle, it became apparent that Edward's arrows and strategy had prevailed. A young knight fighting on the side of the English, seeing the guard surrounding the king of France set upon by a last, decisive offensive by the Black Prince, called to John: "'Surrender yourself, surrender yourself, or you are a dead man.' The King, who found himself very disagreeably situated . . . then gave him his right-hand glove, and said, 'I surrender myself to you.'"

The capture of the king caused great consternation among what remained of his forces and resulted in a general exodus of the French from the field. Among those who fled (ignominiously, in the populace's eyes) was John's eldest son, Charles; his youngest, Philip, only fourteen at the time of the battle, was apprehended with his father. Edward treated his royal prisoners with exquisite courtesy, escorting them to England with great fanfare. The king of France was soon installed at Windsor Castle, where, Froissart observed, "he was treated with the greatest possible attention, and hunting, hawking, and other amusements were provided for him," while he awaited payment of the crippling ransom demanded of his subjects as the condition of his release.

Thousands who had fought on the side of the French were not as lucky as the king; the countryside surrounding Poitiers was littered with the banners and bodies of those killed, among whom were some 2,426 knights and noblemen. This annihilation of the French aristocracy and their allies produced a strange footnote to Neapolitan history. The ill-luck of Robert of Durazzo, which had previously caused him to spend so much of his life in one dungeon or another, had persisted, and the young man, evicted from Avignon the year before, had arrived in France just in time to be recruited into the service of King John and marched to Poitiers. He was slain in the heat of battle during a particularly fearsome skirmish with Edward's forces. The Black Prince himself recognized the body and had Robert's corpse placed upon a shield. "Present it . . . to the cardinal of Périgord, saying, 'I salute him by that token,'" ordered Edward, who had noticed that members of Talleyrand's suite, although supposedly neutral, had fought that day on the side of the French, by way of a grim jibe.

Fate having dispensed with yet another of Joanna's most dangerous opponents, the male members of the Durazzo family dwindled to one last survivor, Louis.

❧

To cement her rule in Sicily, Joanna continued to reside in Messina with her court for a further eight months. A local government loyal to the new king and queen was established and efforts made to rout the Catalan faction from its remaining strongholds on the island, but the opposition party, long entrenched, remained exceedingly difficult to eradicate. The Neapolitan fleet attempted a raid on Catania at the end of May 1357 but had to turn back before reaching its target due to hostility along the shore, which threatened supply lines. Then, on June 29, Niccolò's galleys were ambushed near the coast by a Catalan force that drew heavily on the population from just outside Messina. Although the fleet managed to escape to the safety of the harbor, Joanna recognized the need for a diplomatic initiative to supplement the military effort. She began a series of negotiations with Frederick III, which led directly to the offer of a marriage alliance—the Angevins' preferred method of integrating rivals into the realm—with Margherita of Durazzo, Maria's youngest daughter. This transaction highlights the political importance of the crown's continuing to act as guardian for Maria's daughters—with no children of her own, Joanna's nieces, as the only direct descendants of Robert the Wise, were irreplaceable as diplomatic bargaining chips.

Holding on to the girls and their assets, however, only served to further alienate and incense Louis of Durazzo, who continued to petition Innocent VI for redress. But the outcome of the battle of Poitiers had significantly altered the political landscape. The king of France was a prisoner of the English and in his place was his eighteen-year-old son, Charles, weak and inexperienced, and at the mercy of conflicting forces unleashed by the military disaster. The combination caused by the absence of strong political leadership and the presence of large numbers of mercenaries left over from the battle with no discernible employment, resulted in, among other social evils, the formation of yet more bands of roving criminals. The most notorious of these was a free company of some four thousand ruffians led by Arnaud de Cervole, nicknamed "the Archpriest," a soldier of fortune and native of the county of Périgord. By May 1357, the Archpriest's forces had pillaged and rampaged their way across France and were preparing to invade Provence.

Innocent was frantic. Matteo Villani claimed that Talleyrand, seeking to strike out against Louis of Taranto for the injustice done to his nephews, was behind the attack, but this seems unlikely, as the cardinal of Périgord was in England trying to arrange for the ransom of King John at this time. The pope himself believed the Archpriest to be working for King John's son Charles and wrote numerous letters to the prince as well as to his father to try to halt the invasion, but these were in vain. Arnaud's forces attacked in July, murdering, burning, and looting much of the county. Concerned, Joanna and her court returned to Naples from Sicily, and the pope had the gates of Avignon reinforced and hired his own mercenaries to guard the papal court. Additionally, that autumn, Philip of Taranto's marriage to Maria was hastily sanctioned by Innocent.

This was no time to quibble over niceties with Louis of Taranto, the titular overlord of Provence—the pope needed all the allies he could get.

But by September 1358, Arnaud had been bribed with a thousand florins from the papal coffers to withdraw his forces permanently from Provence, and in April of the following year the cardinal of Périgord had returned to Avignon from his diplomatic mission abroad and renewed his appeals on behalf of his sole remaining nephew. Once again under the cardinal's influence, Innocent VI was reminded that Louis of Taranto had in fact not returned control of Maria's daughters' assets to Louis of Durazzo, as he had been instructed by the papacy, and that the crown of Naples was still in arrears on the annual tribute. The pendulum abruptly swung back in Louis of Durazzo's favor. The pope renewed the sentence of interdict over Naples and, by letters of April 21, 1359, went so far as to name a legate, Cardinal Gil Albornoz, to take control of the kingdom.

Albornoz was a polarizing and feared figure in Italy. Where Clement had been content to cede effective control over the Papal States to the local baronage so long as a steady stream of bribes made its way to Avignon, Innocent VI was far more aggressive in his approach toward church overlordship of the patrimony. As early as 1353, the Holy See had ordered Albornoz to Italy and instructed him to wrest authority from the various indigenous lords who had seized power during Clement's somewhat lax regime to ensure that official church government and income were once again enforced in the towns surrounding Rome. In the ensuing six years, Albornoz, who had been supplied by the pope with a small militia supplemented by local troops, had achieved no small measure of success. Within three years he had recaptured Orvieto, Viterbo, Romagna, the March of Ancona, and Rimini, and his reputation as a military commander and force to be reckoned with soared. By 1359, control had been reestablished sufficiently in the Papal States that the cardinal was able to turn his attention to the growing territorial threat from Milan, which, under the aggressive leadership of Bernabò Visconti, had expanded its military campaign as far south as Bologna.

Taking on Bernabò, a brutal warmonger prone to both violent rages and deviant sexual activity, required significantly more reinforcements than Albornoz had at his disposal, but the cardinal was willing to employ villains from within the free company who were still in Tuscany terrorizing the local population. Albornoz's policy, however, ran contrary to that of Florence, which, sick of the scourge of criminality, had appealed to Naples to help rid Italy of the free companies. When Joanna and Louis of Taranto sided with Florence instead of Albornoz on this question, Innocent punished them by appointing the cardinal legate of Naples.

The resentment and wrath of the royal court at this demeaning tactic was as pronounced as it had been when Clement VI had appointed Aimeric, but Joanna was no longer a political neophyte; also, Innocent had been in power long enough that by this time she understood him. With Clement, she would have sent warm regards and a sumptuous bribe, but Innocent preferred taxes and deference, so Niccolò Acciaiuoli was hastily recalled from Achaia, where he had gone to look after his and Robert of Taranto's interests after his triumph in Sicily. Dispatched to Avignon, he brought as much of the derelict tribute as she and Louis of Taranto could muster. Acciaiuoli, by this time an experienced diplomat, arrived in March 1360 and succeeded in having the legate revoked and the interdict lifted by May. The pope was so impressed with the Neapolitan envoy that he even presented Niccolò with the Golden Rose and sent him off to Milan as a papal ambassador, to see if war with Albornoz could be averted. Niccolò tried his usual tactics, offering Bernabò Visconti one hundred thousand florins to surrender Bologna to church authority, but Bernabò refused. Despite his failure, Innocent's evident regard for Niccolò greatly increased the grand seneschal's reputation as a statesman throughout Italy, a perception he quickly turned into tangible gain. When, on October 15, 1360, Albornoz succeeded in taking Bologna with the help of a free company and a seven-thousand-man army recruited by Innocent from Louis of Hungary at the last minute, Niccolò was named rector of the city in recognition of his service.

Seeing his advantage slipping away, Louis of Durazzo, in combination with a group of Neapolitan noblemen still loyal to his house, again tried to launch a rebellion from his base in Apulia during the spring of 1360. With Niccolò out of the kingdom, Louis of Taranto himself led a force against the revolt. The king of Naples besieged and destroyed the castles of many Durazzo partisans, forcing his antagonists to surrender and sign a truce. Additionally, Louis of Durazzo was compelled to relinquish his only child, Charles, to the crown of Naples, to be brought up at Joanna's court, as hostage to his father's good behavior in the future. The boy was only three years old when he arrived at the Castel Nuovo, and the queen took to him immediately. Perhaps he reminded Joanna of her own small son, Charles Martel, who had been very close to this age the last time she had seen him, before war with the Hungarians had forced her to flee Naples without him.

Joanna's problems, however, were inconsequential in comparison with those of her Valois cousins during this period. The queen of Naples's rule, though challenged, was stable, and her kingdom essentially secure. France, on the other hand, was in danger of imploding. In addition to the scourge of the free companies, King John's eldest son, Charles, faced threats to his authority from all sides including a peasant uprising in 1358, known as the Jacquerie, and a rebellion by his brother-in-law, Charles the Bad, who, though imprisoned before the battle of Poitiers, "found means to escape during these disturbances, and having collected an army, declared war against France."

The political disintegration of his adversary's kingdom did not go unnoticed by Edward III. Seeking to press his advantage, the king of England demanded huge territorial and financial concessions as a condition for releasing his royal hostage and renouncing any future claim to the throne of France. When the French refused the exorbitant terms, he prepared once again for war. "Edward, on receiving their answer, resolved that he would enter France with a more powerful army than ever, and remain there until the war should be honorably and satisfactorily ended. He made accordingly such great preparations, that the like were never seen before; large numbers of Germans, Bohemians, Brabanters, Flemings, Hainaulters, rich as well as poor, flocked to Calais to assist him; and Edward, on landing at Calais, lost no time in arranging this immense army, and in marching through Picardy and Rheims." The selection of Rheims was no accident; the kings of France were traditionally crowned by the archbishop at the cathedral there. Edward wanted his own coronation ceremony, and all that stood between him and the kingship of France were the gates of the city.

But in his hurry to strike while his enemy was vulnerable, he had not taken account of the weather. Instead of waiting for spring, as was customary, Edward III's forces landed in December 1359, very late in the year for an offensive. "The weather was bad and rainy; and, on arriving before Rheims, the English found no very comfortable quarters," Froissart reported. "The men were miserably housed, and their horses hardly treated and ill fed; the last two or three years' war had so destroyed the country that the ground had remained untilled; and so great was the scarcity of corn of all sorts, that parties were sent to forage as much as ten or twelve miles off." Moreover, Rheims closed its doors firmly against the invader and refused to surrender. After about forty days of mucking around disconsolately in the cold and the mud, the king of England decided the prize was not worth the contest. After a few more months of pillage to the south and then more inclement weather near Chartres, including one notable hailstorm in April, Edward was ready to reopen peace negotiations.

On May 8, 1360, England and France signed the Treaty of Brétigny. In exchange for Edward's definitive renunciation of the French crown, this agreement, while not meeting all his former demands, nonetheless ceded him sovereignty over Calais and the duchy of Aquitaine, which had not been in English hands for almost two centuries. King John's ransom was fixed at three million écus (about £500,000),* and the prisoner was finally released from captivity—although John's sojourn in England was so agreeable, and his relations with his jailor so congenial, that this hardly seems an appropriate description of his condition. "When everything relative to the peace was concluded, the King of France left England for Calais. Here he was met by King Edward, who entertained him at a most magnificent supper in the castle . . . after supper the two kings took a final leave of each other in a most gracious and affectionate manner." Then Edward sailed back to England.

The king sailed back—but the majority of his huge army, frustrated, hungry, deprived of spoils, and hankering for warfare now that the rain had cleared up and the warm weather had arrived, remained. Having absorbed the example set in the aftermath of the

---

*   This ransom was never paid in full, although John went to great lengths to raise it, both by increasing taxes and by other, more unconventional means. For example, Galeazzo Visconti, brother of Bernabò, contracted to marry eleven-year-old Isabelle, a royal princess of the house of Valois, to his nine-year-old son at this time. "His [Galeazzo's] proposals were listened to because they knew he was rich," Froissart sniffed. "He therefore bought the daughter of King John for 600,000 francs." Matteo Villani went even further: "Who could imagine that because of the assaults of the king of England—small and poor in comparison—the king of France should be reduced to such straits as virtually to sell his own flesh at auction . . . Thrusting into oblivion her royal dignity and nobility of blood, she made reverence to messer Galeazzo and to messer Bernabò and to their ladies."

battle of Poitiers, the disgruntled mercenaries formed once more into ad hoc brigades intent on pillage and destruction. The largest and most notorious of these, the White Company, was led by an Englishman, Sir John Hawkwood, with a businesslike efficiency that would have done credit to the managing partner of one of the Florentine super-companies. Hawkwood did not allow the concepts of loyalty or professional contracts to interfere with his pursuit of wealth; he was willing to fight for anyone who paid, which often resulted in his switching allegiance from one day to the next as opposing sides entered into a bidding war for his services. The White Company, consisting of 3,500 horsemen and 2,000 foot soldiers, was even more fearsome than the free company formerly commanded by the Archpriest Arnaud de Cervole. And, just like its predecessor, this terrifying force set its sights on the wealth of the papal court. On December 28, 1360, Hawkwood and his men thundered into Pont-Saint-Esprit, just across the Rhône from Avignon, and occupied the town.

Again, Innocent VI frantically called for help, even preaching a crusade against the ruffians; again, the citizens of Avignon barricaded the city and posted twenty-four-hour watches along the ramparts; again, the situation was resolved by the extortion of a large sum of money from the papal treasury. At the end of March, Innocent agreed to pay Hawkwood the impressive sum of 14,500 gold florins to leave Provence and sent him off to Italy to employ the special talents of the White Company against Bernabò Visconti of Milan.

And so in the spring of 1361, Hawkwood's evil mob, a peripatetic man-made pestilence, filed out of Pont-Saint-Esprit under the ennobling auspices of the church and lurched inexorably toward Italy, leaving a trail of death and destruction in its wake.

So alarming was the specter of the White Company's descent on Milan that it caused a ripple effect throughout Italy even before the actual event took place. Anxious to establish a line of defense in advance of the expected assault, Bernabò Visconti and his army withdrew precipitously from their conflict with Cardinal Albornoz in Bologna. With the decampment of their Milanese foes, the members of the large Hungarian army recruited to protect the church's interests in Bologna suddenly found themselves lacking gainful employment, an unhappy state of affairs that was soon rectified by the soldiers banding together into yet another mercenary company, which then struck out on its own in search of easy spoils to the south. News of the availability of this formidable fighting force, eager to sell its services to the highest bidder, soon reached Louis of Durazzo, still smarting from his earlier defeat at the hands of Louis of Taranto. He invited Hanneken von Baumgarten, one of the leaders of the Hungarian Company, to a secret meeting at a Durazzo castle in Foggia, and a deal was struck. By March 1361, 2,500 members of the Hungarian Company were in Abruzzi, prepared to aid in a revolt against the crown.

This was the third time Louis of Durazzo had provoked a rebellion in seven years. Niccolò Acciaiuoli would later write of this period that Joanna and Louis of Taranto "had always to eat their fruits green . . . They have been so harassed by troubled circumstances and by continually changing and costly events, overt or covert, from internal or external causes, that as soon as a storm erased another appeared in its place immediately." The situation was sufficiently perilous for Louis of Taranto, under whose jurisdiction matters relating to the military fell, to issue a proclamation summoning his vassals to fight on the side of the crown. Both the king and queen of Naples felt an urgency to engage the enemy as soon as possible in order to minimize loss to the citizenry, who would undoubtedly be the object of pillage and looting so long as the Hungarian Company remained within the realm. "So our intention might be known to all," Louis of Taranto wrote in an edict published throughout Naples, "we have promised solemnly by our King's faith and word as witnessed by the magnificent Niccolò Acciaiuoli, Grand Seneschal . . . to do all we can to bring this battle about as will be shown by the event itself; as we prefer to give our life for our sheep, rather than wait about for the enemy's ruin, which would then be harder to achieve because of the country's ruin."

Again the grand seneschal, recalled hurriedly from Bologna, took charge of the kingdom's defense. On May 25, 1361, he managed, by a substantial payment in silver, to coax the Hungarian Company away from Louis of Durazzo's service and into that of Joanna and Louis of Taranto's. Although the bandits made for comically unreliable allies—much to their employers' consternation, they changed allegiance back and forth between Louis of Durazzo and Louis of Taranto several times over the course of the next few months—Niccolò, working through diplomatic channels with the court of Hungary, eventually succeeded in having the mercenaries' energies redeployed once more against Milan. In December 1361, the company permanently departed the kingdom and made its way north. Louis of Durazzo, deprived of the majority of his military support and pursued by a band of knights led by Niccolò's son, the count of Melfi, sought refuge at the Sanctuary of Monte Sant'Angelo sul Gargano, a revered holy shrine, but the local population turned against him. Compelled to escape by night, he was captured and delivered to the royal court of Naples. On February 6, 1362, conceding defeat, he humbled himself before the king and queen and did obeisance to the crown. Then the last surviving brother of the once-powerful house of Durazzo was escorted to the royal prison at the Castel dell'Ovo, where he remained indefinitely at the crown's pleasure.

The incarceration of Louis of Durazzo marked the end of the pitched struggle for ascendancy between the competing factions within Joanna's family. Catherine of Valois' ruthless scheme to place one of her sons on the throne of Naples, set in motion during her lifetime and then engineered after her death by her protégé Niccolò Acciaiuoli, seemed at long last to have definitively triumphed over the ambitions of her rival, Agnes of Périgord. With Louis of Taranto married to the queen, and his brother married to her younger sister, a succession favoring the house of Taranto over that of the Durazzo seemed assured.

But fate has a way of upsetting even the most obvious outcomes. Within two months of Louis of Durazzo's imprisonment, to the terror of the general population, the plague suddenly returned to Naples, and this time claimed a royal victim. On May 24, 1362, at the age of thirty-five, Louis of Taranto, having contracted the fatal disease, received the final sacrament at the hands of a priest and died.

CHAPTER XIV

The Queen *and*
Her Court

ALTHOUGH LOUIS OF TARANTO'S brutal behavior
toward and infringement of his wife's prerogative ensured that
she did not mourn his passing—the queen would write to Innocent
VI in June, officially informing him of the death of "such a
husband"—Joanna was experienced enough by this time to anticipate that there would be challenges to her government once news
of the king's demise was made public. "Our position . . . [is] perhaps
imperfectly protected by perverse intentions," she observed to the
pope in the same letter. Louis' two brothers, Robert and Philip,
would no doubt wish to influence the direction of the realm and to
maintain the position and power they had achieved while their
brother was alive; there was even a possibility that Philip, now legit-
imately married to Maria, would attempt a coup to replace Joanna
with her sister and, citing precedence, have himself crowned king.
To buy herself some time to prepare for any possible resistance, the
queen kept her husband's death a secret while she made arrangements to take full control of the court. Because plague was highly
contagious, she gave orders for Louis' corpse to be smuggled out
of the Castel Nuovo under cover of night and deposited temporar-
ily in the nearby church of San Pietro, so she could remain in the

Castel Nuovo without fear of contracting the disease herself. Later, the king of Naples would be given a state funeral at the important church of San Domenico Maggiore before his body was finally buried beside that of his mother at a monastery near Avellino.

The swiftness of her husband's illness and demise aided her conspiracy. Louis succumbed so quickly that no one outside the palace had any reason to suspect that anything was amiss. For ten days Joanna was able to shut herself up in the Castel Nuovo without detection while she considered her options. Louis of Taranto had left no will, saying, according to Matteo Villani, "that he owned nothing that he could personally bequeath, and that all belonged to Queen Joanna," an indication that, in the end, the king recognized his wife's superior rank and legitimacy. Perhaps regretting his harsh treatment of his cousin, however, with his dying breath he had issued an order freeing Louis of Durazzo from captivity. Joanna honored this request and liberated Louis of Durazzo from his cell, thereby securing her cousin's gratitude. Having gained an ally against her husband's formidable brothers, she then called a meeting of the Grand Council, and on June 5, in the presence of the archbishop of Naples and the most important barons and prelates in the realm, Joanna announced the king's death and publicly assumed her throne as sole ruler of the kingdom, a state of affairs she evidently intended to perpetuate.

Robert and Philip of Taranto reacted to the news of Joanna's widowhood with predictable antipathy. Although the queen had made clear her resolve to manage her government without interference, at thirty-six, she was still capable of childbirth and so would undoubtedly remarry. Since, as married men, neither Robert nor Philip was able to capitalize on this unique opportunity, it meant a new and powerful player would once more be introduced into Neapolitan politics. Above all, the brothers were adamant that Louis of Durazzo should not be chosen to fill the vacancy left by the recently deceased king. According to a chronicler, "They obtained letters from her [Joanna] with the assurance that she would not" marry Louis, but even this attestation proved insufficient to allay their fears. "Still not content, they imposed a guard who then poisoned him with some concoction."

Whether Louis of Durazzo, who died on either June 25 or July 22, 1362 (both dates are cited by chronicles), was actually poisoned or, weakened from his imprisonment, had succumbed to disease is unclear, but what is transparent is Joanna's loathing of her deceased husband's family and her desire to temper their influence within the realm. Upon Louis of Durazzo's death, she made a point of singling out his five-year-old son, Charles of Durazzo, for special favor. Appointing an important nobleman as the boy's seneschal, the queen also ordered that in future little Charles was to be treated with "all honors due to the royal household and to maintain him in a royal state," a signal of her intention to elevate the house of Durazzo at the expense of that of Taranto. Then, having thrown down the gauntlet, and recognizing that she was going to need all the help she could get (which adds credence to the poisoning story), she sent an urgent courier to Niccolò Acciaiuoli, notifying him of the late king's death and requesting that he return at once to Naples.

Niccolò, who was at this time in Messina trying once again to subdue the Catalan opposition in Sicily, answered her summons immediately. "Hearing with great sadness (while in Messina) that conspiracies and leagues of neither small nor unimportant nobles had arisen in Naples at the expense of the Lady Queen, my mistress, I left the affairs of Sicily in good order in the hands of my son . . . and returned to Naples with four armed galleys, to give my most loyal support to my mistress and her needs, with no other limit than my life," he later wrote rather melodramatically in his autobiography. "And in truth my return was much more profitable to the Lady Queen my mistress than to me, because my actions were so obvious and consistent, supported the just cause of my queen, and, with her other loyal followers, undertook whatever was necessary against her enemies' actions, that violent hatreds, dangerous enmities and infinite jealousies befell me."

The arrival of the grand seneschal, not to mention his four warships, in Naples that fall proved sufficient to forestall further mutinies on the part of the Taranto brothers. For the first time, Joanna was able to rule her kingdom without having to ward off a husband's or her family's attempts to interfere with her government. Alone in Europe, she was a woman exercising absolute power. The archbishop of Naples, who was present at court and had ample opportunity to observe Joanna during the period immediately following the death of her husband, captured her mood at this time for posterity. "The queen delights in governing," the archbishop wrote in a letter to the pope. "She wants to do everything because she has waited so long for this moment."

❦

The archbishop's remark notwithstanding, Joanna had not been idle during the years preceding her husband's death. As early as 1352, when she was just crowned, the queen had resumed the policy of perpetuating and legitimizing her own and her family's image through public building and decoration in the Angevin tradition. She had begun by erecting a new church, intended as a reliquary to house some shards from the crown of thorns, in thanksgiving for her throne, just as her grandmother Sancia had ordered the construction of Santa Chiara after her own coronation. Also at this time, in June of 1352, the queen organized and attended a ceremony in which Sancia's remains were removed to an elaborate tomb at the convent of Santa Croce before an august body of bishops and other church officials. Joanna, in describing this event in a letter to the pope, made an (ultimately unsuccessful) effort to obtain sanctity for her grandmother, citing the miracle that, upon the transfer, Sancia's seven-year-old corpse was discovered "whole and not decaying, immune from rottenness and stench."

Joanna's own sanctuary, the church of Santa Maria Incoronata, was completed in the early 1360s. Although not constructed on the same grand scale as the vast monastery of Santa Chiara, the Incoronata was nonetheless an important addition to the city's architecture. The queen made every effort to ensure the beauty of the interior, hiring Roberto Oderisi, a disciple of Giotto and one of the most celebrated masters of his day, to create the frescoes on the walls and ceiling. Giotto, the most revered artist in Italy during the first half of the fourteenth century, had been Robert the Wise's court painter from 1328 to 1332. During his tenure at court, Giotto had taken the highly unusual step of including women in his depiction of famous heroes on the walls of the *sala grande* (the great hall) of the Castel Nuovo; this was clearly in recognition of Joanna's having being named heir to the throne after the death of her father. An amusing but apocryphal legend has the eminent king in conversation with the equally renowned artist. "Whilst Giotto was engaged upon his work King Robert would often come and chat with him, for he appreciated his shrewd speeches as much as his art. 'If I were you, Giotto,' he remarked one summer day, 'I would stop painting now it is so hot.' 'And so would I, Sire,' replied the painter, 'if I were you.'"*

For Joanna, Roberto Oderisi created brilliant images of the seven sacraments using contemporary figures, including a scene depicting the marriage and coronation of the queen and Louis of Taranto, and another, painted after 1362, of the death of the king. In addition to the Incoronata, Joanna completed construction of the monastery of San Martino, a project originally undertaken by her father in 1325 but left unfinished at his death in 1328. The queen

---

* Giotto was famously known for both his wit and his homely appearance. Another medieval folktale reported that Dante had once asked the painter in jest how "his children could be so ugly when his paintings were so beautiful." Without missing a beat, Giotto answered that "he painted by daylight but procreated in the dark."

herself, as well as all the surviving members of the royal family and many influential barons of the court, attended the consecration of this monastery in 1369. The grandeur accompanying this ceremony is telling: Joanna's ability to finish the monastery both honored her father's memory and placed her in an unbroken line of powerful Angevin rulers. During this period the queen also erected another church, dedicated to Saint Anthony, to which was attached a hospital.

The gift of a hospital, rather than a monastery or nunnery, as would have been the preferred manner of largesse during King Robert's reign, reflects an obvious attempt to cope with the recurring horror of the plague. The queen's approach to public health care, particularly as it concerned the poor, was strongly influenced by the doctrine of benevolence practiced by the Spiritual Franciscans, a tradition handed down to her by her grandmother Sancia. Under Joanna, all licenced doctors and medical practitioners were obliged to treat the poor free of charge. This enlightened approach to the general welfare was uncommon for Europe. In nearby Florence, for example, "only the rich could call in a physician."

The practice of medicine in Naples under Joanna was unique in other ways as well, owing in large part to the presence within the kingdom of the University of Salerno, the oldest and most respected medical school in Europe. As early as the eleventh century, this port city was celebrated as a center of learning. "Salerno then flourished to such an extent in the art of medicine that no illness was able to settle there," boasted its archbishop in 1075; a hundred years later, a Spanish Jew traveling through Italy described Salerno as the place "where the Christians have schools of medicine." As a result, the medical profession flourished in Naples, and between the years 1273 and 1409 a remarkable 3,670 medical licenses were issued within the kingdom, dwarfing those in other parts of Italy. Even more novel was the number of these licenses issued to women.

Again, this anomaly can be traced to the medical school at

Salerno, which in the twelfth century produced a famous text dedicated to women's health, the *Trotula*. There are strong indications that at least parts of the *Trotula* were authored by a woman, and that a woman actually taught at the medical school during this period. But it was highly unusual for women to be licensed. Only four women matriculated as doctors in Florence in the fourteenth century, and two of these were daughters of doctors who "could not claim to be physicians in the strict sense, lacking doctorates." From 1100 to 1400, the kingdom of France recognized seventy-four women as some form of physician, but a large percentage of these were untrained and unlicensed. England listed only eight women in eight centuries as "healers"; the crown of Aragon recognized none.

By contrast, in the fourteenth century alone, Naples conferred thirty-four medical licenses on twenty-four women. Since a test or inquiry of some sort was involved for each medical condition, this meant that some of the women obtained expertise in multiple specialties. The license issued to a woman named Raimonda da Taverna in 1345, for example, read: "The aforesaid Raimonda . . . has been examined by our surgeons . . . and has been found competent to cure the aforesaid illnesses ['cancers,' wounds and fistulas]. Although it is unsuitable for women to associate with men, lest they compromise their feminine modesty and fear the blame of forbidden transgression, [nonetheless] they have a legal right to practice medicine." Thirteen of the twenty-four women licensed as practitioners were specifically authorized to treat other women, although they were apparently not limited to standard female ailments. Some of those who matriculated were trained to perform surgery.

Historians, confronted with the anomaly of so many licensed female physicians in fourteenth-century Naples, have struggled to explain the data. "Indeed, the relative independence of southern Italian women practitioners . . . may have been fostered in part by heightened southern Italian concerns about the modesty of female patients at the hands of male doctors." The hypothesis of an excessively demure female population would seem to be challenged by Boccaccio's eyewitness descriptions of the licentious behavior of the upper classes, and certainly Charles of Durazzo had no such qualms about having a male physician examine his mother when she fell ill in the summer of 1345. Another, more plausible explanation for the large number of female doctors in southern Italy might just be that, during the period in question, the kingdom of Naples was ruled by a queen.

⁂

Joanna had also made an effort to reestablish the ambience of high culture for which Naples had been known during her grandfather's reign. To achieve this meant luring to court at least one of the handful of celebrated scholars or writers who constituted intellectual society in Italy during this period. Petrarch, the reigning luminary, was the obvious choice, more particularly as, to the great scandal of his friends, the poet laureate had been living off the hospitality of the ruthless Visconti family of Milan since 1353. "I would wish to be silent," wrote an aghast Boccaccio when he first learned of his friend's new patrons, "but I cannot hold my peace . . . My indignation obliges me to speak out. How has Silvanus [Petrarch] acted? He has forgotten his dignity; he has forgotten all the language he used to hold respecting the state of Italy . . . and his love of liberty; and he would imprison the Muses in that court. To whom can we now give our faith, when Silvanus, who formerly pronounced the Visconti a cruel tyrant, has now bowed himself to the yoke which he once so boldly condemned! How has the Visconti obtained this truckling, which neither King Robert, nor the pope, nor the emperor, could ever obtain?" As early as 1360, both Joanna and Niccolò, an accepted member of Petrarch's highly selective circle of correspondents, tried to coax the scholar to Naples, offering him the prestigious position of royal secretary, but the poet, fleeing the return of the plague, chose instead to settle at Venice. Casting around for another distinguished candidate to fill the post, the court instead chose Niccolò's old acquaintance Boccaccio.

Lacking a rich and powerful benefactor like his friend Petrarch enjoyed, Boccaccio was living in poverty in Certaldo, about twenty miles southwest of Florence. *The Decameron*, his masterwork, a collection of one hundred stories told by a fictitious group of aristocrats fleeing the plague, had been finished in 1351 to popular acclaim and had made its author's name if not his fortune. The book was held in such high esteem in Naples that Niccolò's own nephew begged for a copy from his cousin the archbishop-elect of Patras in a July 1360 letter: "Reverend Domine, here is Monte Bellandi writing to his wife that she is to give you the book of the tales of messer Giovanni Boccaccio, belonging to me; wherefore I beseech you that you have it delivered to you; and if the Archbishop of Naples has not left I beg that you send it by him—by his servitors, that is—and he is not to give it to Messere Niccolò Acciaiuoli nor to any other person than myself. And if the Archbishop has departed, have it given on my behalf to Cenni Bardella . . . otherwise, do you send it to me yourself by one who you believe will deliver it to my hand; and do be most careful that messer Neri shall not get hold of it, for then never would I have it . . . and do be careful not to lend it to anyone because there are many who would be dishonest." Despite *The Decameron*'s many admirers, however, Boccaccio's standing as an intellectual and a man of letters was no match for that of Petrarch, nor even of the previous Neapolitan royal secretary Zanobi, who had succeeded Petrarch as poet laureate and subsequently advanced to apostolic secretary under Innocent VI. Boccaccio was even more inferior in reputation to Acciaiuoli, whose many diplomatic, political, and military achievements had put him on a familiar footing with popes and heads of state, causing even Petrarch to address him with fawning servitude. "With my entire soul I reverently embrace you, O man most rare in every age and unique in ours, and legally lay claim to you as to a discovered treasure . . . When you offer your greatness to a man of my insignificance . . . you honor not me but yourself, thereby seeming perfect in every respect," Petrarch wrote to Niccolò by way of congratulations for the grand seneschal's victory over Sicily. Still, the kingdom—or rather, Niccolò, to whose household this position was assigned—needed a secretary, and in the summer of 1362, on the recommendation of Francesco Nelli, a mutual friend, an invitation to accept this posting was extended to Boccaccio. The author of *The Decameron* confirmed this appointment by writing to Nelli that he had received an "epistle written by the hand of Maecenas [Acciaiuoli]," asking him "to share with him his joys."

Boccaccio had every reason to be suspicious of the grand seneschal's invitation. Two decades earlier, the writer had been forced by financial necessity to leave an idyllic existence in aristocratic Naples and withdraw to bourgeois Florence. In his desperation to find a way back to the kingdom, Boccaccio had turned to his good friend Niccolò, who was then, like himself, a young Florentine of modest origins.* "Niccolò . . . I am writing you nothing about my being in Florence unwillingly, for that would have to be written with tears rather than ink: only this can I tell you, that, just as Alexander changed the ill fortune of the pirate Antigonus to good, so am I hoping that mine will be changed by you," he pleaded in a letter of August 28, 1341, the first of a long series of entreaties to Acciaiuoli to use his influence to obtain a position at court for Boccaccio, all of which were ignored. Now, however, it seemed that his hopes would finally be realized. Nelli too had written, urging Boccaccio

---

* Both men were illegitimate, of undistinguished middle-class birth, working as relative underlings in their fathers' businesses when they first met, although Acciaiuoli, several years older, would very quickly worm his way into Catherine of Valois' household as a financial adviser and tutor to her young sons, among his other, less respectable du-

to accept, to which the writer replied: "Finally thy epistle removed every doubt from me, till then untrusting, and, by thy Maecenas' leave be it said, in thee I believed."

At the end of October 1362, Boccaccio packed up his meager belongings—the greater part of which was represented by his library, among which were two new books that the grateful secretary had written specially to dedicate to Niccolò and his sister as gifts— and left Certaldo for Naples. His reception by Acciaiuoli provides a glimpse of the grand seneschal's behavior and the workings of his household uncorrupted by the filter of self-aggrandizement so carefully cultivated by Niccolò in his official memoirs. Boccaccio's new employer was then at one of his grand estates in Campania, where the secretary now journeyed at his own expense. He found the grand seneschal at home, but when Boccaccio attempted to greet him, "no differently was I received by your Maecenas [Acciaiuoli] than if I were returning from a jaunt to the towns or countryside near Naples: not with smiling face nor friendly embrace and gracious words; on the contrary he barely extended his right hand as I entered his house. Surely no happy augury this!" Boccaccio wrote soon after to Nelli. The situation went immediately from bad to worse, for, although the villa was grand and filled with "glittering things," the royal secretary found himself quartered in the "bilge," a tiny, filthy room with holes in the walls and a cot "just then brought up from the nether regions by a mule driver, and half-covered by a stinking bit of rug. In this self-same bilge with its disreputable cot is kept the domestic ware, the splendid service for dining." As for Niccolò himself, Boccaccio asserted that he

frequently goes into closed assembly and there, so that it may appear that he has much to do with the serious affairs of the Kingdom, he places doorkeepers, according to the royal customs, at the exits of the room, and no one who asks for him is allowed to enter . . . and in the closet, by his command a seat was placed, for there, no differently than on his majesty's throne, he sits ... amid very discordant sounds of the belly and the expelling of the stinking burden of the guts, high Councils are held and the proper business of the Kingdom is disposed of ... The simpletons who wait in the courtyard, think that he, admitted to the Consistory of the Gods, in company with them holds solemn Parliament upon the universal state of the republic.

Boccaccio spurned the bilge and stayed instead with a kind friend, but soon after his arrival, his benefactor decided to move again, this time to his elegant estate near Baia, and his secretary and all his household were obliged to move with him. Again, Boccaccio was placed in quarters humiliating to his position—a young Neapolitan nobleman of his acquaintance was so appalled by *The Decameron* author's sleeping arrangements that he had his servants transport one of his own beds to Niccolò's house for Boccaccio's use. Worse, no sooner had the disillusioned writer dragged his library and luggage to this new location than the grand seneschal and all his retainers, forgetting all about the new secretary, relocated again, this time journeying to the royal court of Naples. Boccaccio was left "alone, with the load of books ... on the shore together with the manservant ... without the necessities of life and without any counsel." He waited more than a month, living at the house of a poor friend, while "he [Acciaiuoli] pretended not to notice" before finally quitting the kingdom and his position in March 1363, "to be no longer tormented by that Maecenas ... having taken leave of the Great Man with what moderation he was capable of."

Joanna was no doubt kept in ignorance of the reasons for Boccaccio's disgruntlement; the queen was extremely busy with diplomatic matters during this period, and this was not the sort of information Niccolò would have been apt to impart. Most likely, she was simply told that the writer was a "man of glass," as his friend Nelli chided him in a letter dated April 22, 1363, and had decided to leave. Certainly the queen did not share her grand seneschal's disdain for his former friend, as she tried to coax Boccaccio to her court again in 1370 when he came to visit his friend Hugo of San Severino. At that time, Joanna went so far as to offer to subsidize his stay in Naples so he would be free to devote himself to his work. "The wonderful man [Hugo] was caring [for me] . . . with all his powers, so that when help arrived from the most serene majesty Joanna, queen of Jerusalem and Sicily, he placed me in leisure among the peaceful Parthenopeii [Neapolitans]," Boccaccio remembered later in gratitude. When the writer graciously declined Joanna's offer, "once again the queen made a great effort to hold him," although again he refused.

History has a way of settling old scores, however. Despite his many undeniable diplomatic and military achievements and his attempt to perpetuate his fame beyond his death, which included the construction of a vast monastery in Florence where he was buried, Niccolò Acciaiuoli never achieved the lasting fame he desired. Instead, the immortality of universal recognition would be reserved for the impoverished, slighted author of *The Decameron*, whose haunting imagery and brilliant evocation of an era produced a masterpiece that would remain in print for nearly seven centuries.

⚬⚬⚬

In the months succeeding Louis of Taranto's death, Joanna's principal concern was not with art and culture but with matrimony. Remaining single was not an option for the queen of so desirable a kingdom as Naples, and Joanna needed an heir. The animosity and ambition of her late husband's brothers threatened her rule internally. External forces, like maintaining her hard-won sovereignty over Sicily and the necessity of keeping the kingdom's boundaries secure from the brutality of the free companies, demanded that she move quickly to take a husband who could command an army. Joanna was at no loss for suitors; on the contrary, she was so beset by offers that her main difficulty was in fending off potential candidates as diplomatically as possible. King John of France, seeing such a prize as the throne of Naples suddenly become available, sent a series of ambassadors to Naples in August, including the bishop of Nevers and the French royal secretary, to coax Joanna into marrying his youngest son, Philip, just twenty years old. The Visconti family of Milan was no less eager to add southern Italy to the roster of their possessions.

The queen's refusal of Ghibelline Milan was supported by the papacy, but the French proposal had church backing and had to be treated with delicacy. Joanna did not want such a young husband, and she worried that France might try to absorb Naples, which above all she wished to remain an independent monarchy. In a letter to the pope she emphasized the kingdom's need of obtaining someone capable of "governing wisely and of defending the kingdom in a manly fashion." To put John off, she wrote thanking him for the great honor he thought of bestowing on her, but regretfully declined Philip's proposal on the grounds that matrimony between blood relations inhibited conception. Her union with the son of Catherine of Valois had already left her kingdom devoid of heirs, a vacuum the queen blamed for the realm's many misfortunes, including "the conflicting wishes of the nobles and of the people, seditions, invasions, pathetic mutilations imposed to certain people, innumerable ransoms and countless tragedies and other evils too great to recount." Just to make sure there was no confusion about her position on this matter, Joanna also informed John's ambassadors that she had taken an oath to retire to a nunnery rather than perpetuate the misery of her infertility by wedding another member of the house of Valois.

But the king of France was not easily put off and sought to force the union on Joanna by putting pressure on her through the Holy

See, which was in a state of flux due to the death of Innocent VI. The old man, weakened and depressed by a series of foreign policy failures, had expired on September 12, 1362. For all his virtuous commitment to reform, Innocent's bellicose approach to his opponents had left the church far less wealthy and powerful than it had been under his corrupt predecessor, Clement VI, a state of affairs that did not go unnoticed by the cardinals. In their first ballot, taken on September 22, the Sacred College elected Clement's brother, Hugues Roger, by a margin of fifteen to five.

Hugues, however, did not want to be pope, and emphatically declined the honor, forcing another vote. Again, the rivalry between cardinals Talleyrand of Périgord and Guy of Boulogne ensured that neither of the two could claim a majority, and the papal ambitions of both men died with this election. Instead, on September 28, the Sacred College, casting about for someone acceptable, chose another older, compromise candidate, fifty-one-year-old Guillaume of Grimoard, the abbot of Saint Victor of Marseilles.

Guillaume happened to be fulfilling the post of papal nuncio to the court of Naples at the time of his election. Informed by confidential envoys of the cardinals' decision, he hurried back to Avignon. He was crowned on November 6, 1362, taking the name of Urban V.

The elevation of the abbot of Saint Victor to the papacy was fortuitous for Joanna. Her relationship with Innocent VI, whom the queen had never met personally, had been prejudiced from the first by Innocent's evident dislike (fully reciprocated) of Louis of Taranto, which had resulted in her kingdom suffering through years of interdict and unnecessary papal intervention. The cornerstone of Angevin foreign policy had always been a partnership with the papacy, but while her husband was alive, Joanna had never been able to establish the strong, mutual, working alliance with Innocent that she had had with Clement. The queen had been forced to rely on a surrogate, her grand seneschal, whose efforts, while ultimately helpful, were also self-serving. When it came to the papal court, Niccolò was always more interested in promoting himself than he was in forging a genuine understanding between Naples and Avignon.

All this changed with the election of Urban. Between Joanna and her former nuncio existed a mutual respect and sympathy born of familiarity with each other's personality and religious and cultural perspectives. Although personally austere like his predecessor—throughout his tenure, Urban held firmly to the discipline of his monastic order, including eschewing traditional papal garb in favor of a simple monk's habit and sleeping on the bare floor—the new pope's temperament was far more easygoing, attractive, and obliging than Innocent's. When dealing with supplicants, Urban's first choice was to accede as much as possible to everyone's requests; in this his approach to his duties was reminiscent of Clement VI's (although he did not have Clement's predilection for graft). Urban was also exceedingly generous and a great patron of the arts. As pope, he improved his former abbey in Marseilles, personally supervising the work of the architects and decorating the church with fine tapestries and religious objects cast in gold and adorned with precious jewels. He built a cathedral and priory in southern France, among other projects. His commitment to letters and learning was no less passionate. Urban actively supported universities and students and even founded a school of music. Petrarch admired him and wrote him fawning letters later in his career.

That Urban was someone with whom the queen felt comfortable was evident from the very beginning of his pontificate. Before he was even enthroned, she asked for official permission to remarry and was rewarded with letters bearing his consent, issued on November 7, the day after his coronation. According to Matteo Villani, when King John of France subsequently arrived in Avignon on November 20 to pay his respects to the new pope, and immediately put forward his son Philip as a candidate for marriage with Joanna, Urban at first promised to pursue the matter "as long as the prince would reside in the kingdom, took the oath, and paid its dues to the church, and that the queen, whom he would exhort, would agree." But the queen most vehemently did not agree. Responding to a November 29 papal letter, in which Urban observed that refusal of her French cousin's suit might be harmful to herself and her kingdom, Joanna flashed back: "After all, the decision to marry is free, and I can't see why this should no longer be the case at the expense of my freedom . . . I beg your Holiness as respectfully as I can to forgive my thoughtlessness for my excessive and possibly offensive words, but this is a topic which incites me to express my thoughts undiminished . . . I hope that I have taken such counsel in this that my posterity will be fully preserved in the blood of my royal house, far from (and I would rather die) passing it on to other nations," she concluded passionately.

In fact, the queen, forced by the pressure from France to act quickly, had already made her choice. On December 14, without waiting for Urban's response, Joanna officially committed herself through emissaries to wed James IV, king of Majorca, son of Sancia's nephew James III, who had succeeded to the throne of Majorca when Sancia's brother Sancho died in 1324. It was James III who, having lost his kingdom to the crown of Aragon, had come to seek papal aid in 1348 at exactly the same time that Joanna had stood trial before Clement VI; James III to whom Joanna had lent her fleet in 1348 in gratitude for his having championed her cause with the pope. The future James IV, twelve years old at the time, had been with his father in Avignon; presumably, Joanna met him there.

The queen of Naples might have kept her Provençal ships for all the good they had done her cousin. In 1349, having acquired an army to go with his borrowed fleet, James III, accompanied by his son, had launched an attack against his Aragonese enemies in Majorca. This invasion failed spectacularly. The king was killed and his son, James IV, was captured and imprisoned, remaining "shut up for the next fourteen years in an iron cage." He finally managed to slip away in 1362, just in time to marry Joanna by proxy on

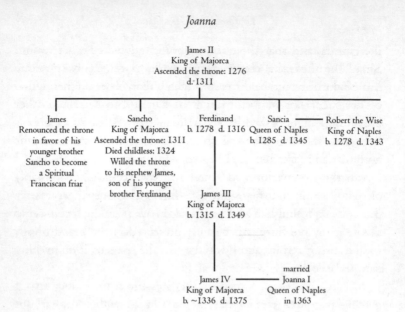

James II
King of Majorca
Ascended the throne: 1276
d. 1311

James	Sancho	Ferdinand	Sancia ——— Robert the Wise
Renounced the throne	King of Majorca	b. 1278 d. 1316	Queen of Naples King of Naples
in favor of his	Ascended the throne: 1311		b. 1285 d. 1345 b. 1278 d. 1343
younger brother	Died childless: 1324		
Sancho to become	Willed the throne		
a Spiritual	to his nephew James,		
Franciscan friar	son of his younger		
	brother Ferdinand	James III	
		King of Majorca	
		b. 1315 d. 1349	

married
James IV ——— Joanna I
King of Majorca   Queen of Naples
b. ~1336 d. 1375   in 1363

December 14. The timing of his breakout is coincidental enough to suggest that the court of Naples may have had something to do with his escape.

For Joanna, at least on paper, James IV of Majorca had all the attributes she was looking for in a husband. She would not have to worry about his being envious of her title and have to placate him by raising him to the crown of Naples, as she had had to do with both Andrew and Louis of Taranto. James was already a king, and therefore of equal rank to his wife. Moreover, he brought his own kingdom (albeit one that for the moment was ruled by someone else) to the marriage, a kingdom he was absolutely committed to regaining, so he would not feel the need to rule hers. At twenty-seven, he was the perfect age to lead her armies, not so young that he would not be listened to and not too old to fight himself. He could keep both her brothers-in-law at bay and her boundaries secure. He was not a blood relation, yet an alliance with Majorca was completely in keeping with Angevin tradition, as established by her grandfather, and added the legitimacy of history to her reign. Should he recover his kingdom with her help, as she clearly expected him to do, he would be the perfect ally to defend her dominion over Sicily and buffer Naples from the acquisitive tendencies of the crown of Aragon. Niccolò Acciaiuoli, who was hardly a political neophyte and had a vested interest in maintaining Neapolitan authority in Sicily, also approved of this choice.

The king of Majorca had every reason to embrace this alliance as well. After spending so much of his youth in hopeless captivity, he suddenly found himself free and paired to a provocative woman who was desired throughout Europe for her large and strategically located realm and who could afford him the means to revenge himself on his enemies.

Joanna had her way. Urban bowed to her wishes and approved the marriage in a bull dated February 8, 1363. On May 16, the bridegroom and his retainers sailed into the harbor accompanied by a flotilla of seven ships. There was the usual period of rejoicing involving banquets, processions, and other public festivities and then, in a solemn ceremony at the Castel Nuovo, Joanna took as her third husband James IV, the king of Majorca.

※

CHAPTER XV

The Quest for an Heir

FOURTEEN YEARS IN A DARK, cramped prison cell does not always produce the healthiest or most well-adjusted marriage partners.

Naples was still struggling with the remnants of the plague when James of Majorca arrived in May. Weakened physically from his long confinement, the king now faced the oppressive heat of a southern Italian summer. James's run-down constitution must have been well known within the realm, because almost before the bride and groom had a chance to become acquainted, Robert of Taranto challenged Joanna's government. In the middle of June, the emperor of Constantinople, with the full support of his brother Philip, seized a castle in a display of strength against the queen, using as his excuse a dispute over property Maria claimed was still due her from her original dowry.

Ordinarily, the task of subduing Robert and Philip would have fallen to Joanna's new husband, but James was too ill to fight. "The Sire the King suffers from tertian fever,"* the archbishop of Naples observed to Urban in a letter dated July 1, 1363. "The doctors

---

* An illness that occurs every other day or every third day.

increased the prescriptions in view of the malicious nature of the times and the epidemic, which has already caused the death of many people." By July 5, James's health showed signs of improvement but "I doubt that he will get better because his hygiene is very poor," the archbishop informed the pope in a further update. "He slept with the queen even though he had been drinking water and despite the contagion, such that this third fit of fever redoubled and exhausted him, causing him to suffer a fourth fit on July 2."

Fortunately, Robert also fell seriously ill around this time, and Joanna was able to resolve the crisis by settling three cities and a castle on Maria, thereby dividing Philip's monetary interests and subsequently his political allegiance from those of his ailing brother. Although the threat of violence was removed, the emperor of Constantinople continued to interfere with the queen's admin-istration. "He has already become very grand with me four times in the presence of the entire Council," wrote the archbishop of Naples to the bishop of Avignon on September 3, "especially when the question came up of revoking grants unwisely made by the Queen, for she is very poor and does not have the resources where-with to pay the census [to the Church]. [Robert] has done this so much that the business remains just about desperate, and yet all men are of the opinion that if the advice of the Count of Nola [another of Joanna's counselors] had been followed in collecting and saving funds and in certain other respects, the Queen would have plenty of money."

James of Majorca's ill health was but one component of a far larger problem confronting Joanna. Early in the marriage, the queen discovered that her new husband was mentally unbalanced and given to violent episodes. Although James had signed a marriage contract specifically waiving any right to encroach upon his wife's authority, or to meddle in any way with the government of her realm, within days of arriving in Naples he began demanding that he be ceded control of the kingdom. When Joanna refused, he flew into feverish rages, ranting irrationally and threatening both his wife and the kingdom. "The Queen, even though like the dead from his conduct towards her, has not had the courage to reveal it to others and told me only with great effort," the archbishop later apprised the pope. "She fears the king as her husband and dreads him as the devil, as not only did his lengthy incarceration affect the soundness of his mind but also because he is, according to the doctors, eccentric by nature and like mad, which his words and deeds show, alas! only too much, and it would be much worse if he came to drink any wine . . . In particular we have not been able to convince him to sleep in a separate bed from the Queen's, considering his impairment and despite his serious fits of fever, his heavy sweating, his enemas and other inconveniences."

Joanna covered up these incidents of aggression and tried to be patient, but James persisted, going so far as to conspire with his brother-in-law, the marquis of Montferrat, to bring John Hawkwood's White Company to Naples in support of a revolt against the queen. The White Company had arrived in Tuscany in July and had been hired for six months by the Pisans at a rate of 150,000 florins to strike against Florence, Pisa's perennial adversary. By September, Hawkwood had scored a significant victory for his employer, capturing many Florentine noblemen in a single battle at Incisa. The specter of an invasion by this criminal band, reported by Matteo Villani to consist of some 3,500 heavily armed horsemen and 2,000 infantrymen, hung heavily over the kingdom of Naples, especially when members of the free company were discovered to have infiltrated to the north in December and had only been dissuaded from attacking by the presence of heavy snows. "The Lady Queen has suspected for some time that her husband has been responsible for the coming of the free companies, and for this reason there is today a scandalous dissension between them," the archbishop of Naples wrote to the bishop of Avignon on January 18, 1364.

Joanna concealed her husband's dementia from all but her most intimate counselors for as long as possible, but privacy became impossible on January 4, 1364, when James engaged in a very public display of domestic violence, which caused a great scandal at court and throughout the capital. Forced to concede that her third marriage was a disaster, the queen unburdened herself in a long letter to the pope, which reveals the depth of her despair. "Most Holy Father, the importance of this matter compels me to reveal to your conscience, with most displeasure, what I wish Heaven had allowed me to keep to myself in complete silence," Joanna began. "Eight days after I had joined my spouse in matrimony by God's permission, Your Holiness's consent, and the necessary exemption, he began to engage in insane behaviors, about which I did not excessively worry, thinking that they were caused by his youth and the filth of a long imprisonment which might have dulled his sensuality. But after several days, afflicted with a fit of fever, he carried out even more outrageous deeds such that, on the doctors' advice, I removed from his room the weapons, stones, wooden clubs and all such objects he could lay his hands on. But this too I kept silent, presuming that the infection from his disease was the cause of this. Later and as a result of the familiarity caused by a more intimate association I began to notice that every month, sometimes at the change of the moon and sometimes just after the full moon he would have an outbreak of madness, with some clear-sighted moments at intervals."*

The queen observed that many famous physicians were consulted in an effort to cure James. She herself watched his diet carefully, which evidently meant inhibiting his consumption of fruit, as the archbishop of Naples also observed to the pope that James

---

* Joanna's reference to the moon is most likely meant to underscore that James's ailment was psychological, not physical. In the Middle Ages, insanity ("lunacy") was frequently thought to be affected by the phases of the moon.

frequently overindulged, which resulted in "the flux and vomiting." Nonetheless, despite her husband's obvious lack of improvement and her understanding of the danger she faced, Joanna continued, with misgivings, to share James's bed, she reported to Urban.

"But most recently, at the last change of the moon, one morning, suddenly, like a lunatic grinding his teeth, he began to say that he intended to be the master and general reformer of the justice of the kingdom, as I remember I had written to you previously, and that he would implement all the measures he intended in spite of me, and that I should immediately present to him a report on all pensions and privileges, as he wanted to know all," Joanna continued in her letter. "I agreed so as to contain his madness and, to please him and against the advice that I had been given, gave the order to provide him with this report. Abusing my good intentions and my kindness, he took an arrogant tone and said that all beneficiaries of whatever privileges had been granted from as far back as one could remember until today would be deprived of these without delay." When Joanna pointed out that there were several clauses within their marriage contract specifically prohibiting James from interfering in the realm, and that by signing this document, which had been further legitimized by a pontifical decree, he had agreed to these conditions, James flew into a rage.

"Bearing my answer with great impatience, he answered as he had often done publicly, with many gestures of contempt, that if he could be the master and lord, he would never relinquish this power either for the pope or for the Church, as he didn't care to obey them. I counseled him not to speak this way in public. He turned to me and said he would do what he had to do. I asked him what he would dare do; he answered that he would even strike the body of Christ with a knife. The fact is, dear Father and Master, that he has already easily drawn fifty letters of donation to his acquaintances, of three thousand, two thousand, one thousand florins or more, to be collected each year on the royal treasury."

Then Joanna described the incident that had caused such scandal in the realm. "Throwing himself impetuously at me, he seized me by the arm in the presence of several witnesses who thought I might fall to the ground.* Even though these witnesses were many, I bore with extreme patience the insult that was made to me, and so nothing worse could ensue I expressly ordered that no one move, feigning to give the impression that he hadn't done this with evil purpose but rather for amusement, and that he hadn't intended to pull me so violently. He turned to me and indulged in insults slanderous to my reputation, saying out loud that I had killed my husband, that I was a worthless courtesan, that I kept near me go-betweens who brought men to me at night, and that his revenge would be exemplary . . . I realized that such things could not be kept secret and that they were the topic of conversation in the entire town. Very quickly, the illustrious emperor of Constantinople, prince of Achaia and Taranto, learning of this, sent me this night the empress his wife with the duchess of Andria his sister to keep me company. They slept with me in my room, showing me much concern and with the thought that my husband's fit of madness would pass, but in the morning we found him in a worse state. Thus, in the evening of the second day, this same emperor came to me in person, along with my sister, wife of lord Philip of Taranto, accompanied by a goodly number of armed men, not to engage in any inappropriate action but rather to refrain the impudence of the king's acquaintances [retainers] . . . had they the temerity to indulge themselves in insolent behavior . . . Finally, we decided that my lord and husband and I would never meet alone in a bed or in a room . . . until we could fully determine what needed to be done to ensure my safety . . . As for me, I openly go during the day, at appropriate hours and with the appropriate escort, from my room to the room where

---

* Other observers reported that James had in fact "struck the Queen, injuring her badly," during this incident.

he lives to comfort him, giving him all honors due and bringing familial gifts," she concluded sadly.

That Robert of Taranto, who six months previously had threatened Joanna's rule, should have been the one to come to the queen's rescue in her extremity is an indication of just how seriously the threat from the king of Majorca and the free companies was perceived at court. It took a madman to do it, but in their detention of James, Joanna's family, famously and historically renowned for discord, finally seems to have found a subject on which everyone could agree.

Her husband's breakdown and the danger posed by a possible invasion by the White Company were by no means the only challenges Joanna faced during this period. As she was trying to temper and hide James's outbursts (for these, if known, would only add to the perception of potential weakness), the queen was also confronted with a crisis in Sicily.

Despite the treaty and coronation of 1356, Neapolitan hold over the island had never been fully realized. The Catalan party had remained in opposition, slowly building strength, although the strategically critical city of Messina, under the governorship of Niccolò Acciaiuoli's son, remained loyal to Naples. As early as 1359, Joanna had recognized that she did not have the military resources necessary to secure a lasting victory over Sicily and that consequently some sort of diplomatic arrangement would have to be made with the Catalans and their hereditary monarch, Frederick III, if she wished to continue to exert influence over the territory. Accordingly, she had offered to marry Maria's youngest daughter, Margherita, to Frederick III, aspiring in this way to wrest the Catalans away from their traditional ally, the crown of Aragon. Joanna was especially eager to negotiate this compact while Naples still held Messina, as possession of that city represented a tactical advantage that allowed her to press for much more favorable terms. But the Catalan advisers surrounding Frederick the Simple had rejected the Neapolitan offer and instead had surreptitiously smuggled Constanza, daughter of the king of Aragon, to Sicily to wed Frederick in 1361, hoping that the marriage would encourage her father to send an army to help topple the Neapolitan government in Messina.

The desired Aragonese military support never materialized, however, dampening Catalan prospects. The party was just at the point of considering reopening peace negotiations with Naples when plague reemerged on the island in the summer of 1363, claiming the life of Frederick's new young wife. Suddenly, a marriage alliance with the Neapolitan royal family was again a possibility, and this time, both sides leaped at it. The only problem was that Frederick wanted not Margherita, but her older sister, Jeanne.

Jeanne, duchess of Durazzo,* was Maria's eldest daughter and the likely heir to the throne, given the queen's childless condition, a situation for which there was not much prospect for improvement considering the current state of Joanna's third marriage. As Jeanne happened also to be the wealthiest woman in the kingdom, she made for a most attractive potential bride and was the focus of a number of matrimonial intrigues. One of these schemes, by far the most damaging to Neapolitan interests, originated at the highest level of the papal court.

Cardinal Guy of Boulogne had not forgotten that as early as 1355, Philip of Taranto had promised that Jeanne would be married to Guy's brother Godfrey, in return for Guy's active intervention in support of Taranto interests with Innocent VI. To Guy's displeasure, this alliance between his family and the duchess of

---

* Actually, in English, the duchess of Durazzo was also named Joanna in honor of her aunt, Joanna I, but I have used the French spelling of her name to avoid confusion with the queen.

Durazzo had never come to fruition, owing to Louis of Taranto's having, in the cardinal's opinion, reneged on Philip's promise by later stipulating that Godfrey could have Jeanne but not her money. With Louis dead and Urban V in the papacy, Guy now thought to resurrect a variation on this ménage, substituting his nephew Aimon of Geneva for Godfrey as the prospective bridegroom. To ensure that this time he was not thwarted by internal politics at the Neapolitan court, the cardinal, seeking a local surrogate, secretly enlisted the archbishop of Naples as his personal representative in this matter, charging the clergyman with the delicate task of closing the deal.

The archbishop had his work cut out for him. Aimon, who was so poor that the archbishop had to put up his own money as collateral against a seven-hundred-florin loan to allow the eager suitor to finance a trip to Naples, was the least impressive of the candidates for Jeanne's hand. In addition to Frederick III, the duchess of Durazzo was also pursued by Louis, count of Navarre, brother of the powerful Charles the Bad, king of Navarre; and by Louis II, duke of Bourbon, whose mother, Isabella of Valois, had been Joanna's mother's sister. "The lord Louis of Navarre has been much praised here," wrote a worried archbishop to his sponsor Guy of Boulogne on July 5, 1363, "and the lady [Jeanne] has stood up for him, until now, and has set her heart upon him quite remarkably until she heard that our candidate is handsomer, about which matter she is quite unwilling to believe anyone until she sees him . . . And so I would by all means have him [Aimon] come here quickly, for she has secretly indicated to me that she will expect him within two months, during which time she will become betrothed to no one else, nor even after that will she become betrothed to anyone except the lord Louis, and this only after deliberation with me." The archbishop further suggested that Cardinal Guy secure a bishopric for Jeanne's chancellor and some other method of bribery for the chancellor's brother, Jeanne's seneschal, as the archbishop considered the support of these two men to be instrumental to the happy conclusion of "the business of the marriage."

Taking the archbishop's advice, Aimon hurriedly traveled south, arriving in Aversa, where the court was staying, on November 15. He was greeted graciously by the royal family, including Joanna, who granted him an audience, and by Jeanne herself; afterward everyone took part in a dance hastily organized in celebration of the marriage of one of Joanna's servants. The next day, Aimon was treated to lunch by James of Majorca, who must have been having one of his good days, and danced again with Jeanne. Aimon made an extremely good impression on Jeanne, particularly after he had presented her with some expensive jewelry (supplied by the archbishop) as a token of his affection. There is no way to tell if he was in fact handsomer than Louis of Navarre, as Louis, of higher rank, declined to make a trip to Naples simply to woo Jeanne. He must have been good-looking enough, because the duchess's overly attentive manner toward the visitor from Geneva prompted the rumor that she was already secretly married to Aimon. Joanna herself raised this suspicion the next day with the archbishop, who denied the gossip and pressed for a decision regarding Aimon's suit. "The next day I addressed the Queen," the archbishop wrote to Cardinal Guy on November 23, "in the presence of all her Council . . . The Queen then finally said some things. Her answer is, in effect, that the Sicilian undertaking still hangs over us, and in the event that marriage should not take place, there remains the question of Duke [Louis] of Bourbon, her own near relative . . . But if this marriage should also not take place, and if our lord the Pope should approve of the lord Aimon, she would for her own part be content, and so, as I believe, she is writing to our lord the Pope." In other words, Aimon was in third place.

Unfortunately for the archbishop, Cardinal Guy's interference in the duchess's nuptial arrangements had by this time come to the attention of Cardinal Talleyrand of Périgord, who had no intention of marrying his great-niece, possibly the future queen of Naples, to his chief rival's impoverished nephew. Talleyrand did not bother with surrogates; he went straight to Urban. As a result, the archbishop had also to regretfully inform Cardinal Guy that Jeanne had received "a letter which the lord of Périgord [Talleyrand] has recently written to her, in which among other things I read that the Sicilian marriage had the approval of our lord the Pope, and in the event of this marriage's not taking place, he was himself sending the Archbishop of Patras to negotiate for the Duke of Bourbon, and he encourages her to fix her mind upon one or the other of these, despite the fact that that consummate swindler, the Archbishop of Naples,* who is generally regarded as such by all who know him, was intriguing for some other marriages, as he said, which were not consistent with the distinction of her royal blood, and that she was in no wise to be induced to accept such a marriage."

Urban, too, wrote to both Jeanne and Joanna. To Jeanne, the pope expressed his strong approval of her projected marriage with the king of Sicily "as a means of bringing back Frederick to obedience and devotion to the Holy Roman Church" and warned her not to bind herself to anyone else. "Your own uncle [Talleyrand], who is a man of great prudence and loves you like a father . . . will guide and assist you loyally and wisely in this matter and in your other undertakings," Urban noted in a letter dated November 28. To Joanna, in a letter written the same day, the pope went further: "Because it would not be fitting that the famous title of the house of Durazzo . . . should pass into alien hands, which we have learned is being attempted [a reference to the prospective marriage with Aimon], we wish and command you that, if the aforesaid Duchess

---

* This part must have been difficult to forward, as it was the archbishop of Naples himself who was transmitting this information.

should wish to transfer the city and duchy to another outside the aforesaid house, you should in no wise consent thereto, but expressly forbid her to do so, and impede her with all your strength."

But Jeanne, who was already twenty years old by this time, and more interested in sex appeal than state policy, did not want to marry the king of Sicily, whom she had heard was not as attractive as either Aimon or Louis of Navarre, and who had furthermore acquired the unpromising nickname of Frederick the Simple. To promote her own agenda, the duchess took steps to sabotage the prospective alliance. Secretly, she sent one of her servants to Sicily to "see and learn about certain things which were being generally said both about the miserable state of the kingdom and the poverty of the King and the late Queen as well as about the person of the said King," wrote the archbishop of Naples. The servant's mission went beyond mere surveillance, however, as was discovered when he was taken into custody at Messina by soldiers loyal to Joanna and the grand seneschal. Jeanne had also given him letters addressed to Frederick III in which she warned the king of Sicily that Niccolò Acciaiuoli was not to be trusted in the peace negotiations, as he intended to seize the island of Malta for himself "and some other things . . . touching the city of Messina to the prejudice of the said Lady Queen," reported the archbishop.

Joanna, although of course intent on the Sicilian marriage as a way of salvaging the one great foreign policy achievement of her reign, had nonetheless tolerated her niece's unhelpful attitude up until now. ("I would marry him [the king of Sicily] myself if I could!" Joanna is reported to have exclaimed on more than one occasion.) But this was treason. The queen, who had correctly identified the archbishop of Naples as the catalyst for Jeanne's obstinacy, moved quickly to punish the culprits. On December 22, 1363, Jeanne's seneschal and others of her household staff were arrested on the charge of conspiring against the crown (or "using their influence with her [Jeanne] in favor of our business," as the archbishop put it in a December 29 letter to Cardinal Guy). Jeanne herself was placed under house arrest at the Castel dell'Ovo. "The said lady Duchess . . . is still detained, in the strictest custody, to such an extent that no one, however great or small, familiar or outsider, has access to her; so that she did not even hear the divine office on Christmas day," wrote the archbishop. Although the archbishop was protected by his position, he was accused of deliberately undermining the treaty with Sicily, which by this time had been negotiated on terms highly favorable to Naples. "Open war" existed between the archbishop and Niccolò Acciaiuoli. The former feared his correspondence was being intercepted and read, and took the precaution of writing in cipher. He also begged Cardinal Guy to get the pope to assign a legate to the kingdom to aid him in his task.

To the queen, the idea that her niece would rebel against a marriage that would help cement one of the principal goals of all the Angevin rulers, and would furthermore bring peace and stability to the kingdom, was unthinkable. And so, on January 16, 1364, she had Jeanne brought to Robert of Taranto's house, and there the duchess of Durazzo broke down before an audience consisting of her aunt, the queen; her mother, Maria; and her uncle, the emperor; and consented to marry Frederick III. It looked as if the Neapolitan alliance with Sicily had been saved after all.

And then, the next day, Cardinal Talleyrand of Périgord unexpectedly died.

The speed with which the papal court reversed itself on the subject of Jeanne's marriage was marvelous. Overnight, Urban, who until this point had been busy appeasing Talleyrand, found himself suddenly relieved of this responsibility, leaving ample opportunity for accommodating the now-dominant cardinal, Guy of Boulogne. On February 27, ten days after the cardinal of Périgord's demise, Urban wrote to Joanna ordering her to release Jeanne from custody in order to permit her to marry Aimon, threatening sanctions if the queen did not obey his commands. At the end of April, at Cardinal

Guy's behest, Urban signed bulls excommunicating both Joanna and Maria for failing to allow Jeanne to marry whom she pleased and sent them to the archbishop of Naples for publication. The archbishop did not dare present the bulls at court. "Because there is no wickedness greater than the wickedness of a woman, especially of those two, in truth I now begin to be afraid, above all because they put on such a good face when they see me: since Easter the Queen has invited me to dine with her four times, and always I have presented my excuses!" Eventually, the kingdom was threatened with interdict for failing to allow Jeanne to marry Aimon. As Cardinal Guy of Boulogne wrote in a letter to Niccolò Acciaiuoli, "And in truth, my very dear friend, up to now we have not heard that in the land of any other prince in Christendom people are compelled by force to contract marriage," a stirring statement of feminist principle that would no doubt have been of great interest to Christendom's many female subjects, had the Curia felt the slightest need to apprise them of it.

With the marriage arrangements thus stymied, popular opinion in Sicily swung away from the Latin party and toward the opposition. Emboldened by Naples's apparent weakness, and insulted by Jeanne's disparagement of their sovereign, the Catalan faction struck. On June 1, 1364, Frederick III's forces retook Messina with aid from within the city itself. The fall of Messina brought an end to the Latin party's dominance, the prospective marriage alliance, and Joanna's all-too-brief reign as queen of Sicily.

Stunned and furious, the ruling elite of Naples turned on the archbishop. On June 18, the highest-ranking barons and court officials, with the full endorsement of the queen, sent a sharply worded grievance to the pope complaining of interference in the kingdom's affairs and calling the archbishop "the great deceiver, who got around one man with flattery, another with promises . . . [who] had succeeded in blocking the marriage of the Duchess with Frederick, destroying every hope of peace and tranquility in the kingdom . . .

[The nobles further swore] to resist to the bitter end the marriage of Jeanne of Durazzo with Aimon of Geneva." Guy of Boulogne fought back by convincing Urban to send a papal legate, who arrived in the kingdom in early July with new bulls excommunicating Joanna and Maria if Jeanne was not handed over to papal authority by August 20; these were made public in the capital on July 11. Joanna coldly informed Urban's representative in a private audience that evening that the duchess of Durazzo was under her mother's care, and not the queen's. Maria, incensed by this tampering with what she considered to be a private family affair, harangued the archbishop in front of the papal legate, and then had her servants attack the archbishop's palace, kidnapping two of his retainers who were subsequently rescued by other church officials. Faced with such open hostility, the archbishop judged it prudent to withdraw, and he fled the kingdom. The papal legate waited until the deadline of August 20, and when Jeanne was not released into his custody, he pronounced the bans of excommunication and placed the kingdom under interdict. Then he, too, fled.

In defiance of the papal court, Jeanne was eventually betrothed on November 23, 1365 "on the advice of Queen Joanna, her aunt, and . . . her mother [Maria]" to Charles the Bad's younger brother Louis of Navarre, and married him the following year. "On the 18th of June, 1366, the lord Louis of Navarre entered Naples with three galleys and the next day married the lady Jeanne, duchess of Durazzo, and that same night slept with her," reported an official chronicle. For his part, Aimon, having failed to secure his heiress, instead embarked on a crusade against the Turks in Constantinople in 1366. Although he returned safely to Venice in the summer of 1367, he fell ill on the journey home to Geneva and died on August 30. Jeanne's new husband was similarly cursed: intent on asserting his authority over his wife's property, he hired a free company of Navarrese mercenaries and in 1372 launched a carefully prepared attack against the city of Durazzo, which had fallen into enemy hands. No sooner had he arrived at the port than, in the process of achieving his military objective, he fell ill or was wounded (the record is unclear) and promptly died.

The true victim of the Holy See's marital meddling, however, was undoubtedly the kingdom of Naples, which lost its one chance to hold on to its long-sought territorial gains in Sicily. By 1372, Joanna was forced to concede Catalan supremacy on the island and sign a peace treaty with Frederick III. Although the queen managed to negotiate a number of concessions—Frederick III was to pay homage to the crown of Naples in perpetuity; he was not to use the title "king of Sicily," which she reserved for herself and her heirs, but rather was to style himself "king of Trinacria"; the island was to pay an annual tribute of three thousand ounces of gold, which made up about half the amount Joanna needed to supply the church each year as part of the original contract with Charles of Anjou—the agreement nonetheless represented a final surrender of Neapolitan ambitions in Sicily. On October 31, 1372, this compact was further amended to Naples's detriment by the pope, who demanded that Sicily fall under his dominion and that both Joanna and Frederick do homage to the church for the island. Frederick's acceptance of this and other papal stipulations led to his being crowned king of Sicily on March 30, 1375; thereafter he was known by this designation, and not king of Trinacria. Since Joanna also retained the title of sovereign of Sicily, the double billing might have caused some confusion, but the medieval world was nothing if not resourceful and neatly resolved the difficulty by simply coining the appellation the "Kingdom of the Two Sicilies," an ingenious solution that would endure for the next five hundred years.

~❦~

Despite the excommunications, the acrimony surrounding the duchess of Durazzo's marriage represented a distinct anomaly in the queen's overall relationship to the pope. In almost every other aspect of their affiliation, Joanna maintained a congenial rapport with Urban. This affinity was based on a shared purpose and understanding. Each recognized in the other an advocate for what both believed was the critical issue of the age: the necessity of physically returning the papal court to its former seat of authority in Italy.

To return to Rome was a cherished objective of Urban's pontificate. Almost every evil plaguing Italy was, he believed, attributable to the removal of the papal court to Avignon, and certainly the best way to capitalize on Cardinal Albornoz's considerable military achievements was to reinhabit the patrimony. Urban knew that there would be vociferous opposition to his plan, both from within the Sacred College, a majority of whose members were French, and from external sources like the crown of France, which had become used to wielding significant influence over church policy by virtue of the papacy's proximity in Avignon. To accomplish his dream, Urban needed powerful allies in Italy who would be willing to provide material support in the form of ships to transport the court to Rome, and soldiers to guard its members and implement its policies once they arrived.

In this aspiration, the pope had no more stalwart champion than the queen of Naples. A return of the papal court to Italy meant the resumption of the close collaboration that had characterized papal relations during earlier Angevin reigns. Moreover, Joanna herself was very religious, and for this reason also desired the seat of church power to be close at hand. And so, although they quarreled about Jeanne's marriage, and certainly Joanna's frustration at the loss of Sicily was real, the issue never caused a significant rift between Joanna and Urban, the way similar arguments had alienated Innocent VI from Louis of Taranto.

Instead, Urban often went out of his way to assist Joanna as a means of cementing her reign. In May 1364, when the queen could not raise the money for the yearly tribute—the archbishop of

Naples reported that the kingdom as a whole produced some 290,000 florins in revenues that year, but due to the alienation of the realm, the crown's share of this was so small that the queen could barely afford to buy bread, a bit of hyperbole which nonetheless made the point—Urban forgave nine tenths of the debt and then lent Joanna the remaining balance of 15,000 florins through an intermediary. When Robert of Taranto, who had been gravely ill, finally died on September 17, 1364, and Philip of Taranto tried to prevent Joanna from reclaiming lands and income formerly belonging to the crown from his brother's estate, Urban again supported the queen's position, particularly after she promised to earmark the revenues generated by these properties toward the payment of the annual tribute.

The following year, 1365, marked a turning point for the queen. Evidently, despite her fear of James's outbursts, Joanna had resumed sleeping with her husband, an indication of just how desperately she sought to provide a child of her own as heir to the kingdom. In January 1365, her efforts were rewarded. The thirty-nine-year-old queen of Naples was pregnant.

Joanna's joy and relief over having conceived is not difficult to imagine. Urban, too, was pleased and in a February 5 letter revoked her excommunication (still in force due to the court's resistance to Jeanne's marriage with Aimon) to accommodate the prospective birth of the child. But jubilation turned to despair in June when the queen miscarried.

The abrupt termination of this pregnancy, so ardently wished for, had a profound impact on Joanna. She had only endured the trial of her third husband because she believed she could still bear children with someone who was not a near relation. When events dictated otherwise, she turned to the church. That summer, as soon as she recovered, she wrote to Urban, inviting him to resettle the papal court in Naples, under her protection, and offering him her fleet as a means of transportation.

The choice of Naples, rather than Rome, was not without precedent. Joanna knew that Pope Celestine V had been induced by her great-grandfather Charles the Lame to be crowned at Aquila in 1294 and to reside for his entire pontificate (albeit abbreviated to five months) in a little room at the Castel Nuovo. Moreover, Joanna's kingdom promised to be a much safer destination than Rome, whose notoriously aggressive citizens had only recently agreed to submit once again to papal authority, and then only under the stimulus provided by the presence of Cardinal Albornoz and his mercenaries.

With the queen's encouragement and that of the Holy Roman Emperor, Charles IV, who was concerned that the Viscontis were becoming too powerful and wanted a strong local papacy as a counterpoint, Urban came to a decision. On October 1, 1365, he wrote to Joanna, thanking her for her invitation and offer of assistance and informing her that he intended to return the papal court to Italy as soon as political conditions seemed favorable. Although it was clear the pope meant to inhabit Rome and not Naples, Joanna expressed no disappointment, only joy—a further indication her motives were spiritual rather than political. "I have only one regret," the queen wrote in response to Urban's letter, "that the Creator did not see fit to make me a man; because if my gender had allowed me to do so, upon seeing my lord [the pope] arrive . . . like Peter before me, I would have hurried on foot to greet him in complete and trusting faith."

Even the sudden, unexpected death of Niccolò Acciaiuoli on November 8 did not adversely affect plans for this transition. Or, perhaps, it was not so unexpected. According to Matteo Palmieri, a fifteenth-century historian and one of Niccolò's early biographers, the grand seneschal's death was foretold by Saint Bridget of Sweden, who happened to be staying with Niccolò's sister Lapa in Naples that autumn. Frightened by her houseguest's prophecy, Lapa hurried to find her brother and discovered him in council with Joanna. He seemed perfectly healthy, and Lapa returned to her own castle vastly relieved, only to have Niccolò subsequently fall ill and die a few days later. For this reason, Saint Bridget, Lapa, and Joanna were all painted into the *Via Veritatis*, a magnificent fresco by Andrea da Firenze (also known as Andrea di Bonaiuto) in the Spanish Chapel of Florence's Santa Maria Novella church in 1366, the year after Niccolò's death.

The corpse of the grand seneschal was transported to Florence and interred at the Certosa of Galluzzo, the cavernous Carthusian monastery he had built with the proceeds of his highly lucrative career, and the repository of much of this wealth. There, surrounded by many precious works of art and a library rivaling that of King Robert, an impressive shrine depicting Niccolò in full armor was installed and the tomb decorated with the royal Angevin fleur-de-lis, an honor ordinarily strictly reserved for immediate members of Joanna's family. Niccolò was laid to rest beside his son, who had predeceased him, and whose equally splendid statuary was reputed to have cost his father fifty thousand florins. The remaining family held on to both Niccolò's fabulous riches and control of the principia of Achaia well into the next century in the name of Robert of Taranto's widow and her subsequent heirs. "Acciaiuoli," Edward Gibbon would later pronounce. "Plebian at Florence, potent at Naples, and sovereign in Greece."

❧

The loss of the man who was, at least in his own estimation, the single most important influence in the kingdom of Naples, had surprisingly little effect on the state of the realm, causing none of the usual plays for power that characterized most medieval political transitions. Instead, the queen, very much in control of her government, simply replaced Acciaiuoli with Niccolò Spinelli, formerly a Neapolitan ambassador to the papal court. While lacking Acciaiuoli's undeniable gift for self-promotion, Spinelli was nonetheless an extremely able administrator who served the queen with great distinction. The next several years were among the most peaceful, prosperous, and prestigious the kingdom had known in decades.

Unquestionably, much of the tranquility resulted from a slightly improved economic position. Joanna had made a deliberate effort to foster security, and thereby promote material gain, by protecting the rights and livelihoods of the common people from the excesses of the aristocracy, as witnessed by her decree in favor of the townspeople of Chieti, issued on August 6, 1362, immediately after the death of Louis of Taranto:

> Joanna, by the grace of God, queen of Jerusalem and Sicily . . . to the Captain general and justiciar of the province of Abruzzi . . . On behalf of the whole community [*universitas*] of the men of Chieti . . . It has recently been shown by their petition to our Majesty that a dispute arose between the count of San Valentino and the men of Chieti on account of some men from the count's lands who had gone to live in Chieti. The count demanded them back, and two envoys were sent to the count to negotiate a settlement. The count detained them and refused to release them until the community obliged itself on pain of 400 onze [about 30 tarius] to remit and expel his vassals from the city. This the community, keen to liberate its citizens, undertook to do, under duress . . . In the same petition, it is added that the count busied himself . . . to proceed against the community and notified you, as royal justiciar, of the penalty and pressed you to exact it . . . Mindful that if the undertaking was made under duress, as claimed, the community is not legally held to observe it, we . . . therefore order that if you find the matter corresponds to this petition . . . you are . . . not to trouble the community at the request of the count in any way.

Similarly, the queen tried to introduce the production of silk as a means of offsetting the losses from grain. Other sources of income came from the sale of lumber from the kingdom's many forests and the export of sweet wine. The queen was not above putting pressure on her trading partners to exact economic concessions. In 1363, Niccolò Acciaiuoli had written to the Florentines on her behalf: "You know well . . . the great difficulties faced by my lady the queen, and the dangers she faces by not paying her tribute [to the Holy See]; hence the officials of the treasury have investigated many ways of finding the funds she needs, and the method everyone approved was to impose a tax of two ounces per piece on Florentine cloth brought by sea or by land into this kingdom. And meanwhile it is the Genoese who provide help and offer to bring as many French, Genoese, and Milanese cloths into the kingdom as we might need, if it is forbidden for Florentine cloths to enter the kingdom without payment of two ounces per piece; by acting thus they [the treasury officials] want to increase the taxes and to obtain no small sum of money."

The redistribution of Robert of Taranto's assets also served to relieve the financial stress on the crown, which aided the cause of stability. Because Robert died childless, Philip inherited the title of emperor of Constantinople, and Maria styled herself empress, even though Robert's widow, Marie of Bourbon, kept all the property in Achaia and haughtily refused to recognize the transferal of rank, so that for a time there were two empresses of Constantinople. And although Philip of Taranto remained obdurate, refusing to do homage to Joanna after she appropriated lands from his brother's estate, he lacked sufficient support to contest her rule and was effectively marginalized.

The first months of the year 1366 were bittersweet for the queen. James of Majorca, frustrated at his exclusion from his wife's government, abruptly left Naples at the beginning of January to seek allies willing to help him recover his former kingdom. His departure signaled an end to the queen's hopes of producing an heir, but the pain of this reality was no doubt tempered by her relief at his absence. James's withdrawal from the field of Neapolitan politics was followed soon after by the loss of yet another of Joanna's perennial opponents, her sister, Maria, who died on May 20.* Maria, always second, did not live to see her daughter Jeanne married to Louis of Navarre that fall, but her eldest daughter's recalcitrance had apparently brought her closer to Joanna, as evinced by the burial arrangements. Maria was interred at the church of Santa Chiara, in a position of honor next to King Robert. Her funeral statuary featured her figure crowned and clothed in imperial robes, under which ran the inscription "imperatrix Constantinopolitana a ducissa Duracii" (empress of Constantinople and duchess of Durazzo), a parting gift from the queen, who allowed her sister to occupy in death the sphere of majesty that had been denied her in life.

❧

Two months later, on July 20, 1366, Urban V upended the balance of power in Europe by publicly announcing his intention of leaving Avignon in order to return the papal court to its rightful place in Italy.

---

* There is some confusion as to when, exactly, Maria died, as another chronicler wrote that she lived until June 5, 1367, and a third indicated that she was still alive in Viterbo on September 5, 1367. However, as May 20, 1366, is the date of Maria's death as inscribed on her sepulcher at Santa Chiara, and there are strong indications that Joanna, rather than Maria, acted in a mother's capacity to Jeanne at her wedding to Louis of Navarre on June 19, 1366, the earlier date seems the most likely.

✦

CHAPTER XVI

Queen *and* Pope

S O BEGAN THE period of Joanna's greatest influence, when the kingdom of Naples again assumed the position of primacy it had occupied during the halcyon years of King Robert's early reign.

Although Urban's decision was announced in the summer of 1366, the actual transfer of the Holy See was delayed by a number of factors and did not take place for another nine months. Despite Cardinal Albornoz's efforts, the Papal States had not yet been completely pacified. The criminal activities of the free companies, particularly John Hawkwood's mercenary bands,* threatened church rule and raised questions as to whether sufficient protection existed to move the papal court to Rome. Then, too, there was the problem of the deplorable condition of the holy city itself. "For more than sixty stormy years there had been no court life, no pilgrims worth

---

* Hawkwood's forces went through a number of transformations. The White Company disbanded in 1365, only to be reconstituted as the Company of Saint George, which also dispersed after a year. Although known primarily as a leader of expatriate English mercenaries, Hawkwood also utilized Italian and Hungarian knights and soldiers in his companies. "It was the peculiarity of Italian warfare that the captains Hawkwood fought against one day fought with him the next," observed medieval scholar William Caferro.

mentioning, no great religious festivals, none, in fact, of the ordinary sources of Roman prosperity. The nobles had shunned the dismal city, the mercenaries had sacked it, and even the priests had fled, leaving their deserted cloisters to add to the surrounding desolation." Urban was informed that the most famous and important buildings, including Saint Peter's and the Lateran Basilica, had been allowed to fall into ruin and that the papal palaces were completely uninhabitable. Lastly, great opposition to the move was voiced by the French crown and from within the Holy See itself. Six decades in Avignon had produced a Sacred College heavily weighted toward France. Only three of Urban's twenty cardinals were Italian by birth; Albornoz was Spanish; the rest were all French. These sixteen did not want to give up their immense, splendid homes, nor the fashionable company, excellent wines, and temperate climate of Provence to take up residence in a dilapidated, dangerous city whose climate was as notoriously unhealthful as its citizenry and where they could not even speak the language.

But Urban quietly persisted in the face of every obstacle. Security was established on September 18, 1366, when the kingdom of Naples joined together in a league with Florence, Pisa, and Siena and committed to sending 650 horsemen and 650 foot soldiers to resist the free companies and ensure the protection of the papal court. Similarly, an army of architects, masons, marble cutters, and carpenters descended on Rome to restore the city to its former glory. Urban spent 15,569 florins on repairs to the papal palace alone. A fleet of sixty galleys provided by Naples, Venice, Genoa, and Pisa was assembled to convey the vast wealth and material goods accumulated by the members of the papal court. One cardinal needed space to transport his stable of more than two hundred horses, and some sixty-five barrels of wine were conveyed in order to ensure an adequate drinking supply during the first months of relocation.

Opposition from France was considerable, but again Urban prevailed. King John had died in 1364 and was succeeded by his eldest son, Charles V. Desperate to hold on to the papacy, Charles sent a delegation of his most learned clerics and prestigious nobles to Avignon armed with scholastic arguments refuting the decision to move. Incorporated in one of the speeches enunciated by the French ambassadors was a fictional conversation between king and pope. "'Lord, where goest thou?' asked the son [Charles]. 'To Rome,' replied the father [Urban]. 'There thou wilt be crucified,' rejoined the son," the ambassador finished ominously, thereby providing a succinct summation of the prevailing opinion of a majority of the cardinals. Indeed, on May 6, 1367, when all was finally prepared and the galleys waiting at Marseille, the cardinals refused to board the ship and were only induced to sail when Urban diluted their power by raising an underling to a cardinalship on the spot and assuring them "that he could produce other cardinals from underneath his cowl." Even with this persuasion, only five members of the Sacred College embarked with Urban that day, and when the fleet finally set off "like a floating city," the cries and moans of the despondent cardinals—"Oh, wicked Pope! Oh, Godless brother! Whither is he dragging his sons?"—trailed in its wake and were distinctly audible to the citizenry of Marseille.

By June 1, Urban had landed at Pisa and on June 9 entered Viterbo, where he found Joanna's new grand seneschal, Niccolò Spinelli, awaiting him, along with other high-ranking members of her court and an armed force sent by the queen to protect him. Here the papal court settled for the hot summer months, and Spinelli and the Neapolitan soldiers distinguished themselves by quelling a rebellion against the papacy on September 5. Finally, on October 16, 1367, Urban fulfilled his promise by making a triumphant entrance into Rome, albeit one accompanied by a significant military escort. The Neapolitan delegation held a prominent place of honor in the procession.

In March of the following year, Joanna, regally surrounded by an entourage consisting of senior members of her baronage, and accompanied by a procession of sumptuously clad retainers, paid a state visit to Rome. The pope met the queen on the outskirts of the city and they rode together into the center of town, where she was formally greeted by the cardinals on the steps of a somewhat restored Saint Peter's and then taken to hear Mass. On March 17, the fourth Sunday of Lent, as a mark of special favor, Urban presented Joanna with the golden rose, a highly unusual gesture that caused comment. "Some of the Cardinals afterwards protested that this coveted honor had never before been granted to a woman. The ready Pontiff replied, 'Neither has any of you ever seen an Abbot of St. Victor [Urban's former position] in the chair of St. Peter.'" The presentation of this ornament must have been deeply satisfying for the queen. Robert the Wise never got a golden rose.

Joanna's triumphs were never completely unblemished, however. Just before the queen knelt at the pope's feet to receive her honor, word arrived that her husband, James of Majorca, had been captured in battle and was being held for ransom.

─❧─

In the two years he had been away, James's odyssey had taken him first to Avignon, and then westward to Gascony in search of an ally willing to assist him in a campaign against the king of Aragon for control of Majorca. Finding none, James had instead found himself drawn into a completely unrelated conflict that happened to occupy a position of prominence at the time: the hereditary struggle for the crown of Castile.

The war for Castile had its origins in the amours of its former sovereign Alphonso XI. Alphonso had been married to Maria of Portugal, by whom he had a son, Pedro. Having fulfilled his duty as a husband by providing an heir, Alphonso, who seems to have been less than enchanted with his wife, had remedied the situation by taking another woman, Leonora de Guzmán, as his lover.

Leonora also provided Alphonso with a son, Enrique, sensibly known as "the Bastard." There was nothing unusual about this arrangement except that Alphonso so made a point of favoring his illegitimate family that Maria felt humiliated. To appease his mother's wounded sensibilities, Pedro's first act upon assuming the throne after his father's death was to murder Leonora and banish Enrique, a maneuver that earned the new king the sobriquet "Pedro the Cruel."

Enrique fled to France, where he found a powerful ally in Charles V. Pedro the Cruel was a partisan of Edward III; if Charles put Enrique the Bastard on the throne of Castile instead, England would lose (and France would gain) a valuable ally. Although France had ostensibly been at peace with England since the Treaty of Bretigny in 1360, Charles was only too willing to harass the English through surrogates. The king of France introduced Enrique to his best general, Bertrand du Guesclin, who secured an army of several thousand men by redirecting the energies of those free companies that had not already left France for Italy. Together with Enrique, Bertrand invaded Castile and successfully removed Pedro from the throne in 1366. "It seems all but certain that the campaign of the companies under Du Guesclin . . . was part of a brilliant French strategy designed by Charles V to take the English in the rear."

Finding himself on the run, Pedro remembered his English ally and turned up in Bordeaux, where Edward III's son the Black Prince, now styled prince of Aquitaine, kept a magnificent court. The ousted king of Castile asked for help, offering to pay all expenses and to reward his collaborators handsomely. Pedro had brought what treasure he could with him and made a point of mentioning that there was quite a bit more back in Castile but that he hadn't had room on his ships to carry it all. "My dear cousin [Edward], as long as my gold, my silver, and my treasure will last, which I have brought with me from Spain, but which is not so great by thirty times as what I have left behind, I am willing they should be divided among your people," said Pedro. The Black Prince, his interest piqued, called a war council, which was attended by Charles the Bad, king of Navarre. Charles's participation was necessary as Navarre held the only reliable pass through the Pyrenees between Spain and France. "They all, and the king of Navarre as well, agreed to help king Pedro to win back Spain; since he had so humbly asked them he deserved to be helped; on this they were unanimous," reported the chronicler Chandos Herald.

Into this mix stumbled Joanna's husband. "At this period Lord James, King of Majorca, came to visit the prince [Edward] in the city of Bordeaux, and to request his assistance in order that he might recover his possessions from the King of Aragon, who had driven him from them, and put his father to death," wrote the chronicler Jean Froissart. The Black Prince instead enlisted James in the Castile campaign, saying, "Sir King . . . I promise you, most loyally, that upon our return from Spain, we will undertake to replace you on your throne of Majorca, either by treaty or by force of arms." Thrilled to have found so forceful an advocate, James agreed to join the expedition and fight with the Black Prince on the side of King Pedro. As a special sign of favor, just before they left, James was selected to stand as godfather to Edward's second son, Richard, born on January 6, 1367, the feast of the Epiphany, "the day of the three kings." Much was made of the miraculous occurrence that, by coincidence, three kings were in Bordeaux on the day of the birth—Pedro, king of Castile; Charles the Bad, king of Navarre; and James IV, king of Majorca—a biblical allusion only slightly tarnished by the fact that only one of the three sovereigns could be said to be in actual possession of his kingdom at the time.

The Black Prince and his allies put together a massive army of thirty thousand men and departed for Spain on Valentine's Day 1367. The cost of maintaining so many men and supplies exceeded the value of the treasure Pedro had brought with him, so Edward fronted the money for the expedition, which eventually amounted to approximately 2.7 million florins. Enrique had been warned that they were coming, and although his generals advised avoiding a direct confrontation with so large an aggressor and instead suggested that the Bastard simply cut off Edward's supplies "to famish them without striking a blow," Enrique, goaded by the chivalric notion of warfare, which prized honor above all, stubbornly insisted on fighting. The result was the battle of Najera, which took place on April 3, 1367. James of Majorca led the rear guard, which was stationed "on a little hill to the left," for the Black Prince. Enrique's forces were outnumbered, and Edward and his longbows won easily. The Bastard was forced to flee, and Pedro was restored to the throne. "My dear cousin, I must thank you, for today you have done so much for me that I can never repay it in my lifetime," said Pedro to Edward when it was all over. This turned out to be a highly accurate assessment of the situation, as the restored king of Castile subsequently reneged on the vast sum of money he owed to the prince.

But although the battle had been won, the war was soon lost. Edward, who had his own notions of chivalry, insisted that Pedro pardon most of those taken prisoner and ransom the rest, a gesture to which the new king of Castile grudgingly acquiesced. Du Guesclin, who had escaped the battle but was subsequently apprehended, won his freedom through wiliness. "They say in France," said Du Guesclin to the prince [Edward], "that you are so much afraid of me, that you dare not set me free." "What! Sir Bertrand," said the prince, "do you imagine that we keep you a prisoner for fear of your prowess? By St. George it is not so; for, my good sir, if you will pay one hundred thousand francs you shall be free at once." Charles V immediately forwarded the ransom, and Bertrand du Guesclin, an extremely able opponent, was free in a month.

The real problem was Pedro, however. The restored king left for Seville soon after the battle, promising to return with sufficient treasure to repay the Black Prince and his army for their service. He never returned. Edward waited six months "and his army suffered great hardship, hunger and thirst, for lack of wine and bread," reported Chandos Herald. With famine came illness. Of course, James of Majorca, with his delicate constitution, was one of the first to sicken. When it became clear that Pedro had defaulted on his obligations, Edward ordered the army to withdraw "and all prepared for departure except the King of Majorca, who was so ill that he could not be moved," said Froissart. As a result, when Enrique and Du Guesclin regrouped, as it was inevitable they would, and invaded Spain with a second army in autumn 1367, the hapless James, having been left behind in the city of Valladolid, was captured easily and held for ransom. "As soon as the King [Enrique] was entered into the town, he demanded where the King of Majorca was? The which was showed to him. Then the King entered into the chamber where he lay, not fully whole of his disease. Then the King went to him and said, 'Sir King of Majorca, you have been our enemy and have invaded this our realm of Castile with a great army; wherefore, we set our hands on you; therefore yield yourself as our prisoner, or else you are but dead.' And when the King of Majorca saw himself in that case, and that no defense would help him, he said, 'Sir King, truly am I but dead, if that it please you; and, sir, gladly I yield me unto you, but to none other. Therefore, sir, if your mind be to put me into any other man's hands, show it me; for I had rather die than to be put into the hands of my bitter enemy, the King of Aragon.' 'Sir,' said the King, 'fear you not; I will do you but right; if I did otherwise, I were to blame. You shall be my prisoner, either to acquit you, or to ransom you at my pleasure.' Thus was the King of Majorca taken by King Henry [Enrique], and caused him to be well kept there."

Pedro tried to rally, but deprived of Edward's support, his forces were defeated. He was ultimately cornered by Du Guesclin and transferred to the care of his half-brother. The gracious consideration displayed by the new king of Castile to James of Majorca did not extend to his own family. On the evening of March 22, 1369, an unarmed Pedro was viciously stabbed to death by a group of men led by Enrique the Bastard, whose notion of chivalry had obviously evolved in the wake of his previous defeat.

Nor did the Black Prince emerge unscathed from this adventure. Heavily in debt, he was forced to raise taxes on his subjects in Gascony, and his rule became even more unpopular among the conquered French nobility. Worse, while in Spain he had evidently fallen prey to the same disease that had afflicted James of Majorca, and the sickness grew worse after he returned to Bordeaux. By the following year, the Black Prince was so ill that he could no longer mount his horse.

⁂

Joanna was thus forced to scrape together a large sum of money from within her already overtaxed resources to liberate a husband from whom she had only just succeeded in honorably separating herself. Urban, who was well acquainted with the most intimate details of Joanna's third marriage, was sufficiently concerned she might refuse to aid James altogether that he felt the need to write to her, urging her to produce the funds with alacrity. "Even though we trust, without our ever doubting it, that you bring all of your care and concern to his release," the pope wrote on January 30, 1368, as soon as the news of the king of Majorca's imprisonment was known, "we urge your sublimity to apply yourself with persistence, and bring all the attention you can to the . . . ransom, or to any other means of freeing your husband." Still, Joanna recognized her responsibility to her spouse and, working with James's sister, the marchioness of Montferrat, eventually came to terms with Enrique. The ransom demanded—sixty thousand golden doubloons, the Spanish coinage—was so considerable that the only means of raising it was for the queen to discontinue salary payments to her government in Provence for a year, a solution that, not unreasonably, caused considerable discontent among the local officials. "The which ransom these two ladies [Joanna and James's sister] paid so courteously, that King Henry [Enrique] was well content," Froissart concluded. James was released into the care of his ally Charles the Bad to ensure that the king of Aragon did not take advantage of the king of Majorca's weakness during the transition. He was back in Naples by 1369 in time for the solemn consecration ceremony of the church of San Martino, the monastery Joanna completed for her father.

The issue of her husband's ransom was not the only exigency Joanna wrestled with during this period. Of equal concern to the queen was the heirless condition of the realm. Uncertainty over the succession of the crown of Naples was too tempting not to invite interference. By 1368 the most insistent meddling issued from a voice from the past, and hailed from a part of the world that she most wished to forget: Hungary.

Eighteen years had passed since the king of Hungary, stymied in his original conquest of Naples, had abandoned his hereditary interests and departed the kingdom, seemingly for good. In the interim, King Louis' stature had swelled. His own people dubbed him "the Great" for having built Hungary into a regional power through aggressive military policies. Louis found the business of governing too tame for his tastes and much preferred warfare "since it is not the kingship itself that is desirable but the fame that goes with it," as one of the king's clerics, who knew him well, reported. But despite the renown he achieved, nature (or, more likely, the Angevin genetic structure) had contrived against him, so that, ironically, he faced exactly the problem Joanna did: at forty-two years old, the same age as the queen, the king of Hungary was still childless. The succession crisis in Hungary mirrored that of Naples still further: Like Joanna, Louis the Great's nearest blood relation was a girl, his niece, Elizabeth, the daughter of his younger brother Stephen, Stephen himself having died in 1354.

The king of Hungary did not want to leave the realm to his niece, but nor did he wish to forgo his Angevin bloodline. Searching for a candidate who embodied both these requirements, he discovered only one: Charles of Durazzo, son of Louis of Durazzo, the little boy who had first come to Joanna's court as a hostage to his father's good behavior and who was subsequently raised to a high position by the queen after Louis of Durazzo was murdered by Robert and Philip of Taranto in 1362.

Intent on establishing a viable succession while he was still at the peak of his power, Louis the Great invited Charles of Durazzo to Hungary so that he and his young kinsman could become acquainted, and Charles introduced to the customs of the kingdom. This invitation was accepted, and Charles was brought to the Hungarian court, possibly as early as 1364, when he was still only seven years old. From this point on, Charles was more or less adopted by the man who had imprisoned his father and murdered his uncle. Although there seems to have been no official ceremony or announcement, it was implied that the boy would someday inherit the throne. Certainly, judging by later events, much of the Hungarian nobility and Charles himself believed this to be the case. Furthering this speculation, the king showed every consideration for Charles, had him brought up in splendor and luxury, and arranged a prestigious marriage for the boy with the daughter of the Holy Roman Emperor. The engagement was broken off, however, when Hungary abruptly severed relations with this former ally; among the other political and strategic reasons for the break, the emperor was accused of having insulted Louis' mother, Elizabeth, the dowager

---

*   Elizabeth was not only still alive; she was managing much of the Hungarian government. "Due to her influence over Louis, she gained the upper hand at court and for several decades acted as a sort of co-regent," wrote Pál Engel. "The king clung to her with boyish affection . . . Even the barons were afraid of her." When Louis the Great inherited the kingdom of Poland on his uncle's death in 1370, he sent his sixty-five-year-old mother to govern it for him.

queen, "with impudent words."* Seeking another suitably illustrious partner for Charles, Louis and Elizabeth remembered Naples. In an instant was revived the old idea of combining the two kingdoms through the marriage of the next generation, prompting Louis to propose an engagement between Charles of Durazzo and Charles's first cousin, Margherita, the youngest of Maria's daughters and the only surviving niece of Joanna's who was still unattached.

Despite her fondness for Charles, this was definitely not the marriage the queen of Naples had envisioned for Margherita, or for the kingdom. Joanna was particularly concerned about her young cousin's new affinity with the king of Hungary and the influence Louis would have over Charles. The queen balked, demanding that Louis the Great give assurances he would not use the marriage as a pretext to interfere in her government. The king of Hungary agreed to this stipulation, but still Joanna stalled, so he appealed once again to the papacy. Urban V was in favor of the match. The free companies, employed by Milan, were once again threatening the Papal States, and the pope hoped to encourage the king of Hungary, who had offered to send troops to fight on the side of the church, to make good on his promise. On June 15, 1369, Urban issued a bull approving the marriage and making the necessary allowance for consanguinity, since the principals were within the ordinarily proscribed degree of kinship.

Despite Joanna's many misgivings, Urban's approval carried great weight with her, and she reluctantly agreed to the marriage—it is unlikely that, saving perhaps Clement VI, she would have done so for any other pope. On January 24, 1370, in a bizzare imitation of the past, Charles of Durazzo, just thirteen years old, returned to Naples accompanied by an elaborate Hungarian escort and was wed to twenty-two-year-old Margherita of Durazzo in a grand ceremony hosted by Joanna at the Castel Capuano, another of the royal palaces. Charles does not seem to have been inhibited by the age difference between himself and his bride. When he left Naples a short time later to return to Hungary (King Louis and the dowager queen Elizabeth having learned their lesson, there was no chance of the bridegroom's residing in Italy and risking another assassination attempt), Margherita was already pregnant. She remained behind alone to have the baby, a girl, Marie. Sadly, the child died soon after birth and was buried in the church of Santa Chiara. Having suffered this wrenching loss, Margherita was then obliged to leave her life-long friends and family in Naples to take her place beside her boy husband at the royal court at Visegrád, under the patronage and benevolent care of the man who had murdered the father she had never known.

But succession schemes and rights of inheritance are as subject to the vagaries of fate as any other political agenda. No sooner had the marriage of Charles and Margherita been consummated than the king of Hungary's wife, who in seventeen years of marriage had failed to conceive a child, suddenly produced three daughters in quick succession: Catherine, born in 1370, Mary, in 1371; and Hedwig, in 1374.

～✦～

Joanna's prestige, and correspondingly that of her kingdom, continued to swell. In 1369, the queen entertained the Byzantine emperor, John V Palaeologus, who had come to Rome to mend the rift within Christianity between East and West in exchange for Urban's promise of money and troops to fight the growing threat to Constantinople from the Turks.* John Palaeologus so enjoyed his stay at the Castel Nuovo that he made a repeat visit and, prior to Charles of Durazzo's wedding, offered to promote an alliance between the Byzantine Empire and the kingdom of Naples by marrying his son to Margherita instead, a proposal Joanna diplomatically

---

* Unlike Philip of Taranto, who held the title of emperor of Constantinople, John Palaeologus actually *was* the emperor of Constantinople.

declined. Additionally, in May 1370, following the wedding of Charles and Margherita, the kingdom of Naples hosted a meeting of the Chapter General of the Friars Minors at the feast of Pentecost. Some eight hundred Franciscan friars descended on the capital to discuss the issues of their order at the church of San Lorenzo and partake of Joanna's generous hospitality. "The Lady Queen gave in their honor the most splendid banquet at the Castel Nuovo, to which all the friars went in procession," reported a chronicler. Spectacles like these, so reminiscent of the celebrated reign of Robert the Wise, indicate just how far the kingdom of Naples had recovered its former brilliance under Joanna.

But in Rome the situation was much more precarious. For all their initial joy over the return of the papacy, the native population soon became disenchanted with Urban V, suspecting that the pope harbored a distinct preference for Frenchmen over Italians. This suspicion was confirmed in September 1368, when the pope raised six Frenchmen to the cardinalate and only one Roman. The Italians loathed the French, whom they regarded as haughty and mendacious, while the French despised the Italians, whom they considered coarse and barbaric. Urban's policy of placing French cardinals and members of their retinues in positions of power was particularly galling. In 1369, this tactic provoked a crisis. The citizens of Perugia rebelled against church authority and drove away the Frenchman recently appointed as papal legate. When Urban raised an army to meet the challenge, Bernabò Visconti, alive to any opportunity to whittle away at church authority in Italy, magnified the conflict by sending John Hawkwood and a free company of two thousand horsemen to fight on the side of the Perugians. The two militias met outside the city in June 1369. The papal forces gained an initial success, even capturing Hawkwood himself, but the victory was short-lived. Two months later, Hawkwood was released. Reunited with his former company and bent on revenge, the English mercenary targeted the papal residences at Montefiascone and Viterbo, where Urban had retreated for safety during the hot summer months. The criminal band thundered through the countryside, robbing and murdering at will, setting fire to the fields and vineyards, and volleying arrows at the pope's front doorstep. Even more disturbing from Urban's point of view was that the majority of the citizens of Rome actively took the side of the Perugians against him.

Frightened, exhausted, and desperately homesick for the peace and civility of Avignon, an ailing Urban capitulated. Citing as a pretext a new outbreak of hostilities between England and France that required his presence, the pope made plans to return home. Too late, the Romans saw their error and sent an embassy to Viterbo to beg him to stay, but, much to the relief of the French cardinals, he refused. In a document written on June 26, 1370, Urban, under the guise of praising his Roman hosts, obliquely referred to the hostility of the populace to the Holy See and hinted at the need to maintain a cooperative spirit, "so that, if we or our successors decide for adequate reasons to return to Rome, we be not deterred by any troubles that may exist there."

Joanna, who had answered the pope's call and contributed troops to the army Urban had sent out against Hawkwood and Perugia in 1369, remained loyal to Urban, although she was regretful of the decision to leave Rome. Together with the kings of France and Aragon, she provided the thirty-four galleys required to ferry the papal court out of Italy on September 5, 1370. To ensure that her relationship with the pope retained its intimacy, Joanna promoted Niccolò Spinelli, who was also on familiar terms with the papal court, to seneschal of Provence, and accorded him powers superior to those of his predecessor, so that he might act as her surrogate in Avignon. Three weeks later, on September 27, to the delight of the citizenry, who envisioned a renewal of wealth and prestige in the pope's return, the papal court entered Avignon in solemn procession and once again took up residency in the grand châteaux that had stood empty for the past three years.

Urban unfortunately did not have much time to enjoy the sooth-ing atmosphere of peace he craved. The Roman experiment had vis-ibly taken its toll on the pope's health. Bridget of Sweden had prophesied, just before he sailed, that Urban would die if he left Italy. The pope obligingly added to her mystique by passing away on December 19.

The reaction to the pontiff's death in Guelphic Italy, where most people felt betrayed by the return to Avignon, was harsh. Petrarch was among the most lacerating. "Pope Urban would have been num-bered among the most honored men if, when dying, his litter had been carried before the altar of St. Peter, and if with tranquil con-science he had there fallen asleep in death, invoking God and the world as witnesses that if ever any Pope forsook this place the fault was not his, but that of the author of his disgraceful flight," the scholar wrote acridly. The news, however, was a blow to Joanna, who genuinely mourned Urban's passing. That her affection had been reciprocated was made plain in the official letter sent by the Sacred College to the queen announcing the death. "The pontiff cherished a sincere love for your Serenity," the cardinals made a point of not-ing.

The Holy See, determined to extinguish any possibility of repeating the misguided Roman adventure, made sure to elect a rel-atively youthful Frenchman, Gregory XI, to succeed Urban. But hav-ing been rekindled however briefly by Urban V, the desire for a Roman pontificate among the Italians stubbornly refused to go away. A bitter struggle for control over the papacy between France and Italy had been provoked and would end in a conflict that would prove every bit as destructive to Europe as the devastation of the Hundred Years' War. As this violent political storm gathered strength and careened ominously forward, Joanna and her kingdom stood directly in its path.

~∞~

CHAPTER XVII

Six Funerals *and a* Wedding

"THE PAPAL CHAIR was governed by Gregory XI," Machiavelli would later write of the new pope. "He, like his predecessors, residing in Avignon, governed Italy by legates, who, proud and avaricious, oppressed many of the cities."

This state of affairs was exactly what members of the Sacred College had in mind when they chose Urban V's successor. Crowned on January 5, 1371, by Guy of Boulogne, who had also orchestrated his unanimous election, Gregory XI had been singled out for his nationality, his youth, and his family connections. Although he had spent much of his career in Italy studying law under the tutelage of a master jurist, Gregory was Clement VI's nephew, which made him a Frenchman both by birth and inclination. His election reflected the nostalgia the cardinals harbored for the heady days of Clement's reign, when the pope had ruled as a great lord and the grandeur of the Holy See rivaled even the French royal court in prestige and glamour. Only forty-two years old, Gregory was the youngest of all the Avignon popes. Although he suffered from an unidentified ailment, it was not life-threatening, and he could therefore reasonably be assumed to rule for many years, by which time the cardinals, still shaken by the perils and inconvenience of their recent Roman adventure, devoutly hoped to extinguish forever the notion of an Italian papacy.

The new pontiff, schooled in law, was a firm believer in strong, autocratic rule and sought to extend church authority in Italy to the fullest extent possible. Joanna's government was an early victim of the papacy's new expansionist policies. It was Gregory who, on October 31, 1372, rewrote the original Neapolitan treaty with Sicily, subverting the queen's position and demanding instead that the island become a fief of the church; Gregory who later crowned Frederick the Simple and allowed his new vassal to style himself "king of Sicily." Although these events did nothing to recommend the new pope to the queen, Joanna overlooked these grievances and tried to maintain a supportive attitude in an effort to establish a cooperative alliance with the Holy See. When, in April 1371, Gregory reconfirmed the Guelphic league established in 1366 to fight the free companies, the queen of Naples endorsed his decision by once again agreeing to participate, and she later sent a troop of three hundred lance men at the pope's request to aid the coalition.

Gregory's territorial and political objectives soon put Joanna to the test, however. Determined to control the Papal States and other traditional Guelph cities, many of which, in the wake of Urban's departure, had rebelled against church officials, the pope went to new lengths to establish his authority. Correctly identifying the powerful Visconti family of Milan as the church's primary antagonist for control of Italy after Bernabò brazenly took possession of the former church territory of Reggio in the spring of 1371, Gregory excommunicated Bernabò and declared a crusade against Milan. The war with the Visconti family was intensely personal to Gregory; a Sienese ambassador who knew him reported that the pope was "completely disposed to the destruction of the lords of Milan." Gregory made no secret of his hatred. "Either I will destroy the Visconti such that there will not be a single one left, or they will destroy the Church of God," he declared. For their part, the Visconti were no less implacable; when Bernabò was duly served by one of Gregory's legates with the papal bull of excommunication, the dictator forced the man to eat the document right down to its "silken cord and seals of lead."

The papal war against Milan, orchestrated from Avignon, was aggressively comprehensive in a manner that dwarfed Cardinal Albornoz's previous military efforts. Gregory dispatched four separate armies from different locales—Savoy, Bologna, Naples, and Provence—to try to encircle and capture the Milanese city of Pavia. Joanna, the pope's principal ally in Italy, signed a treaty with other members of the coalition against Milan pledging support. In 1372 she acted on this promise by sending James of Majorca to Avignon to participate in the war effort and authorizing Niccolò Spinelli to raise and captain the papal force emanating from Provence. Neapolitan troops were also assigned to a combat unit headed by the papal legate from Bologna.

At this point, the outcome of the conflict was still uncertain, for, although the pope had managed to coordinate a number of separate militias under an umbrella strategy, the troops at his disposal were by no means overwhelming. Bernabò was an experienced warrior; additionally, he had hired John Hawkwood and his mercenary band to fight on the side of Milan. Before a single blow was struck, however, Gregory was the recipient of an enormous piece of luck. Hawkwood worked by the job, and his contract with Bernabò was due to expire in September 1372. The two entered into negotiations for a renewal of the Englishman's term of employment. Giovanni Pico, a Mantuan nobleman familiar with the details of the haggling, explained the situation in a September 12 letter. "Bernabò wanted to sign him again according to the previous agreement, by which the English were to have 100 lances in Cremona and 100 lances elsewhere," Pico wrote. "The English [Hawkwood] did not want that, but wanted to augment their band by 200 lances and 200 archers. According to the general opinion, they are coming toward

Saint Benedict and will stop there and sign an accord either with my lord Bernabò or with whoever will give them the best terms."

Just before the outbreak of a serious war would seem an odd time to antagonize the mainstay of one's mercenary army, but Bernabò chose to refuse to meet Hawkwood's demands, insisting instead on the original military formula. Rather than continue to bargain with the Visconti, Hawkwood, a shrewd businessman, simply changed sides and opened negotiations with the papacy. In an instant, the Holy See went from being the leading persecutor of the free companies in Italy to their most lucrative employer. Gregory not only promised Hawkwood the requested lances and archers but also threw in a salary of forty thousand florins. The resources of the church being somewhat overtaxed at this time, Gregory turned to Joanna for the money. The queen must have had dealings with Hawkwood in the past, because the pope mentioned in a letter that he was aware that the Englishman had extorted an annual pension out of Naples some years earlier as a price for leaving the kingdom unmolested. "Most dear daughter in Christ," Gregory wrote in September. "Recently it has reached our ears that you made or gave . . . to our beloved son, the noble John Hawkwood, knight now for many years, a certain annual provision . . . Since, however, the same John, whom we take from the services of Bernabò Visconti, enemy and persecutor of the whole church, intends to come over to the church and not to offend, invade or damage its subjects, and lands . . . we strongly ask and urge your Serene Highness that you make good to the said John Hawkwood his provision which you previously so liberally granted."*

Aided by Hawkwood's free company, the papal forces scored a number of victories. In October 1372, fighting in Piedmont, the

---

* No record survives as to how much Joanna paid to Hawkwood, what year the annuity began, or when it ended, but possibly Joanna was forced to bribe the Englishman to stay out of Naples in January 1364, when James of Majorca invited Hawkwood and the White Company to Naples in order to overthrow her.

count of Savoy took Cuneo and by January 1373 had captured many other castles and towns in the surrounding area, all of which he was legally obligated by treaty to hand over to Joanna, who claimed them as part of her original legacy from Robert the Wise. As the count of Savoy was naturally reluctant to do this, wishing to keep the gains for himself, the queen was compelled on January 8, 1373, to notify her government in Provence of her intention to take back Piedmont, at which time she authorized Niccolò Spinelli to receive, or recover by force, the captured territory from the count of Savoy. Aware that the queen of Naples was his most important ally in the struggle against Milan, Gregory intervened, and the count of Savoy handed Cuneo over to Spinelli on February 14. Spinelli, who proved to be every bit the warrior his predecessor, Acciaiuoli, had been, also recaptured Centallo in the queen's name on August 2, 1373, and for the first time since the days of King Robert, Naples again ruled a substantial portion of Piedmont.

Faced with mounting losses from papal forces to the west and south, and a renewal of the plague, the Visconti family sued for peace. Gregory, who lacked the money necessary to continue prosecuting the war—Hawkwood's men were already owed back wages, a dangerous situation—agreed to come to terms, and a treaty was signed in June 1374. As a result, although some territory changed hands, Milan remained a potent force in Italian politics. For all Gregory's military effort, the only tangible outcome of the conflict was the perception that the pope intended to take and hold fiefs in Italy much more aggressively than in the past, an unsettling image that would in the end prove far more destructive to Europe than the bloody warfare that precipitated it.

The period following the cessation of hostilities between Milan and the church was marked by a series of deaths that altered the cultural and political landscape of Europe. The ink was not yet dry on the parchment of the Visconti peace treaty when the world learned to its great sorrow of the passing of Francesco Petrarch, probably on the evening of June 18, 1374, at his home in Arquà, between Venice and Ferrara. His political judgment might have been flawed, but no man in history did more for the promotion of learning. Petrarch's great love of reading, his devotion to the classics, and his contagious enthusiasm for a life of letters spawned a generation of scholars equally committed to intellectual pursuits and laid the foundation for the Renaissance. Fittingly, the seventy-one-year-old was discovered to have died in his chair "with his head and arms resting on a pile of books." In recognition of his many accomplishments, his corpse was dressed in red satin and his casket hidden beneath a cloth of gold bordered with ermine, as it would have been for an emperor or king. "Now art thou risen, dear my lord / unto the kingdom, to mount to which still waits / every soul chosen [thereto] for that by God / on its departure from this wicked world . . . Now with . . . Dante livest thou, sure of eternal rest . . . Ah! If thou didst care for me wandering about here below, / draw me up to thee," penned a passionate Boccaccio upon hearing the news. Perhaps Petrarch did hear his plea, for the next year, on December 21, 1375, Boccaccio followed his mentor to the grave. Unlike the world-renowned Petrarch, Boccaccio was buried simply, leaving instructions in his will for a very modest epitaph, but one of his mourners, who shared a love of literature with his friend, added the following lines:

Why, O illustrious poet, do you speak of yourself so humbly?
You with your limpid notes have exalted pastoral verses;
You with your arduous labors have numbered the hills and
 the mountains;
You have described the forests and springs and the swamps
 and marshes; . . .

You bring before us great princes, relating their trials and
    downfalls, . . .
Labors past counting have made you famous among all the
    people
Nor will an age ever come that will pass over you in silence.

Sandwiched between the burials of these two literary lions was a third loss, less noted by history, but of significance to the kingdom of Naples. In February 1375, Joanna's third husband, James IV of Majorca, passed away at the age of thirty-nine. Although he participated in the early maneuvers against the Visconti in Piedmont in 1372, by 1373 James had drifted away to France, intent on organizing yet another foray against his eternal nemesis, the king of Aragon, for control of Majorca. With the help of the king of Navarre, he had managed to obtain an army of some twelve hundred knights, and actually succeeded in invading Aragon, where he "took little fortresses, and sore-travailed the plain country, and ransomed men and took prisoners," reported Froissart. With victory in his grasp, the unfortunate James was felled not by his rival but by the ill health that had dogged him since his youthful incarceration in Spain. "And while this war was thus begun, cruel and fell, King James of Majorca fell sick again in the vale of Soria, of the which sickness he died; and so therefore the Aragoneses had peace and rest for a great season after; and the companions that had made war departed and returned into France," the chronicler concluded. James was buried in Soria, in northeast Spain, the closest the king of Majorca ever came to the longed-for island domain he had known as a boy but never ruled.

Word of her widowhood reached Joanna just as a new threat from her old enemy, Hungary, surfaced. In 1374 Louis the Great's third daughter, Hedwig, was born, and the king had begun to re-examine the plans for the royal succession. Charles of Durazzo was no longer his primary heir; that honor now fell to Catherine, Louis' eldest daughter. Her younger sisters would have to be provided with an inheritance as well, and Louis had only two dominions— Hungary and Poland—to bestow. The king needed a third realm.

With this in mind, Louis the Great, in his correspondence with the pope, began to revive the old issue of Hungarian rights to the kingdom of Naples. For the first time in more than two decades, he characterized Joanna's government as illegal, claiming that, by the law of primogeniture, first King Robert and then the queen had "usurped" the realm from the true heir, Louis' father, Carobert.* The king of Hungary then acted on his demand by entering into a nuptial agreement with Charles V, king of France, whereby Louis' daughter Catherine, four at the time of her engagement, would wed one of Charles's younger sons, two-year-old Louis, duke of Orléans. The marriage contract of 1374 stipulated that Catherine of Hungary was to be dowered with the domains of Naples, Provence, and Piedmont.

This alliance between Louis the Great and the French monarchy against Joanna was particularly ominous. Under Charles V's leadership, France was in the process of reclaiming its role as the predominant power in Europe. The French king was aided enormously in this endeavor by the unpopular tax policies and steadily deteriorating health of his principal opponent, the Black Prince. Members of the Gascon nobility, infuriated at being required to foot the bill for Edward's Castilian adventure, had rebelled. By 1371, a seriously ill Edward had been forced to return to England. Charles V had taken advantage of his absence to mount a military campaign in Aquitaine and succeeded in taking back much of the occupied territory, including Saintes, La Rochelle, and Poitiers. "As soon as it was known that the prince was ill and at death's door, his enemies

---

* Interestingly, Louis did not attempt to reacquire the kingdom of Naples by revisiting the notion that Joanna had murdered Andrew, an indication that her innocence on this point was an accepted matter of record. The king of Hungary would most certainly have tried this gambit if he thought it would have any hope of success.

decided to start the war again," wrote Chandos Herald. "Then the war between France and England began again, and then towns and cities changed sides, and many counts and barons as well, . . . all renounced their allegiance to their lord the prince on the same day, because he was ill and could not look after his interests." Prince Edward lived just long enough to see almost all the territory he had fought for revert to France. By 1375, when a truce was declared, the English were left with little more than Calais and a narrow piece of coastland between Bordeaux and Bayonne. On June 8, 1376, a week before his forty-sixth birthday, "that flower of English knighthood, the Lord Edward of England, Prince of Wales and Aquitaine, departed this life in the palace of Westminster," Froissart reported. "Here ends the lay of the most noble Prince Edward, who had never a coward's heart," mourned Sir John Chandos. The Black Prince's body was buried with great pomp before parliament, and even the king of France recognized the warrior's death by ordering a funeral service performed in his honor in Paris. Twelve months later, Edward III, king of England, old and grieving, also expired, leaving the field to Charles V.

Emboldened by his success against England, the king of France sought to expand the kingdom's borders still further, and Provence, just to the south, made a tempting target. Even before the alliance with Hungary, Charles V had sent his younger brother Louis of Anjou, who had been very helpful to Gregory in the war against Milan, to the papal court at Avignon to press for the royal family's claims to Provence. The 1374 agreement with the king of Hungary was merely an extension of existing French policy.

But by this time, Joanna had a strong supporter in Gregory, who recognized and appreciated the effort she had made to come to his assistance against Milan. When the king of Hungary sent a team of ambassadors to Avignon in the summer of 1374 to inform the pope of the marriage arrangement with France, Gregory refuted the usurpation accusation by referring to the original 1301 agreement between Charles the Lame and the church, whereby thirteen-year-old Carobert had been sent to Hungary and King Robert named legitimate ruler of Naples. The pope also wrote to the queen on September 22, 1374, to warn her of the scheme to deprive her of her birthright and to solicit further legal evidence substantiating her position. Joanna immediately fired back, citing as precedent the much more recent Neapolitan-Hungarian peace treaty of 1351, signed by Louis the Great himself, in which the king of Hungary had officially abandoned all claim to the kingdom of Naples and the county of Provence in exchange for a compensation payment of three hundred thousand florins, monies he had subsequently also voluntarily renounced in an excess of chivalry.

Moreover, in the months following James of Majorca's death, the pope and the queen were deeply involved in a plan that would bring them even closer together. By the spring of 1375, the Holy See recognized that church control of the Papal States would never be more than nominal without a physical presence in Italy. Milan's influence, coupled with the growing desire among the city-states for independent government, would eventually erode the military gains Gregory had acquired at such cost to the papal treasury, and this attrition the pontiff was determined to prevent. In May, with the active approval of the queen of Naples, whose logistical support was essential to the journey, Gregory officially announced his intention to return the papal court once more to Rome.

～⋇～

The prospective return of the papal court to Italy for the second time represented another diplomatic triumph for Joanna over the interests of her enemies. No monarch in Europe had harnessed the power of the church or managed his kingdom's relationship with the pope as effectively as had the queen of Naples since the death of Louis of Taranto in 1362. To have Gregory ensconced in Rome as Urban had been, where he would be even more reliant on Neapolitan troops for protection, and where she could be in close personal communication with him, ensured the safeguarding of Joanna's prerogative and increased her already potent influence.

But this time, unlike previously, sentiment throughout the rest of Italy was decidedly hostile to Gregory's plan. The pope was widely viewed as grasping and intent on enlarging church dominion over formerly independent territory. Florence, in particular, nursed a number of grievances against the papacy. In early 1375, the city had suffered from famine and had pleaded with Gregory to be allowed to import grain from the Papal States; inexplicably, permission had been withheld by the local legate even though Gregory had approved the Florentines' request. Then that summer, following hard upon the denial of grain, came an invasion by John Hawkwood's mercenaries. The signing of the papal peace treaty with Milan on June 4, 1375, had left the free company without an obvious means of support, and so the bandit army had descended south in search of spoils. Eyewitnesses reported that Hawkwood's militia, composed of thousands of soldiers of fortune and all the ominous accoutrement of war, including massive siege engines and catapults, made up "a vast army . . . a good ten miles long" as it trundled its way into Tuscany. Terrified, Florence sent emissaries to intercept the band of outlaws and on June 21 agreed to pay them the staggering sum of 130,000 florins to leave the commune in peace for five years. Pisa followed suit on July 3 with a bribe of 30,500 florins; Lucca on July 13 with 7,000 florins; and Siena a few days later with 30,500 florins. In total "John and his society received 200,000 florins in tribute from the time they formed the company," wrote Giovanni Pico, one of the ambassadors involved in the negotiations. "The magnificent figure was more than five times greater than the operating capital of the businesses of the famous merchant of Prato . . . It was three times greater than the operating capital of the great Medici bank of the next century; and more than the combined yearly revenue of the cities of Lucca and Siena," agreed a later scholar.

Nothing agitated a commercial town like Florence more than an out-of-pocket expense, particularly one of this magnitude, and in fury the citizenry turned on Gregory. Everybody knew that Hawkwood was in the pay of the pope, and it was widely believed that the church deliberately sent the free company into Tuscany to expand its territorial domain in preparation for its return to Rome. In retaliation, on July 24, 1375, Florence, historically a staunch supporter of Guelphic policies, did an abrupt about-face and joined with Gregory's archenemy, Milan, to raise an army of "2,350 lances with accompanying units of archers, crossbowmen, and infantrymen" in a league to defend themselves against incursions by the pope. Within a month, Siena, Pisa, and Lucca, following Florence's cue, also fell in with Milan and signed the anti-papacy pact.

Naples, as Florence's primary trading partner and ally, was caught in the middle. Joanna, convinced that Gregory was not behind Hawkwood's attack, did all she could to heal the rift between the Holy See and the disgruntled city-states. Beginning in August, as soon as she was informed of the league's existence, the queen sent a series of her most trusted and highly placed ambassadors to Florence to try to calm the commune's fears and to reassure her ally of the pope's peaceful intentions. Gregory, too, protested his innocence; and there is no evidence that Hawkwood's invasion of Tuscany was the result of any impetus other than the mercenary's own. But that was the problem with the pope's having accepted the aid of the free companies in the first place; Gregory was powerless to control his employees' actions and perception went against him. Joanna's first embassy failed; the queen tried again in October, and then a third time in November. Additionally, she kept Tommaso Sanseverino, a member of one of the most important aristocratic families in Florence, by her side at court in an effort to convince her former ally of her good intentions.

Joanna's efforts at mediation were reinforced by those of another figure central to the growing political turmoil in Italy: Catherine of Siena, later Saint Catherine. The youngest of twenty-five children, Catherine had demonstrated an early affinity for the church; at the age of five, she began the habit of ascending and descending the staircase of her family home on her knees, as though in prayer. At seventeen she took the vows and black mantle of the Church of Saint Dominic, becoming one of the youngest members of the sister order. Adding to her mystique, Catherine reported many visions where God appeared before her and spoke to her; during one of these visitations, as a sign of divine favor, she was presented by Jesus with a magnificent diamond and pearl ring, which afterward she wore continually, although only she could see it. Additionally, and perhaps more impressively, while in seclusion, Catherine taught herself to read and write in the vernacular.

Having acquired this skill, the future saint, dedicated to good works and the promotion of peace, aggressively inserted herself into the diplomatic process between Florence and the papacy by engaging in an extensive letter-writing campaign. Fueled by religious zeal, her passionate missives bombarded every combatant, dignitary, and potential ally who might be induced to further her cause. Among her correspondents were the pope; Bernabò Visconti and his wife, Regina della Scala; Elizabeth, the dowager queen of Hungary; Charles V, king of France, and his brother, Louis, duke of Anjou; the eight Florentine magistrates, known as the "Eight of War," charged by the commune with conducting hostilities against the pope; and Joanna. Catherine even wrote to John Hawkwood, urging the mercenary to stop harassing the Florentines and go on crusade instead. "My dearest and very loved brothers in Christ Jesus," Catherine wrote to the English brigand. "I Caterina, servant and slave of the servants of Jesus Christ, am writing to you in his precious blood . . . Oh dearest gentlest brother in Christ Jesus, would it be such a great thing for you to withdraw a little into yourself and consider how much pain and anguish you have endured in the devil's service and pay? Now my soul wants you to change your course and enlist instead in the service and cross of Christ crucified, you and all of your followers and companies . . . You find so much satisfaction in fighting and waging war, so now I am begging you tenderly in Christ Jesus not to wage war any longer against Christians (for that offends God), but to go instead to fight the unbelievers, as God and our holy father have decreed."

To the queen of Naples, too, Catherine appealed for help with her crusade, and received a sympathetic response. Calling Joanna "honorable and dearest mother, milady the queen," in a letter dated August 4, 1375, Catherine wrote: "I want you to know, my revered lady, that my soul is jubilantly happy after receiving your letter. It gave me great consolation because, it seems to me, you have a holy and wholesome readiness to give both your possessions and your life for the glory of the name of Christ crucified. You can show no greater sacrifice or love than to be ready to give even your life, if necessary, for him. Oh what a great joy it will be to see you giving blood for blood! May I see the fire of holy desire so growing in you at the remembrance of the blood of God's Son that you may be leader and patroness of this holy crusade just as you bear the title of queen of Jerusalem." It is unlikely that forty-nine-year-old Joanna would have been willing to go quite so far as to lead the military expedition herself, but encouraging the free companies to divert their attention to the Holy Land made political and diplomatic sense, and both the queen and the pope added their endorsement to Catherine's plan. Evidently proud of Joanna's support, but clearly unaware that her backing might not be the most tactful recommendation, Catherine specifically mentioned Joanna in a letter to her former mother-in-law the queen mother of Hungary: "I want you to know, dearest mother," Catherine informed Elizabeth, "that I have written to the queen of Naples and to many other rulers in regard to what I am asking you here. All have responded kindly and graciously, offering to help both with their possessions and personally."

Joanna's solicitude for Catherine of Siena's entreaties reflected her growing absorption with matters of the spirit. At this point in her life the queen was profoundly religious, with a tendency toward superstition, an inclination somewhat at odds with her opulent and eccentric court, which included a white deer and a parrot, as well as African, Saracen, and Turkish servants; an incident is recorded whereby the queen had her African servants present a prayer book to a chapter of Franciscan friars. Joanna was also profoundly affected by the extended visit to Naples, from 1365 to 1372, of the mystic Saint Bridget of Sweden. Legend portrays the queen of Naples as lusting after Bridget's handsome son, twenty years her junior, who only escaped the lascivious queen's clutches by a premature death, but this story, like so much of the gossip attached to Joanna, was a myth. In fact, Bridget characterized the relationship between herself and the queen as one of a mother instructing an obedient daughter. At Bridget's urging, Joanna issued decrees warning of the dangers to the soul of wearing too much makeup or dressing in too overtly sexual a fashion ("modifying male and female bodies by dishonest styling in clothes"), which were subsequently read aloud in Neapolitan churches. The saint also favored the queen with many prophecies, often with obscure meanings. In one, "Saint Bridget had a vision of Joanna seated on her golden throne, with two Black men facing her. One of them said to her: 'O woman lioness, I bring this blood to you, take it and spill it,' and the other said: 'I bring to you this vase filled with fire, take it, you who have the spirit of fire.'"

Catherine of Siena's passionate approach to religion and politics was similar to Bridget's, and the queen of Naples, understanding and sympathizing with Catherine's motives, respected and encouraged her. Although later events would divide them, in the beginning these two shared a common purpose. Like Joanna, Catherine also wished to see the papal court reinstated in Rome, and she made a special trip to Avignon to beg Gregory to act on his intention. Subsequent church lore recounts that it was this visit that induced the pope to make the journey, but Catherine's role seems overstated. "We know how Saint Catherine went to Avignon to urge Gregory IX to leave, and how she persuaded herself that she was the one who had ultimately convinced him to do so. Yet before she had even reached the County [of Provence], the first travel arrangements had been made, galleys had been rented in Marseille, and the journey of the Holy See had been organized together with Queen Joanna."

Despite the efforts of both women, the Florentines remained obdurate, and by her adherence to Gregory, Joanna forfeited the goodwill of her former partisans. Seeking allies in an attempt to escalate hostilities, the commune deliberately turned to Charles of Durazzo, the assumed heir to the kingdom of Naples, to undercut the queen's position. On September 2, 1375, the Florentine chancellor wrote to Charles, now a manly eighteen years old and schooled in the art of warfare by Louis the Great, complaining of the pope's antipathy. "It was necessary that we seek grain for our sustenance from Flanders, Burgundy, Spain and—still more merciless—from the Turks and islands of the Saracens," the chancellor informed his correspondent. "We found more charity from foreigners and infidels than from the Church! . . . While we were exhausted from famine, the Church set their eyes on us and all of Tuscany . . . They held a colloquium and offered remedy by hiring the company of soldiers so that they would—or so they said—not vex us. In this way, they prepared for our destruction . . . Within one day [Hawkwood's band] was united into a pestilential 'society' and sent upon Tuscany."

Inspired by Florentine rhetoric, which characterized the conflict as a heroic struggle for liberty rather than as retaliation for past grievances, the rebellion soon spread to the Papal States. One by one the cities of Perugia, Viterbo, Orvieto, and Bologna expelled their legates and joined the anti-papal league. With each defection,

Florence grew bolder, and despite Joanna's ongoing efforts, the chance for a diplomatic resolution diminished. It was against this dangerous backdrop of rising aggression, isolated from her former allies and faced with the intrigues of powerful enemies, that the queen of Naples chose her fourth husband.

~&~

His name was Otto, duke of Brunswick. He was fifty-five to Joanna's forty-nine, a career warrior and experienced statesman who had come to the Piedmont region from his home in Germany a dozen years before and fallen into the service of his cousin, the marquis of Montferrat. In 1372, upon his cousin's death, Otto had been named guardian of the marquis' eldest son and had thereby undertaken responsibility for maintaining the child's inheritance against incursions made by the Visconti family, who sought to expand into Piedmont. The duke of Brunswick subsequently performed brilliantly in the papal war against Milan, holding the important town of Asti against a prolonged siege, which prompted Gregory to write of "our dear son and noble lord Otto, duke of Brunswick, descendant of the imperial line of Otto of Saxony, also cousin of our dear son and noble lord John, Marquis of Montferrat [married to James of Majorca's sister], whose armies he has led and still leads with great energy . . . universally known as most valorous, magnificent and honorable, and able to secure foreign help, albeit not through his personal power but with his prudence and empathy." The duke of Brunswick was brought to the queen's attention by Niccolò Spinelli, who knew the German commander personally from his own recent experience on the battlefields of northern Italy, and who recommended the alliance as a means by which both to cement Neapolitan control of Piedmont and to secure the talents of a professional soldier in defense of the realm at large.

As a member of the minor German nobility, Otto was of a vastly inferior rank to the queen. There was never any real choice but that Joanna would marry again—to have remained single would merely have invited the unwanted attention of many suitors, some of them armed, which would have placed the kingdom at unnecessary risk— but the fact that the queen was willing to consider a spouse so beneath her represented the triumph of pragmatism over the traditional medieval preference for prestigious lineage. The queen had had enough experience by this time with younger, elite princes who, despite prenuptial promises to the contrary, tried to make inroads into her prerogative by bullying her into submission. Spinelli's word carried great weight with her, and she accepted the denigration associated with a marriage to the duke of Brunswick for the sake of the realm. For once there was no question of her new husband's being crowned king, as the Neapolitans would never have accepted as sovereign an outsider of such inferior rank. The pope alluded as much to this when he addressed a general proclamation to the citizenry, recommending that the kingdom receive the news of the alliance "with joy" and requiring that they "honor him as the true husband of the queen." On December 28, 1375, Joanna and Otto were married by proxy. Three months later, on March 25, 1376, the duke of Brunswick arrived in Naples, and "that very night slept with the queen," according to the *Chronicon Siculum*.

Otto would prove to be the most loyal and cooperative of all Joanna's husbands. Never did he interfere in her government or try to take power away from her. At their marriage, the queen graciously bestowed on her new spouse the customary title of duke of Calabria and also accorded him the principia of Taranto.* Grateful for the recognition, and conscious of the slurs his wife had been exposed to by marrying him, Otto worked and fought tirelessly in the queen's

---

* Philip of Taranto, the last surviving brother, had died in 1373, at which point the Taranto family holdings had reverted to the crown.

interest. (The Florentines, hoping to provoke Hungarian intervention, complained of the alliance in a letter to Louis the Great, in which they accused Joanna "of humiliating Italy by mixing the blood of the glorious Angevin race with the detestable blood of a German prince.") If she had had him from the beginning, the queen of Naples might have spared herself and her kingdom years of turmoil.

~✦~

During the winter months, while her marriage was being negotiated, the conflict between Gregory and Florence had continued to escalate. Joanna's nuptials had barely concluded when, on March 31, 1376, the pope signed a papal bull placing the Florentines under interdict, at the same time demanding that their citizens be expelled from all states loyal to the church and that their goods be confiscated. This last measure, aimed at the Florentine economy, the commune's most vulnerable quarter, was extremely effective. "Few princes could resist the temptation to enrich themselves with the confiscated property of outlaws, while also gaining credit for obeying their spiritual lord," observed a later historian. The cardinal of Limoges wrote that "not one Florentine dares to remain in the kingdom [of France], and all of their goods have been confiscated; likewise in the kingdoms of England, Spain, Scotland, Aragon, Portugal, Navarre and in the county of Flanders." Joanna, too, enforced the papal ban by evicting the many Florentine merchants operating in the kingdom's borders and seizing their money and property. Even Louis the Great of Hungary complied with Gregory's orders.

Determined to retake papal territory lost to the uprising and bring Florence to heel, the pope did not limit himself to the traditional spiritual weapons at his disposal. In May, he asked Robert of Geneva to mount a military effort against the rebellious Italian league. Robert, who had been made a cardinal by Gregory in 1371, was the nephew of Guy of Boulogne. Soon to become one of the most divisive figures of his age, there are conflicting reports of Robert's physical presence. Italian chroniclers, intensely antagonistic, claimed the cardinal was a hunchback; other observers asserted that he was merely lame and squinted. Those who supported him, on the other hand, insisted that, like his older brother Aimon of Geneva (unsuccessful suitor of Joanna's eldest niece, Jeanne), Robert was "handsome and well formed." There was no disagreement at all as to his character, however: the cardinal of Geneva was universally acknowledged as cultivated, imperious, and arrogant. When his powerful uncle finally passed away in 1373, Robert assumed Guy's mantle of leadership among the French cardinals at the Sacred College.

In response to the Florentine revolt, Robert, with Gregory's approval, recruited an army of Breton mercenaries numbering some ten thousand men and left the area around Avignon with this intimidating force on May 20, 1376. They crossed the Alps and made their way slowly into central Italy. Upon reaching the Papal State of Romagna, the cardinal augmented his host by once again enlisting the services of John Hawkwood and his free company in the cause of the church, for the respectable fee of 13,520 florins, payable in cash. The force was by this time so overwhelming that when Gregory inquired of one of the Breton generals whether he thought the papal troops would succeed against Florence, the mercenary replied, "Does the sun enter there? If the sun can enter there, so can I."

But it was already fall, which was late in the year for the sun. Not wanting to fight in the cold weather, the army didn't go straight to Florence; instead, the mercenaries settled for the winter outside the town of Cesena, on the eastern coast of Italy. When supplies ran short in November, Robert of Geneva allowed the army to invade the town, even though Cesena had not joined the anti-papal league. "They came inside the city," reported a chronicler from nearby Rimini, "where they devoured, consumed, and forced everything out of men and women." By February, the local citizenry had had enough. There was a riot and several hundred of the mercenaries were killed. In retaliation, the papal army, under the command and with the explicit approval of Robert of Geneva, turned on the city and massacred its inhabitants, an event that shocked Italy. "Everyone— women, old and young, and sick, and children and pregnant women were cut to pieces at the point of a dagger," wrote a chronicler from Siena. "Babies were taken by the feet and dashed against the town wall." In all, some four thousand people were killed and by the end "there remained neither man nor woman" in Cesena.

Apparently, even the unrepentant Hawkwood had qualms about attacking a predominantly unarmed, civilian population. A Sienese chronicle reported that the following conversation took place between the English brigand and Robert of Geneva just prior to the slaughter:

> "I command you to descend on the land and do justice," said the cardinal.
>
> "Sir, when you want, I will go and prevail upon the inhabitants, so that they give up their arms and render them to you . . ." Hawkwood replied.
>
> "No," the cardinal said, "I want blood and justice."
>
> "Please think about it," Hawkwood protested.
>
> "I command you thus," said the cardinal.

Into this poisoned atmosphere Gregory XI, prepared at last to carry through on his resolve to return the papal court to Italy, set sail for Rome.

~⚜~

The Holy See departed from Marseille on October 2, 1376, in a fleet of galleys once again provided mostly by Joanna. Events leading up to the papal removal from Avignon were reminiscent of the drama connected with the earlier embarkation of Urban V. Again, the king of France sent a team of prominent ambassadors, led by his brother Louis, duke of Anjou, to the pope's side, to present the old arguments against the plan; again, the dismayed and fearful cardinals pleaded with their master to change his mind; again "never were seen so many tears, lamentations and groanings," as the day the ships were boarded and the fleet pushed off from the dock. Inconsolable, Gregory's own father, the elderly count of Beaufort, in a final act of desperation, threw himself on the ground in his son's path in an attempt to halt the proceedings. But the pope, mindful of a recent speech by Cardinal Orsini, one of the few Italian members of the Sacred College—"Who has ever seen a kingdom well directed and wisely governed in the prince's absence? It is certain that if the king of France left his kingdom and went to Greece, his own realm would not be well governed. I cannot foresee how peace can come to his domains, if the pope does not reside in his own see"—merely stepped over the prone body of his parent, and continued on his way.

The journey itself was plagued by terrible storms, which caused considerable delay. The pope did not arrive in Rome until January 17, 1377, when, heralded by trumpets, he entered the city at the head of a procession that included dancers, musicians, notable ecclesiastics, a company of knights and soldiers for protection, and delegations of high-ranking barons, among whom were many representatives from Joanna's court. The citizens of Rome, attracted by the festive air and the promise of an increase in income, cheered.

The queen of Naples's support, both diplomatic and financial, was even more vital to the pope after he arrived in Italy. Joanna sent Spinelli to Gregory in March, and the grand seneschal agreed to take control of church efforts to separate Bologna from the Florentine league and return the city to papal control, a task accomplished in August 1377. This latest military effort, reliant as before upon the recruitment of mercenaries, was expensive. In desperation, Gregory, who had exhausted his funds, wrote to Joanna asking for money "to help us carry the weight we bear on our shoulders." The queen responded generously with a payment of fifty thousand florins on April 15, but by fall this had all been spent and the pope was forced to plead again for financial aid. "We don't know who to turn to besides you," he wrote in an October 12 letter. Gregory went on to thank Joanna for "the treasure of your compassion and for the immense royal charity towards us."

By year's end, the partnership between the papacy and the kingdom of Naples had begun to yield results. Faced with Gregory's physical proximity, which highlighted in a visceral and highly public manner the failure of the anti-papal league to achieve its goal of eradicating church dominance over the politics of Italy, Florence agreed to participate in talks aimed at mediation. In February 1378, a peace conference was convened in Sarzana, about twelve miles west of Carrara. Europe's most powerful heads of state—the Holy Roman Emperor, the sovereigns of France, Hungary, and Naples—all sent ambassadors in an international effort to end the conflict. Joanna's place at the peace table was ably occupied by Niccolò Spinelli, whose presence signaled the importance the queen attached to these proceedings. (Gregory had asked the grand seneschal to represent the interests of the papacy at this forum, but the counselor demurred, choosing to act for Joanna instead.) The congress was mediated by Bernabò Visconti, who had been induced by a combination of threat and bribery to accept a separate truce with the pope.

This peace conference, so fundamentally modern in its conception, represented the apex not only of Joanna's foreign policy but perhaps of fourteenth-century European diplomacy. For once using the instruments of détente, rather than the apparatus of war, the assembled dignitaries managed to bring the adversaries to terms in less than two months. The chronicles of the period are unanimous in reporting that during the final week of March 1378, a settlement acceptable to both the Florentines and the church was reached, in which Florence agreed to pay reparations of eight hundred thousand florins over a period of five years.

Then, on March 31, 1378, word suddenly arrived in Sarzana that Gregory XI had died in Rome on the twenty-seventh and in a matter of moments the bright promise of peace was abruptly extinguished.

꘎

CHAPTER XVIII

The Great Schism

T HE DEATH OF the pope created a vacuum of uncertainty into which rushed all the usual competing interests, grabs for power, and general opportunism common to the transition of rule from one medieval monarch to another. Even measured by the chaotic standards of the fourteenth century, however, the confusion and anarchy unleashed in the aftermath of Gregory's demise reached new heights. For the first time in seventy-four years, a pontiff had died not in Avignon but in Rome. At once, the most urgent, vital political struggle of the age—who would run the church, France or Italy—rose to the fore and was boiled down to its essence in the choice of Gregory's successor.

The sixteen cardinals, eleven of whom were of French origin, who were in Rome at the time of Gregory's death and who would be responsible for choosing the next pope were acutely aware of this issue. As early as February 1378, when Gregory had become so ill that his doctors forbade his getting out of bed, rumors had swept through Rome that he had already died and the French cardinals were keeping his death a secret in order to elect one of their own in his place. So upsetting was this gossip that a delegation of several high-ranking members of the city government intent on discovering the truth insisted on seeing Gregory and were granted an audience in his bedchamber. According to an eyewitness observer, these officials, having satisfied themselves that Gregory was still alive but failing fast, and fearful that he, like Urban, was planning to return to Avignon before he died, were overheard plotting as they left the pontiff's presence. "The pope will not escape. The time has come to show ourselves good Romans. We must see to the arrangements so that this time, the papacy remains with the Italians and the Romans." There were mob uprisings at the beginning of February, and then again at the beginning of March, which forced the cardinals to lock themselves into the secure fortress of Castel Sant'Angelo for their own protection, and the French cardinals in particular were warned repeatedly of murderous intrigues against them by members of the Roman populace. "The cardinals feared for their lives months before the election, and with good reason." Even before Gregory's death, the members of the Sacred College, worried about the reaction of their host city to the outcome of the papal election, took the precaution of protecting their property as well as their persons. "Since the cardinals, especially the French, felt somewhat uneasy, they arranged for all their private goods, particularly money, books, jewels, and all other mobile possessions to be brought into the castle of St. Angelo, as soon as Gregory died," reported an official church memorandum of the period.

The pope expired on March 27, 1378, and the next day at the burial ceremony, at the church of Santa Maria Nova, the senator of Rome "and other officials approached them [the cardinals] and humbly and civilly submitted the request that a worthy man of the Italian nation should be elected ... This request was repeated by them on subsequent days when they gave their reasons: that the Roman see ... had suffered greatly through the long absence of the pope; also that the state of the city of Rome itself was ruinous and near collapse ... The only way to remedy this state of affairs was to elect a pope who was a Roman and, furthermore, for the cardinals themselves to reside at Rome and not, as hitherto, to despise the city." The Roman citizenry was not nearly this polite; as soon as the cardinals entered the conclave on April 7, an angry mob gathered just outside the palace doors and began chanting, "We want a Roman!" and sometimes, for variation, "Let's kill them!" at intervals throughout the election.

Adding to the difficulty of the selection was the fact that the eleven French cardinals, while possessing a decisive majority over their four Italian colleagues (the sixteenth cardinal, of Spanish ancestry, voted consistently with the French), were bitterly divided among themselves along regional lines into two parties: the Limousins and the Gallic. The Limousin party consisted of the cardinals of Limoges, Aigrefeuille, Poitiers, Marmoutier, and de Vergne. The Gallic, or French, faction boasted the remaining French cardinals, plus the one Spaniard. The last four popes had all come from the Limousin party. Even before Gregory had died and the electors had secluded themselves in conclave, the Limousins had floated the names of the cardinals of Poitiers and de Vergne as possible candidates.

But the Gallic party, under the leadership of Robert of Geneva (who coveted the papal tiara for himself), was equally determined that the new pope should come from one of their number and rejected the Limousin candidates. "The French strongly declared that they would never consent to such an election: the Limousins must not think that they had rented the papacy because the last four popes had been of their nationality," reported the official church record of these proceedings. The Italian cardinals, of course, wanted an Italian pope, but of the four, the two Romans, Cardinal Orsini and the cardinal of St. Peter, were judged too young and too old, respectively, for the job, and the other two cardinals were declared unsuitable as well because they represented Florence and Milan, cities that had opposed Gregory in the recent war.

Faced with this impasse, the cardinals sought a compromise

candidate who was acceptable to a majority of the electors and whose qualifications also satisfied the chief restraint under which they labored: that is, unless the cardinals wanted to be torn to pieces by the crowd, the new pontiff had to be someone of Italian lineage. Even this was taking a risk as the angry citizenry had specifically requested a Roman pope, but the cardinals decided that it would not do to be seen as caving in too cravenly to the mob's demands. As the cardinal of Limoges pointed out, "a Roman was asked for by the populace, therefore they could not have a Roman."

Under this not inconsiderable constraint, the cardinals could find only one man to nominate who they believed was suited to the position and to the protection of their own interests: the archbishop of Bari. A Neapolitan by birth, the archbishop was a career administrator who had spent many years serving at the papal court in Avignon and was thus familiar with both the bureaucratic workings of the church and the habits and privileges of the Sacred College. Accustomed to dealing with the archbishop in a subservient position, the cardinals had found him to be competent but meek and rather toadying, which suited their purposes; best of all, "a long residence in Avignon had given him the opportunity of acquiring French manners, and ties of equal strength bound him to Italy and to France."

The choice of a Neapolitan pope was no accident. The cardinals well understood the importance of Joanna's support to the Holy See. An Italian papacy was simply not possible without the backing of the queen of Naples, which took the tangible form of Neapolitan money, troops, and diplomats. "He was by birth of the kingdom of Naples which was now ruled by Queen Joanna, a princess very devout and loyal to the Church," read the official paper documenting these events. In choosing the archbishop of Bari, the Sacred College was making a bid to continue the partnership with Naples that had proven so advantageous to the church during the terms of the two previous popes. In this case, however, the desire for continuity with Naples was acute and transcended mere politics. Somebody was going to have to stand up to that unruly Roman mob when it discovered that the cardinals had not elected a Roman pope after all, and by choosing the archbishop of Bari, the electors more or less assured themselves that person would be the most powerful sovereign in the region.

So, although he was by no means anyone's first choice, and would never have been even considered for the position if the election had taken place in Avignon, the archbishop of Bari was chosen as pope by a two-thirds majority on April 8, 1378. The speed with which his selection took place—the cardinals had only entered the conclave the day before—is an indication that this compromise had been haggled out in advance in the weeks before Gregory's death. "It was common knowledge in Rome that, even before the cardinals had entered the conclave, they had in mind the Archbishop of Bari as future pope," the official record noted.

Still, the cardinals, aware of the ugly mood of the crowd, were by no means anxious to inform the city of their decision and put off the announcement until after lunch, which had the added benefit of allowing them time to have the valuable tableware used at the meal transferred to a more protected location. However, when a door of the palace was unlocked to remove the plates, the crowd pushed its way in. Terrified, the other members of the Sacred College convinced the elderly cardinal of Saint Peter, a Roman, to pretend that he was the new pope in order to provide a diversion in the hopes that this would allow the remaining cardinals to make their escape. The masquerade worked: "He [the cardinal of Saint Peter] was placed on the papal throne and arrayed with the papal mitre and cope. The door of the conclave was opened and through this there entered a great crowd of people. Believing him to be the rightful pope, they paid homage to him. The cardinals ... taking advantage of this, disappeared one by one from the palace under the cover of the general commotion."

Once the electors were out of danger and securely barricaded in their fortified castles, the cardinal of Saint Peter informed the mob that the archbishop of Bari, not he, was pope. Perhaps because the news was broken by one of their own, the crowd accepted this decision and quieted down (although, deprived of the dinnerware, they "inflicted much damage on the papal food stores," according to the bishop of Marseille, particularly, it was further reported, the wine cellar). Eventually, the archbishop of Bari, who was hiding in a locked room for fear of his life, emerged, and the city officials were informed. Content that an Italian had been named, the government approved the choice. The next day, assured of protection by the senator of Rome, all the cardinals reappeared at the palace, sang a Te Deum, draped the archbishop in the papal robes, and officially enthroned the new pope, who took the name Urban VI.

The ordeal of the conclave safely over, the cardinals must have congratulated themselves on the wiliness of their choice. Under cover of electing an Italian, they had actually chosen someone as close to a Frenchman as it was possible to be without having in fact been born in France, someone who understood their backgrounds and lofty positions, and who for years had played by the same rules they did. Moreover, by raising the archbishop to an honor he could not have hoped to aspire to under any other scenario, they could be confident of his lifelong gratitude and corresponding solicitude. He was one of their own.

Except he wasn't.

※

At first, there was no inkling of a problem. The citizenry of Naples, proud to have one of their countrymen raised to the highest office in Christendom, celebrated by illuminating the capital city far into the night in honor of the new pope. Joanna, no less pleased, at once dispatched Otto of Brunswick at the head of a high-ranking royal embassy to Rome to convey her private felicity and to offer official congratulations. That the queen of Naples knew the pope personally is confirmed by a letter written four days after the papal election by the ambassador of Mantua, an eyewitness to events in Rome, in which he stated that Urban VI "is on very friendly terms with the Queen of Naples." This observation was additionally supported by the large number of Joanna's courtiers who were subsequently appointed to the papal court—not only Spinelli, who served as a member of the pope's private council, but also, according to a May 10 letter, some of her most important and intimate vassals, such as Niccolò Orsini—and Tommaso Sanseverino, who were appointed as grand marshal and the senator of Rome, respectively. Other Neapolitans among the queen's close acquaintance were also recruited for positions of power in Urban's private household and in the papal treasury.

But soon the volatile and highly unpleasant character of the new pope began to make itself known. In a position that called for nuance, sophistication and diplomacy, the cardinals began to realize that they had placed a crude, obsessive, domineering political neophyte prone to incoherent ravings and violent rages. Urban VI is "considered, both by the majority of contemporary chronicles and by most later historians, one of the most arbitrary and, indeed, insane of all the popes . . . usually described as capricious, arbitrary, deceitful, distrustful, nepotistic and vengeful, even by his defenders." Apparently, during his years of humble servitude in Avignon, the new pope had quietly nursed a number of grievances against his employers, principally directed at the lordly pretensions and opulent manner of living adopted by members of the Curia. Righteous indignation and a burning desire to reform what he considered to be a corrupt style of living now burst out of him, much of it directed at the cardinals. So incensed did the pope become with the cardinal of Limoges during consistory, for example, that he launched himself bodily at his unsuspecting colleague and would have struck him to the ground had not Robert of Geneva intervened, stepping quickly between the two and confronting the pope with incredulity: "Holy Father, what are you doing?" Urban particularly singled out the cardinal of Amiens, who was not in Rome at the time of Gregory's death, and so had not participated in the election, as an object of abuse, accusing him repeatedly of accepting bribes and engaging in treason. The cardinal of Amiens, whose lineage was far superior to that of the new pontiff, retorted: "I cannot answer you back now that you are pope; but if you were still the little Archbishop of Bari—*Archiepiscopellus Barensis*—as you were only a few days ago, I would say that this *Archiepiscopellus* lies in his throat." When the cardinal of Milan, previously a very distinguished doctor of canon law at the University of Naples, and one of the mildest and most reasonable of the members of the Sacred College, objected to one of Urban's pronouncements by explaining quietly, "Holy Father, there can be no lawful excommunication unless you have warned the guilty person three times beforehand," Urban shouted back, "I can do everything—and so I will and decree it."

Urban's provocative behavior extended well beyond his relations with the papal court. In a bit of discourtesy that underscored the depth of the pope's ignorance, or perhaps simply his willful rejection of political realities, Urban made a point of insulting Otto of Brunswick, and indeed the entire Neapolitan delegation sent by Joanna to congratulate him on his elevation to the papal throne. The duke of Brunswick, as befit his status as the consort of the queen of Naples, was given the high chivalric honor of cupbearer at his first meeting with the new pope, a position requiring him to remain on his knees while offering wine to the pontiff. Urban deliberately ignored him, forcing Otto to remain in this humiliating posture, futilely trying to serve the wine in front of the entire assembly, until finally one of the cardinals intervened, saying, "Your Holiness, it is time to drink." When Otto, seconded by Spinelli, later relayed a petition from the queen in which she asked to be given extra time in which to gather the proceeds of the annual tribute (since she had donated so much to Gregory's war effort the previous year), Urban directed his explosive wrath at Joanna. As recorded by a chronicler, the pope not only denied her request but also "threatened to use his power over her and to place her in a nunnery and confiscate all of her goods." This refrain was repeated at a subsequent audience with Otto and the other Neapolitan representatives, at which Urban informed the duke of Brunswick that the kingdom of Naples ought not to be ruled by a woman and that he intended to depose Joanna and give her realm to a son of the king of France, or perhaps to his own nephew, who was later described by Robert of Geneva as "a thoroughly worthless and immoral man." (Urban might rail incessantly against the sin of simony, but nepotism was another matter entirely.) "To lessen the effect of this startling news upon the legation which had come to congratulate him, the pope suggested that the queen should voluntarily enter a nunnery."

The coup de grâce, however, occurred on May 23, 1378, at a dinner given at the papal palace, when Urban tried to publicly demean Niccolò Spinelli by requiring him to give up the seat assigned to him at the table and move to an inferior place. "In a dignified manner the seneschal left his seat, approached the pope and said that he had been sitting there by the arrangement of the master of ceremonies, and added that he had always occupied the same seat in the reign of Urban V and Gregory XI, who had known how to treat the seneschal and chancellor of the queen. Thereupon the Neapolitan embassy left the hall and returned to Naples."

Despite the new pope's overt hostility, neither Joanna nor her infuriated ambassadors, newly returned from Rome, would likely have taken seriously Urban's threat to depose the queen and force her, voluntarily or otherwise, into a nunnery. At fifty-two, with more than a quarter century of experience behind her, Joanna was at the peak of her powers. The reach and breadth of her rule was astonishing. The queen was involved, often in the most meticulous fashion, in every aspect of the administration of her realm. The inhabitants of the smallest village in Naples could not secure the services of a local doctor without first applying to the queen and receiving her approval of their choice. No new product could be brought to market or the time or place of a market day changed without her sanction; no policy or edict implemented unless it bore her seal. Where other rulers, like her cousin Louis the Great, found government tedious, Joanna reveled in it and did her best to adjudicate disputes knowledgeably and with a fairness that accounts in large part for her long success. The queen would rise in the morning, hear Mass in her private chapel, and then throw herself fully into her work, mastering details like those included in this letter pertaining to the importation of wine in Provence:

> We, Joanna, by the grace of God queen of Jerusalem and Sicily, of the duchy of Apulia and of the principality of Capua, countess of Provence, Forcalquier, and Piedmont, to the seneschals of our counties of Provence and Forcalquier or to their lieutenants and to the viguiers of the castle or locality of Tarascon in the aforesaid counties [and to all] our faithful present and future, grace and good will.

> It is our aim and intention unremittingly to protect in a maternal manner the interests of our subjects and as best we can to reduce their expenses through our sovereign love. Now a respectful petition on behalf of the community of the citizens of the said locality of Tarascon, our faithful, recently made to Our Sublimity by their special ambassadors and messengers sent to our court, stated that although the said locality of Tarascon is so well supplied with vineyards that the wine coming from them is quite sufficient for the use of the petitioners, yet it often happens that some inhabitants of the said locality and others, outsiders, carry and have carried wine to that locality from outside; and they consume it not only for their

own use but also by offering it for sale. As a consequence of this, citizens there who have surplus wine cannot sell it, and the foreign wine is sold, from which the mentioned petitioners draw no profit. And because of this Our Majesty was humbly entreated on behalf of the petitioners that we should be good enough . . . to take action with them on this matter, and to order that the import and sale in the aforesaid locality of wine coming from outside the territory and district of the said locality of Tarascon be forbidden.

We, then, being eager through our sovereign love [to promote] the profit and advantage of our faithful . . . consented to these supplications presented to us, as follows: We thought it fit . . . out of our certain knowledge and special grace, to grant . . . to the same community and citizens that so long as it pleases us no wine may be or is permitted to be imported or sent into the said locality of Tarascon by any outsider, of whatever status and condition he be, for sale or merely for his own consumption, exception being made only for citizens and inhabitants of the said locality who own vineyards outside the territory of the aforesaid locality. And this wine coming from vineyards which the latter have and own outside the territory of the said castle they may send into the said castle, and sell, or convert to their use at their will, provided that whenever it will seem expedient, fit, or opportune, a certain suitable tax on the sale of wine—especially retail [sale]—may be imposed and ought to be imposed by the aforesaid council . . .

Issued in Aversa by the magnificent man Ligurio Zurullo of Naples, knight, logothete, and protonotary of the kingdom of Sicily, our relative councilor, and beloved faithful of ours, in the year of the Lord 1377, December 14, first indiction, thirty-fifth year of our reign.

This was not the letter of a woman who was ready to give up her rule.

The queen had had rocky beginnings with pontiffs in the past and had still managed to forge enduring relationships over time. She understood, if Urban did not, that he would need her help if he hoped to remain in Rome. This fact was brought home to the pope when later that summer he was forced to appeal to the queen of Naples for troops to guard him against Breton and Gascon mercenaries hired by his enemies. Luckily for him, she had not taken his advice and retreated to a monastery and so was able to send him two hundred lances and one hundred Neapolitan foot soldiers in July to protect his person.

The cardinals, who bore the full force of Urban's behavior, were not as tolerant, however, particularly as the pope did not limit his ravings to insults but began very soon to issue decrees aimed at reforming their opulent lifestyles. One of his first acts was to forbid the members of the Sacred College from taking money or goods offered as presents by those seeking to influence the workings of the church, a measure that severely threatened the cardinals' interests, as it struck at the source of much of their wealth. But when Urban ordered that his colleagues' meals be limited to a single course, a majority of the cardinals agreed that he had gone too far and began to look for a way out of their predicament.

Their first thought was to amend the situation by a change of locale. Dietrich of Nieheim, a firsthand observer to these events, reported that "the Cardinals came to the conclusion that the sudden elevation to the supreme dignity had completely turned his [Urban's] head," and that this troublesome condition might be remedied by a return to the intimidating, luxurious surroundings at Avignon (where they much preferred to live in any event). But Urban had no intention of leaving Rome and rejected their petition. Frustrated, many of the cardinals, using the heat as a pretext, slipped away from Rome and reassembled at Agnani to plot. By June 21,

1378, all the cardinals, with the exception of the four Italians, had deserted Urban and joined their co-conspirators at Agnani.

The Sacred College had only three ways to rid itself of an unwanted pope. The first was to induce the pontiff to step down of his own accord. This Urban had already shown himself disinclined to do. The second was to kill him, a remedy the cardinals were perfectly happy to carry out; Urban, however, informed by a sympathetic bishop of the danger, thwarted their efforts by refusing to accept their gracious invitation to visit Agnani.

The third and most promising alternative took advantage of a loophole in the electoral proceedings. If it could be proven that the cardinals had been constrained in any way during the election—if they had felt fear, for example, which subsequently compromised their decision-making process—then that election could be held null and void, and they could legally depose the pope and choose another. It was at this point that the cardinals suddenly remembered that they had been pressured by a Roman mob to provide an Italian pope, and that this was the reason they had chosen the archbishop of Bari, a candidate whom, they were by now utterly and absolutely convinced, they would never have even considered otherwise, a clear case of constraint.

By this time, the antipathy between the pope and his cardinals was public knowledge, so Joanna, in an effort to reconcile the two parties, sent a new embassy, again headed by Otto of Brunswick, back to Rome to attempt arbitration. The Neapolitan ambassadors were received by Urban on July 15; Niccolò Spinelli was present at this audience. Joanna's diplomatic initiative was unfortunately overshadowed by the invasion of Breton and Gascon mercenaries, rumored to have been hired by the cardinals, who won a decisive victory over the Roman soldiers sent out to defend the city and the pope on July 16. This was the battle that forced Urban to beg Joanna for troops; later, the arrival of the queen's forces forestalled further incursions by the ruffians.

Emboldened by the success of the mercenaries, the French cardinals at Agnani issued an invitation to their Italian counterparts to meet, ostensibly to begin negotiations for a possible reconciliation. Much more inclined toward accommodation in the light of his soldiers' defeat, Urban sent the three Italian cardinals (the cardinal of Saint Peter, who would die in September, was too weak to travel) to a rendezvous on July 26 with Robert of Geneva, armed with a proposal to call for a general council to resolve the differences within the Curia. This suggestion was rejected by the opposition party. Instead, Robert used the occasion of these talks to acquaint the three Italian members of the Sacred College with their colleagues' plan to depose Urban by declaring the election null and void. The Italian cardinals would then be able to participate in a subsequent election, at which a new pope would be chosen. Robert strongly hinted that if the Italians were to go along with this proposal, the new pope might well be selected from one of their number, the obvious candidate being Cardinal Orsini, who had a Roman heritage.

The upshot of this meeting was that Cardinal Orsini, accompanied by Niccolò Spinelli, who was well acquainted with all the French cardinals from his many years of papal service and was especially intimate with the cardinal of Amiens, who loathed Urban and was one of the first to call the election invalid, left for Naples the next day with the intention of apprising the queen of these new developments in the hopes of gaining her protection and support.

～✄～

The meeting with the queen of Naples, which took place on July 30, 1378, marked a turning point in the crisis. Joanna's acceptance of the premise that Urban's election had been tainted by fear of reprisal by the Romans, and so could not be considered legitimate, was crucial. As the most powerful ruler in the region, only the queen could provide the Sacred College with the protection they would need in order to see this strategy through to its successful conclusion. The support of the king of France would also be necessary eventually, but Charles V was too far away to offer immediate military aid; the cardinals would not send an emissary to Paris until August.*

The audience with the queen was witnessed by Nicholas de Brancaciis, who had accompanied Cardinal Orsini and Niccolò Spinelli to Naples. Joanna had obviously been informed of the circumstances of the case prior to this interview, as Nicholas recorded that her principal focus was to ascertain the veracity of the intelligence provided to her. The queen seems already to have submitted the question of the election's legality to the expertise of her legal counsel, which included many prestigious masters of law at the University of Naples. During the interview, Joanna went directly to the heart of the issue by questioning Orsini as to whether what she had been told about the abnormalities surrounding the election of Urban VI was true. In reply, "Orsini put his hand upon his heart and swore that Urban was not the true pope," Nicholas wrote. "The queen then took his hand and kept it in hers until he swore again that he was telling the truth."

The testimony of Cardinal Orsini was critical to Joanna's decision. He was an Italian cardinal and so (as Robert of Geneva well knew) could not be accused of bias toward the French. Additionally, his statement was supported by Spinelli, the man who had represented her in all her dealings with the previous two popes, who knew

---

* "It doesn't seem to me that modern historians who have examined the schism have paid this point the required consideration," wrote Italian scholar Giacinto Romano. "Looking to identify the distant and direct reasons of this grave conflict, they didn't think it necessary to speculate how Joanna's stance might have contributed not perhaps to provoke, but to facilitate and hasten it. It cannot be denied, however (since this stands out in the chronology of facts) that if the French cardinals had not been certain of the immediate and neighborly support of the queen of Naples . . . they would have found it difficult to dare spur the fight against Urban and accelerate events in such a public way."

the papal court intimately, and whom she trusted implicitly. The grand seneschal's extended sojourn in Rome during the preceding months and position as papal adviser had given him an opportunity to observe these matters firsthand. Whether he in fact believed that the cardinals had experienced sufficient fear at the time of the conclave to taint the election, or whether he more likely simply understood that the rift between Urban and the Sacred College was too pronounced to be repaired, is not certain; what is clear is that by adopting the cardinals' version of events, Spinelli unquestionably believed he was acting in his sovereign's best interests. The desire to replace Urban with a new, more diplomatic pope was first and foremost a bid to return to the old, established ways that had served the kingdom of Naples so well in the past. The Sacred College functioned primarily as an old-boy network, and Spinelli was much more a member of the establishment than was Urban, whom the grand seneschal, in company with the cardinals, considered dangerous to the status quo. Spinelli's loyalties were bound equally to the queen and the church; by adopting the viewpoint that the election was illegitimate, he satisfied both, and so he worked tirelessly to achieve this end.

Most important to the queen's decision was her own reverence for the church. Joanna's faith bordered on superstition by modern standards. According to her beliefs, Orsini risked eternal damnation if he lied to her about something so holy. This made his avowal all the more persuasive and was likely what convinced the queen that the papal election had, in fact, been fraudulent. Later Joanna affirmed that, as he was one of her own subjects, her initial personal feeling inclined her to side with Urban, but that after the meeting with Orsini, "we took the advice of distinguished masters of theology, of doctors in civil and canon law, and of other experts in other relevant disciplines; above all, we received truthful information from our Reverend Fathers and Lords the Cardinals, recorded in their own hand and under their seal in their letters and writs, and without a single member of the Sacred College being of a different opinion." From this point on, the queen of Naples was never shaken from this conclusion, an indication that her acceptance of the cardinals' explanation was genuine.

Assured of Joanna's patronage, the members of the Sacred College moved quickly to implement their chosen course. On August 9, in a lengthy document laying out in detail the evidence justifying their actions, the cardinals publicly declared Urban's election null and void and called on the pope to accept this decision and step down voluntarily in order to avoid conflict. The French cardinals then prudently abandoned Agnani for the town of Fondi, which had the advantage of being within the boundaries of the kingdom of Naples and so was subject to Joanna's protection. The three Italian cardinals were induced to join them and participate in a new conclave by intrigues, which took the form of secret promises made to each that the other cardinals intended to make him pope; Spinelli took an active part in this conspiracy. On September 20, 1378, a new election was held, at which the three Italian cardinals, each believing that he was to be raised to the highest office of the church, refrained from voting. The remaining electors then voted unanimously for Robert of Geneva, who, leaving nothing to chance, was immediately crowned, taking the name Clement VII. Joanna was again the first monarch to be informed of the decision; it took less than twenty hours for an emissary from Fondi to appear at her court with the news.

The choice of Robert of Geneva as the new pope could not have pleased the queen. Joanna had not forgotten that she had lost Sicily as a result of the romantic interference of Robert's older brother Aimon in Jeanne of Durazzo's marriage plans, nor could she have been favorably disposed toward the man responsible for the recent massacre of the inhabitants of Cesena. Nicholas de Brancaciis reported that "she didn't like Clement VII when he was a cardinal." But the queen put aside her own personal feelings and previous experience with Robert's family and sent a magnificent procession of courtiers and noblemen, led by Robert of Artois,* Jeanne's new husband, to congratulate the new pontiff on October 31.

The Great Schism, which would bitterly divide the church for the next forty years and be as damaging to Europe, and especially to the kingdom of Naples, as any war, had begun.

---

* Jeanne of Durazzo, having lost her first husband, had just married Robert, another member of the extended Valois family, on April 6, 1378, in Naples.

CHAPTER XIX

The Fall *of the* Queen

THE ELECTION OF Clement VII was obviously a victory for France, and so, almost by habit, the Christian world divided up once again along the lines previously established by the Hundred Years' War; in fact, in some ways, the schism may be viewed as merely an extension of that conflict. The king of France was positively gleeful. "I am now Pope!" Charles V exulted and declared himself an official supporter of Clement VII on November 16. The majority of the theological masters at the University of Paris, who were originally in favor of calling a general council, took a little longer to accept the decision, but under pressure from the king, they too endorsed Clement. Because France was in favor, England was naturally against, as was the Holy Roman Emperor and the king of Hungary. Two years later Castile (which had been reclaimed with French aid) also decided in Clement's favor as did Aragon and Navarre.

Italy, in general, was dismayed by this turn of events. Although Spinelli wrote personal letters recommending Clement VII to the governments of Pisa and the other Tuscan city states, very few wanted a continuation of French dominance within the church. Rome itself remained staunchly supportive of Urban, particularly after he replaced the entire Sacred College with twenty-six new cardinals, twenty-four of whom were Italian, right after Clement was elected at Fondi. To further buttress his position, Urban asked Catherine of Siena to come to Rome to help counsel him during this period of turmoil; she had written to him in the immediate aftermath of the crisis, "I hear that those incarnate demons have elected an anti-Christ, whom they have exalted against you, the Christ on earth, for I confess, and deny not, that you are the Vicar of Christ."

Catherine did not limit her support of Urban to vigorous denunciations of the disgruntled cardinals; she once again inserted herself directly into the conflict by writing a long letter to Joanna on October 7, 1378: "Dearest mother,—in so far as you are a lover of truth and obedient to Holy Church I call you mother, but in no otherwise, nor do I speak to you with reverence, because I see a great change in your person . . . You who were a legitimate daughter, tenderly beloved of her father, the Vicar of Christ on earth, Pope Urban VI, who is really the Pope . . . have divided yourself from the bosom of your mother, Holy Church, where for so long a time you have been nourished . . . It appears that you have not known God's truth in the way I spoke of . . . nor have you known truth about your neighbor; but in great ignorance, moved by your own passion, you have followed the most miserable and insulting counsel—having acted according to it—that I ever heard of . . . I am quite sure that the counsel came from someone beside yourself. Will, will to know the truth; who those men are, and why they make you see falsehood for truth, saying that Pope Urban VI is not true Pope, making you consider that the antipope, who is simply an antichrist, member of the devil, is Christ on earth. With what truth can they say that to you? Not with any; but they say it with entire falsity, lying over their heads." For all her passion, Catherine showed herself to be a practical negotiator, cognizant of the political realities. Later in the same letter she made an attempt to, if not convert Joanna to Urban's side, at the very least remove the queen of Naples's influence from the process by writing, "If you said to me, 'My mind is not clear as to all these things,' why do you not at least stay neutral?"

Catherine arrived in Rome in November. The future saint was well aware that the intolerance of the pope was at least partly responsible for the situation in which he now found himself. In her first letter to him, at the very beginning of his reign, Catherine had pointed out the need for diplomacy and moderation. "Act with benevolence and a tranquil heart," she had written, "and for the love of Jesus, restrain a little those too quick movements with which nature inspires you." Catherine counseled mediation, and Urban, still hoping for reconciliation, decided to send her to Joanna, along with Bridget of Sweden's daughter, who was also in Rome at the time. "It was hoped that the two virgins, who were well known to Joanna, would make her renounce her great errors," wrote Raymond of Capua, Catherine's friend and confessor, who was present at this meeting. Catherine approved the idea, but Bridget's daughter, also called Catherine, balked. "The other Catherine, however, the Swedish one, would not hear of it, and in my presence refused point blank," reported Raymond. Swedish lore recounts that Bridget's daughter declined this assignment because she dreaded further contact with the depravity of the queen of Naples and her court, but Raymond, who was there, never mentioned this objection. Rather, he noted that his own and Urban's principal reservations had to do with the possibility that the two women would be taken hostage, or worse. "The queen whom they had been asked to go and see, egged on by the followers of Satan—and there were plenty of them around her!—could easily have ordered unprincipled men to do them some injury on their way and stop them from ever reaching her, whereby we should both fail in our purpose and they lose their good name," he wrote. In this, both Raymond and Urban did Joanna an injustice; there is nothing whatever in the queen's background to suggest that she countenanced violence against nuns; it was quite the opposite. The queen revered Bridget of Sweden. She would never have knowingly allowed either woman to be harmed. Catherine, who wanted to go in spite of Raymond's fears, fought for the embassy. "If . . . other holy virgins had thought of things like that they would never have gained the crown of martyrdom! Haven't we a Heavenly Bridegroom, who can free us from the hands of the ungodly and keep our purity intact even in the midst of a shameless mob of men? Your arguments are quite worthless and were suggested by lack of faith, not prudence," she told him. In the end, though, Urban decided not to send Catherine to Joanna, and she remained in Rome.

Although her followers lamented this decision, and wondered if events might have turned out differently if she had gone, there is no evidence that Catherine would have succeeded in her mission. Joanna was unlikely to have taken the word of an unschooled spiritualist, even one purporting to possess mystical powers, over that of the cardinals. Catherine had not even been in Rome during Urban's election. Her knowledge of what occurred was acquired secondhand. As a point of canon law, this rendered her opinion worthless. Only the testimony of the members of the Sacred College mattered, and each and every one of them avowed that he spoke the truth. Joanna was not alone in rejecting the saint's interference; none of the monarchs and scholars to whom Catherine wrote, including those who favored Urban, took the least note of her many appeals.

And so the conflict continued, a war waged, at least for the time being, with sweeping declarations for weapons and ceremonial, largely symbolic acts for battles. On November 22, 1378, Joanna formally declared herself in favor of the new pope and handed over the annual Neapolitan tribute of sixty-four thousand florins to Clement VII, a jab that struck Urban far more effectively than any sword point. Urban countered on November 29 by publishing a long list of people officially branded as enemies of the church; Robert of Geneva's name headed the register. Niccolò Spinelli's name also appeared near the top of this index, as did the names of four other members of Joanna's court, although the queen herself was omitted. Spinelli and the other Neapolitans were ordered stripped of their goods and honors, an act much more pernicious in word than fact, as Urban had not the slightest ability to carry it out. In retaliation, Joanna, who did have the power to implement her commands, replaced all the church officials in the kingdom of Naples who were sympathetic to Urban with priests who were allied to Clement. She also arrested the ambassadors Urban had sent to her court to persuade her to relinquish her allegiance to Clement, so Raymond of Capua had done well in advising against Catherine of Siena's making the trip to Naples, as she, too, would likely have been detained.

But, although the queen of Naples, her court and government, and the learned masters of law at the University of Naples were all agreed as to the illegality of Urban's papacy, the vast majority of the kingdom's population saw the case very differently. To the average citizen of Naples, their sovereign's embracement of a French pope over an Italian one—and a Neapolitan at that—was a crime against the church, akin to treason. There were riots in the streets of Naples, and something very like civil war broke out in the important city of L'Aquila, in Abruzzi, which was on the road to Florence. For the first time since the immediate aftermath of the murder of Andrew so many years before, Joanna did not have the support of her people.

By spring of 1379, the rupture within the church had escalated to the point where both Clement and Urban had actually raised armies in the hopes of settling the question by force. A battle between the two regiments took place on April 30 on the outskirts of Rome. Clement had his Breton mercenaries, but Urban had a Roman militia led by a veteran general, the count of Cuneo; there were also rumors that Hawkwood, who was in the vicinity, would join on the side of the Italian pope. Fearful of the participation of the English free company, some of the Bretons, who were holding the Castel Sant'Angelo and its huge store of treasure for Clement, abruptly defected to Urban. Although Hawkwood and his men never materialized, the Roman forces were able to take advantage of the enemy's confusion to deliver such a resounding defeat to the army of the French pope that Clement found it necessary to vacate his position at Fondi in search of safer quarters to the south. He and his cardinals fled to Joanna's court, arriving in the capital city on May 10.

With the arrival of the French pontiff, the events of Joanna's tumultuous life came full circle. Where once she had stood before a pope, Clement VI, to plead for her crown and her legitimacy, Clement VII now stood before her seeking protection for his tiara and throne. Joanna granted this favor in a manner entirely reflective of her belief and commitment to his cause. The Castel Nuovo was at once given over to the pope and his entourage, and the queen ceremonially knelt to kiss Clement's foot at a spectacle of such pomp, luxury, and grandeur as to leave no doubt of its majestic intentions.

But again the condemnation of her subjects interfered. Led by Ludovico Bozzuto, a militant cleric who had been named archbishop of Naples by Urban VI and subsequently deprived of his position by the queen when Clement VII was elected, violence broke out in the streets of the capital city. The palace of the new archbishop of Naples was attacked and looted by a mob, as was a monastery. A large crowd, including a number of armed men brandishing their weapons, assembled ominously outside the Castel Nuovo, chanting threatening slogans derogatory to Clement and demanding that the queen recognize Urban as the true pope.

Under the circumstances, Clement, while appreciating Joanna's support, felt that Naples was perhaps not the best place to set up his court. Much to the satisfaction of the French cardinals, it was decided that the papacy should return yet again to Avignon. Joanna agreed and offered to provide transportation. Three days later, on May 13, Clement and his suite hastily withdrew from Naples and returned to Fondi to await the promised ships. These appeared some days later, and on May 22, to their evident relief, the French pope and his court left Italy for good in a Neapolitan galley and sailed back to Provence. They reached Marseille safely on June 10, 1379, and were soon ensconced once again in their splendid châteaux in Avignon, amid the sumptuous surroundings and elegant company for which they had pined while in Rome, and where in short order the privations and discomforts they had endured in Italy, particularly the limitation on the number of courses that could be served at any one meal, faded into the background.

Unfortunately, the violence in the streets of Naples persisted even after Clement's exit, and threatened to escalate. The situation became so critical that the queen, deprived of military support— her husband, Otto of Brunswick, was in northern Italy overseeing her Piedmont territories—was forced to resort to subterfuge in order to pacify the kingdom. On May 18, by royal proclamation, Joanna suddenly reversed her position and officially recognized Urban as the true pope after all. To further placate her subjects and perpetuate the charade, the queen sent ambassadors by ship to Rome on June 30, charged with conveying her obedience to Urban.

The scheme worked; the rioting quelled and civil order was restored. But this short-term domestic stability was purchased at the price of the kingdom's trust. In July, when Otto returned with troops, Joanna immediately recalled her ambassadors to Rome and again officially recognized Clement as pope. In the wake of the reversal, her subjects, disgusted by the deception, turned against the queen in a manner from which she would not recover. Joanna had never done anything like this in the past and must have felt herself severely threatened to have resorted to such a measure, but it was a mistake that in the end would cost her dearly.

In Rome, Urban, aware of the unrest in Naples and infuriated by the royal reception Joanna had lavished on his competitor, was again preparing to lash back at the queen. On June 17 he issued a proclamation in which he accused Joanna, "the new Jezebel and the height of impiety," of the crimes of heresy and schism. Then, in what would ordinarily have been just another toothless order, Urban officially excommunicated and deposed Joanna from the throne of Naples in favor of her heir, Charles of Durazzo, and his wife, Margherita, the queen's niece.

Except this time, the gesture had potency. For waiting in the background for just such an opportunity was an opponent who did have the means to dispossess the queen of Naples of her kingdom: Louis the Great, king of Hungary.

~~~

Louis the Great had been monitoring events in Italy closely. The king of Hungary had officially pronounced Urban to be the legitimate pope at the beginning of June 1379, just prior to the Italian pontiff's deposal of Joanna; the timing of these announcements would seem to indicate collusion between the two courts. In any event, this latest pontifical act served Louis' interests very well. The king of Hungary's eldest daughter, Catherine, originally engaged to the son of the king of France, had unfortunately died the year before, leaving her father with a problem. His two remaining daughters, Mary and Hedwig, were slated to inherit his two kingdoms, Hungary and Poland, respectively, but this arrangement had left Charles of Durazzo, his previously adopted heir, without a realm, a situation Louis recognized as inherently dangerous. Charles was now an adult, an experienced warrior with long-standing expectations of sovereignty, and since the king of Hungary's daughters were still children, he could easily overpower his female cousins in the event of Louis' death, thus disrupting the legitimate line of succession. Louis of Hungary understood that he needed to find his ambitious kinsman a kingdom of his own to divert Charles's attention from the crown of Hungary.

Urban conveniently provided one. Louis had already dispatched Charles in the autumn of 1379 to Venetia, in northern Italy outside Venice, with an army to interfere in Hungary's favor in a skirmish between Venice, Padua, and Genoa. When Urban instead urged Charles through emissaries to march his company south and conquer Naples, Louis the Great agreed to allow Charles to use his Hungarian troops for this purpose in exchange for Charles's sworn renunciation of any future right to the throne of Hungary. Charles accepted this condition, and plans were made to invade Naples.

In Avignon, Clement VII heard of these developments with mounting concern. Although Joanna believed Otto of Brunswick was fully capable of protecting her and her kingdom—she would later write that her husband would "fill the world with the renown of his victories"—the French pope was much less sanguine about the Hungarian threat and sought an ally to champion her cause. The obvious choice was Louis, duke of Anjou, younger brother of the king of France, an ambitious, energetic, and experienced warrior. More important, as a member of the French royal family, he had access to the resources necessary to raise an army of sufficient size to challenge Charles of Durazzo. Louis could not be expected to mount a war effort on Joanna's behalf without some form of compensation, but Clement was confident a suitable incentive could be found and invited Louis to meet with him in Avignon in January 1380 to discuss the matter.

The upshot of this negotiation was a detailed agreement whereby the duke of Anjou offered to undertake to protect the sovereignty of the queen of Naples in exchange for Joanna's adopting him as her legal heir. Louis was specific about what he was prepared to do for the queen. He would put four armed galleys and a supply of money at her immediate disposal, in case she needed to flee Naples and required transportation or financing. He promised to take up arms in her defense in a timely and effective manner and to raise an army at no expense to the queen. (In a side agreement, Clement pledged to fund the entire enterprise out of church income raised by taxes on France and Spain.) Cleverly, Louis also agreed never to impinge on Joanna's authority, or that of her husband, while she was alive. The queen would continue to rule as she always had. Only at her death would Louis claim his inheritance and take over the government of the kingdom. The duke of Anjou's proposals seemed so reasonable, and the foreign situation so threatening, that without even waiting for Joanna's response, Clement went ahead and issued a bull on February 1, 1380, officially appointing Louis as the heir to the kingdom of Naples and county of Provence.

Despite the danger, the queen was loath to take this step. Her realm had been established by her illustrious great-great-grandfather Charles of Anjou to rival the kingdom of France, not be incorporated into it. The loss of independence implied by an acceptance of the count of Anjou's proposal would be as much an admission of defeat as a loss in battle to the Hungarians. Joanna did not like it and knew her subjects would also be opposed. She was not yet so desperate as to clutch at straws. Accordingly, she stalled. No official proclamation in support of the arrangement with France was issued by the queen of Naples at this time.

Joanna may also have been unable to accept that Charles and Margherita, whom she had protected and raised to the highest position of nobility as children, would turn against her in this way. She had already as much as made them her heirs; she had stood host at their wedding and ensured that they were married in grand style; she had shown them nothing but affection; they owed her their gratitude and obedience. This was especially true of Margherita, who had been living in Naples with her children for the previous four years, having returned from Hungary in the summer of 1376. And Margherita's behavior in the aftermath of the schism indicated that, at least initially, she supported her aunt's position. Margherita displayed no outward partiality for Urban; on the contrary, she had been present at the welcoming ceremony for Clement VII at the Castel Nuovo in May 1379 and had willingly done obeisance to the French pope, along with Joanna and the rest of the court, at that time. There was no evidence whatsoever of a break or quarrel between the queen and her niece. In fact, by her continued separation from Charles, Margherita gave every indication of preferring her aunt's company to that of her husband.

Yet Margherita suddenly left Naples with her children on June 6, 1380. The chroniclers offer conflicting accounts of her departure. One report asserts that Joanna had her niece under surveillance but that Margherita, taking advantage of an outbreak of violence on the streets of the capital city that day, managed to slip away with her children unnoticed in the confusion. But another source indicates that Margherita asked permission to leave in order to join her husband, and that Joanna granted her request, even providing a military escort to ensure her safety and that of her children on the journey. Whichever of these versions is closer to the truth, the withdrawal of her niece from the royal court at Naples jolted Joanna into acceptance of the danger at hand. In a letter to Clement written on June 29, 1380, the queen officially adopted Louis, count of Anjou, as her successor and granted him the rights and title to the duchy of Calabria, the traditional honorific accorded to Neapolitan heirs to the throne. Clement VII quickly ratified her decision in bulls of July 22 and 23.

The queen's acceptance of assistance came not a moment too soon. By July, Charles of Durazzo, at the head of an army of five thousand Hungarian horsemen and some two thousand foot soldiers, was in Romagna, moving rapidly toward Tuscany. By August, he had taken the towns of Gubbio and Arezzo without a struggle, and by late September was on the outskirts of Florence. Joanna reacted by sending the brother of Cardinal Orsini as an emissary to Tuscany to hire mercenaries and seek an alliance with Florence against the aggressor. But the Florentines favored Urban in the schism and much preferred to get out of Charles's way than to fight on the side of the queen of Naples, so recently their opponent in the struggle against Gregory XI. At the beginning of October the city-state proclaimed its neutrality "with benevolence towards the invader." (Sensing that good wishes, however well meant, might not be enough to ensure their safety in this instance, the Florentine government also prudently bribed Charles with forty thousand florins to leave the city alone.) By November 11, 1380, in an eerie replication of the first Hungarian invasion, without ever engaging in battle, Charles and his army had made their way to the Eternal City, where Urban immediately rewarded his new ally by naming him senator of Rome.

Naples prepared for war. Some minor skirmishes occurred on the border of the kingdom over the next few months, but for the most part Charles's forces remained quiescent during the winter. Although Joanna's troops acquitted themselves well in these initial clashes, the size of the Hungarian company was sufficiently disheartening to provoke great fear in the capital. Bowing to necessity, the queen called on Louis of Anjou to make good his promise and come quickly to Naples to relieve her in her moment of need.

But the count of Anjou was unprepared to answer her summons. His eldest brother, Charles V, king of France, had died on September 16, 1380, and Louis had been required to hurry to Paris to act as regent on behalf of Charles's eldest son, the future Charles VI. To leave comfortable France, where for the moment he enjoyed considerable power, in order to undertake a dangerous and expensive adventure to Naples was highly inconvenient. Louis remained in Paris.

The final preamble to armed conflict occurred with the advent of summer. On June 1, 1381, the pope, who had so inveighed against the corruption of the French cardinals that he had provoked a schism, officially invested Charles of Durazzo with the kingdom of Naples on the condition that, once Charles and his army had removed Joanna from her throne, Urban's nephew would receive the lucrative towns of Capua, Caserta, Aversa, Nocera, and Amalfi, along with a few other rich demesnes. Charles agreed to everything, just as he had with Louis the Great, and the next day, June 2, he was further rewarded by Urban with a solemn coronation ceremony. Six days later, Charles of Durazzo, now Charles III of Naples, Sicily, and Jerusalem, rode out of Rome at the head of a fierce Hungarian army, which had been supplemented over the course of the winter by an additional company of Italian mercenaries numbering some one thousand men. The entire fighting force, consisting of approximately eight thousand hardened warriors and all the cruel machinery of medieval warfare, including three massive catapults, lumbered out of the city and took the road south to Naples.

Joanna made one last, desperate attempt to enlist the aid of Louis of Anjou. In response to the crowning of Charles III, the queen issued a royal proclamation on June 4 publicly announcing the adoption of the duke of Anjou as her heir and promising him a say in her government during her lifetime but only if he kept to the original agreement and appeared in Naples with an army. She also dispatched a private, high-ranking ambassador, the count of Caserta, to Provence and Paris with an urgent message to Louis and Clement to release the promised galleys and to send these, along with a fighting force, to her as quickly as possible.

Then Otto of Brunswick left the queen within the thick-walled fortress of the Castel Nuovo and bravely led a regiment of Neapolitan lances and foot soldiers out of the capital city to try to block the road and repel the invasion.

~☙~

The two armies met at Palestrina, twenty-five miles southeast of Rome, on June 24. Otto's forces were hopelessly outmatched, and the Neapolitans were forced to withdraw. The Hungarians did not even bother to pursue their fleeing opponents but continued their single-minded, unrelenting march forward. Four days later, Charles of Durazzo penetrated the northern border of Joanna's kingdom.

Otto regrouped and fell back on the capital, hoping to make a last stand outside the Porta Capuana, one of several locked gates to the city. He and his knights arrived on July 16, the same day that Charles of Durazzo and his army reached the outskirts of the city of Naples. As night was falling and it was too late to fight, both armies made camp—Otto at the Porta Capuana, Charles at a different gateway, the Porta del Mercato—and prepared to do battle the next day.

But Charles did not have to wait until morning. Under cover of darkness, partisans of Urban VI betrayed the queen's forces. According to seventeenth-century Italian historian Pietro Giannone, referring to earlier chronicle accounts of these events, "then Palamede Bozzuto [brother of Ludovico, Urban's choice for archbishop] and Martuccio Ajes, two Neapolitan knights and captains of the horse, advanced with their troops; and being guided by certain of those who had come out of the city, they moved to the seaside, waded, and entered by the Porta della Conceria; for those within, having trusted to its being washed by the waves, it was neither locked nor guarded; and from thence having marched to the market-place, with a great 'Huzza,' they shouted 'God save King Charles and Pope Urban!' Then, being followed by those who were in the market-place, they easily beat off those of the Queen's party, and forced them to retire to the castle, while they opened the Porta del Mercato, at which Charles with his army entered; and having posted a strong guard at that gate, he [Charles] marched to the Porta Capuana, where he also posted a good guard, and sent another to that of St. Gennaro, while himself and the rest of the army took up their quarters at Santa Chiara, so that they could hinder the enemy from entering by the Porta Donnoroso and the Porta Reale."

Otto was informed of the treachery only after Charles of Durazzo had secured the portals. Although the Neapolitan forces managed to pick off members of the Hungarian rear guard who were late making camp, the queen's champions were effectively locked out of the capital. But for the stone walls of the palace, Joanna was suddenly without defense.

Charles left nothing to chance, and the next morning began a violent siege of the Castel Nuovo. Using his three catapults, he bombarded the fortress with boulders while his engineers tunneled under the walls; when there were no rocks convenient, the Hungarians flung sewage and other filth, including the bodies of the dead, in an effort to intimidate those inside. Many were killed and wounded by the barrage. Even so, Joanna herself might have withstood the assault for months had she not previously opened her doors to some five hundred of her subjects, including her two remaining nieces, Spinelli and the other members of her government, and two cardinals who had remained behind when Clement returned to Avignon. "The next day Charles laid siege to Castel Nuovo, whither, besides the Duchess of Durazzo [Jeanne] with Robert of Artois her husband, almost all the ladies of the best quality had flocked, who, because of their sincere affection for the Queen, were afraid of being ill-used; there was likewise a vast number of noblemen with their families, which occasioned so sudden destruction; for the Queen, partly out of the mildness of her disposition, and partly because she hoped that the galleys of Provence would quickly arrive, received and fed them all with the provisions of the castle, which perhaps would have been sufficient for the garrison for six months, but were consumed in one," Giannone recounted.

The heinous siege conditions ground on. By the third week of August, the food stores had dwindled to the point where it was clear that unless help arrived quickly, those huddled within the shelter of the castle would be forced to surrender or face starvation. Still, the queen, at the age of fifty-five, believed she could repeat the experience of her youth by once again making the journey to Avignon to appear before the papal court and appeal for aid. "She not only designed to make her escape, but to go in person to persuade . . . Pope Clement to give her powerful assistance, in order to return with her adopted heir [the count of Anjou] and drive out the enemy." On August 20, to bargain for time, Joanna sent a personal emissary, the count of San Severino, to Charles of Durazzo to negotiate the terms of a truce. Charles agreed to give her five days "after which time, if Prince Otto did not come to relieve the castle and raise the siege, the Queen must deliver herself up into his hands."

To encourage her submission, Charles adopted a charmingly chivalric attitude and expressed concern for her person. "And San Severino being returned with these conditions, Charles sent after him some servants with a present to the Queen of some fowl, fruit, and other eatables, and ordered daily to be sent whatever she should think fit to command for her own table . . . But what is more . . . to excuse himself . . . he [said] that he sincerely esteemed her as Queen, and would continue to do so, and respect her; that he would not have taken the kingdom by force of arms, but would have waited till it had fallen to him by succession, if he had not seen the Prince, her husband . . . kept up a powerful army; whence it appeared very plain that he [Otto] would have been in a position to keep possession of the kingdom, and to deprive him [Charles] the only branch of the race of Charles I." Joanna's reaction to this ingenuous explanation is not known; most likely she was far more interested in having achieved a postponement of captivity, however slight, than in her persecutor's rationalizations. The first day of the five passed, and then the next, and the next, and still the ships from Provence did not arrive.

Then suddenly, on the fourth day, Otto struck. Down from the Castel Sant'Elmo, which overlooked the city, he and his horsemen thundered toward Piedigrotta and the waterfront to break through

Charles's fortifications and open a supply line to the Castel Nuovo to lift the siege. The Hungarians mobilized quickly, and the army marched out to meet the threat. The Neapolitan forces under Otto made a valiant effort. "They fought with so much bravery, that for a great while the victory was doubtful. At last the Prince [Otto] rushed forward towards King Charles' royal standard with so much boldness, that none durst follow him; so that being surrounded by the best of the enemy's cavalry, he was forced to surrender, and by his being made prisoner his army was routed."

In the wake of the defeat of the Neapolitan forces and the capture of her husband, Joanna had no choice but to surrender. She sent the count of San Severino again to Charles to arrange a parley. On the morning of August 26, the queen descended to the garden of the Castel Nuovo and met her former ward to bargain for terms. The chroniclers indicate that Charles maintained his chivalric posture throughout these discussions. Negotiations between the two continued until evening, at which time a document was apparently drawn outlining the terms of Joanna's surrender. Her first concern was for the safety of those of her subjects and vassals who had supported her in the crisis. "The Queen sent Hugo San Severino to surrender, and to beg of the conqueror to take those who were in the castle with her under his protection. The same day the King [Charles], with his guard and San Severino, entered the castle and saluted the Queen, assuring her that he would perform whatever he had promised, and would have her remain in an apartment of the castle, not as prisoner, but as Queen, and to be served by the same servants as formerly." The terms of her capitulation having been established, Joanna went back inside the Castel Nuovo and had Charles's colors and flag displayed outside the walls of the palace to indicate that he now held possession of both the fortress and the government of Naples. Then she officially surrendered herself to him.

What happened in the immediate aftermath of Joanna's capture is not altogether clear. There is a chronicler's report, sufficiently detailed as to be credible, claiming that on September 1, 1381, less than a week after the queen's surrender, the promised galleys—ten armed ships under the command of the count of Caserta, the personal ambassador whom she had sent to Clement and Louis of Anjou to beg for help—at last appeared. According to this account, Charles of Durazzo allowed the captains of these galleys to visit Joanna in her confinement on condition that the queen announce to the Provençals that she had decided to make him, and not Louis of Anjou, her legitimate heir. Joanna then tricked Charles by agreeing to speak to the captains without specifying what she intended to say:

> As soon as they [the Provençals] were entered, the Queen spoke to them thus: "Both the behavior of my ancestors, and the sacred tie under which the county of Provence was to my crown, required greater dispatch than you have made in coming to relieve me, who, after having suffered all those hardships which are not only grievous to women, but the most robust soldiers, even to the eating of the filthy flesh of unclean animals, have been forced to deliver myself up into the hands of a most cruel enemy. But if this, as I believe, has been through negligence, and not out of any ill intention, I conjure you, if there be remaining in you the least spark of affection toward me, or the smallest remembrance of your oaths, and of the favors you have received from me, that by no means you ever accept of this ungrateful robber [Charles of Durazzo] for your lord, who from a Queen has made me a slave; and even if ever any writing shall be mentioned to you or shown you whereby I may have appointed him my heir, believe it not, but look upon it as if it were a forgery, or extorted from me against my will; because my will is that you should have the

Duke of Anjou for your lord, not only in the county of Provence and my other dominions beyond the mountains [Piedmont], but likewise in this kingdom, to all which I have already appointed him my heir, and to be my champion in order to revenge this treason and violence. Go, then, and obey him; and if you are not void of all sense of gratitude for the love I have showed to your country, and of pity for a Queen under such calamity, you will go and take revenge with your arms, and pray to God for my soul, and I not only advise you so to do, but as you are yet my subjects, I command you."

Her visitors, the chronicler continued, "with sad lamentation excused themselves [for not having arrived sooner] and appeared most sensibly affected with her captivity, and promised to do what she had ordered them, and then ventured abroad of their galleys, and set sail for Provence."

Although the sentiments and commands expressed in Joanna's speech are certainly in keeping with her previous attitude and behavior, other records indicate that the ships in question were still being outfitted in Marseille on September 8, and seem never to have been launched at all. And yet, lending further credibility to the story, on September 2, the day after this incident supposedly took place, Charles of Durazzo abruptly reneged on all his promises to the queen. Instead of allowing Joanna to live at the Castel Nuovo, where a number of high courtiers and members of the royal family, including Otto of Brunswick, Niccolò Spinelli, Jeanne of Durazzo and her new husband, Robert of Artois, were also being held, he suddenly separated the queen from her court and had her transferred to much more austere quarters at the Castel dell'Ovo, accompanied by just a few of her ladies-in-waiting. Nor was she treated with the respect due her position, as was specified by the terms of her surrender. Instead, Joanna was relegated to the position of prisoner. She was held in isolation, unable to communicate with anyone, another indication that she had refused to legitimize Charles's occupation by publicly naming him her heir.

Joanna's situation became even more desperate in December when Robert of Artois, who had earlier feigned homage to Charles in order to gain his freedom, was arrested and accused of plotting to assassinate the usurper and rescue the queen. After that, Joanna was hastily moved during a violent storm to the castle of Nocera, in the interior of the kingdom southeast of Naples, closer to Salerno. Charles allowed her only one lady-in-waiting and three Tartar servants for company.

~❧~

The queen was not without powerful international allies, however. In Avignon, agitated by the news of Joanna's surrender and imprisonment, Clement sent emissaries to Paris to put pressure on Louis of Anjou to honor his obligations under the recent agreement with Naples. By January 1382, the French pope had succeeded in wresting a promise from the duke that an army would be raised and ready to leave for Italy by May 1. That this time Louis was serious was made clear when the duke of Anjou left his regent's post in Paris to travel to Avignon to meet with the pope, arriving on February 22. Sufficient progress was made during these discussions that the next week Clement officially awarded Louis the title of duke of Calabria and threw church support and monies behind the effort to assemble a legion strong enough to defeat the Hungarians.

French preparations for an assault on Naples were noted with some trepidation by Charles of Durazzo. In reaction, the queen's Nocera prison was suddenly judged insufficiently secure in the event of a rescue attempt. On March 28, 1382, the new king of Naples ordered that Joanna be forcibly removed again, this time to the desolate castle of Muro, in the remote, mountainous region of the Apennines of Basilicata, near Venosa, about halfway between Naples and Bari. For good measure, Otto was also transferred out of the capital at this time to the fortified castle of Altamura, in Apulia, inland of the city of Bari.

With this latest move, Joanna's situation deteriorated alarmingly. To act as her warden at the castle of Muro, Charles appointed Palamede Bozzuto, the Neapolitan captain who had been instrumental in opening the gates of the city to the Hungarians. Palamede was a ferocious Urban partisan whose brother Ludovico had recovered his position as archbishop of Naples under Charles's regime. He despised the queen for her espousal of Clement. Under Palamede's direction, Joanna's incarceration took on a new and frightening level of brutality. Her jailer treated her with scorn, at one point tearing the rings from her fingers. Her food was limited and of poor quality, and even this could be denied at any time based on her tormentor's whim. She saw no one but Palamede, her one lady-in-waiting, and her three servants.

Yet time was running out for the Hungarians. Joanna in her isolation could not have known it, but help was on the way. With Clement's backing, Louis of Anjou had raised a huge army and on June 13, 1382, led his force out of Carpentras and toward Italy. Although Florence, Bologna, and Genoa remained loyal to Urban and refused to lend their support to the invasion, Louis and Clement had succeeded in convincing both the count of Savoy and the Visconti family of Milan to contribute men and arms, and the result was a massive force—some sixty thousand men by Louis' own estimation, the largest army ever to cross the Alps (although recent scholarship has put the number closer to fifteen thousand). For his expenses, which included the possibility of hiring mercenaries and further encouraging Italian defections from Urban, it was rumored by the chroniclers that the duke of Anjou carried with him more gold than could be found in the vaults of the rich city of Milan. War was now inevitable, and the advantage in men, arms, and money was on the side of those allied with the queen, still recognized by the majority of Europe as the legitimate ruler of Naples.

This threat signed her death warrant. Without Joanna, Charles's legal claim to the kingdom was much stronger. He was a direct descendant of the original patriarch, Charles of Anjou, as was his wife, Margherita, the queen's niece. Joanna's subjects were far more likely to accept—in fact they had accepted—Charles and Margherita as rulers than they were to support the claims of a member of the French royal family. However, if the queen lived and was freed from captivity, she would undoubtedly legitimize the duke of Anjou's enterprise and might yet swing popular opinion away from Charles, particularly if stories of her ill treatment became known.

On July 27, 1382, just as the duke of Anjou's massive army was making its ponderous way into Italy to rescue her, Joanna I, queen of Naples, Sicily, and Jerusalem, and countess of Provence, was secretly assassinated somewhere within the confines of the castle of Muro. Although Charles of Durazzo, in his official announcement, claimed that she died of natural causes, other documentary sources are unanimous in reporting that the queen was murdered. Because the violence was committed clandestinely, in a remote location, the accounts of the manner in which she was slain vary. As with any sensational event, the chroniclers were perhaps prone to exaggeration and sometimes to outright fantasy. Some say she was poisoned; others that she died of self-imposed starvation. Since only Joanna and her assailants were present at the act, it is impossible to say definitively which of the differing reports is accurate. Still, from within the multitude of rumor, two accounts may be distinguished as having the advantage of some measure of authenticity.

The source of the first of these is Thomas of Niem, who held the position of secretary to Urban VI. According to his version, which was probably supplied by Hungarian informants associated with Charles of Durazzo, Joanna was kneeling in prayer at the private chapel to which she had access within the castle of Muro when four Hungarian soldiers rushed in behind her, took the queen by surprise, and strangled her with a silken cord. The use of strangulation in this instance was obviously intended to replicate the death of Andrew of Hungary and may be seen as retribution for that act.

The second credible source is Marie, wife of Louis of Anjou, who later reported the circumstances of Joanna's death, based on information received from sources within the kingdom, in a letter of August 20, 1385. Marie, like Thomas of Niem, affirmed that Joanna was killed by four men, presumably Hungarian, who overpowered her. But in Marie's version, instead of going to the trouble of strangling her, the thugs simply tied the queen's hands and feet and then smothered her between two feather mattresses. Although no mention is made of the crime's taking place in any particular part of the castle, the presence of the mattresses would indicate that Joanna was killed in her bedroom, which functioned as her cell, and not in the chapel, as was indicated in Thomas of Niem's statement. Marie's story is more prosaic, less loaded with the sort of symbolic detail—the chapel, the strangulation, the silken cord—so favored by storytellers of the period, which perhaps gives it more of the ring of truth.

Whatever the specific circumstances, what can be said with certainty is that, after months of hardship, Joanna died violently and alone, bereft of friends or family, deprived even of the final sacraments from which this most religious of queens would have found solace.

Although Charles announced her passing in an official proclamation, this seems not to have been enough to satisfy the capital, so to settle the matter, the new king of Naples had Joanna's corpse transported by litter from the castle of Muro to the church of Santa Chiara, where for several days the queen's body, surrounded by candles, was displayed to the public to prove she was dead. However, this had the opposite effect, as the privations and anxiety Joanna had suffered during the months of her captivity, coupled with the brutality of her murder, had evidently greatly altered her appearance.

A large number of the people who crowded in to see her corpse reportedly did not recognize her. As a result, one of the chronicles asserted that "many people thought she was dead but others thought she was not," which fueled gossip that Joanna was still alive and that Charles was trying to cover up this fact by substituting another woman's body for the queen's. Because of the confusion, Joanna's death would not be officially recognized in Provence for nearly two years.

After the viewing there followed the problem of what to do with her remains. Since Urban had excommunicated Joanna, the queen could not be buried in consecrated church property, nor did Charles of Durazzo feel the need to honor in death the woman who had, at least until recently, been his benefactor in life. There would be no great funeral statuary erected for Joanna to memorialize the many achievements of her long reign as there had been for her grandfather King Robert, or even a place for her by his side or by that of her sister, Maria, or her father, Charles of Calabria, or her mother, Marie of Valois, all of whom lay in state in the great gloom of the sanctuary of Santa Chiara.

In the end, a compromise solution of sorts was settled on, apparently at the initiative of the Poor Clares, to whom the queen had been so generous throughout her reign. Just outside the edge of the nave, in the lowly space that occupies the entranceway to a back door that leads from the main body of the church of Santa Chiara to the cloister behind, was a deep well covered by a stone slab, into which the bones of the dead were often discarded. Into this well went the remains of Joanna I, to lie unmarked and forgotten through the centuries.

Epilogue

TWO MONTHS LATER, Louis of Anjou's army invaded the kingdom.

The duke of Anjou's journey southward had been prolonged by his decision to avoid Tuscany, and particularly Florence, which still favored Urban in the schism. To protect themselves from attack by the French, the Florentine government had hired John Hawkwood and his men, and Louis, aware of the Englishman's reputation, had no wish to engage him in battle prior to tackling Charles of Durazzo's Hungarian forces. So Louis instead went east and took the long, out-of-the-way, Adriatic coast route to Naples, an unfortunate choice that had the dual effect of cutting significantly into provisions while dividing the army from its supply ships, which had been sent by Clement from Provence and were consequently on the Mediterranean. By the time the duke of Anjou finally made it to the northeastern edge of Joanna's realm, his battalions were already hungry and disease-ridden. Still, on September 17, 1382, he had no difficulty occupying L'Aquila, where he was recognized as king by the local aristocracy. He was in Caserta by October.

But by then Hawkwood's contract with the Florentines had run out, and Urban was able to hire the English commander for the princely sum of forty thousand florins to fight on Charles of Durazzo's side against Louis. Hawkwood, accompanied by 2,200 highly experienced, well-fed cavalry, arrived in Naples in November. Hearing of this, and being by this time also aware that Joanna was dead, Louis chose not to march on the capital but instead retreated to Benevento in the interior to make camp for the winter. There, deprived of food and other supplies, sickness and starvation decimated his ranks. "They are all barefoot and nude and in the greatest poverty," wrote one eyewitness of the invading army. Louis spent Christmas Day composing his will. When his principal ally, the count of Savoy, died of illness in late February 1383, the duke of Anjou broke down and cried.

Cognizant of his advantage, in April 1383, Charles of Durazzo, accompanied by Hawkwood, led an army of some sixteen thousand men toward Benevento to finish off his opponent. Although Louis' forces were by this time reduced to eight thousand soldiers, of whom only two thousand were mounted, the encounter was not decisive. Instead, the duke of Anjou retreated to Bari, where he had himself crowned king of Naples on August 30, 1383, and called for reinforcements from France. For the next year the realm was split in two, with Louis ruling Apulia and Charles installed in the capital.

With Clement's help, a new army, led by the powerful French nobleman Enguerrand Coucy, was hastily organized. By July 1384, this force had entered Italy and was ready to assist Louis. But it was too late. The duke of Anjou, weakened along with his men, caught a chill and died at the castle in Bari on September 20, 1384. Relieved of its commander, what remained of the once-mighty French force scattered. Upon hearing the news, Coucy, too, turned his troops around and made for home, leaving the field and the kingdom of Naples to the victorious Charles of Durazzo.

He did not hold it for long. Emboldened by his success, the new king of Naples turned his sights on Hungary. On September 11,

1382, two months after Joanna was murdered, Louis the Great had also died, of a disease similar to leprosy. The day after his burial, Louis' eleven-year-old daughter, Mary, had been crowned queen, with her mother, Louis' widow Elizabeth,* governing as regent. Many Hungarian nobles were unhappy at the prospect of being ruled by a woman and urged Charles to depose Mary.

In September 1385, Charles heeded their call, left Naples by sea, and landed in Dalmatia. He marched to Buda and called a council of his supporters, who agreeably declared him king. Mary was forced to abdicate, and on December 31, 1385, Charles was crowned sovereign of Hungary, establishing himself at the royal residence at Buda. There, what Louis of Anjou and an army of fifteen thousand warriors had been unable to do, Elizabeth accomplished with dispatch. Feigning motherly warmth and noble family feeling, she waited until the great coronation festivities had passed and everyone had gone home. Then, on February 7, 1386, just thirty-nine days into Charles's reign, she sent a select band of loyal knights into the castle at Buda to assassinate him. A scuffle ensued in which the new king was severely injured. Elizabeth immediately reestablished her rule, and Charles was taken to Visegrád, where, two weeks later, on February 24, 1386, in a fittingly symmetrical display of medieval retribution, the man responsible for the murder of the queen of Naples died of his wounds.

History has not been kind to, or even honest about, Joanna. Her story, when it is recounted at all, focuses entirely on her notoriety, as the queen who murdered her husband, and not on the many impressive accomplishments of her reign. Only Clement VII, who

* Not to be confused with Louis' indomitable mother, Elizabeth, who had finally passed away in 1380, predeceasing her son by only two years.

remained loyal and never forgot that he owed his position and power to her, thought to praise her publicly. "Of all the illustrious women of this world, Joanna, radiant rose among thorns, enfolded us, the whole Roman Church and her subjects in an amazingly sweet scent . . . She passed on from the misery of this world to the beatitude of God's kingdom where she lives and reigns and where, despising and mocking her adversaries, she recovers the scepter that has been taken from her and receives her crown among the saint martyrs," he wrote several years after her death.

But the facts are these. During her long, eventful reign, Joanna held together a large and far-flung dominion, which included Provence and all of southern Italy, and even expanded her rule, however briefly, into Sicily and Piedmont. She was the last medieval ruler to do so; after her death, Provence broke away from the kingdom and was ruled by Louis of Anjou's heirs, who eventually incorporated the county into France, while Naples came for a short time under the sway of first Charles of Durazzo's son and then his daughter, before falling in the next century to the crown of Aragon. For more than thirty years, this queen fed the poor and cared for the sick; built churches and hospitals; reduced crime and promoted peace; protected trade and introduced new industry within her borders. She guided her subjects to recovery from the many instances of plague, war, famine, and depression endemic to the second half of the fourteenth century. The odds against her securing her reign were enormous; that she would survive to rule for thirty years impossible. And yet she did. She has earned the right to be remembered for what she was: the last great sovereign in the Angevin tradition, a worthy successor to Charles of Anjou and Robert the Wise.

To this day, there is still no monument or funeral statuary commemorating Joanna I at the church of Santa Chiara, and the ban of excommunication remains in force.

Acknowledgements

B ECAUSE OF THE destruction of records and the paucity of translated primary source material, *Joanna* represented by far the most challenging (and rewarding) work of my career. It is no exaggeration to say that this book simply could not have been written without the generous help of some wonderfully talented individuals. First and most important among these is my dear friend Marie-Paule de Valdivia, a native Frenchwoman transplanted to suburban Connecticut, who is responsible for the majority of the translated material appearing here in English for the first time. I knew Marie-Paule was the perfect person for the job from the very first day, some two years ago, when I brought over the dowager queen Elizabeth's instructions to her papal ambassadors regarding the inferiority of Andrew's position at the Neapolitan court, and Marie-Paule took one look, laughed, and said "What a mother-in-law! She's not interfering too much in her son's marriage!" To Marie-Paule I owe, among her myriad translations presented here, nearly every long passage from the chroniclers Domenico da Gravina and Giovanni Villani; Louis of Hungary's infuriated missive to Clement VI in which he presents his plan for taking over Naples after his brother's murder; and Joanna's extensive letter to Urban V in which she breaks down and confesses James of Majorca's insanity and ill-treatment of her, and by implication the failure of her third marriage. I may have provided the window by which to view Joanna's world, but Marie-Paule opened it and let in the air of that time; she brought the voices of the past to life in a way that I never could, and I am eternally grateful to her.

For most of the Latin translations I am indebted to Dr. Clement Kuehn, a classical scholar who teaches at Hopkins School in New Haven, Connecticut. Despite a full teaching schedule and his own research, Dr. Kuehn always generously and immediately made time for me. Reviewing my pathetic attempts at translation, in the most chivalrous manner possible, he unfailingly responded with "Your interpretation is very good, but you might just consider . . ." Dr. Kuehn is responsible for most of the elegant translations associated with the *Chronicon Siculum*; for demystifying portions of some of Joanna's and Clement VI's letters; and for the knowledgeable rendering of the queen's laundry list of jewels and enamels purchased for her coronation ceremony with Louis of Taranto in 1352. Hopkins School is exceedingly fortunate to have such an accomplished and gifted classicist as a member of its faculty; I only wish I could have been one of Dr. Kuehn's students. Thank you again, so much, for all your help.

Also, a special nod to Tobias Wildman Burns, lately of Harvard and the New York International Fringe Festival, for his Latin translation of those lines from *De Casibus* and the *Chronicon Siculum* pertaining to the torture of Philippa the Catanian and her granddaughter Sancia immediately after the two were surrendered to Hugo del Balzo in March 1346. Similarly, I am once again, as always, indebted to the staff at the Westport Public Library and particularly to Sue Madeo, the interlibrary loan coordinator, for her valiant efforts on my behalf to secure the loan of dozens of books, many of them obscure and valuable, from research libraries. Having the opportunity to live with a source book for three weeks at a time, rather than simply take notes on it for a few hours a day at a distant library, made understanding the material so much easier and helped enormously when it finally came time to write. And to Wendy Kann, who took time away from her own writing to read the manuscript, and who was always there to bounce ideas off, and to offer insight, advice, and unfailing encouragement, a profound thank you.

Several of the beautiful color illustrations for *Joanna* came from Italy, and I want to emphasize how extremely grateful I am for the aid I received in obtaining images and permissions for this project. I am especially proud and thrilled to have been able to reproduce here the image of Joanna that appears in the lunette above the chapel door of the Certosa di San Giacoma, a fourteenth-century monastery in Capri. There are only two surviving portraits of Joanna painted in her lifetime, and this one is by far the more detailed, defined, and prominent. The other image of Joanna, also reproduced here, may be found in *Via Veritatis (Way of Salvation)* by Andrea da Firenze in the Spanish Chapel of the Church of Santa Maria Novella in Florence, but in that fresco the queen is half hidden by a crowd of familiars and other medieval figures. To include the Certosa di San Giacoma illustration, it was necessary to have a high-quality photograph taken, a daunting endeavor that would simply not have been possible without the active and enthusiastic intervention of Fawn Wilson White, international chairman of the Friends of the Certosa di Capri; Dr. Sara Oliviero, assistant director of the Certosa and special assistant to Professor Nicola Spinosa, superintendente speciale per il patrimonio storico, artistico, etnoantropologico e per il Polo Museale della Citta di Napoli; and Annalisa Ciaravola at Pedicini Luciano. I am also indebted to Professor Spinosa for granting me permission to reproduce this unique and exceptional image.

A special photo also had to be taken of the four miniatures from Andrew's book of saints. Twenty-six leaves of this manuscript, known officially as MS M.360, *Hungarian Anjou Legendary*, are held at the Pierpont Morgan Library, and I want to thank Heidi Hass, head of the Reference Collection; Carolyn Vega, cataloger for medieval and renaissance manuscript images; reading room assistants Sylvie Merian and Maria Isabel Molestina T.; and Eva Soos, photography and rights, for helping me with my research and for making it possible for me to reproduce this image for *Joanna.* I am especially grateful to the curator Dr. William Voelkle, head of the Department of Medieval and Renaissance Manuscripts, for allowing me access to the original illustrations in the reading room. For those interested, images from all twenty-six leaves of MS M.360 are now available through Corsair on the Morgan Library Web site (http://corsair .morganlibrary.org).

My deepest gratitude as well to all the people at Walker & Company who worked so hard to bring this project to fruition: to Amy King for her gorgeous cover design; Margaret Maloney for all her administrative help, especially with the illustrations; Greg Villepique and Maureen Klier for all of their hard work on the manuscript; and Peter Miller for his efforts to promote my book. And to my editor, George Gibson, who was there every step of the way and who, despite the overwhelming number of calls upon his time, devoted so much painstaking attention to *Joanna,* my most heartfelt and sincere thanks. Your experience and insight were invaluable and resulted in a much improved manuscript.

Joanna would not be in print today without the efforts of all those at Inkwell Management who worked so hard to sell the book in America and abroad. To Ethan Bassoff, Mairead Duffy, Susan Hobson, and Patricia Burke, thank you! And to my fabulous agent and friend Michael Carlisle, who I knew instantly was the only person I ever wanted to represent my work, my heartiest thanks and appreciation.

At last I come to my family. To my daughter, Emily, who endured way too much takeout Chinese food for dinner these past few years and was burdened in high school by a mother who started every other sentence with "Back in the fourteenth century ...," my total and absolute love. I am so proud of you. And to my brilliant husband, Larry, who often put down his own work to help me with mine, thank you for your love, generosity, unfailing encouragement, and JSTOR password.

A Brief Explanation of Fourteenth-Century Money

THE FOURTEENTH CENTURY was all about gold—
Hungarian gold, to be specific. Previously, the vast majority
of coins struck in Europe were made of silver. Throughout the thirteenth century, for example, kings and queens had always used silver
in coins, bars, and sometimes even plates and other decorative items
to finance their wars and pay royal dowries; merchants had reckoned
their accounts in silver; and peasants had scraped together small
tarnished silver pennies, known as denari in Italy and deniers in
France, to buy bread and the other necessities of life.

All this changed when Carobert discovered gold in the 1320s
and began minting Hungarian gold florins and aggressively
importing goods and services, mostly from Venice and Florence.
Hungarian gold suddenly flooded into Italy, and from there,
thanks to the super-companies, to the rest of Europe. Gold, intrin-
sically more valuable than silver, was a much more convenient
medium for large transactions, and it quickly became the specie
of choice for the aristocracy and international merchant class.
Although the average medieval citizen or peasant never saw a gold
coin, let alone handled one, the great payments of the age—the
ransom of King John of France, the financing of the Hundred

Years' War, the huge transactions associated with the super-companies—were all paid in gold florins.

It is easy to see why. It took, on average, fourteen times as much silver by weight to equal the purchasing power of gold, and because gold was also denser than silver, silver coins took up twenty-six times more room in a saddlebag or a wagon than their equivalent in gold. So, for example, when a member of one of the Florentine super-companies was sent to England to lend money to Edward III in exchange for licenses to import wool, he could take gold florins, which weighed approximately 3.5 grams per coin, or silver grosso, which were large silver coins, each weighing 1.7 grams. But to use silver meant taking twenty-eight grosso in place of each florin, as two grosso equaled the weight of one florin, and then you needed fourteen times as many to get the same purchasing power. And, obviously, carrying twenty-eight large light silver coins instead of one small heavier gold coin meant taking a *much* larger bag, particularly when dealing with sums in the hundreds of thousands, or, in the case of England, the one and a half million florins Edward III borrowed from the Bardi and Peruzzi families.

Naturally, every kingdom minted its own coins, with the name, weight, and quality of fineness varying from place to place, although Florentine gold florins were accepted everywhere as the principal international currency. The kingdom of Naples continued to mint large silver coins, called gigliati or carlini, and used them to pay sailors and other militia in the never-ending war for Sicily, or exchanged them for gold florins, at an approximate rate of twelve gigliati per florin, for the annual payment to the pope. France began striking its own gold coins, the franc à cheval, largely equivalent to a florin, in the 1360s, but before that the kingdom minted primarily small silver deniers (pennies) and, like Naples, exchanged them for florins when the crown needed money for large political payments. England began striking its first gold coin, "the noble," which was more than twice the size of a florin (the English always had to be different), in 1351 but also minted pennies. Dauphiné, near Avignon, began striking its own gold florins as early as the 1340s to accommodate the many bribes and purchases made to and by Pope Clement VI's lavish court.

All the sums mentioned in *Joanna* are denominated in Florentine florins unless otherwise indicated. For more on this subject, I strongly recommend Peter Spufford's *Money and Its Use in Medieval Europe* and its companion book, *A Handbook of Medieval Exchange*. And if you are interested in the super-companies, you simply cannot do better than Edwin S. Hunt's *The Medieval Super-companies: A Study of the Peruzzi Company of Florence*.

One last point of interest: A stable and strong currency is generally accepted as a measure of a sound political regime. To meet the many pressing financial needs associated with the Hundred Years' War, Catherine of Valois' brother, King Philip VI of France, much to the detriment of his kingdom, chose to devalue the national money supply *seven times* over the course of his reign, so that where sixty silver coins were struck from a weight of silver in 1336, two hundred and forty coins were struck from the same weight in 1342. By contrast, Joanna, whose need for money was certainly equally urgent to that of her cousin, never resorted to devaluation to meet her expenses. The currency of Naples remained stable, and even strengthened from twelve gigliati per florin in 1350 to ten gigliati per florin toward the end of her reign, another intelligent policy decision for which the queen is never given credit.

A Note on the Sources Cited and Used to Research *Joanna*

I THINK THAT ONE of the reasons Queen Joanna I has not been written about in English in more than a century may be attributed to the difficulty in obtaining primary source material relating to her reign after the wanton destruction of the Angevin register by the German army during World War II. This is a sad story, which bears repeating, particularly in the light of the recent lootings of antiquities and other valuable artifacts in Iraq. An eyewitness account of what happened, titled "Report on the Destruction by the Germans, September 30, 1943, of the Depository of Priceless Historical Records of the Naples State Archives," written by Count Riccardo Filangieri of the Royal State Archives of Naples, may be found in the *American Archivist*, vol. 7, no. 4 (October 1944), pp. 252–55. Count Filangieri was the Neapolitan official responsible for overseeing the safety of a large trove of historical documents during the war. The following summary is taken from his report:

At the beginning of World War II, worried about the vulnerability of the thousands of years' worth of historical documents that made up the State Archives of Naples to Allied bombing, Count Filangieri was asked by the Italian Ministry of the Interior to oversee the transfer of the oldest and most valuable of these to a place of safety. Count Filangieri accordingly packed up some thirty thousand books and an additional fifty thousand parchments into 866 strong wooden crates and had these removed to a quiet villa about twenty miles outside Naples. There they remained undisturbed through most of the war.

In September 1943, however, the Germans knew that an Allied invasion was imminent and discipline seems to have broken down. The area near the villa was plagued by small bands of German soldiers armed with submachine guns intent on stealing food and other valuables and destroying both public and private buildings. (I think of them as the twentieth-century version of the free companies.) On the afternoon of September 28, one of these bands, consisting of three privates, appeared at the villa and found, not the calves they were hoping for, but the 866 wooden crates. It was explained to the soldiers that the crates held documents of scholarly interest only, and the soldiers went away.

The next morning, a German officer appeared and ordered one of the boxes opened. The director of the depository stood with the officer and explained the contents of the box and impressed upon him the irrelevance of the collection to the current war effort, at the same time emphasizing its importance for historical research. The officer, apparently satisfied, said, "All right," and left.

Although not seriously worried, Count Filangieri, who lived nearby, at this point wrote a letter to the local German commander again stressing the purely scholarly nature of the documents. This letter was delivered to the villa the next morning, September 30, just as another three-person squad of soldiers, this time armed with incendiary materials, arrived. The director tried to read them the letter, but one of the Germans grabbed it and threw it away, shouting, "Commander know everything, order burn." The soldiers then proceeded to spread straw and gunpowder throughout the villa and set it ablaze. The collection went up in flames in minutes. The staff heroically worked to save a few cartons, but for the most part, everything was destroyed, including what remained of the records of the thirteenth-century reign of Frederick II, known as the "Wonder of the World," one of the greatest of the *German* emperors.

Count Filangieri wrote of this tragic episode: "Their [the documents'] destruction has created an immense void in the historical sources of European civilization, a void which nothing will ever be able to fill." First among the most precious of the documents lost, the count listed the 378 registers of the Angevin Chancery, covering the years 1265 through 1435—the annals relating to Joanna's reign. Gone were the records of what the queen ate and wore, the edicts she directed, the letters she wrote, the money she took in and spent—all the tools a biographer needs to re-create a life lived in the long-ago past—senselessly, needlessly, appallingly destroyed.

This is where an unlikely hero, but a hero nonetheless, Émile-G. Léonard, steps in. In 1932, Léonard, then a graduate student at the University of Paris, decided to do his doctoral dissertation on Joanna I. Because this was before the war, Léonard, who spent time in Naples to do his research, had available to him all the documents later destroyed, and he used these at length in his dissertation. His thesis, titled "La Jeunesse de Jeanne Ire, Reine de Naples, Comtesse de Provence" (The Youth of Joanna Ist, Queen of Naples, Countess of Provence), is written entirely in French and Latin and runs over thirteen hundred pages in two volumes. Although it covers only the early years of Joanna's life and reign, up to her crowning, with Louis of Taranto, in 1352 when she was twenty-six, Léonard's work is invaluable. To make his many points, as would any graduate student, Léonard quoted long passages from primary sources and reprinted in full many letters and other documents, as well as lists of the accounts from the Angevin registers of the period. By doing so, not only did he earn his degree, but he also defeated the ignorance of the German army. More than this, after the war, understanding that he was one of the few scholars who had studied the lost documents, he published other works on the period based on copies he had made and notes he had taken while writing his dissertation, including *Les Angevins de Naples*. Today, every international scholar interested in this period relies on and refers to Léonard's research in his or her own work.

I am fortunate to live by Yale University, which owns one of the few published copies of Léonard's thesis, and so he was my source, too, for much of the primary documentation on Joanna's life. Although the queen had earlier English-language biographers—most notably St. Clair Baddeley in the late nineteenth century—none were nearly as rigorous in their approach as Léonard, and so their books lack much of the material that I am pleased to be able to provide for the first time in English in *Joanna*.

This is not to say that my book merely parrots Dr. Léonard's work. I disagree strongly in many ways with his portrait of Joanna. To name just one point, Léonard asserted that the queen was illiterate and could not even read or write her own name. He based this idea on a letter Joanna sent to Pope Clement VI in 1346, in which, in response to Clement's asking her to defend herself against the charge of conspiracy in Andrew's death, the queen wrote that she was only a lowly woman and was not capable of writing well enough to do this. Since this letter was written in Latin, and Joanna and Clement had by this time been corresponding with each other in Latin for three years, I believe Joanna simply used the standard "I'm only a lowly woman" excuse as a ploy not to have to put down on paper arguments that could be twisted, taken out of context, or later used against her by lawyers. Her grandmother Sancia also referred to herself as only a lowly woman in her letter to the Franciscans, a letter that she nonetheless made a point of noting "was written in her own hand." If Sancia, who was in no way particularly brilliant or accomplished, and who was responsible for Joanna's education, could read and write, it is likely that Joanna could do so as well. Also, the Latin used in Joanna's letters was often not polished, another indication that she composed them herself. There were very few eloquent writers in the fourteenth century, Petrarch being the great exception. Cardinal Talleyrand of Périgord, for example, communicated notably poorly in Latin and was always begging Petrarch to write more simply, so he could understand him.

The other principal difficulty I have with Léonard's work is his obvious prejudice against his subject. Reading his thesis, it is pretty clear that he undertook the project as a reaction to St. Clair Baddeley's portrayal of Joanna. Baddeley made the common biographical mistake of falling in love with his subject; his is an overly romantic, paternalistic, almost quaintly chivalrous view of her person and reign. Léonard, not without some justification, found this approach offensive and used his dissertation to volley many scathing remarks in Baddeley's direction. This is not quite fair, as Baddeley, who seems to have relied primarily on papal records and chroniclers, was accurate on many points. But Baddeley was an Englishman and Léonard a Frenchman, and so there was inevitable competition in this arena as well, which resulted in Léonard's taking an unnecessarily harsh interpretation of Joanna's life. Somewhere between Baddeley's fawning and Léonard's criticism lies the true nature of Joanna's reign, and although more research needs to be done about this important figure, I hope this book, which seeks to navigate between these two extremes, is a first step in this direction.

Of course, there were many other primary sources available to me. Petrarch's *Letters on Familiar Matters* has been translated into English and published in three volumes by Aldo S. Bernardo, and almost all Boccaccio's work has been published in translation as well (although it would be nice if someone would collect and publish all his letters in one place as Bernardo did with Petrarch's). Letters and documents relating to the Avignon papacy are currently available in French and Latin but only sporadically in English; now there's a project for some enterprising church scholar, as I'm sure there would be great interest in America in this material. Excerpts from *Villani's Chronicle* up to the year 1321 were translated into English and published in 1906, but there is no English text of the material covering Joanna's reign—another oversight—so the passages attributed to the Villanis in *Joanna* came from other sources, including Léonard. (There were actually three Villanis—the first, Giovanni, began writing in 1300 and died of plague in 1348; he was succeeded by his brother, Matteo, who wrote the chronicle until his death, also of plague, in 1363. Filippo Villani, Matteo's son, then took over from his father and finished the chronicle in 1364.) Excerpts from Domenico da Gravina's chronicle (who also died of plague in 1348) occasionally appear in English in academic articles but these are mostly paraphrased—so the long passages attributed to this chronicler in *Joanna* are again from Léonard because he quoted them in full. Lastly, all the primary source material pertaining to the Hundred Years' War, including Froissart's marvelous chronicle, have been published and are readily available in English.

Notes

The Trial

1 **"The plague began with us"** Cohn, "The Black Death: End of a Paradigm." http://www.historycooperative.org/journals/ahr/107.3/an0302 000 703. html.

2 **"In a treatise titled"** Wood, *Clement VI*, p. 66.

4 **"From the upper end"** Baddeley, *Queen Joanna I of Naples*, p. 88.

Epigraphs

6 **"Joanna, queen of Sicily"** Boccaccio, *Famous Women*, p. 467.

6 **"Giovanna Regina"** Baddeley, *Robert the Wise*, p. 264, translation by N. Goldstone.

Chapter I: The Kingdom of Naples

7 **"This city [Naples]...is joyful"** Boccaccio, *The Elegy of Lady Fiammetta*, p. 34.

9 **"an earthly paradise"** Croce, *History of the Kingdom of Naples*, p. 45.

9 **"My lady, as you know"** Boccaccio, *The Elegy of Lady Fiammetta*, p. 72.

9 **"I saw Baia"** Petrarch, *Letters on Familiar Matters, I-VIII*, p. 239.

16 **"Robert...asked him"** Bruzelius, *The Stones of Naples*, p. 133.

16 **"a thousand horse"** Machiavelli, *History of Florence and the Affairs of Italy*, p. 76.

16 **"his army prevented"** Ibid., p. 76.

17 **"In the year 1326"** Panache, *Historical Life of Joanna of Sicily*, vol. 1, p. 107.

17 **"two female children"** Ibid., p. 109.

19 **"In this manner"** Bell, *A Short History of the Papacy*, pp. 211–212.

20 **"The crown has fallen"** Headlam, *The Story of Naples*, p. 267.

20 For documentary evidence relating to the death of Marie of Valois, Joanna's mother, see Léonard, *La jeunesse de Jeanne I*, tome 1, p. 142.

Chapter II: The Court of Robert the Wise

22 **"Who in Italy"** Petrarch, *Letters on Familiar Matters I-VIII*, p. 182.

22 **"He seems to have tried"** Toynbee, *S. Louis of Toulouse and the Process of Canonisation in the Fourteenth Century*, p. 59.

23 **"the tears and terrors"** Ibid., p. 69.

27 **"sons"** and herself as their **"mother"** Musto, "Queen Sancia of Naples," p. 207.

28 **"4,012 loaves of bread"** Mollat, *The Popes at Avignon, 1305–1378*, p. 311.

29 **"I … consider it"** Musto, "Queen Sancia of Naples," pp. 213–214.

31 **"They smashed the holy"** Norwich, *Byzantium: The Decline and Fall*, p. 179.

32 **"They do have one city"** *An Anonymous Description of Eastern Europe*, http://www.albanianhistory.net/texts15/AH1308.html.

34 **"very handsome"** Branca, *Boccaccio: The Man and His Works*, p. 23.

35 **"He [Niccolò] began to frequent"** Bergin, *Boccaccio*, p. 33.

35 **"It was said openly"** Branca, *Boccaccio: The Man and His Works*, p. 24.

36 **"the daughter of a poor fisherman"** Boccaccio, *The Fates of Illustrious Men*, p. 236.

36 **"remained among the other servants"** Ibid.

37 **"to him almost all the duties"** Ibid.

37 **"he began to attract"** Ibid.

37 **"the African soldier"** Ibid.

37 **"towns, estates, villas"** Ibid., p. 238.

38 **"She [Philippa] helped them"** Ibid., p. 237.

38 **"What a ridiculous thing"** Ibid.

38 **"Philippa was honored"** Ibid.

39 **"You would think"** Ibid., p. 238.

39 **"nothing serious, arduous, or great"** Ibid.

Notes

Chapter III: The Kingdom of Hungary

40 **"The barons did not concede"** Engel, *The Realm of St. Stephen*, p. 129.

41 **"with great solemnity"** Ibid., p. 130.

42 **"one third of the total production"** C. A. Macartney, *Hungary: A Short History*, p. 41.

43 **"habit of granting privileges"** Engel, *The Realm of St. Stephen*, p. 141.

44 **"His head was sent"** Ibid., p. 138.

48 **"Maria was ... looked upon"** Baddeley, *Robert the Wise*, p. 240.

49 **"Truly the Angevins"** Ibid., p. 216.

50 **"Italy, as always,"** Miskimin, *The Economy of Early Renaissance Europe*, p. 135.

51 **"could only be afforded"** Jones, *The New Cambridge Medieval History*, vol. 6, p. 167.

51 **"There more than anywhere"** Boccaccio, *The Elegy of Lady Fiammetta*, pp. 72–73, 84.

53 **"I recall"** Petrarch, *Letters on Familiar Matters, XVII-XXIV*, p. 165.

54 For Joanna's crown, see Hoch, "The Franciscan Provenance of Simone Martini's Angevin St. Louis in Naples," p. 32.

Chapter IV: A Royal Apprenticeship

58 **"It often happened that"** Boccaccio, *The Elegy of Lady Fiammetta*, p. 83.

60 **"Alas, what a shame"** Petrarch, *Letters on Familiar Matters, I-VIII*, p. 234.

61 **"Who of sane mind doubts"** Baddeley, *Robert the Wise and His Heirs*, p. 131.

64 **"that men of the city"** Dean, *The Towns of Italy in the Later Middle Ages*, p. 167.

65 **"In 1338 there began"** Ibid., pp. 165–166.

66 **"All the important additions"** Coulter, "The Library of the Angevin Kings at Naples," p. 154.

66 **"Naples therefore in his reign"** Baddeley, *Robert the Wise*, p. 272.

67 **"I find myself at a difficult crossroads"** Petrarch, *Letters on Familiar Matters, I-VIII*, pp. 188–189.

68 **"The King's [Robert the Wise's] hand was absent"** Ibid., p. 196.

68 **"How much the study"** Ibid., p. 193.

69 **"by fair speeches"** Froissart, *Chronicles*, vol. 1, p. 12.

70 **"and they did not hesitate"** Hunt, *The Medieval Super-companies: A Study of the Peruzzi Company of Florence*, p. 49.

70 **"collected taxes, transported cash"** Ibid.

73 **"wonderful"** Léonard, *La jeunesse de Jeanne I*, tome 1, p. 175.

73 For documentary evidence relating to Robert of Taranto's birth date see Léonard, *La jeunesse de Jeanne I*, tome 1, p. 178.

73 **"Our princes [Robert and Louis of Taranto] arrive on horses"** Boccaccio, *The Elegy of Lady Fiammetta*, pp. 85–87.

74 **"indolent; prefers food"** Baddeley, *Queen Joanna I of Naples*, p. 36.

74 **"The young prince"** Godkin, *History of Hungary and the Magyars*, p. 74.

75 **"He [Andrew] was manifestly"** Baddeley, *Queen Joanna I of Naples*, p. 36.

77 **"sound of mind"** Baddeley, *Robert the Wise*, p. 282.

77 *"Rex ... instituit sibi"* Ibid.

78 **"The before mentioned duke and duchess"** Ibid., p. 284; and Léonard, *La jeunesse de Jeanne I*, tome 1, p. 224.

Chapter V: The Foolish Legacy of Robert the Wise

81 **"on the day of Wednesday"** Léonard, *La jeunesse de Jeanne I*, tome 1, p. 221, translation by N. Goldstone.

81 **"devised to silence doubts"** Hoch, "The Franciscan Provenance of Simone Martini's Angevin St. Louis in Naples," p. 35.

81 **"The altarpiece's significance"** Ibid.

84 **"He himself denies it"** Zacour, "Talleyrand: The Cardinal of Périgord (1301–1364)," p. 21.

84 **"for it was openly said"** Giovanni Villani, *Villani's Chronicle*, p. 427.

85 **"It was probably this close association"** Zacour, "Talleyrand: The Cardinal of Périgord (1301–1364)," p. 20.

87 **"No one should go out"** Mollat, *The Popes at Avignon*, p. 38.

87 **"A pontiff should make"** Ibid.

87 **"even in prohibited places of worship"** Baddeley, *Robert the Wise*, p. 289.

89 **"having intercourse"** Ibid., p. 290, translation by Dr. Clement Kuehn.

90 **"we have granted"** Ibid.

90 **"by reason of their tender years"** Ibid., p. 291.

90 **"You, as her only sister"** Ibid.

90 **"The marriage did please"** Ibid., pp. 291–292.

90 **"As to the arrangement"** Ibid., p. 292.

92 **"corresponding to 1,449,000 florins"** Engel, *The Realm of St. Stephen*, p. 156.

94 **"There would be no downside"** Léonard, *La jeunesse de Jeanne I*, tome 1, p. 265, translation by Marie-Paule de Valdivia.

Notes

Chapter VI: Papal Politics

100 **"Most of the shareholders"** Hunt, *The Medieval Super-companies*, p. 240.

100 For information on the super-companies' workforce, see ibid., p. 105; and Hunt and Murray, *A History of Business in Medieval Europe, 1200–1550*, p. 109.

101 For information on grain production, see Hunt and Murray, *A History of Business in Medieval Europe*, p. 104.

101 **"The Angevins remained dependent"** Hunt, *The Medieval Super-companies*, p. 47.

102 For statistics on rainfall, see Hyde, *Society and Politics in Medieval Italy*, p. 184.

103 **"the scourge of Apulia"** Baddeley, *Robert the Wise*, p. 245.

103 **"kindling civil war"** Ibid., p. 294.

104 **"The elder queen"** Petrarch, *Letters on Familiar Matters, I-VIII*, p. 237.

104 **"Letting the Pipini go free"** Léonard, *La jeunesse de Jeanne I*, tome 1, p. 319, translation by M-P. de Valdivia.

105 **"seductive band of courtiers"** Petrarch, *Letters on Familiar Matters, I-VIII*, p. 235.

105 **"Relying not as much on eloquence"** Ibid., p. 155.

105 **"I am really alarmed"** Ibid., p. 228.

105 **"I consider what Plautus says"** Ibid., p. 227.

105 **"A single law governs"** Ibid., p. 181.

106 **"Perhaps last night I might have"** Ibid., p. 249.

106 **"in mockery of the King's justices"** Bellamy, *Crime and Public Order in England in the Later Middle Ages*, p. 77.

106 **"Here human blood flows"** Petrarch, *Letters on Familiar Matters, I–VIII*, p. 250.

107 **"And you will have to share"** Ibid., p. 235.

108 **"the age of the queen"** Léonard, *La jeunesse de Jeanne I*, tome 1, p. 301, translation by M-P. de Valdivia.

108 **"praying him to treat no further"** Baddeley, *Robert the Wise*, p. 299.

109 **"Pleading with confidence"** Léonard, *La jeunesse de Jeanne I*, tome 1, p. 322, translation by M-P. de Valdivia.

109 **"certain things, which they"** Zacour, "Talleyrand: The Cardinal of Périgord (1301–1364)," p. 34.

110 **"Your Holiness will deign"** Baddeley, *Robert the Wise*, p. 316.

110 **"tanquam vir ejus"** Léonard, *La jeunesse de Jeanne I*, tome 1, p. 339.

112 **"lofty mind"** Petrarch, *Letters on Familiar Matters, I-VIII*, p. 249.

113 **"his praise sounds like"** Léonard, *La jeunesse de Jeanne I*, tome 1, p. 397, translation by M-P. de Valdivia.

Chapter VII: Nest of Vipers

114 **"vainglorious"** . . . **"always ripe for deceit"** Mollat, *The Popes at Avignon*, p. 102.

116 **"he persists in his inflexibility"** Léonard, *La jeunesse de Jeanne I*, tome 1, p. 354, translation by M-P. de Valdivia.

117 **"Being puffed up with triumph"** Baddeley, *Robert the Wise*, p. 310.

117 **"Sometimes toward the Queen"** Ibid., p. 304.

121 **"For Joanna was given in marriage"** Boccaccio, *The Fates of Illustrious Men*, pp. 238–239.

122 **"When there is the least familiarity"** Ibid., p. 239.

122 **"Good God!"** Petrarch, *Letters on Familiar Matters, I-VIII*, pp. 245–246.

123 **"Since all power over these States"** Léonard, *La jeunesse de Jeanne I*, tome 1, p. 410, translation by M-P. de Valdivia.

123 **"certain others whom we do not"** Baddeley, *Robert the Wise*, p. 335.

124 **"If you deem either untimely"** Léonard, *La jeunesse de Jeanne I*, tome 1, p. 410, translation by M-P. de Valdivia.

126 For information concerning the size of the Hungarian bribe, see Baddeley, *Robert the Wise*, p. 321; and Panache, *Historical Life of Joanna of Sicily*, p. 230.

126 **"an honorable role"** Léonard, *La jeunesse de Jeanne I*, tome 1, p. 455.

128 **"Madame the duchess of Durazzo was . . . gravely ill"** Léonard, *La jeunesse de Jeanne I*, tome 1, p. 437, translation by M-P. de Valdivia.

133 **"Immediately he [Andrew] was summoned by them"** Baddeley, *Robert the Wise*, pp. 343–344.

134 **"It was further related to us"** Ibid., p. 343.

Chapter VIII: Under Siege

136 **"When morning came"** Léonard, *La jeunesse de Jeanne I*, tome 1, pp. 482–483, translation by M-P. de Valdivia.

137 **"honorably interred"** Baddeley, *Robert the Wise*, p. 357.

138 **"Tommaso was prevented"** Ibid., p. 347.

140 **"the nobles, statesmen, and Governing Council"** Ibid., pp. 345–346.

141 **"They [Andrew and his guards] had supped gaily"** Ibid., p. 353.

141 **"We have received your Majesty's letters"** Ibid., p. 351.

143 **"Your envoys will confirm"** Léonard, *La jeunesse de Jeanne I*, tome 1, p. 491, translation by M-P. de Valdivia.

144 **"[If] after the loss of such a consort"** Baddeley, *Robert the Wise*, pp. 360–361.

146 **"My brother's infamous death"** Léonard, *La jeunesse de Jeanne I*, tome 1, p. 516, translation by M-P. de Valdivia.

147 **"Your Holiness knows"** Ibid., translation by M-P. de Valdivia.

150 **"If his marriage [to Joanna] is accomplished"** Ibid., p. 503, translation by N. Goldstone.

152 **"conspired with all of the princes"** Ibid., p. 533.

154 **"Death to the traitors!"** Ibid., p. 525.

154 **"Nobis absentibus abinde"** Ibid., p. 526, translation by Dr. Clement Kuehn.

156 **"In front of the whole city"** Ibid., p. 531, translation by Toby Burns.

156 **"Whoever was a friend"** Ibid., translation by Toby Burns.

Chapter IX: The World at War

159 **"This letter very closely"** Léonard, *La jeunesse de Jeanne I*, tome 1, p. 573, translation by M-P. de Valdivia.

161 **"The prisoners were sentenced to death"** Ibid., p. 587, translation by M-P. de Valdivia.

161 **"The semi-burned corpses"** Ibid., p. 388, translation by M-P. de Valdivia.

163 **"marched on foot"** Froissart, *Chronicles*, vol. 1, p. 40.

163 **"There is no man"** Ibid., pp. 39–40.

164 **"return to those that sent you"** Ibid., p. 43.

164 **"11 princes, 1,200 knights"** Ibid., p. 45.

164 **"It was not merely a victory"** Harvey, *The Black Prince and His Age*, p. 84.

165 **"always, inasmuch as he was able"** Wood, *Clement VI*, p. 138.

165 **"At this time, Pope Clement"** Léonard, *La jeunesse de Jeanne I*, tome 1, p. 640.

165 **"We will freely give both counsel"** Baddeley, *Robert the Wise*, p. 372.

167 **"certain quantities of silver"** Léonard, *La jeunesse de Jeanne I*, tome 1, p. 606, translation by Dr. Clement Kuehn.

168 **"If you attend to our admonitions"** Baddeley, *Robert the Wise*, p. 392.

170 **"bound to poles"** Léonard, *La jeunesse de Jeanne I*, tome 1, p. 628, translation by M-P. de Valdivia.

170 **"Sancia, who had endured torture"** Ibid., translation by M-P. de Valdivia.

170 **"After that, she [Sancia]"** Ibid., translation by M-P. de Valdivia.

171 **"the Princes are innocent"** Ibid., p. 633.

171 **"It is most important that you"** Ibid., p. 634, translation by M-P. de Valdivia.

172 **"nothing would lead to a suspicion"** Ibid., p. 635, translation by M-P. de Valdivia.

Chapter X: The Scales of Justice

180 **"In the same year"** Léonard, *La jeunesse de Jeanne I*, tome 2, p. 44, translation by Dr. Clement Kuehn.

181 **"The king greeted the princes graciously"** Ibid., p. 38, translation by M.-P. de Valdivia.

184 **"A night of violence followed"** Ibid., p. 41, translation by M-P. de Valdivia.

191 **"When first the King of Hungary"** Baddeley, *Robert the Wise*, pp. 433–434.

193 **"according to the ceremonial protocol"** Léonard, *La jeunesse de Jeanne I*, tome 2, p. 89.

194 **"Consistory was … the supreme court"** Wood, *Clement VI*, p. 97.

195 **"Joanna arrived in Provence"** Panache, *Historical Life of Joanna of Sicily*, vol. 1, pp. 313–314.

195 **"You know of the wretched situation"** Léonard, *La jeunesse de Jeanne I*, tome 2, p. 93, translation by M-P. de Valdivia. See also Wood, *Clement VI*, p. 97.

196 **"Not only innocent"** Panache, *Historical Life of Joanna of Sicily*, vol. 1, p. 313, translation by M-P. de Valdivia.

196 **"She spoke at length"** Ibid., p. 314, translation by M-P. de Valdivia.

196 **"As far as the murder of her first husband"** Ibid., pp. 314–315, translation by M-P. de Valdivia.

Chapter XI: The Return of the Queen

197 **"However, and even though in point of fact"** Léonard, *La jeunesse de Jeanne I*, tome 2, pp. 99–100, translation by M.-P. de Valdivia.

198 **"Nor was any mercy"** Ibid., p. 117, translation by M.-P. de Valdivia.

198 **"was put to the question"** Ibid., translation by M-P. de Valdivia.

198 **"Assuredly it was"** Baddeley, *Robert the Wise*, p. 330.

199 **"The violence of this disease"** Boccaccio, *The Decameron*, pp. 3–6.

202 **"Since the castles of Naples"** Léonard, *La jeunesse de Jeanne I*, tome 2, p. 144, translation by M-P. de Valdivia.

203 **"ostentatious outfits"** Ibid., p. 145, translation by M-P. de Valdivia.

203 **"The Florentine, Sienese and Luccan merchants"** Ibid., translation by M-P. de Valdivia.

206 **"Although of royal birth"** Baddeley, *Robert the Wise*, pp. 456–458.

206 **"Most blessed Father (in Christ)"** Ibid., p. 460.

208 **"The quarrel between Louis and the queen"** Léonard, *La jeunesse de Jeanne I*, tome 2, p. 245, translation by M-P de Valdivia.

208 "After deliberation with the royal family" Ibid., p. 264, translation by M-P. de Valdivia.

210 "Long Live the Pope!" Ibid., p. 266.

210 "best love" Ibid., p. 268.

211 "The king of Hungary" Ibid., p. 269, translation by M-P. de Valdivia.

212 "As for Louis of Taranto" Ibid., translation by M-P. de Valdivia.

213 "On September 29" Ibid., p. 280, translation by M-P. de Valdivia.

213 "The count went to the castle" Ibid., translation by M-P. de Valdivia.

214 For accounts of Maria's second marriage and the deaths of Hugo and Robert del Balzo, see Ibid., p. 281; Baddeley, *Robert the Wise*, p. 481; and Zacour, "Talleyrand: The Cardinal of Périgord (1301–1364)," p. 36.

215 "At the end of the month of February" Léonard, *La jeunesse de Jeanne I.* tome 2, p. 300, translation by M-P. de Valdivia.

215 "The general accord between our masters" Ibid., p. 313, translation by M-P. de Valdivia.

215 "Because he did not go to war" Ibid., p. 331, translation by M-P. de Valdivia.

218 "In conjunction with our festive coronation" Ibid., p. 347, translation by Dr. Clement Kuehn.

219 For details of Louis of Taranto's accident and the death of Françoise, see Panache, *Historical Life of Joanna of Sicily*, vol. 2, p. 17; and Léonard, *La jeunesse de Jeanne I*, tome 2, p. 359.

Chapter XII: Foreign and Domestic Relations

220 For statistics on the plague, see Postan, *The Cambridge Economic History of Europe*, pp. 346, 347, 364; and Miskimin, *The Economy of Early Renaissance Europe*, p. 29.

220 "Is it possible" Larner, *Italy in the Age of Dante and Petrarch, 1216–1380*, p. 265.

221 "I found my Pouilles lands" Léonard, *La jeunesse de Jeanne I*, tome 2, p. 377, translation by M-P. de Valdivia.

221 "Followed by 400 horsemen" Ibid., p. 373, translation by M-P. de Valdivia.

221 "If we examine her domain" Boccaccio, *Famous Women*, p. 471.

223 "My Lords Cardinal" Zacour, "Talleyrand: The Cardinal of Périgord (1301–1364)," p. 21.

223 "No doubt the Sacred College" Mollat, *The Popes at Avignon*, p. 45.

223 "In this way he emptied the Papal Palace" Pastor, *History of the Popes*, p. 93.

226 **"He honored the Queen little"** Léonard, *Les Angevins de Naples*, p. 373, translation by M-P. de Valdivia.

226 **"humiliated"** Ibid.

226 **"sterility in her times"** Ibid., p. 403, translation by M-P. de Valdivia.

227 **"recover the kingdom of Jerusalem"** Ibid., p. 373.

228 **"I swear ... that I have"** Ibid., p. 386, translation by M-P. de Valdivia.

230 **"leave their side"** Ibid., p. 375, translation by M-P. de Valdivia.

232 **"twenty-five hundred well-armed"** Ibid., p. 378, translation by M-P. de Valdivia.

233 **"possibly the richest heiress"** Zacour, "Talleyrand: The Cardinal of Périgord (1301–1364)," p. 40.

Chapter XIII: Queen of Sicily

236 **"The Sicilians had such"** Léonard, *Les Angevins de Naples*, p. 396, translation by M-P. de Valdivia.

236 **"courteous custody"** Setton, "Archbishop Pierre d'Ameil in Naples and the Affair of Aimon III of Geneva," p. 644.

238 **"Know that it was I"** Tuchman, *A Distant Mirror*, p. 136.

238 **"as he shall never"** Ibid., p. 136.

239 **"My lord, as to news"** Barber, *The Life and Campaigns of the Black Prince*, p. 50.

239 **"He gathered all the forces"** Ibid., p. 94.

240 **"out of reverence for holy Church"** Ibid., p. 73.

240 **"The battle that day"** Froissart, *Chronicles*, vol. 1, p. 52.

240 **"the French army increased"** Barber, *The Life and Campaigns of the Black Prince*, p. 73.

240 **"The whole army of the prince"** Froissart, *Chronicles*, vol. 1, p. 53.

240 **"Occasion, time, and dangers"** Barber, *The Life and Campaigns of the Black Prince*, p. 75.

241 **"Surrender yourself, surrender yourself"** Froissart, *Chronicles*, vol. 1, p. 60.

241 **"he was treated with the greatest"** Ibid., p. 65.

242 **"Present it ... to the cardinal"** Ibid., p. 56.

243 For Charles of Durazzo's age see Léonard, *Les Angevins de Naples*, p. 392. Also Engel, *The Realm of St. Stephen*, p. 195, reports that Charles was "brought up in Hungary," after moving there in 1364 (p. 169) which also implies a birth date in the late 1350s.

246 **"found means to escape"** Ibid., p. 67.

247 **"Edward, on receiving their answer"** Ibid.

247 **"The weather was bad and rainy"** Ibid.

248 footnote **"His [Galeazzo's] proposals"** E. R. Chamberlin, *The Count of Virtue*, pp. 33–35.

248 **"When everything relative to the peace"** Ibid., p. 71.

250 **"had always to eat their fruits"** Léonard, *Les Angevins de Naples*, p. 398, translation by M-P. de Valdivia.

250 **"So our intention might be known"** Ibid., p. 393, translation by M-P. de Valdivia.

Chapter XIV: The Queen and Her Court

253 **"such a husband"** Léonard, *Les Angevins de Naples*, p. 401.

253 **"Our position . . . [is] perhaps"** Ibid., p. 401, translation by M-P. de Valdivia.

254 **"that he owned nothing"** Ibid., p. 398, translation by M-P. de Valdivia.

254 **"They obtained letters from her"** Ibid., p. 402, translation by M-P. de Valdivia.

255 **"Still not content"** Ibid., translation by M-P. de Valdivia.

255 **"all honors due to the royal household"** Ibid., translation by M-P. de Valdivia.

255 **"Hearing with great sadness"** Ibid., translation by M-P. de Valdivia.

256 **"The queen delights in governing"** Ibid., translation by M-P. de Valdivia.

256 **"whole and not decaying"** Kirshner and Wemple, *Women of the Medieval World: Essays in Honor of John H. Mundy*, p. 189.

257 Sadly, Giotto's frescoes at the Castel Nuovo are no longer extant. To read more about them, see Joost-Gaugier, "Giotto's Hero Cycle in Naples: A Prototype of Donne Illustri and a Possible Literary Connection," p. 317.

257 **"Whilst Giotto was engaged"** Headlam, *The Story of Naples*, p. 269.

257 footnote **"his children could be so ugly"** Adams, *Italian Renaissance Art*, p. 26.

258 **"only the rich"** Park, *Doctors and Medicine in Early Renaissance Florence*, p. 50.

258 **"Salerno then flourished"** Green, *The Trotula*, p. 9.

258 **"where the Christians"** Ibid., p. 4.

259 **"could not claim"** Park, *Doctors and Medicine in Early Renaissance Florence*, p. 72.

259 For statistics on the percentage of women employed as doctors, see Bennett et al., *Sisters and Workers in the Middle Ages*, pp. 43–47.

259 **"The aforesaid Raimonda"** Judith C. Brown and Robert C. Davis, *Gender*

and Society in Renaissance Italy, p. 135.

259 "Indeed, the relative independence" Ibid., p. 137.

260 "I would wish to be silent" Campbell, *Life of Petrarch*, p. 254.

261 "Reverend Domine, here is" Branca, *Boccaccio: The Man and His Works*, pp. 197–198.

262 "With my entire soul" Petrarch, *Letters on Familiar Matters, XVII-XXIV*, p. 298.

262 "epistle written by the hand" Branca, *Boccaccio: The Man and His Works*, p. 134.

262 "Niccolò ... I am writing you" Ibid., p. 56.

263 "Finally thy epistle" Ibid., p. 134.

263 "no differently was I received" Ibid., p. 135.

263 "just then brought up from the nether regions" Ibid.

263 "frequently goes into closed assembly" Ibid., p. 136.

264 "alone, with the load of books" Ibid., p. 137.

264 "he [Acciaiuoli] pretended not to notice" Ibid.

264 "to be no longer tormented" Ibid.

264 "man of glass" Ibid., p. 138.

265 "The wonderful man [Hugo]" Ibid., 169, translated by Dr. Clement Kuehn.

265 "once again the queen" Ibid., p. 169.

266 "governing wisely and of defending" Léonard, *Les Angevins de Naples*, p. 403, translation by M-P. de Valdivia.

266 "the conflicting wishes of the nobles" Ibid., translation by M-P. de Valdivia.

268 "as long as the prince would reside" Ibid., translation by M-P. de Valdivia.

269 "After all, the decision to marry is free" Ibid., p. 404, translation by M-P. de Valdivia.

269 "shut up for the next fourteen years" Ibid., p. 403, translation by M-P. de Valdivia.

Chapter XV: The Quest for an Heir

272 "The Sire the King suffers" Léonard, *Les Angevins de Naples*, p. 405, translation by M-P. de Valdivia.

273 "I doubt that he will get better" Ibid., p. 406, translation by M-P. de Valdivia.

273 "He has already become very grand with me" Setton, "Archpishop Pierre

d'Ameil in Naples," pp. 655–656.

274 **"The Queen, even though like the dead"** Léonard, *Les Angevins de Naples*, p. 406, translation by M-P. de Valdivia.

274 **"The Lady Queen has suspected"** Setton, "Archpishop Pierre d'Ameil in Naples," p. 668, footnote 73.

275 **"Most Holy Father, the importance of this matter"** Léonard, *Les Angevins de Naples*, p. 407, translation by M-P. de Valdivia.

276 **"the flux and vomiting"** Setton, "Archpishop Pierre d'Ameil in Naples," p. 655, footnote 38.

276 **"But most recently"** Léonard, *Les Angevins de Naples*, pp. 407–409, translation by M-P. de Valdivia.

277 footnote **"struck the Queen"** Setton, "Archpishop Pierre d'Ameil in Naples," p. 655, footnote 37.

280 **"The lord Louis of Navarre"** Setton, "Archpishop Pierre d'Ameil in Naples," p. 653.

281 **"the business of the marriage"** Ibid.

281 **"The next day I addressed"** Ibid., p. 660.

282 **"a letter which the lord of Périgord"** Ibid., p. 662.

282 **"as a means of bringing back Frederick"** Ibid., p. 664.

282 **"Because it would not be fitting"** Ibid.

283 **"see and learn about certain things"** Ibid., p. 682.

283 **"and some other things . . . touching the city"** Ibid.

283 **"I would marry him [the king of Sicily]"** Ibid., p. 656, footnote 44.

283 **"using their influence with her"** Ibid., p. 665.

284 **"Open war"** Ibid., p. 671.

285 **"Because there is no wickedness"** Ibid., p. 689.

285 **"And in truth, my very dear friend"** Ibid., p. 686.

286 **"the great deceiver"** Ibid., p. 690.

286 **"on the advice of Queen Joanna"** Léonard, *Les Angevins de Naples*, p. 418, translation by M-P. de Valdivia.

286 **"On the 18th of June, 1366"** Ibid., translation by M-P. de Valdivia.

290 **"I have only one regret"** Ibid., p. 419, translation by M-P. de Valdivia.

291 **"Acciaiuoli, . . . Plebian at Florence"** Gibbon, *The Decline and Fall of the Roman Empire*, vol. 3, p. 599.

292 **"Joanna, by the grace of God"** Dean, *The Towns of Italy in the Later Middle Ages*, p. 182.

293 **"You know well . . . the great difficulties"** Abulafia, "Southern Italy and the

Florentine Economy," p. 377.

294 "imperatrix Constantinopolitana" Hare, *Cities of Southern Italy and Sicily*, p. 106.

Chapter XVI: Queen and Pope

295 footnote "It was the peculiarity of Italian warfare" Caferro, *John Hawkwood*, p. 147.

295 "For more than sixty stormy years" Bell, *A Short History of the Papacy*, p. 224.

297 "'Lord, where goest thou?'" Mollat, *The Popes at Avignon*, p. 157.

297 "that he could produce other cardinals" Ibid., p. 57.

297 "like a floating city" Bell, *A Short History of the Papacy*, p. 223.

297 "Oh, wicked Pope!" Tuchman, *A Distant Mirror*, p. 250.

298 "Some of the Cardinals" Baddeley, *Queen Joanna I of Naples*, p. 217.

299 "It seems all but certain" Harvey, *The Black Prince and His Age*, p. 106.

299 "My dear cousin [Edward]" Froissart, *Chronicles*, vol. 1, p. 95.

300 "They all, and the king of Navarre as well" Barber, *The Life and Campaigns of the Black Prince*, pp. 109–110.

300 "At this period Lord James" Froissart, *Chronicles*, vol. 1, p. 100.

300 "the day of the three kings" Harvey, *The Black Prince and His Age*, p. 108.

301 "to famish them without striking a blow" Tuchman, *A Distant Mirror*, p. 231.

301 "on a little hill to the left" Barber, *The Life and Campaigns of the Black Prince*, p. 128.

301 "My dear cousin, I must thank you" Ibid., p. 130.

301 "They say in France" Froissart, *Chronicles*, vol. 1, p. 111.

301 "and his army suffered" Barber, *The Life and Campaigns of the Black Prince*, p. 132.

302 "and all prepared for departure" Froissart, *Chronicles*, vol. 1, p. 110.

302 "As soon as the King [Enrique] was entered" Baddeley, *Queen Joanna I of Naples*, p. 205.

303 "Even though we trust" Léonard, *Les Angevins de Naples*, pp. 421–422, translation by M-P. de Valdivia.

304 "The which ransom these two ladies" Baddeley, *Queen Joanna I of Naples*, p. 206.

304 "since it is not the kingship" Engel, *The Realm of St. Stephen*, p. 158.

305 "with impudent words" Ibid., p. 168.

305 footnote **"Due to her influence over Louis"** Ibid., p. 171.

308 **"The Lady Queen gave in their honor"** Léonard, *Les Angevins de Naples*, p. 431, translation by M-P. de Valdivia.

309 **"so that, if we or our successors"** Mollat, *The Popes at Avignon*, p. 160.

310 **"Pope Urban would have been numbered"** Bell, *A Short History of the Papacy*, p. 226.

310 **"The pontiff cherished a sincere love"** Léonard, *Les Angevins de Naples*, p. 428, translation by M-P. de Valdivia.

Chapter XVII: Six Funerals and a Wedding

311 **"The papal chair was governed"** Machiavelli, *History of Florence and of the Affairs of Italy*, p. 110.

312 **"completely disposed to the destruction"** Caferro, *John Hawkwood*, p. 151.

312 **"Either I will destroy the Visconti"** Léonard, *Les Angevins de Naples*, pp. 440–441, translation by M-P. de Valdivia.

313 **"silken cord and seals of lead"** Tuchman, *A Distant Mirror*, p. 240.

313 **"Bernabò wanted to sign him"** Caferro, *John Hawkwood*, p. 150.

314 **"Most dear daughter in Christ"** Ibid., p. 152.

316 **"with his head and arms"** Tuchman, *A Distant Mirror*, p. 259.

316 **"Now art thou risen"** Branca, *Boccaccio: The Man and His Works*, p. 189.

316 **"Why, O illustrious poet"** Bergin, *Boccaccio*, p. 65.

317 **"took little fortresses"** Baddeley, *Queen Joanna I of Naples*, p. 206.

317 **"And while this war"** Ibid., p. 207.

318 **"usurped"** Léonard, *Les Angevins de Naples*, p. 445.

318 **"As soon as it was known"** Barber, *The Life and Campaigns of the Black Prince*, pp. 134–135.

319 **"that flower of English knighthood"** Froissart, *Chronicles*, vol. 1, pp. 148–149.

319 **"Here ends the lay"** Harvey, *The Black Prince and His Age*, p. 117.

321 **"a vast army ... a good ten miles"** Caferro, *John Hawkwood*, p. 163.

321 **"John and his society"** Ibid., p. 168.

321 **"The magnificent figure"** Ibid., pp. 168–169.

322 **"2,350 lances with accompanying units"** Ibid., p. 169.

323 **"My dearest and very loved brothers"** Catherine, *The Letters of Saint Catherine*, vol. 1, p. 106.

324 **"honorable and dearest mother"** Ibid., p. 129.

324 **"I want you to know"** Ibid., p. 133.

325 **"modifying male and female"** Léonard, *Les Angevins de Naples*, p. 432, translation by M-P. de Valdivia.

325 **"Saint Bridget had a vision"** Ibid., translation by M-P. de Valdivia.

326 **"We know how Saint Catherine"** Ibid., p. 451, translation by M-P. de Valdivia.

326 **"It was necessary that we seek"** Caferro, *John Hawkwood*, pp. 169–170.

327 **"our dear son and noble lord"** Léonard, *Les Angevins de Naples*, p. 439, translation by M-P. de Valdivia.

328 **"with joy . . . honor him"** Ibid., p. 450.

328 **"that very night"** Ibid.

329 **"of humiliating Italy"** Ibid., translation by M-P. de Valdivia.

329 **"Few princes could resist"** Brucker, *Florentine Politics and Society*, p. 311.

329 **"not one Florentine"** Ibid.

330 **"handsome and well formed"** Tuchman, *A Distant Mirror*, p. 321.

330 **"Does the sun enter there?"** Caferro, *John Hawkwood*, p. 188.

330 **"They came inside the city"** Ibid., p. 189.

331 **"Everyone—women, old and young"** Ibid.

331 **"there remained neither man"** Ibid.

331 **"I command you to descend"** Ibid., p. 190.

332 **"never were seen so many"** Mollat, *The Popes at Avignon*, p. 63.

332 **"Who has ever seen"** Ibid., p. 169.

333 **"to help us carry the weight"** Léonard, *Les Angevins de Naples*, p. 452, translation by M-P. de Valdivia.

333 **"We don't know who to turn to"** Ibid., p. 453, translation by M-P. de Valdivia.

Chapter XVIII: The Great Schism

336 **"The pope will not escape"** Trexler, "Rome on the Eve of the Great Schism," p. 503.

336 **"The cardinals feared for their lives"** Ibid., p. 508.

336 **"Since the cardinals, especially the French"** Ullmann, *The Origins of the Great Schism*, p. 12.

336 **"and other officials approached them"** Ibid.

337 **"We want a Roman!"** Ibid., p. 16.

337 **"Let's kill them!"** Ibid., p. 36.

337 **"The French strongly declared"** Ibid., p. 16.

338 "a Roman was asked for" Ibid., p. 17.

338 "a long residence in Avignon" Pastor, *The History of the Popes from the Close of the Middle Ages*, vol. 1, p. 118.

338 "He was by birth of the kingdom" Ullmann, *The Origins of the Great Schism*, p. 16.

339 "It was common knowledge" Ibid.

339 "He [the cardinal of St. Peter] was placed" Ibid., pp. 19–20.

340 "inflicted much damage" Ibid., p. 33.

341 "is on very friendly terms" Pastor, *The History of the Popes from the Close of the Middle Ages*, vol. 1, p. 121.

341 "considered, both by the majority" Percy, "Review of *La politica napoletana di Urbano VI* by Salvatore Fodale," pp. 740–741.

342 "Holy Father, what are you doing?" Ullmann, *The Origins of the Great Schism*, p. 46.

342 "I cannot answer you back" Ibid., p. 47.

342 "Holy Father, there can be no" Ibid., p. 48.

342 "Your Holiness, it is time to drink" Curtayne, *Saint Catherine of Siena*, p. 159.

343 "threatened to use his power" Ullmann, *The Origins of the Great Schism*, p. 49.

343 "a thoroughly worthless and immoral man" Ibid., p. 96. See also Pastor, *The History of the Popes from the Close of the Middle Ages*, vol. 1, p. 136.

343 "To lessen the effect" Ullmann, *The Origins of the Great Schism*, p. 49.

343 "In a dignified manner" Ibid., p. 50.

344 "We, Joanna, by the grace of God" Lopez and Raymond, *Medieval Trade in the Mediterranean World*, pp. 331–332.

346 "the Cardinals came to the conclusion" Pastor, *The History of the Popes from the Close of the Middle Ages*, vol. 1, p. 122 footnote.

349 "Orsini put his hand upon his heart" Léonard, *Les Angevins de Naples*, p. 456, translation by M-P. de Valdivia.

349 footnote "It doesn't seem to me" Ibid., p. 457, translation by M-P. de Valdivia.

350 "we took the advice" Ibid., p. 456, translation by M-P. de Valdivia.

351 "she didn't like Clement VII" Ibid., p. 457, translation by M-P. de Valdivia.

Chapter XIX: The Fall of the Queen

353 "I am now Pope!" Pastor, *The History of the Popes from the Close of the Middle Ages*, vol. 1, p. 134.

354 "I hear that those incarnate demons" Drane, *The History of St. Catherine of Siena and Her Companions*, vol. 1, p. 151.

354 "Dearest mother,—in so far" Catherine, *Saint Catherine of Sienna*, http://www.domcentral.org/trad/cathletters.htm.

355 "Act with benevolence and a tranquil heart" Drane, *The History of St. Catherine of Siena and Her Companions*, vol. 1, p. 145.

355 "It was hoped that the two virgins" Raymond of Capua, *The Life of St. Catherine of Siena*, p. 306.

355 "The other Catherine, however" Ibid.

355 "The queen whom they had been asked" Ibid.

356 "If ... other holy virgins" Ibid., p. 307.

360 "the new Jezebel" Léonard, *Les Angevins de Naples*, p. 459, translation by M-P. de Valdivia.

361 "fill the world" Ibid., p. 462, translation by M-P. de Valdivia.

364 "with benevolence towards the invader" Ibid., p. 463, translation by M-P. de Valdivia.

366 "then Palamede Bozzuto" Baddeley, *Queen Joanna I of Naples*, p. 286.

367 "The next day Charles" Ibid., p. 287.

368 "She not only designed to make" Ibid., p. 288.

368 "after which time, if Prince Otto" Ibid., p. 289.

368 "And San Saverino being returned" Ibid.

369 "They fought with so much bravery" Ibid., p. 290.

369 "The Queen sent Hugo San Severino" Ibid.

370 "As soon as they [the Provençals] were entered" Ibid., p. 291.

371 "with sad lamentation" Ibid., p. 292.

376 "many people thought she was dead" Léonard, *Les Angevins de Naples*, p. 467, translation by M-P. de Valdivia.

Epilogue

378 "They are all barefoot" Caferro, *John Hawkwood*, p. 239.

380 "Of all the illustrious women" Léonard, *Les Angevins de Naples*, p. 468, translation by M-P. de Valdivia.

Select Bibliography

Abulafia, David. "Southern Italy and the Florentine Economy, 1265–1370," *Economic History Review*, n.s., vol. 34, no. 3 (August 1981), 377–388.

Adams, Laurie Schneider. *Italian Renaissance Art* (Colorado, Westview Press, 2001).

Ambrosini, Maria Luisa, and Mary Willis. *The Secret Archives of the Vatican* (New York, Barnes & Noble Books, 1996; originally published by Little, Brown, 1969).

Astarita, Tommaso. *Between Salt Water and Holy Water: A History of Southern Italy* (New York, W. W. Norton & Company, 2005).

Audibert, Paul. *Histoire des comtes de Provence: rois de Sicile et de Jerusalem* (Draguignan, Les Presses des Imprimeries Riccobono, 1969).

Baddeley, St. Clair. *Queen Joanna I of Naples, Sicily, and Jerusalem, Countess of Provence, Forcalquier and Piedmont: An Essay on Her Times* (London, William Heinemann, 1893).

———. *Robert the Wise and His Heirs, 1278–1352* (London, William Heinemann, 1897).

Barber, Richard, editor and translator. *The Life and Campaigns of the Black Prince from Contemporary Letters, Diaries and Chronicles, Including Chandos Herald's Life of the Black Prince* (London, Folio Society, 1979).

Barraclough, Geoffrey. *The Medieval Papacy* (New York, W. W. Norton & Company, 1968).

Baxandall, Michael. *Giotto and the Orators: Humanist Observers of Painting in Italy and the Discovery of Pictorial Composition* (Oxford University Press, 1971).

Bayley, C. C. *War and Society in Renaissance Florence: The De Militia of Leonardo Bruni* (University of Toronto Press, 1961).

Bell, Mary I. M. *A Short History of the Papacy* (New York, Dodd, Mead & Company, 1921).

Bellamy, John. *Crime and Public Order in England in the Later Middle Ages* (London, Routledge & Kegan Paul, 1973).

Bennett, Judith M., Elizabeth A. Clark, Jean F. O'Barr, B. Anne Vilen, and Sarah Westphal-Wihl, editors. *Sisters and Workers in the Middle Ages* (University of Chicago Press, 1989).

Berenson, Bernard. *Studies in Medieval Painting* (New York, Da Capo Press, 1975).

Bergin, Thomas G. *Boccaccio* (New York, Viking Press, 1981).

Binns, L. Elliott. *The Decline and Fall of the Medieval Papacy* (New York, Barnes & Noble Books, 1995).

Bisson, T. N. *The Medieval Crown of Aragon: A Short History* (Oxford, Clarendon Press, 1991).

Black, Robert. *Humanism and Education in Medieval and Renaissance Italy: Tradition and Innovation in Latin Schools from the Twelfth to the Fifteenth Century* (Cambridge University Press, 2001).

Boccaccio, Giovanni. *The Decameron.* Translated by Richard Aldington (New York, International Collectors Library, translation copyright 1930 by Doubleday & Company).

———. *The Elegy of Lady Fiammetta.* Edited and translated by Mariangela Causa-Steindler and Thomas March (University of Chicago Press, 1990).

———. *Famous Women.* Edited and translated by Virginia Brown (London, Harvard University Press, 2001).

———. *The Fates of Illustrious Men.* Translated by Louis Brewer Hall (New York, Frederick Ungar Publishing Company, 1965).

———. *Il Filocolo,* vol. 43, series B. Translated by Donald Cheney with the collaboration of Thomas G. Bergin (New York and London, Garland Publishing, 1985).

Boitani, Piero, and Anna Torti, editors. *Intellectuals and Writers in Fourteenth-Century Europe: The J. A. W. Bennett Memorial Lectures, Perugia, 1984* (Cambridge, D. S. Brewer, 1986).

Bouard, A. De, editor. *Documents en Francais: Des archives Angevins de Naples (règne de Charles I) transcrits par P. Durrieu et A. de Bouard* (Paris, E. De Boccard, 1933).

Branca, Vittore. *Boccaccio: The Man and His Works.* Translated by Richard Monges (New York University Press, 1976).

Brodman, James William. *Charity and Welfare: Hospitals and the Poor in Medieval Catalonia* (Philadelphia, University of Pennsylvania Press, 1998).

Brown, Judith C., and Robert C. Davis, editors. *Gender and Society in Renaissance Italy* (London, Longman, 1998).

Brown, Virginia. *Terra Sancti Benedicti: Studies in the Palaeography, History and Liturgy of*

Medieval Southern Italy (Rome, Edizioni Di Storia e Letteratura, 2005).

Browning, Oscar. *Guelphs and Ghibellines: A Short History of Mediaeval Italy from 1250–1409* (London, Methuen & Company, 1894).

Brucker, Gene A. *Florentine Politics and Society, 1343–1378* (Princeton University Press, 1962).

Bruzelius, Caroline. *The Stones of Naples: Church Building in Angevin Italy, 1266–1343* (New Haven, Yale University Press, 2004).

Burckhardt, Jacob. *The Civilization of the Renaissance in Italy.* Translated by S. G. C. Middlemore (New York, Modern Library, 2002).

Caferro, William. *John Hawkwood: An English Mercenary in Fourteenth-Century Italy* (Baltimore, Johns Hopkins University Press, 2006).

Cambell, Thomas. *Life of Petrarch* (Philadelphia, Carey and Hart, 1841).

Cantor, Norman F. *The Civilization of the Middle Ages: A Completely Revised and Expanded Edition of Medieval History* (New York, HarperPerennial, 1994).

Catherine. *Letters of Saint Catherine.* Edited and translated by Suzanne Noffke (vol. 1, New York, Medieval and Renaissance Texts and Studies, 1988; vols. 1 and 2, Tempe, Arizona, Center for Medieval and Renaissance Studies, 2001).

————. *Saint Catherine of Siena as Seen in Her Letters.* Translated and edited by Vida Dutton Scudder (London and New York, J. M. Dent and E. P. Dutton, 1905), http://www.domcentral.org/trad/cathletters.htm.

Chamberlin, E. R. *The Count of Virtue: Giangaleazzo Visconti, First Duke of Lombardy* (New York, Charles Scribner's Sons, 1965).

Cheney, Liana De Girolami. "The Cult of Saint Agatha," *Woman's Art Journal*, vol. 17, no. 1 (Spring–Summer 1996), pp. 3–9.

Cohn, Samuel K., Jr. "The Black Death: End of a Paradigm," *American Historical Review.* http://www.historycooperative.org/journals/ahr/107.3/aho302000 703.htm.

Collins, Amanda. *Greater Than Emperor: Cola di Rienzo (ca. 1313–54) and the World of Fourteenth-Century Rome* (Ann Arbor, University of Michigan Press, 2002).

Contamine, Philippe, editor. *War and Competition Between States* (Oxford University Press, 2001).

Cotterill, H. B. *Medieval Italy During a Thousand Years (304–1313): A Brief Historical Narrative with Chapters on Great Episodes and Personalities and on Subjects Connected with Religion, Art and Literature* (New York, Frederick A. Stokes Company, 1915).

Coulter, Cornelia C. "The Library of the Angevin Kings at Naples," *Transactions and Proceedings of the American Philological Association*, vol. 75 (1944), pp. 141–155.

Cox, Eugene L. *The Green Count of Savoy: Amadeus VI and Transalpine Savoy in the Fourteenth Century* (Princeton University Press, 1967).

Crinelli, Lorenzo, and Anna Rita Fantoni. *Treasures from Italy's Great Libraries* (New York, Vendome Press, 1997).

Croce, Benedetto. *History of the Kingdom of Naples.* Translated by Frances Frenaye (University of Chicago Press, 1965; originally published as *Storia del regno di Napoli*, 1925).

Curtayne, Alice. *Saint Catherine of Siena* (Illinois, Tan Books and Publishers, 1980).

Dean, Trevor, translator. *The Towns of Italy in the Later Middle Ages* (Manchester University Press, 2000).

Dean Trevor, and K. J. P. Lowe, editors. *Marriage in Italy, 1300–1650* (Cambridge University Press, 1998).

Déprez, E., and G. Mollat, editors. *Clément VI (1342–1352): Lettres closes, patentes et curiales interessant les pays autres que la France publiées ou analysées d'apres les registres du Vatican*, Premier Fascicule, Tome 1 (Paris, Éditions E. de Boccard, 1960).

Drane, Augusta Theodosia. *The History of St. Catherine of Siena and Her Companions with a Translation of Her Treatise on Consummate Perfection.* 2 vols., 2nd ed. (London, Burns and Oates, 1887).

Duby, Georges. *France in the Middle Ages, 987–1460.* Translated by Juliet Vale (Oxford, Blackwell Publishers, 1993).

Duby, Georges. *Rural Economy and Country Life in the Medieval West.* Translated by Cynthia Postan (Columbia, University of South Carolina Press, 1968).

Duggan, Anne J., editor. *Queens and Queenship in Medieval Europe: Proceedings of a Conference Held at King's College London, April 1995* (Woodbridge, Boydell Press, 1997).

Dumas, Alexander. *Celebrated Crimes*, vol. 6 (New York, P. F. Collier & Son, 1910).

Dunbabin, Jean. *Charles I of Anjou: Power, Kingship and State-Making in Thirteenth-Century Europe* (London, Longman, 1998).

Engel, Pál. *The Realm of St. Stephen: A History of Medieval Hungary, 895–1526* (London, I. B. Tauris, 2005).

Epstein, Stephan R. *An Island for Itself: Economic Development and Social Change in Late Medieval Sicily* (Cambridge University Press, 1992).

Filangieri, Count Riccardo. "Report on the Destruction by the Germans, September 30, 1943, of the Depository of Priceless Historical Records of the Naples State Archives," *American Archivist*, vol. 7, no. 4 (October 1944), pp. 252–255.

French, Roger, Jon Arrizabalaga, Andrew Cunningham, and Luis García-Ballester, editors. *Medicine from the Black Death to the French Disease* (Aldershot, Ashgate, 1998).

Froissart, Jean. *Chronicles of England, France, Spain, and the Adjoining Countries, from the Latter Part of the Reign of Edward II. to the Coronation of Henry IV.* Translated by T. Johnes (London, 1839–55).

Gibbon, Edward. *The Decline and Fall of the Roman Empire*, vol. 3, A.D. 1185 to the

Fall of Constantinople in 1453 (New York, Modern Library, 1977).

Gies, Frances, and Joseph Gies. *Women in the Middle Ages* (New York, Barnes & Noble Books, 1978).

Gill, Joseph. *Byzantium and the Papacy, 1198–1400* (New Jersey, Rutgers University Press, 1979).

Godkin, Edwin Lawrence. *History of Hungary and the Magyars.* Notable Authors Series (Reprint Services Corp., June 1992).

Goldstone, Nancy. *Four Queens: The Provençal Sisters Who Ruled Europe* (New York, Viking Penguin, 2007).

Goodich, Michael E. *Violence and Miracle in the Fourteenth Century: Private Grief and Public Salvation* (University of Chicago Press, 1995).

Green, Louis. *Castruccio Castracani: A Study on the Origins and Character of a Fourteenth-Century Italian Despotism* (Oxford, Clarendon Press, 1986).

Green, Monica H., editor and translator. *The Trotula: A Medieval Compendium of Women's Medicine* (Philadelphia, University of Pennsylvania Press, 2001).

Hare, Augustus J. C. *Cities of Southern Italy and Sicily* (New York, George Routledge, 1895).

Harvey, John. *The Black Prince and His Age* (London, B. T. Batsford, 1976).

———. *Medieval Gardens* (Oregon, Timber Press, 1981).

Hay, Denys. *Europe in the Fourteenth and Fifteenth Centuries* (New York, Holt, Rinehart & Winston, 1966).

Headlam, Cecil. *The Story of Naples* (London, J. M. Dent & Sons, 1927).

Heers, Jacques. *Parties and Political Life in the Medieval West.* Translated by David Nicholas. Vol. 7 of *Europe in the Middle Ages Selected Studies*, edited by Richard Vaughan (Amsterdam, New York, Oxford, North-Holland Publishing Company, 1977).

Henneman, John Bell, Jr. "The Black Death and Royal Taxation in France, 1347–1351," *Speculum*, vol. 43, no. 3 (July 1968), pp. 405–428.

———. *The Medieval French Monarchy* (Illinois, Dryden Press, 1973).

Hoch, Adrian S. "The Franciscan Provenance of Simone Martini's Angevin St. Louis in Naples," *Zeitschrift für Kunstgeschichte*, 58 bd., h. 1 (1995), pp. 22–38.

Holmes, George, editor. *The Oxford Illustrated History of Medieval Europe* (Oxford University Press, 1990).

Housley, Norman. *The Italian Crusades: The Papal-Angevin Alliance and the Crusades Against Christian Lay Powers, 1254–1343* (Oxford, Clarendon Press, 1982).

———. "King Louis the Great of Hungary and the Crusades, 1342–1382," *Slavonic and East European Review*, vol. 62, no. 2 (April 1984), pp. 192–208.

Hunt, Edwin S. *The Medieval Super-companies: A Study of the Peruzzi Company of Florence* (Cambridge University Press, 2002).

Hunt, Edwin S., and James M. Murray. *A History of Business in Medieval Europe,*

1200–1550 (Cambridge University Press, 1999).

Hunt, John Dixon, editor. *The Italian Garden: Art, Design and Culture* (Cambridge University Press, 1996).

Hyde, J. K. *Society and Politics in Medieval Italy: The Evolution of the Civil Life, 1000–1350* (New York, St. Martin's Press, 1973).

Jamison, Evelyn M. *Studies on the History of Medieval Sicily and South Italy*. Edited by Dione Clementi and Theo Kölzer (Scientia Verlag Aalen, 1992).

Johnson, Eric A., and Eric H. Monkkonen, editors. *The Civilization of Crime: Violence in Town and Country Since the Middle Ages* (Urbana, University of Illinois Press, 1996).

Johnson, Lonnie R. *Central Europe: Enemies, Neighbors, Friends*. 2nd ed. (Oxford University Press, 2002).

Johnson, Paul. *The Papacy* (Phoenix Illustrated, 1998).

Jones, Michael, editor. *The New Cambridge Medieval History*. Vol. 6, *c. 1300–c. 1415* (Cambridge University Press, 2000).

Joost-Gaugier, Christiane L. "Giotto's Hero Cycle in Naples: A Prototype of Donne Illustri and a Possible Literary Connection," *Zeitschrift für Kunstgeschichte*, 43 bd., h. 3 (1980), pp. 311–318.

Jorgensen, Johannes. *Saint Catherine of Siena*. Translated from the Danish by Ingeborg Lund (London, Longmans, Green and Co., 1938).

Kirkham, Victoria. *Fabulous Vernacular: Boccaccio's Filocolo and the Art of Medieval Fiction* (Ann Arbor, University of Michigan Press, 2001).

Kirshner, Julius, and Suzanne F. Wemple, editors. *Women of the Medieval World: Essays in Honor of John H. Mundy* (Oxford, Basil Blackwell, 1985).

Klaniczay, Gábor. *Holy Rulers and Blessed Princesses: Dynastic Cults in Medieval Central Europe*. Translated by Éva Pálmai (Cambridge University Press, 2002).

Kristeller, Paul Oskar. *Studies in Renaissance Thought and Letters* (Rome, Edizioni di Storia e Letteratura, 1969; offset reprint of the 1956 edition).

Landsberg, Sylvia. *The Medieval Garden* (New York, Thames and Hudson, 1995).

Larner, John. *Italy in the Age of Dante and Petrarch* (London, Longman, 1980).

Lasareff, Victor. "A New Panel by Roberto Oderisi," *Burlington Magazine for Connoisseurs*, vol. 51, no. 294 (September 1927), pp. 128–133.

Leff, Gordon. *Medieval Thought: St. Augustine to Ockham* (London, Merlin Press, 1959).

Léonard, Émile-G. *La jeunesse de Jeanne I, reine de Naples, comtesse de Provence, thèse présentée a la faculté des lettres de L'Université de Paris* (Paris, Librairie Auguste Picard, 1932).

———. *Les Angevins de Naples* (Paris, Presses Universitaires de France, 1954).

Lock, Peter. *The Franks in the Aegean, 1204–1500* (London and New York, Longman, 1995).

Lopez, Robert S., and Irving W. Raymond. *Medieval Trade in the Mediterranean World:*

Illustrative Documents Translated with Introductions and Notes (New York, Columbia University Press, 1955, 1990, 2001).

Luzzatto, Gino. *An Economic History of Italy from the Fall of the Roman Empire to the Beginning of the Sixteenth Century*. Translated from the Italian by Philip Jones (New York, Barnes & Noble Books; first published by Routledge & Kegan Paul, 1961).

Macartney, C. A. *Hungary: A Short History* (Chicago, Aldine Publishing Company, 1962).

————. *The Medieval Hungarian Historians: A Critical and Analytic Guide* (Cambridge University Press, 1953).

Machiavelli, Niccolo. *History of Florence and the Affairs of Italy from the Earliest Times to the Death of Lorenzo the Magnificent* (New York, Harper Torchbooks, 1960).

Maginnis, Hayden B. J. "Giotto's World Through Vasari's Eyes," *Zeitschrift für Kunstgeschichte*, 56 bd., h. 3 (1993), pp. 385–408.

Marino, John A. *Pastoral Economics in the Kingdom of Naples* (Baltimore, Johns Hopkins University Press, 1988).

Marongiu, Antonio. *Medieval Parliaments: A Comparative Study*. Translated by S. J. Woolf (London, Eyre & Spottiswoode, 1968).

Martines, Lauro, editor. *Violence and Civil Disorder in Italian Cities, 1200–1500* (Berkeley, University of California Press, 1972).

Mazzaoui, Maureen Fennell. *The Italian Cotton Industry in the Later Middle Ages, 1100–1600* (Cambridge University Press, 1981).

McKisack, May. *The Fourteenth Century, 1307–1399* (Oxford University Press, 1959).

Menache, Sophia. *Clement V* (Cambridge University Press, 1998).

Mesquita, D. M. Bueno de. *Giangaleazzo, Visconti, Duke of Milan (1351–1402): A Study in the Political Career of an Italian Despot* (Cambridge University Press, 1941).

Miskimin, Harry A. *The Economy of Early Renaissance Europe, 1300–1460* (Cambridge University Press, 1975).

Mollat, G. *The Popes at Avignon, 1305–1378* (New York, Harper Torchbooks; originally published by Thomas Nelson & Sons, 1963).

Moorman, John. *A History of the Franciscan Order from Its Origins to the Year 1517* (Oxford, Clarendon Press, 1968).

Muir, Dorothy. *A History of Milan Under the Visconti* (London, Methuen & Co., 1924).

Newton, Stella Mary. "Tomaso da Modena, Simone Martini, Hungarians and St. Martin in Fourteenth-Century Italy," *Journal of the Warburg and Courtauld Institutes*, vol. 43 (1980), pp. 234–238.

Nicol, Donald M. *The Last Centuries of Byzantium, 1261–1453*. 2nd ed. (Cambridge University Press, 1993).

Norwich, John Julius. *Byzantium: The Decline and Fall* (New York, Alfred A. Knopf, 1996).

O'Callaghan, Joseph. F. *A History of Medieval Spain* (Ithaca, Cornell University Press, 1975).

Ormrod, W. M. *The Reign of Edward III* (Charleston, Tempus Publishing, 2000).

Panache, Madame. *Historical Life of Joanna of Sicily, Queen of Naples and Countess of Provence with Correlative Details of the Literature and Manners of Italy and Provence in the Thirteenth and Fourteenth Centuries.* 2 vols. (London, Baldwin, Cradock, and Joy, 1824).

Park, Katharine. *Doctors and Medicine in Early Renaissance Florence* (Princeton University Press, 1985).

Parsons, John Carmi, editor. *Medieval Queenship* (New York, St. Martin's Press, 1993, 1998).

Pastor, Ludwig. *The History of the Popes, from the Close of the Middle Ages,* vol. 1. Edited by Frederick Ignatius Antrobus (St. Louis, B. Herder, 1902).

Pennington, Kenneth. *Popes, Canonists and Texts, 1150–1550* (Great Britain, Variorum, 1993).

Percy, William. "Review of *La politica napoletana di Urbano VI* by Salvatore Fodale," *Speculum,* vol. 51, no. 4 (October 1976), pp. 740–741.

Perkins, Charles C. *Historical Handbook of Italian Sculpture* (New York, Charles Scribner's Sons, 1883).

Perkins, F. Mason. "Andrea Vanni," *Burlington Magazine for Connoisseurs,* vol. 2, no. 6 (August 1903), pp. 309–325.

Petrarch, Francesco. *Letters on Familiar Matters, I–XXIV.* Translated by Aldo S. Bernardo. 3 vols. (New York, Italica Press, 2005).

Petrucci, Armando. *Writers and Readers in Medieval Italy: Studies in the History of Written Culture.* Translated by Charles M. Radding (New Haven, Yale University Press, 1995).

Postan, M. M., editor. *The Cambridge Economic History of Europe,* Vol. 1, *The Agrarian Life of the Middle Ages.* 2nd ed. (Cambridge University Press, 1966).

Power, Eileen. *Medieval People* (BiblioLife, 2008).

Quatriglio, Giuseppe. *A Thousand Years in Sicily: From the Arabs to the Bourbons.* Translated by Justin Vitiello (New York, Legas, 1997).

Raymond of Capua. *The Life of St. Catherine of Siena.* Translated by George Lamb (New York, P. J. Kenedy & Sons, 1960).

Ridder-Symoens, Hilde de, editor. *A History of the University in Europe.* Vol. 1, *Universities in the Middle Ages* (Cambridge University Press, 1992).

Rodax, Yvonne. *The Real and the Ideal in the Novella of Italy, France and England: Four Centuries of Change in the Boccaccian Tale* (Chapel Hill, University of North Carolina Press, 1968).

Ruggiers, Paul G. *Florence in the Age of Dante* (Norman, University of Oklahoma Press, 1964).

Runciman, Steven. *The Sicilian Vespers: A History of the Mediterranean World in the Later Thirteenth Century* (Cambridge University Press, 1982).

Sandys, John Edwin. *Harvard Lectures on the Revival of Learning* (Cambridge University Press, 1905).

Saunders, Frances Stonor. *The Devil's Broker: Seeking Gold, God and Glory in Fourteenth-Century Italy* (New York, Fourth Estate, 2004).

Sedgwick, Henry Dwight. *Italy in the Thirteenth Century*, vol. 2 (Boston, Houghton Mifflin, 1912).

Setton, Kenneth M. "Archbishop Pierre d'Ameil in Naples and the Affair of Aimon III of Geneva (1363–1364)," *Speculum*, vol. 28, no. 4 (October 1953), pp. 643–691.

Sevcenko, Ihor. *Society and Intellectual Life in Late Byzantium* (London, Variorum Reprints, 1981).

Sinor, Denis. *History of Hungary* (London, George Allen & Unwin, 1959).

Smith, Denis Mack. *A History of Sicily: Medieval Sicily, 800–1713* (New York, Viking Press, 1968).

Smith, Lesley, and Jane H. M. Taylor, editors. *Women and the Book: Accessing the Visual Evidence* (British Library and University of Toronto Press, 1996).

Spufford, Peter. *Money and Its Use in Medieval Europe* (Cambridge University Press, 1988).

Starn, Randolph. *Contrary Commonwealth: The Theme of Exile in Medieval and Renaissance Italy* (Berkeley, University of California Press, 1982).

Steele, Francesca M. *The Beautiful Queen, Joanna I. of Naples* (London, Hutchinson & Co., 1910).

Swanson, R. N. *Universities, Academics and the Great Schism* (Cambridge University Press, 1979).

Toynbee, Margaret R. *S. Louis of Toulouse and the Process of Canonisation in the Fourteenth Century* (Manchester University Press, 1929).

Treadgold, Warren. *A History of the Byzantine State and Society* (Stanford University Press, 1997).

Trexler, Richard C. "Rome on the Eve of the Great Schism," *Speculum*, vol. 42, no. 3 (July 1967), pp. 489–509.

Tuchman, Barbara W. *A Distant Mirror: The Calamitous 14th Century* (New York, Alfred A. Knopf, 1978).

Ullmann, Walter. *The Origins of the Great Schism: A Study in Fourteenth-Century Ecclesiastical History* (Hamden, Archon Books, 1967).

Van Buren, A. W. "Art Activities in Italy," *Parnassus*, vol. 2, no. 8 (December 1930), pp. 13–18.

Vardy, S. B., G. Grosschmid, and L. S. Domonkos, editors. *Louis the Great, King of Hungary and Poland* (New York, Columbia University Press, 1986).

Villani, Giovanni. *Villani's Chronicle*. Translated by Rose E. Selfe and edited by Philip H. Wicksteed (London, Archibald Constable & Co., 1906).

Villani, Giovanni, Matteo Villani, and Filippo Villani. *Chroniche di Giovanni, Matteo e Filippo Villani* (Trieste, 1858).

Waley, Daniel. *The Italian City-Republics* (New York, McGraw-Hill, 1978).

Ward, Jennifer. *Women in Medieval Europe, 1200–1500* (London, Longman, 2002).

Welch, Evelyn. *Art in Renaissance Italy, 1350–1500* (Oxford University Press 1997).

Wilkins, Ernest H. "Petrarch's Ecclesiastical Career," *Speculum*, vol. 28, no. 4 (October 1953), pp. 754–775.

Wood, Diana. *Clement VI: The Pontificate and Ideas of an Avignon Pope* (Cambridge University Press, 1989).

Zacour, Norman P. "Petrarch and Talleyrand," *Speculum*, vol. 31, no. 4 (October 1956), pp. 683–703.

———. "Talleyrand: The Cardinal of Périgord (1301–1364)," *Transactions of the American Philosophical Society*, n. s., vol. 50, no. 7 (1960), pp. 1–83.), pp. 1–83.

Illustration Credits

p. 1 *Saint Louis of Toulouse Placing the Crown of the Kingdom of Naples on the Head of His Brother Robert of Anjou*, by Simone Martini (1284–1344), Museo di Capodimonte, Naples, Italy. Photo credit: Alinari/Art Resource, NY.

p. 1 *The Coronation of Pope Clement VII, 1378*, c.1378–c.1400, Roy. 20. C. VII. Folio No: 208v (detail), British Library, London, Great Britain. Photo credit: HIP/Art Resource, NY.

p. 2 *Naval Triumph after the Battle of Ischia*, by Francesco Pagano, left and right sides, fifteenth century, Certosa di S. Martino, Naples, Italy. Photo credit: Scala/Ministero per i Beni e le Attività culturali/Art Resource, NY.

p. 2 Hungarian Anjou Legendary single leaf, MS M.360.6. By permission of the Pierpont Morgan Library. Photo credit: The Pierpoint Morgan Library, New York.

p. 3 Boethius, *De musica*, V.A. 14, Fol. 47, mid-fourteenth century. By permission of Biblioteca Nazionale Vittorio Emanuele III, Naples, Italy. Photo credit: Biblioteca Nazionale Vittorio Emanuele III, Naples, Italy.

p. 4 *Distribution of Grain in the Orsanmichele During the 1335 Famine*, manuscript illumination from *Il Biadiolo (The Grain Merchant)* by Domenico Lenzi, fourteenth century, Biblioteca Laurenziana, Florence, Italy. Photo credit: Scala/Art Resource, NY.

p. 4 *Burying Plague Victims of Tournai, 1349*, from the Annals of Gilles de Muisit, by the Abbot of Saint-Martin, 1352. MS 13076-7, c.24t, Fol. 24v., Bibliotheque Royale Albert I, Brussels, Belgium. Photo credit: Snark/Art Resource, NY.

p. 5 *Scene from the Battle of Crécy, 1346*, from *Les Chroniques de France*, Cotton Nero E. II, fol. 152v (detail), British Library, London, Great Britain. Photo credit: Erich Lessing/Art Resource, NY.

p. 5 *King Jean II Le Bon Surrenders to the Black Prince After the Battle of Poitiers, 1356,* from *The Chronicles of Jean Froissart,* Book 1, MS 873, ex 501, fol. 201v, Musée Condé, Chantilly, France. Photo credit: Erich Lessing/Art Resource, NY.

p. 6 *The Sacrament of Marriage,* by Roberto d'Oderisio, mid1360s, the Church of Santa Maria Incoronata, Naples, Italy. By permission of the Soprintendenza PSAE e per il Molo Museale della città di Napoli. Photo credit: @pedicini luciano.

p. 6 *Royal Court Entertained to a Tilting Match,* from *Le Roman du Roi Meliadus de Leonnoys,* by Helie de Borron, circa 1352–1362. Add 12228. Folio 214v215 (detail), British Library, London, Great Britain. Photo credit: HIP/Art Resource, NY.

p. 7 *Petrarch Appearing to Boccaccio in His Sleep,* by Master François and Master Dunois, from *Les Cas des nobles homes et femmes* by Giovanni Boccaccio, 1465, MS 860, fol. 258r, Musée Condé, Chantilly, France. Photo credit: Réunion des Musées Nationaux/Art Resource, NY.

p. 7 "Via Veritatis," detail of *Church Militant and Triumphant,* by Andrea da Firenze (also known as Andrea di Bonaiuto), 1366–1368, Spanish Chapel, S. M. Novella, Florence, Italy. Photo credit: Scala/Art Resource, NY.

p. 8 *The Queen of Naples Praying to the Madonna and Child for an Heir,* by Niccolò di Tommaso, circa late 1360s, lunette over the chapel door, Certosa di San Giacomo, Capri. By permission of the Soprintendenza PSAE e per il Molo Museale della città di Napoli. Photo credit: @pedicini luciano.

Index

NIGHT STALKER